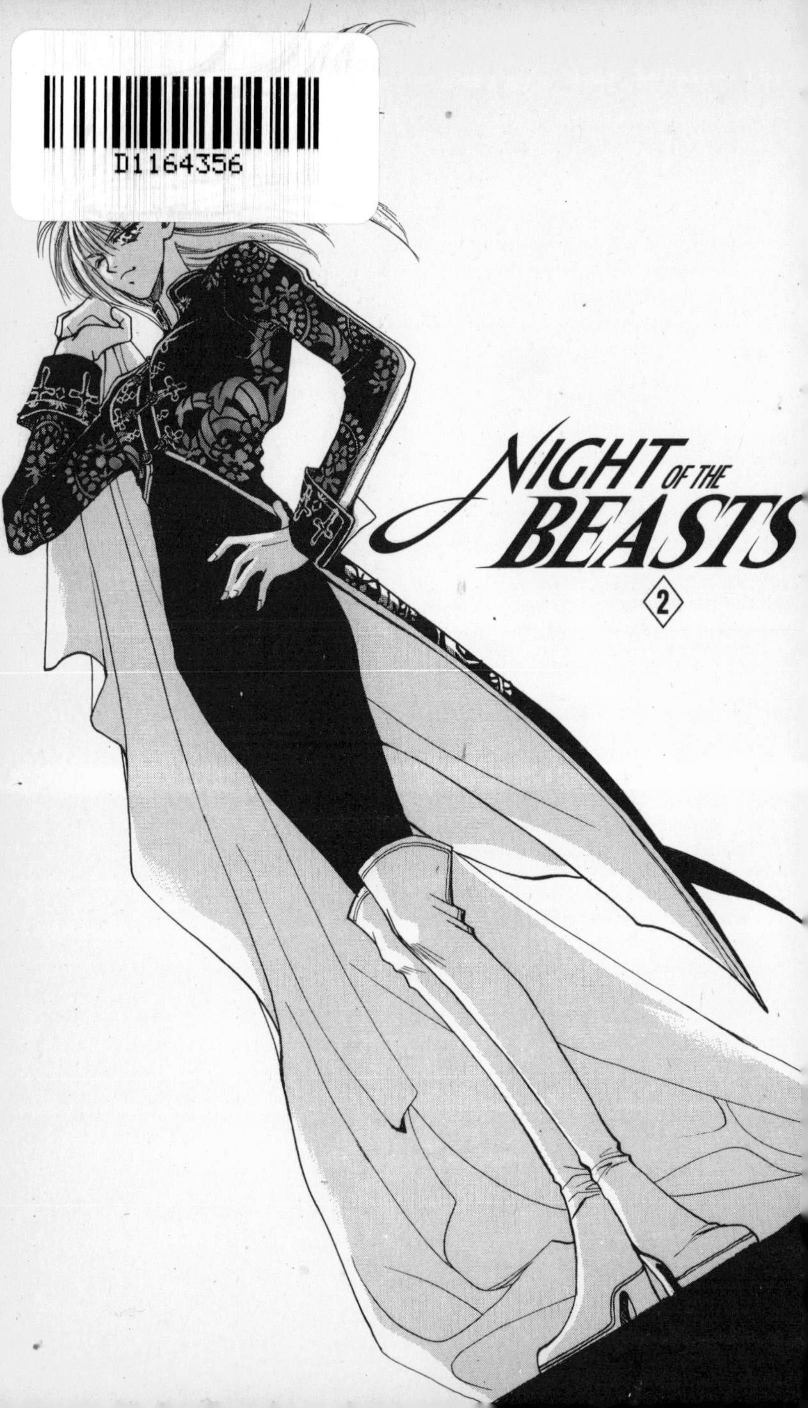
NIGHT OF THE BEASTS
2

Translation – Kathy Schilling
Adaptation – Mallory Reaves
Lettering & Design – Jihye Hong
Production Manager - James Dashiell
Editor -- Brynne Chandler

A Go! Comi manga

Published by Go! Media Entertainment, LLC

Night of the Beasts Volume 2
© CHIKA SHIOMI 1997
Originally published in Japan in 1997 by Akita Publishing Co., Ltd., Tokyo.
English translation rights arranged with Akita Publishing Co., Ltd.
through TOHAN CORPORATION, Tokyo.

Visit us online at www.gocomi.com
e-mail: info@gocomi.com

ISBN 978-1-933617-15-2

First printed in January 2007

1 2 3 4 5 6 7 8 9

Manufactured in the United States of America

NIGHT OF THE BEASTS

STORY AND ART BY
CHIKA SHIOMI

VOLUME 2

go!comi

Concerning Honorifics

At Go! Comi, we do our best to ensure that our translations read seamlessly in English while respecting the original Japanese language and culture. To this end, the original honorifics (the suffixes found at the end of characters' names) remain intact. In Japan, where politeness and formality are more integrated into every aspect of the language, honorifics give a better understanding of character relationships. They can be used to indicate both respect and affection. Whether a person addresses someone by first name or last name also indicates how close their relationship is.

Here are some of the honorifics you might encounter in reading this book:

-san: This is the most common and neutral of honorifics. The polite way to address someone you're not on close terms with is to use "-san." it's kind of like Mr. or Ms., except you can use "-san" with first names as easily as family names.

-chan: Used for friendly familiarity, mostly applied towards young girls. "-chan" also carries a connotation of cuteness with it, so it is frequently used with nick-names towards both boys and girls (such as "Na-chan" for "Natsu").

-kun: Like "-chan," it's an informal suffix for friends and classmates, only "-kun" is usually associated with boys. It can also be used in a professional environment by someone addressing a subordinate.

-sama: Indicates a great deal of respect or admiration.

Sempai: In school, "sempai" is used to refer to an upperclassman or club leader. It can also be used in the workplace by a new employee to address a mentor or staff member with seniority.

Sensei: Teachers, doctors, writers or any master of a trade are referred to as "sensei." When addressing a manga creator, the polite thing to do is attach "-sensei" to the manga-ka's name (as in Shiomi-sensei).

Onii: This is the more casual term for an older brother. Usually you'll see it with an honorific attached, such as "onii-chan."

Onee: The casual term for older sister, it's used like "onii" with honorifics.

[blank]: Not using an honorific when addressing someone indicates that the speaker has permission to speak intimately with the other person. This relationship is usually reserved for close friends and family.

NIGHT OF THE BEASTS

CONTENTS

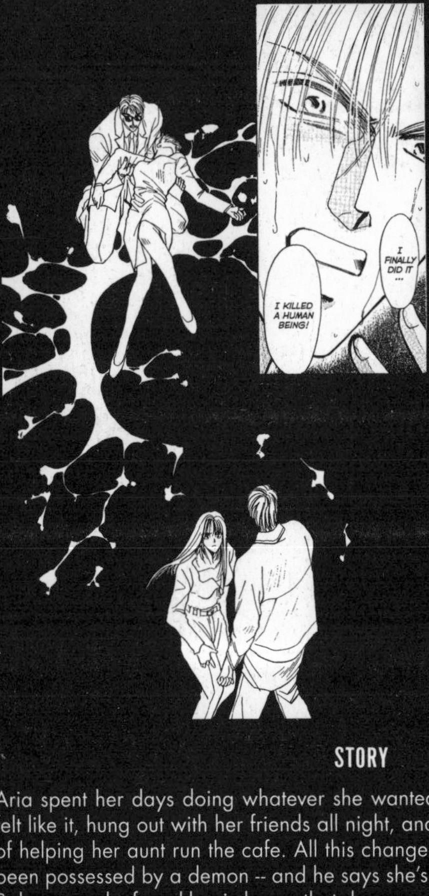
I FINALLY DID IT ...
I KILLED A HUMAN BEING!

STORY

Aria spent her days doing whatever she wanted. She went to school when she felt like it, hung out with her friends all night, and her only worry was getting out of helping her aunt run the cafe. All this changes when she meets Sakura, who's been possessed by a demon -- and he says she's the only one who can save him! Sakura says he found her in hopes that she can calm the demon inside him, before he kills someone. If he does that, he says, something terrible will happen. Though she doesn't understand the whole story, she decides to stay by Sakura's side and try to help him. Following them are some mysterious men who also say they want to "help" Sakura... even if they have to kill him to do it! Even though Sakura is shot during the confrontation, his demonic powers give him the ability to heal quickly. Aria still doesn't know exactly what's going on, but she's determined to get the whole truth out of Sakura... but before she can force it out of him, he is stabbed by a strange woman who seemed to have been driven mad by his very existence. Even faster than Aria can do something, the demon within Sakura surges forth, viciously attacking the woman. Has Sakura killed his first human...?

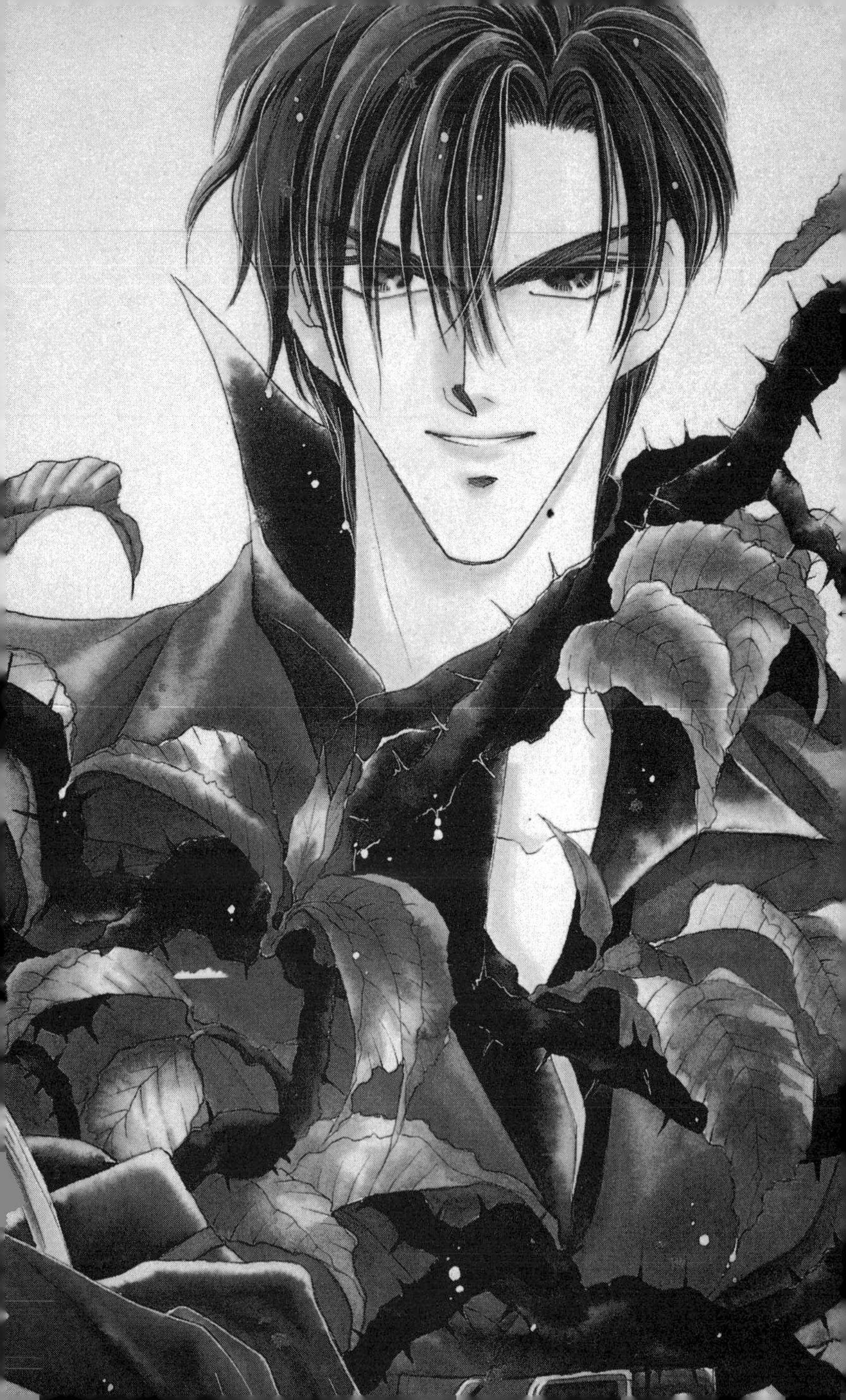

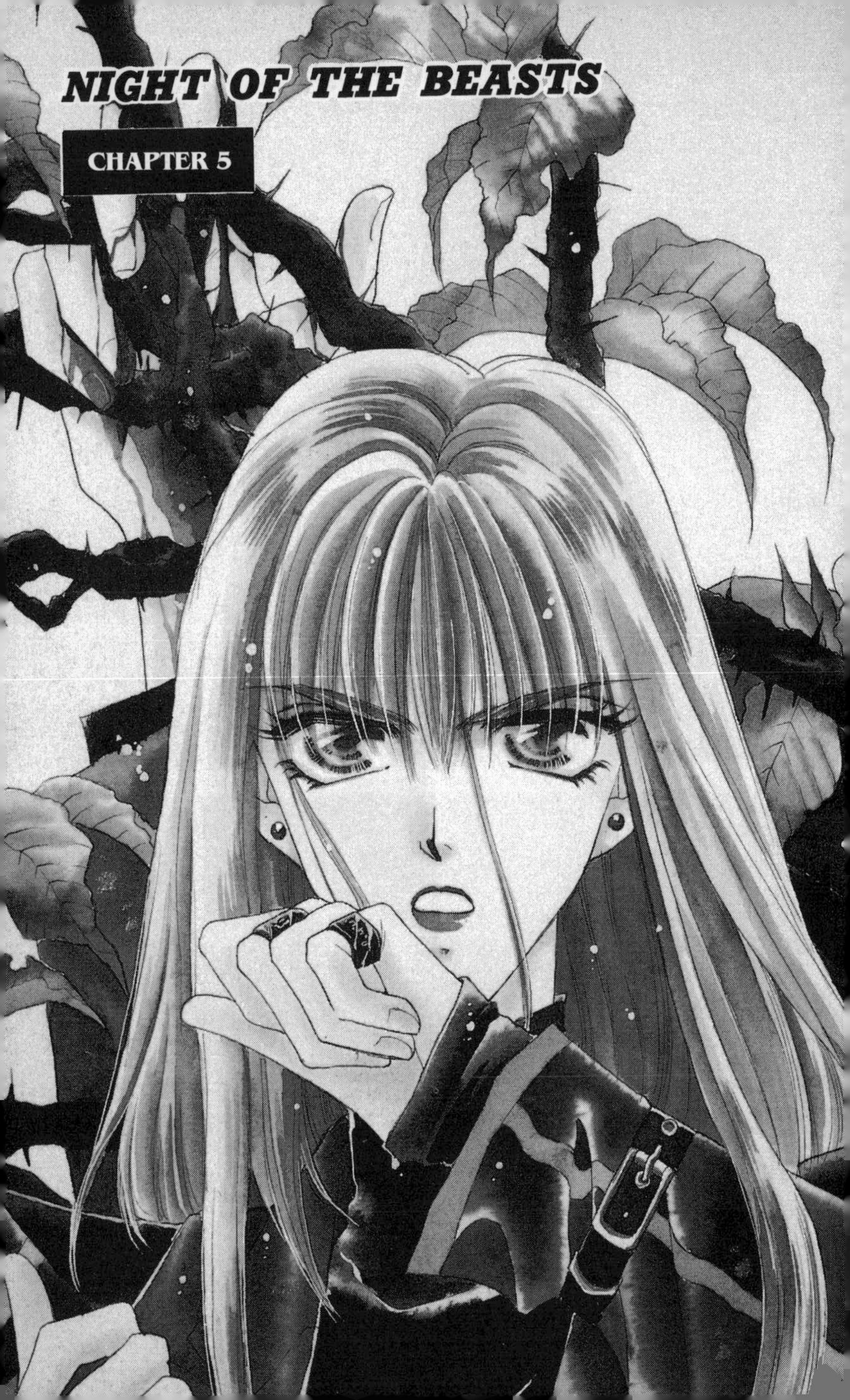
NIGHT OF THE BEASTS
CHAPTER 5

獣(けもの)たちの夜(よる)

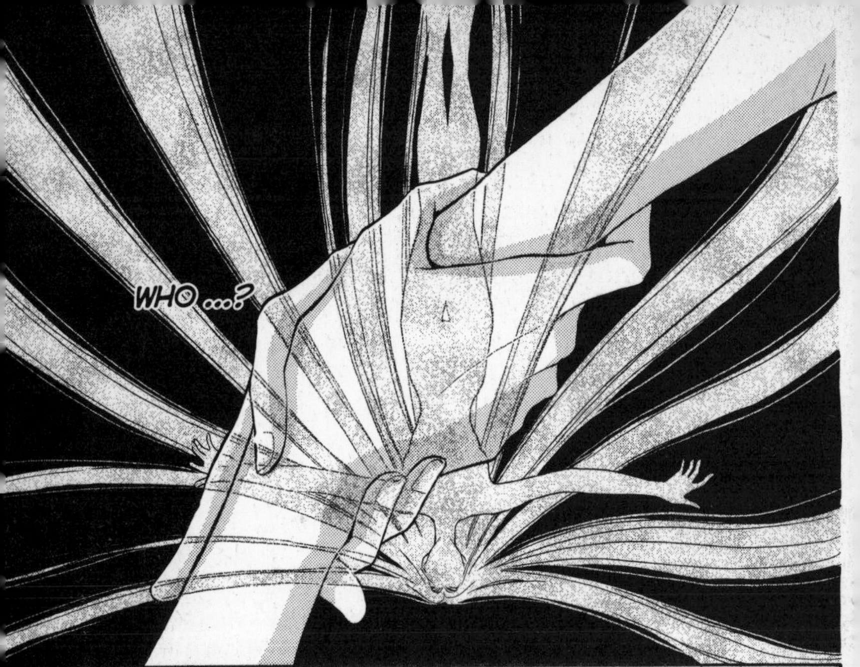
WHO ...?

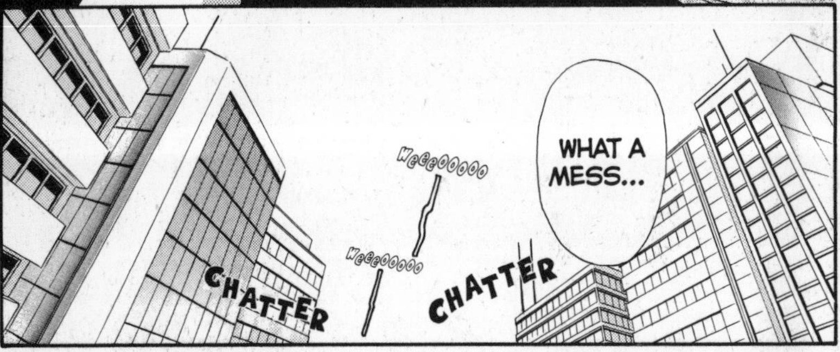
WHAT A MESS...
CHATTER
WEEEOOOOO
WEEEOOOOO
CHATTER

■Aria Yamaguchi■

The main character from my last series was named "Canon." This time it's "Aria," so I get asked a lot by my readers if the names were chosen from music terminology. I never meant for it to turn out that way, but I guess that's how it ended up. ♪ But just to live up to everyone's expectations, I'll be sure to name my next main character "Doremi-chan"! Or how about "Piano-chan"? (What sort of kanji would I use to spell them out, I wonder?)

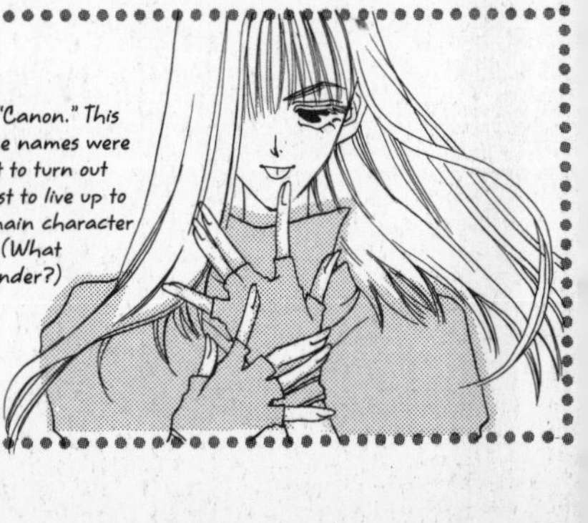

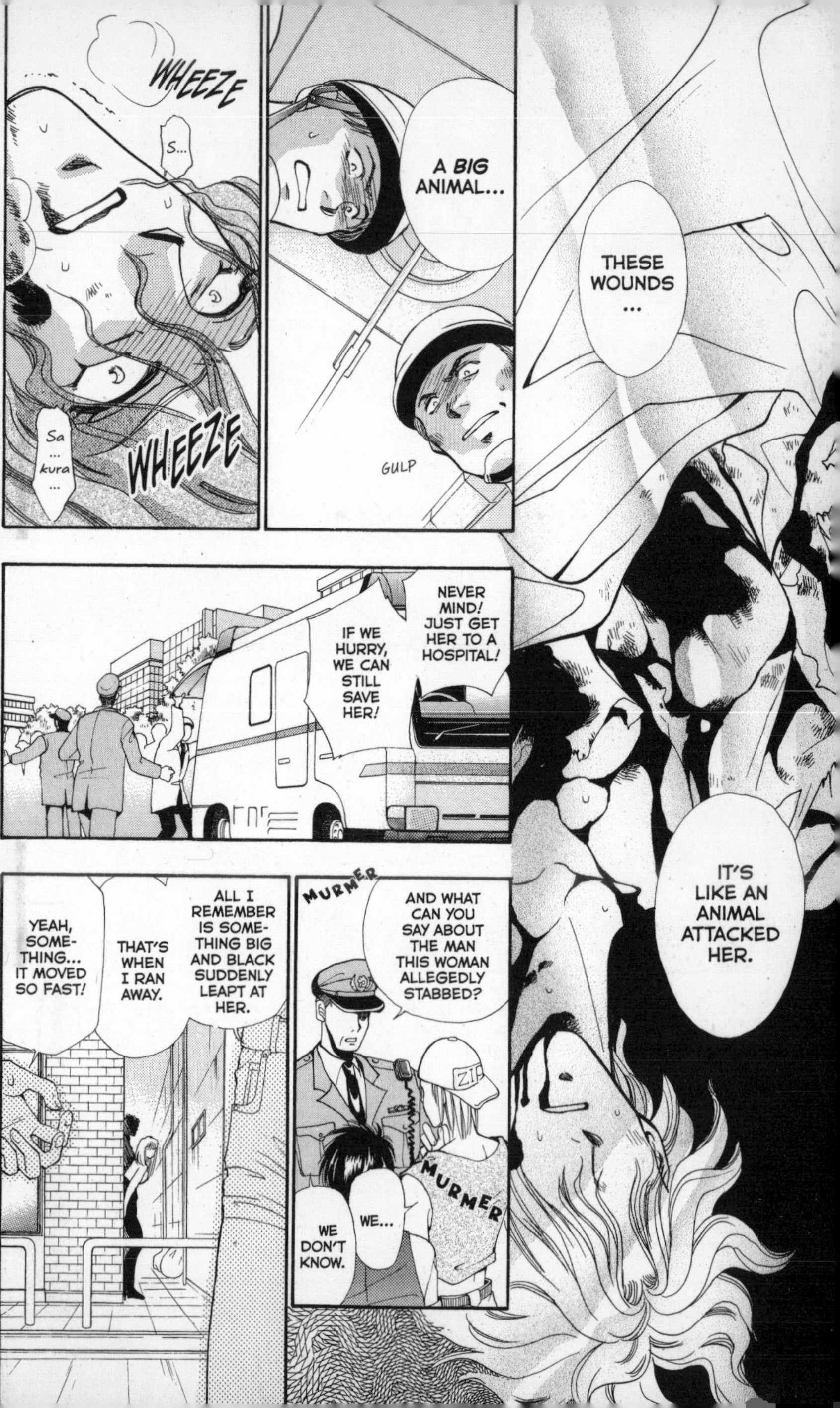
THESE WOUNDS...
IT'S LIKE AN ANIMAL ATTACKED HER.
A BIG ANIMAL...
GULP
WHEEZE
S...
Sa... kura...
WHEEZE
NEVER MIND! JUST GET HER TO A HOSPITAL!
IF WE HURRY, WE CAN STILL SAVE HER!
MURMER
AND WHAT CAN YOU SAY ABOUT THE MAN THIS WOMAN ALLEGEDLY STABBED?
MURMER
WE...
WE DON'T KNOW.
ALL I REMEMBER IS SOMETHING BIG AND BLACK SUDDENLY LEAPT AT HER.
THAT'S WHEN I RAN AWAY.
YEAH, SOMETHING... IT MOVED SO FAST!

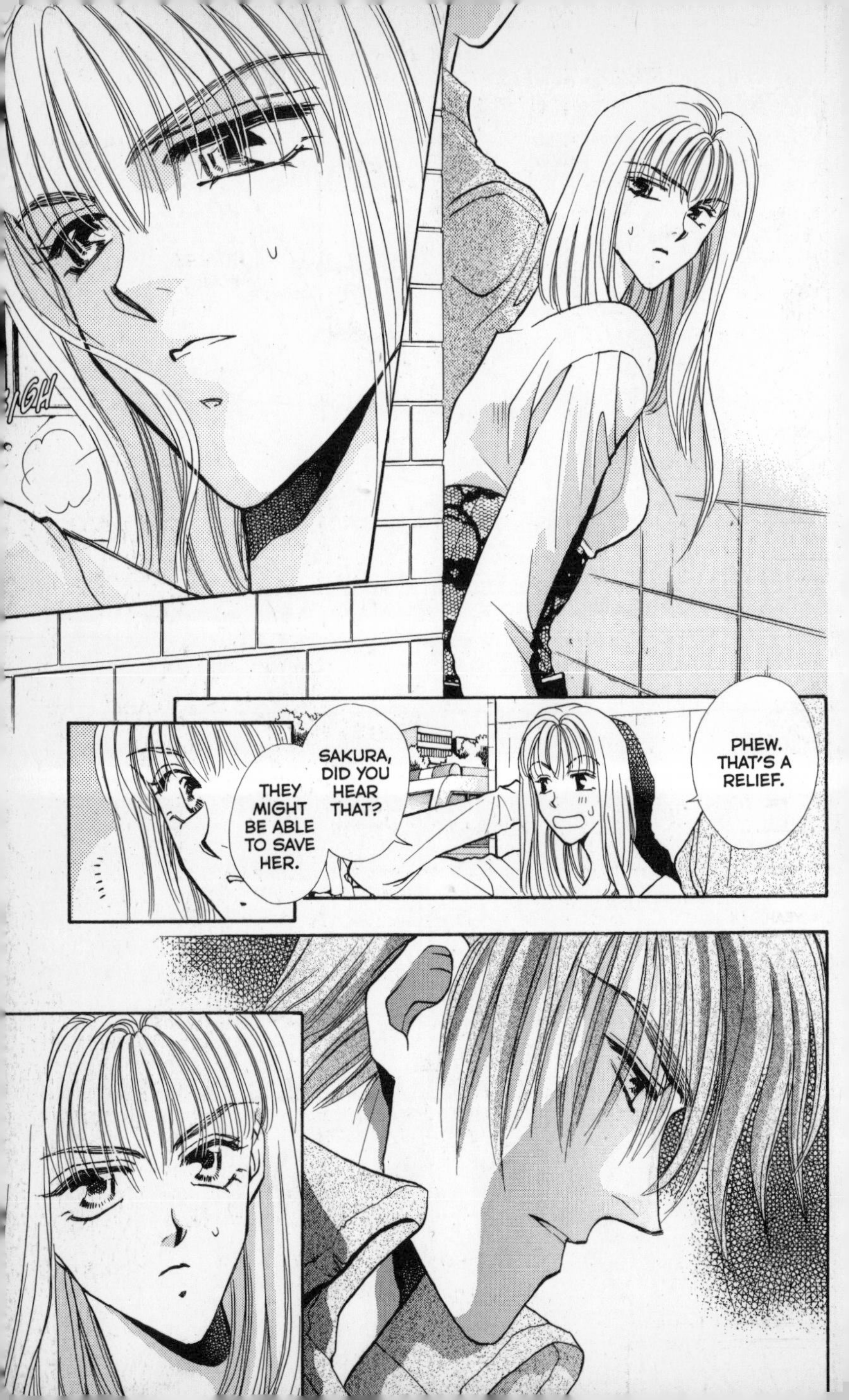
PHEW. THAT'S A RELIEF.
SAKURA, DID YOU HEAR THAT?
THEY MIGHT BE ABLE TO SAVE HER.

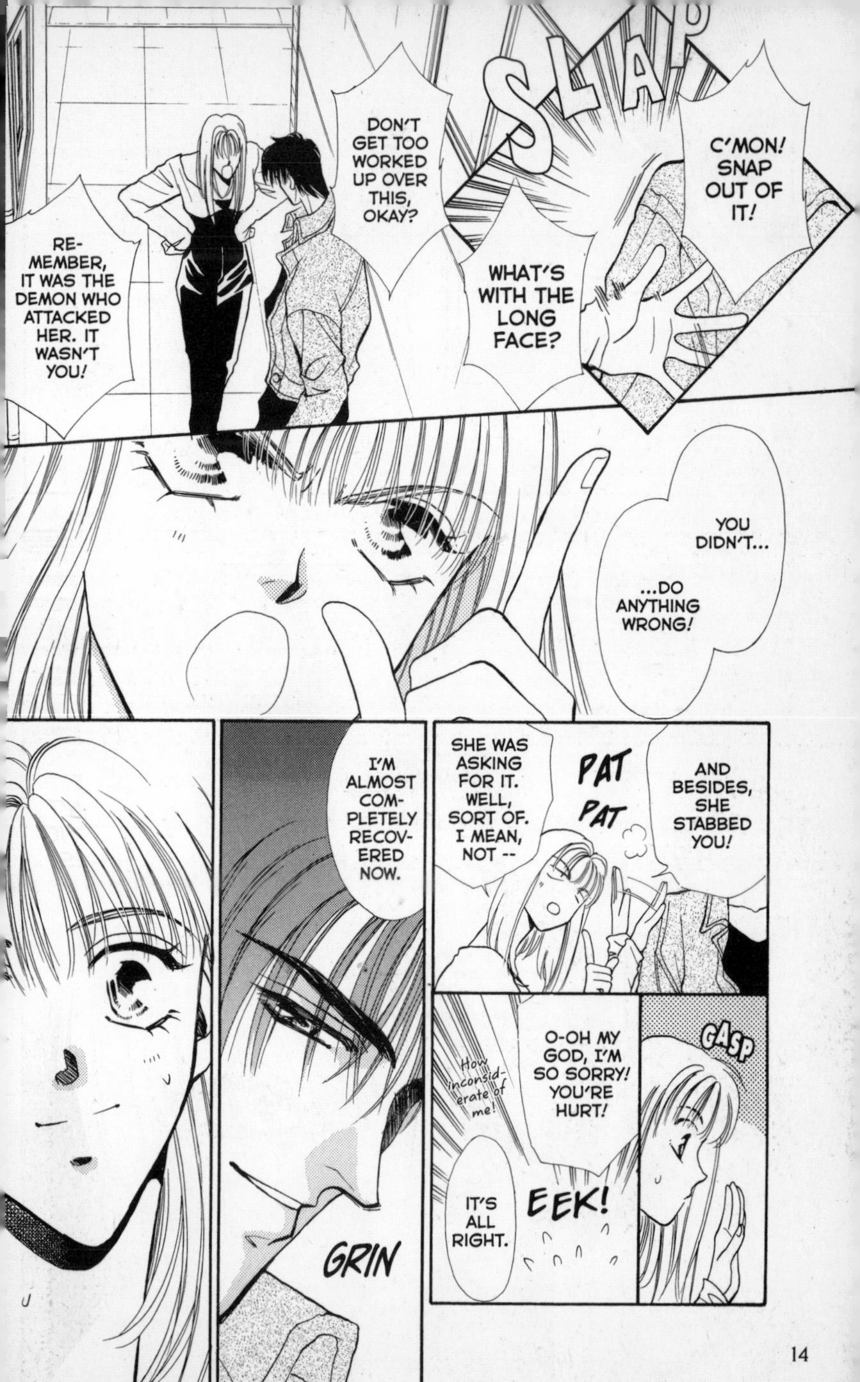
SLAP
C'MON! SNAP OUT OF IT!
WHAT'S WITH THE LONG FACE?
DON'T GET TOO WORKED UP OVER THIS, OKAY?
RE-MEMBER, IT WAS THE DEMON WHO ATTACKED HER. IT WASN'T YOU!
YOU DIDN'T...
...DO ANYTHING WRONG!
AND BESIDES, SHE STABBED YOU!
PAT PAT
SHE WAS ASKING FOR IT. WELL, SORT OF. I MEAN, NOT --
GASP
O-OH MY GOD, I'M SO SORRY! YOU'RE HURT!
How inconsid-erate of me!
EEK!
IT'S ALL RIGHT.
I'M ALMOST COM-PLETELY RECOV-ERED NOW.
GRIN

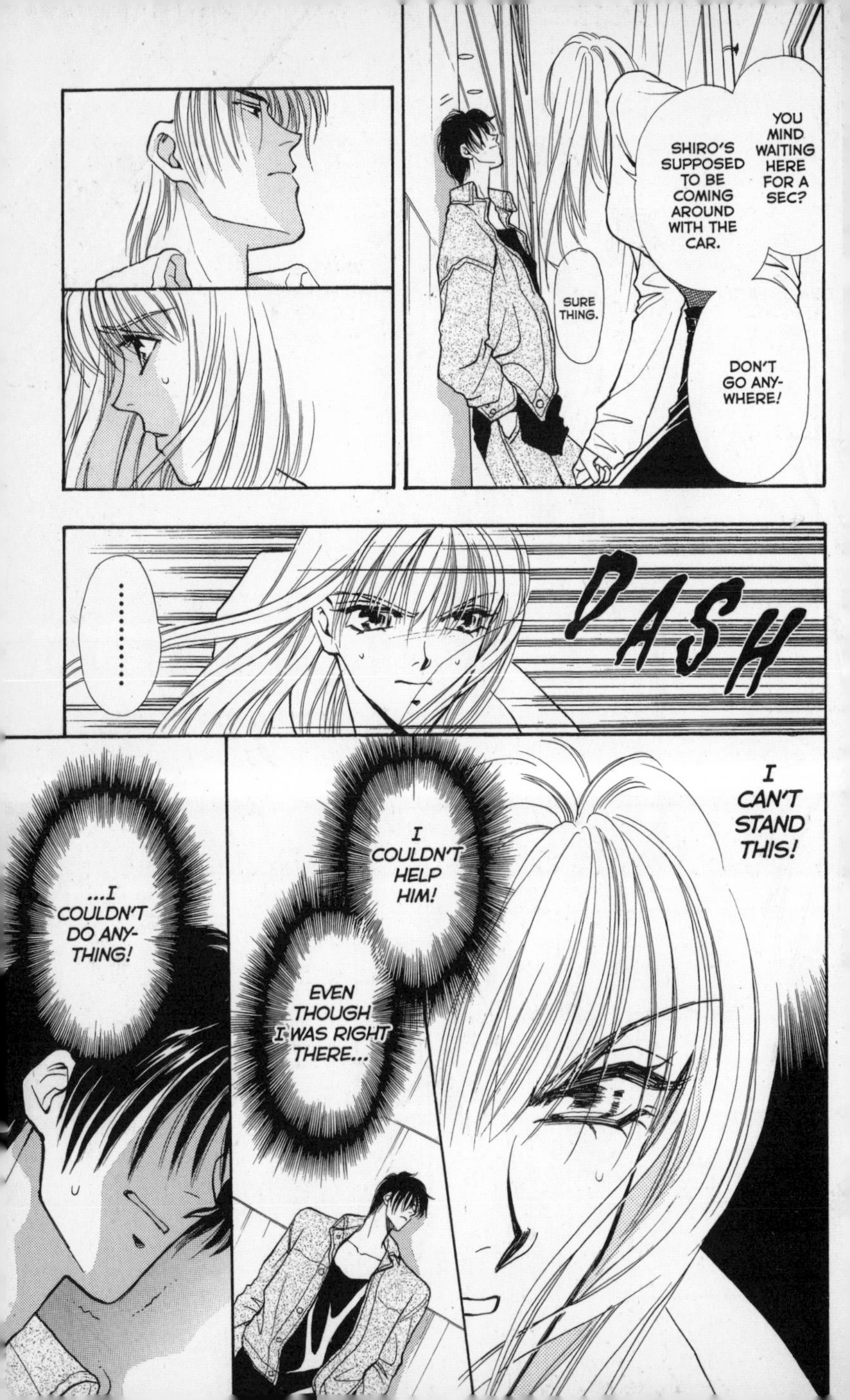
YOU MIND WAITING HERE FOR A SEC?
SHIRO'S SUPPOSED TO BE COMING AROUND WITH THE CAR.
SURE THING.
DON'T GO ANY-WHERE!
DASH
....
I CAN'T STAND THIS!
I COULDN'T HELP HIM!
EVEN THOUGH I WAS RIGHT THERE...
...I COULDN'T DO ANY-THING!

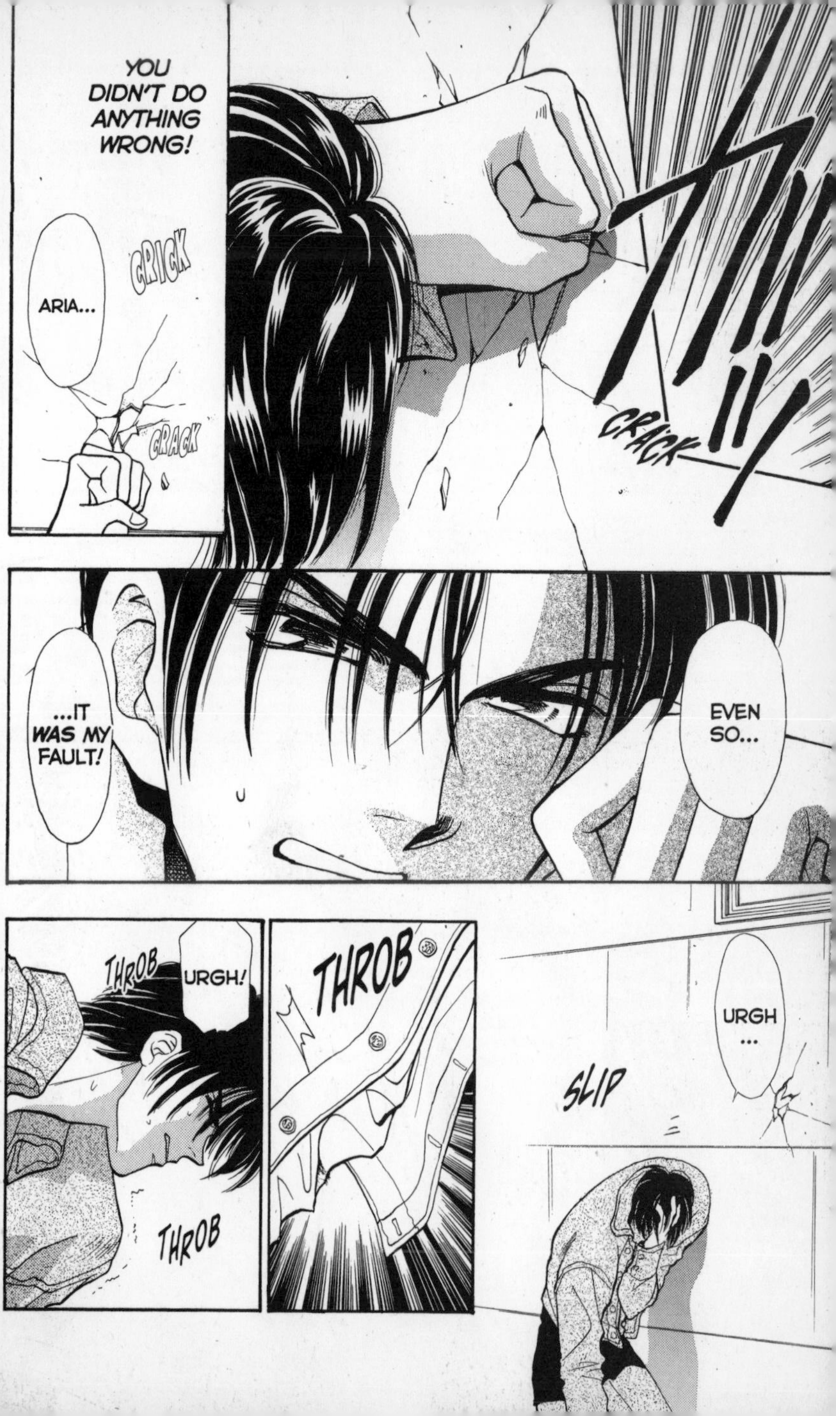
CRACK
YOU DIDN'T DO ANYTHING WRONG!
CRICK
ARIA...
CRACK
EVEN SO...
...IT WAS MY FAULT!
URGH ...
SLIP
THROB
URGH!
THROB
THROB

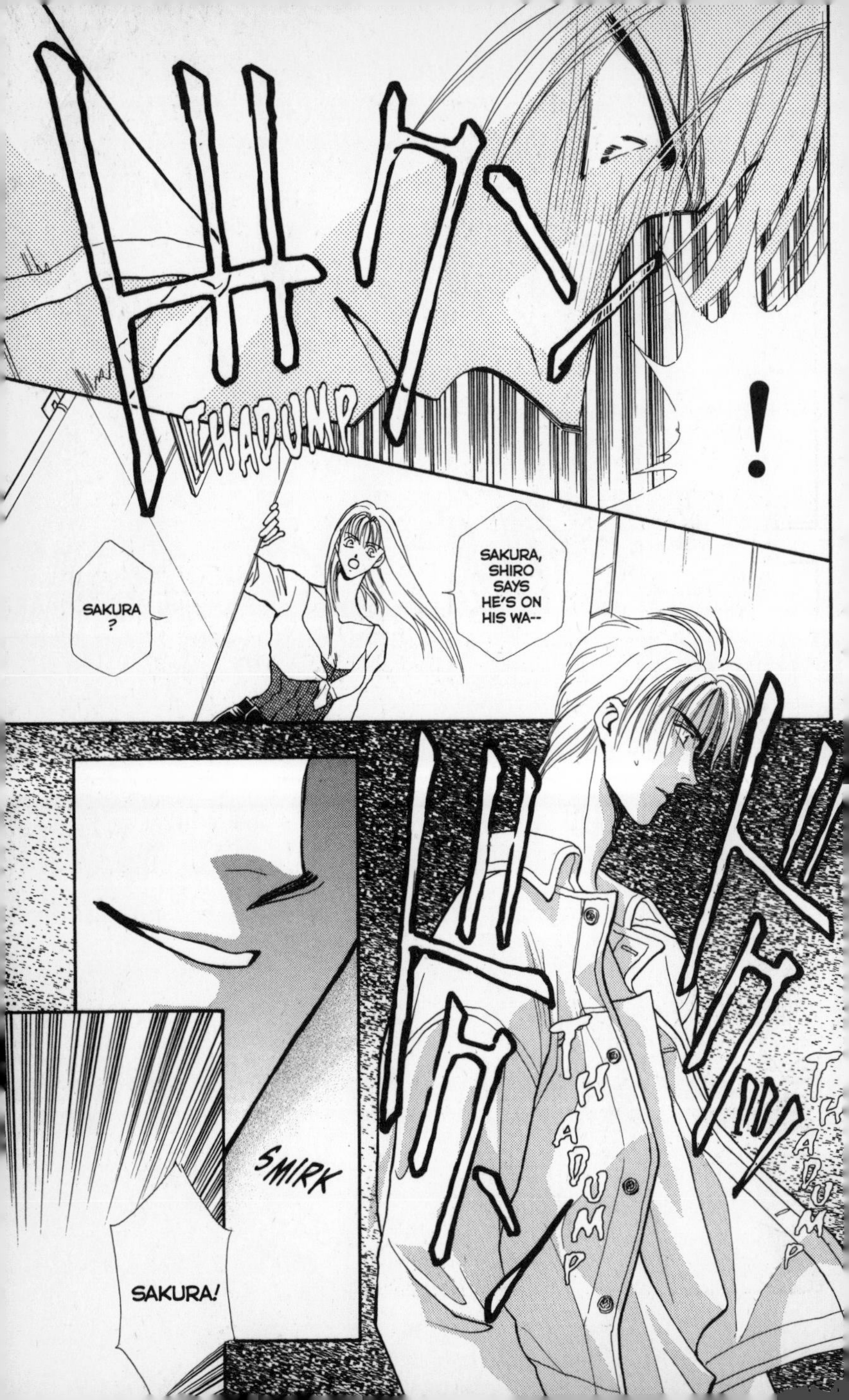
THADUMP
!
SAKURA, SHIRO SAYS HE'S ON HIS WA--
SAKURA ?
THADUMP
THADUMP
SMIRK
SAKURA!

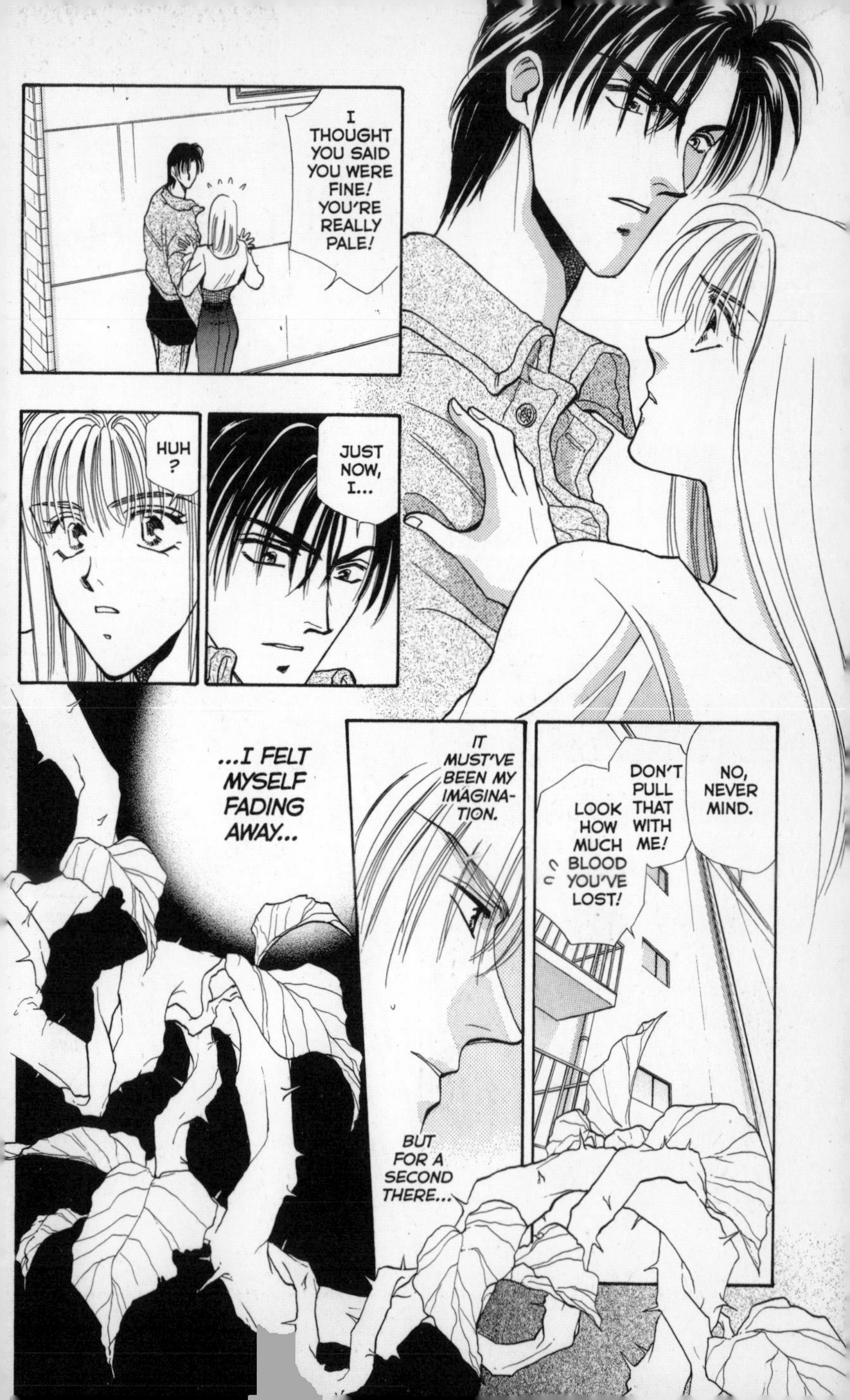
I THOUGHT YOU SAID YOU WERE FINE! YOU'RE REALLY PALE!
JUST NOW, I...
HUH?
NO, NEVER MIND.
DON'T PULL THAT WITH ME!
LOOK HOW MUCH BLOOD YOU'VE LOST!
IT MUST'VE BEEN MY IMAGINATION.
BUT FOR A SECOND THERE...
...I FELT MYSELF FADING AWAY...

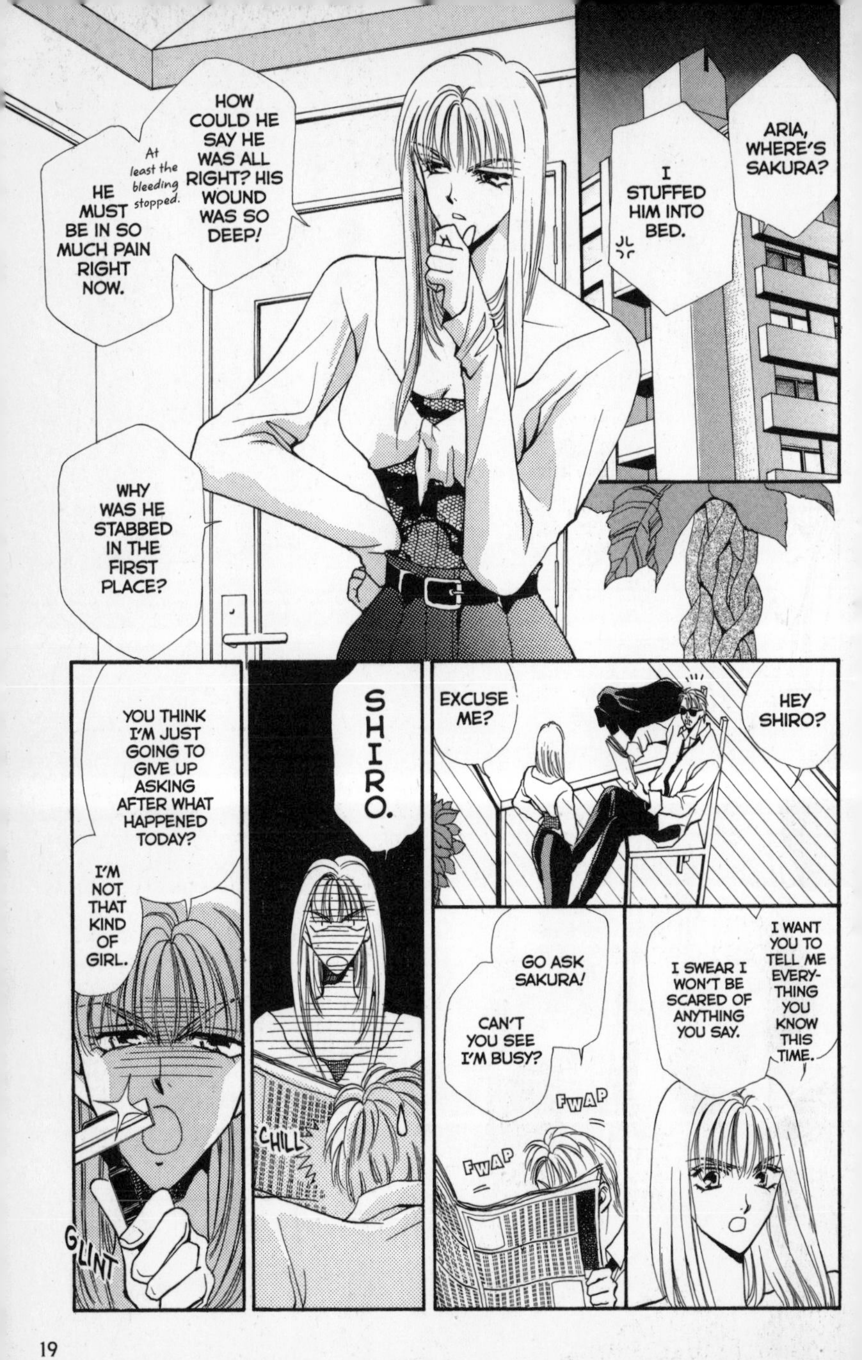
ARIA, WHERE'S SAKURA?
I STUFFED HIM INTO BED.
HOW COULD HE SAY HE WAS ALL RIGHT? HIS WOUND WAS SO DEEP!
At least the bleeding stopped.
HE MUST BE IN SO MUCH PAIN RIGHT NOW.
WHY WAS HE STABBED IN THE FIRST PLACE?
HEY SHIRO?
EXCUSE ME?
I WANT YOU TO TELL ME EVERY-THING YOU KNOW THIS TIME.
I SWEAR I WON'T BE SCARED OF ANYTHING YOU SAY.
GO ASK SAKURA!
CAN'T YOU SEE I'M BUSY?
FWAP
FWAP
SHIRO.
CHILL
YOU THINK I'M JUST GOING TO GIVE UP ASKING AFTER WHAT HAPPENED TODAY?
I'M NOT THAT KIND OF GIRL.
GLINT

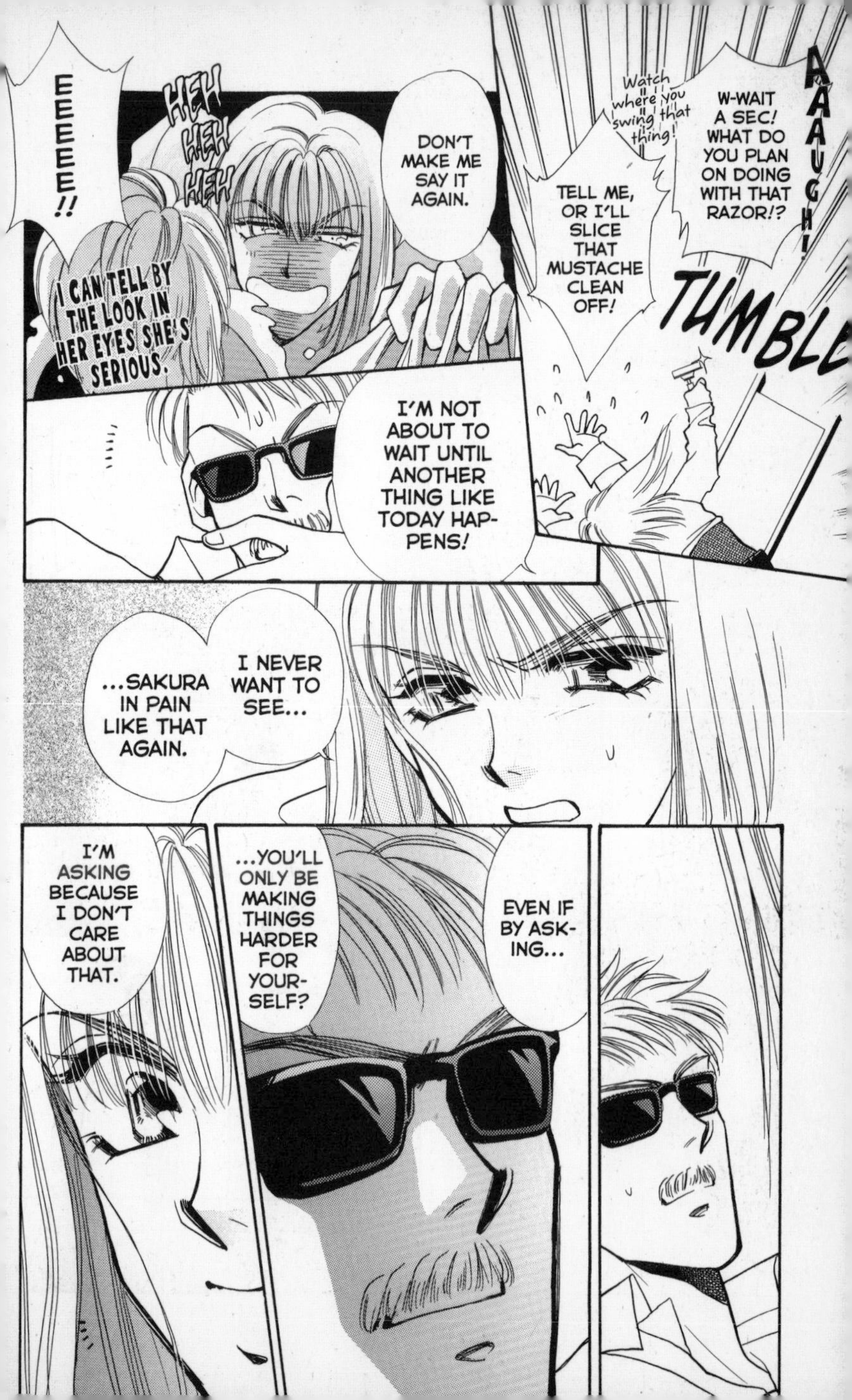
AAAUGH!
W-WAIT A SEC! WHAT DO YOU PLAN ON DOING WITH THAT RAZOR!?
Watch where you swing that thing!
TELL ME, OR I'LL SLICE THAT MUSTACHE CLEAN OFF!
TUMBLE
DON'T MAKE ME SAY IT AGAIN.
HEH HEH HEH
EEEEEE!!
I CAN TELL BY THE LOOK IN HER EYES SHE'S SERIOUS.
I'M NOT ABOUT TO WAIT UNTIL ANOTHER THING LIKE TODAY HAP-PENS!
...
I NEVER WANT TO SEE...
...SAKURA IN PAIN LIKE THAT AGAIN.
EVEN IF BY ASK-ING...
...YOU'LL ONLY BE MAKING THINGS HARDER FOR YOUR-SELF?
I'M ASKING BECAUSE I DON'T CARE ABOUT THAT.
...

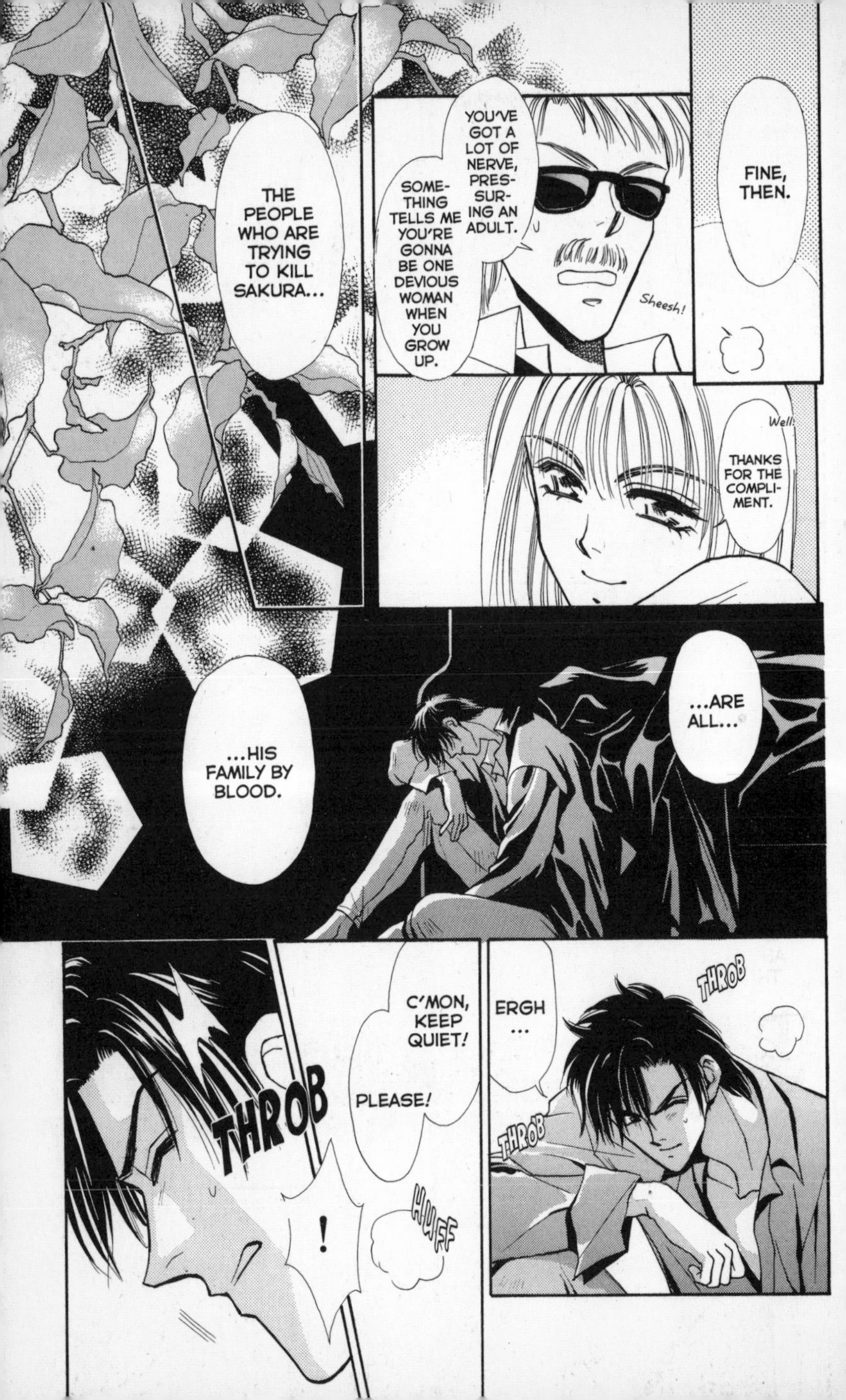
FINE, THEN.
YOU'VE GOT A LOT OF NERVE, PRESSURING AN ADULT.
SOMETHING TELLS ME YOU'RE GONNA BE ONE DEVIOUS WOMAN WHEN YOU GROW UP.
Sheesh!
Well!
THANKS FOR THE COMPLIMENT.
THE PEOPLE WHO ARE TRYING TO KILL SAKURA...
...ARE ALL...
...HIS FAMILY BY BLOOD.
THROB
ERGH ...
THROB
C'MON, KEEP QUIET!
PLEASE!
HUFF
THROB
!

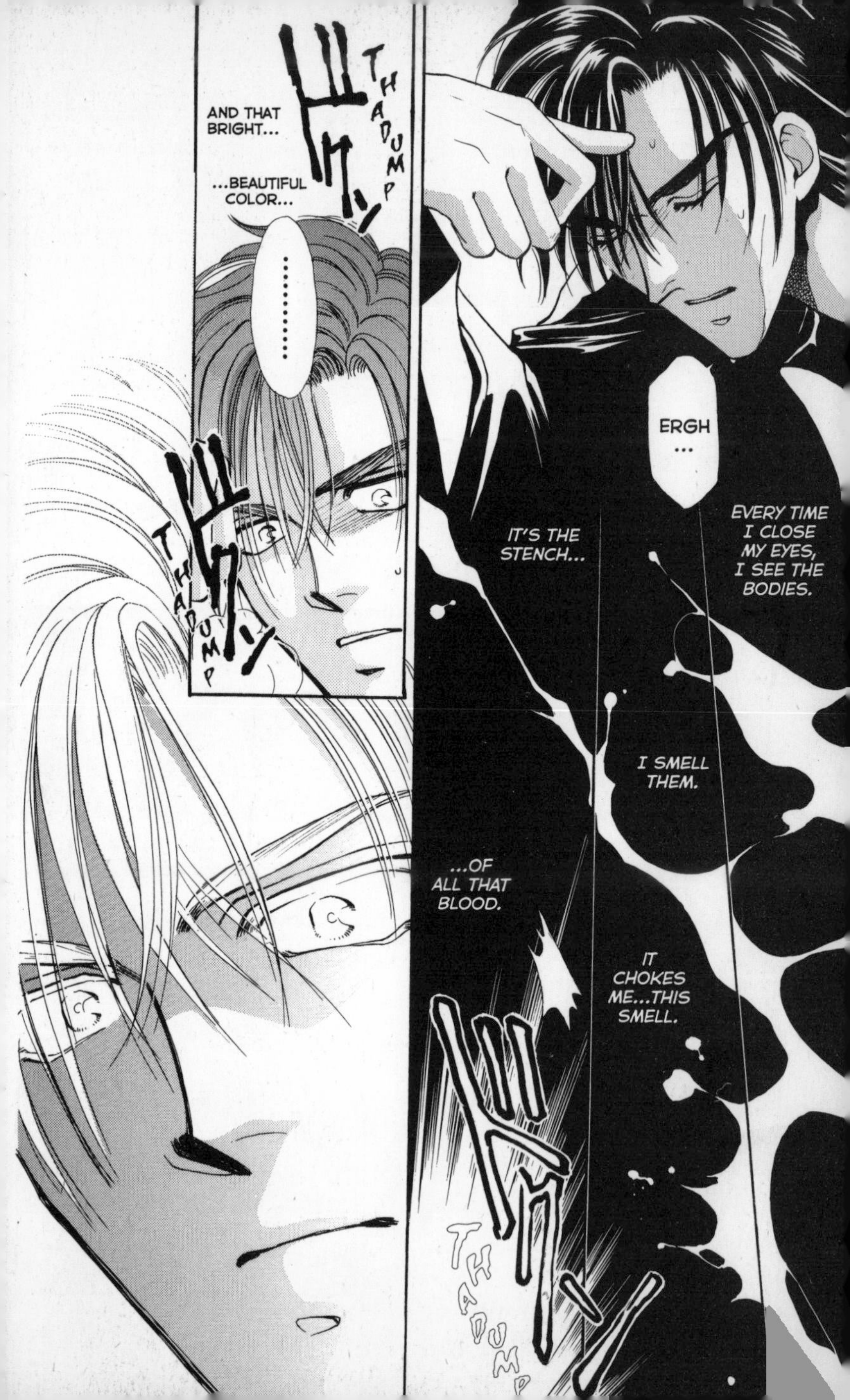
ERGH...
EVERY TIME I CLOSE MY EYES, I SEE THE BODIES.
IT'S THE STENCH...
I SMELL THEM.
...OF ALL THAT BLOOD.
IT CHOKES ME...THIS SMELL.
THADUMP
THADUMP
AND THAT BRIGHT...
...BEAUTIFUL COLOR...
......
THADUMP

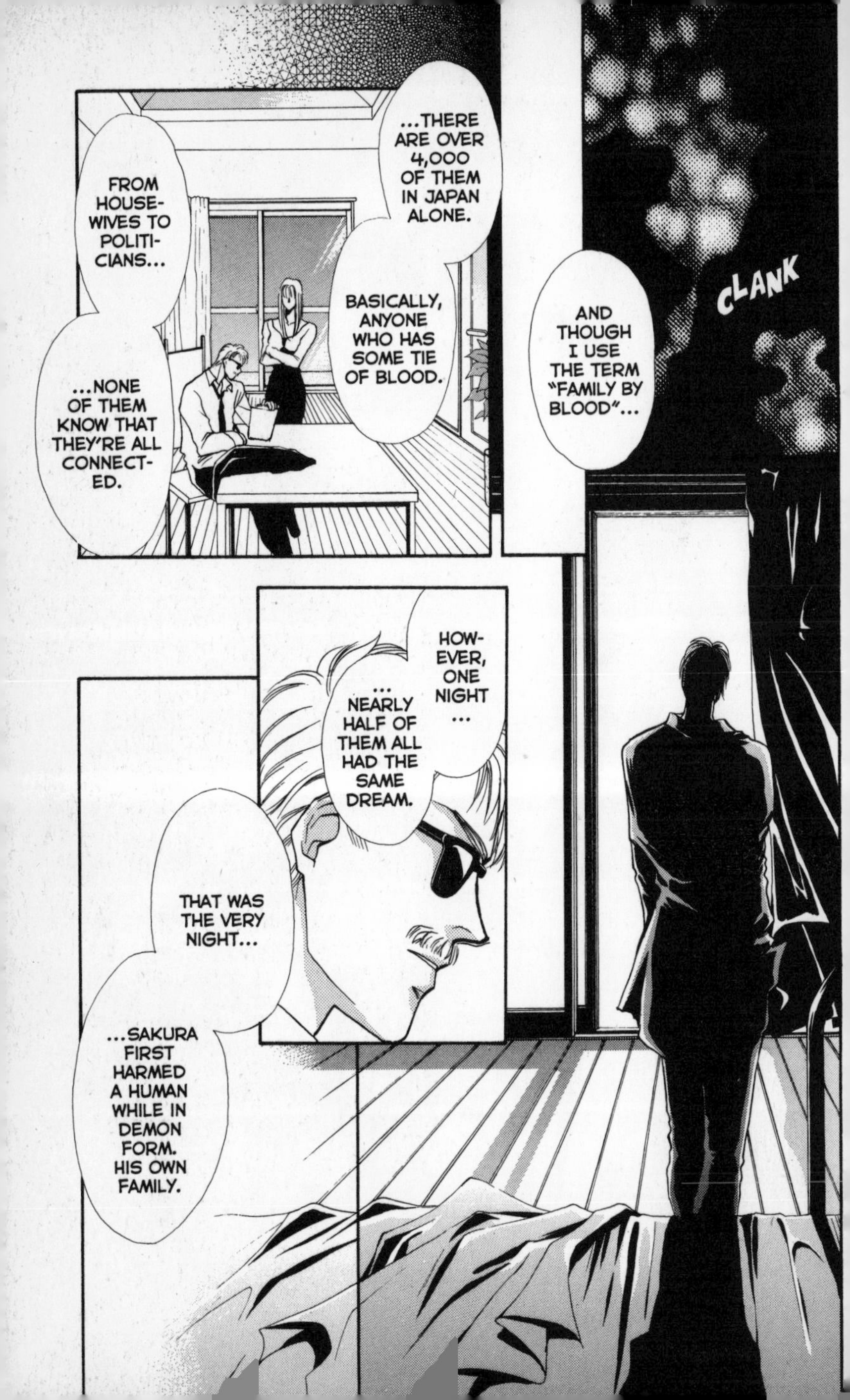
AND THOUGH I USE THE TERM "FAMILY BY BLOOD"...
CLANK
...THERE ARE OVER 4,000 OF THEM IN JAPAN ALONE.
BASICALLY, ANYONE WHO HAS SOME TIE OF BLOOD.
FROM HOUSE-WIVES TO POLITI-CIANS...
...NONE OF THEM KNOW THAT THEY'RE ALL CONNECT-ED.
HOW-EVER, ONE NIGHT...
...NEARLY HALF OF THEM ALL HAD THE SAME DREAM.
THAT WAS THE VERY NIGHT...
...SAKURA FIRST HARMED A HUMAN WHILE IN DEMON FORM. HIS OWN FAMILY.

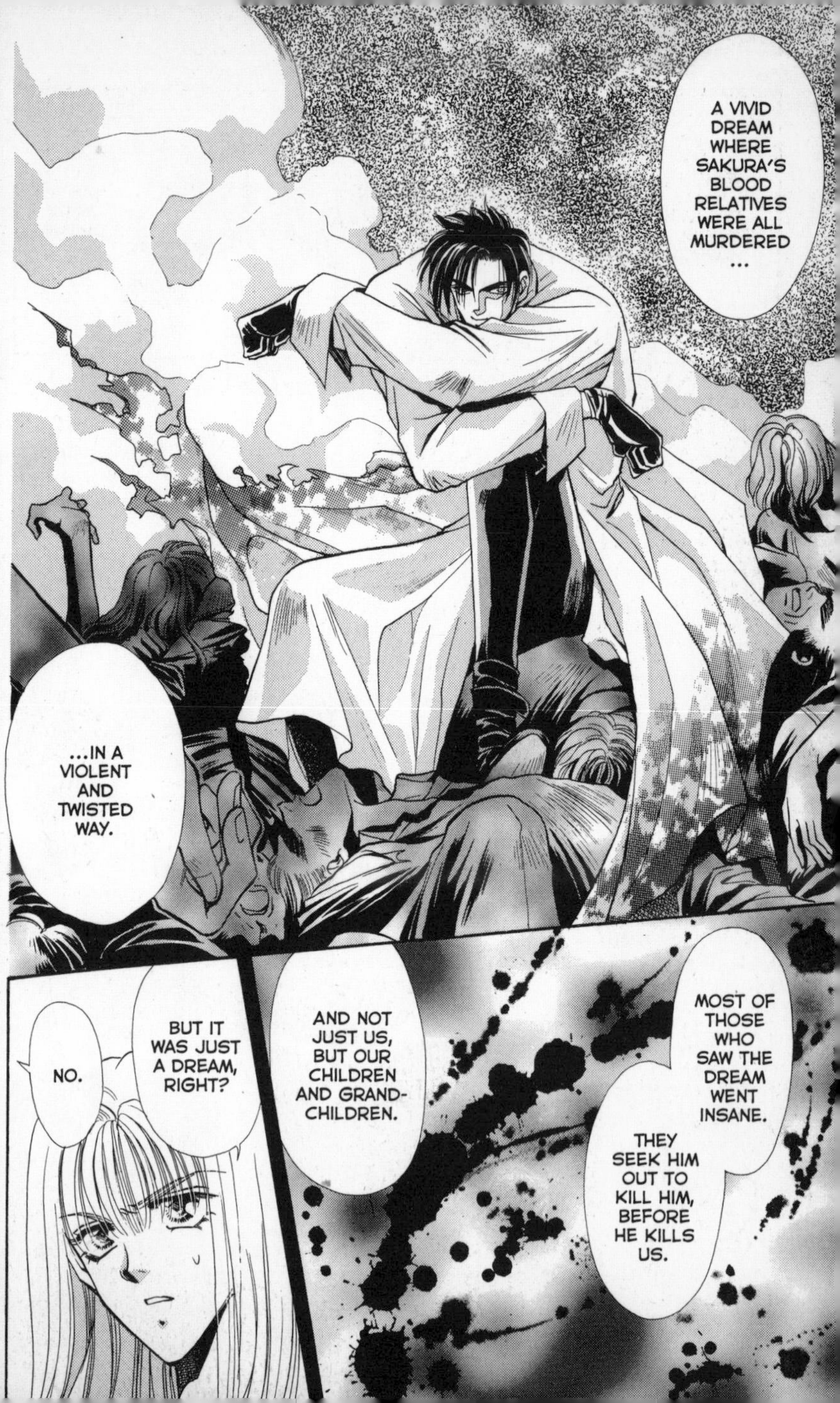
A VIVID DREAM WHERE SAKURA'S BLOOD RELATIVES WERE ALL MURDERED ...
...IN A VIOLENT AND TWISTED WAY.
MOST OF THOSE WHO SAW THE DREAM WENT INSANE.
THEY SEEK HIM OUT TO KILL HIM, BEFORE HE KILLS US.
AND NOT JUST US, BUT OUR CHILDREN AND GRAND-CHILDREN.
BUT IT WAS JUST A DREAM, RIGHT?
NO.

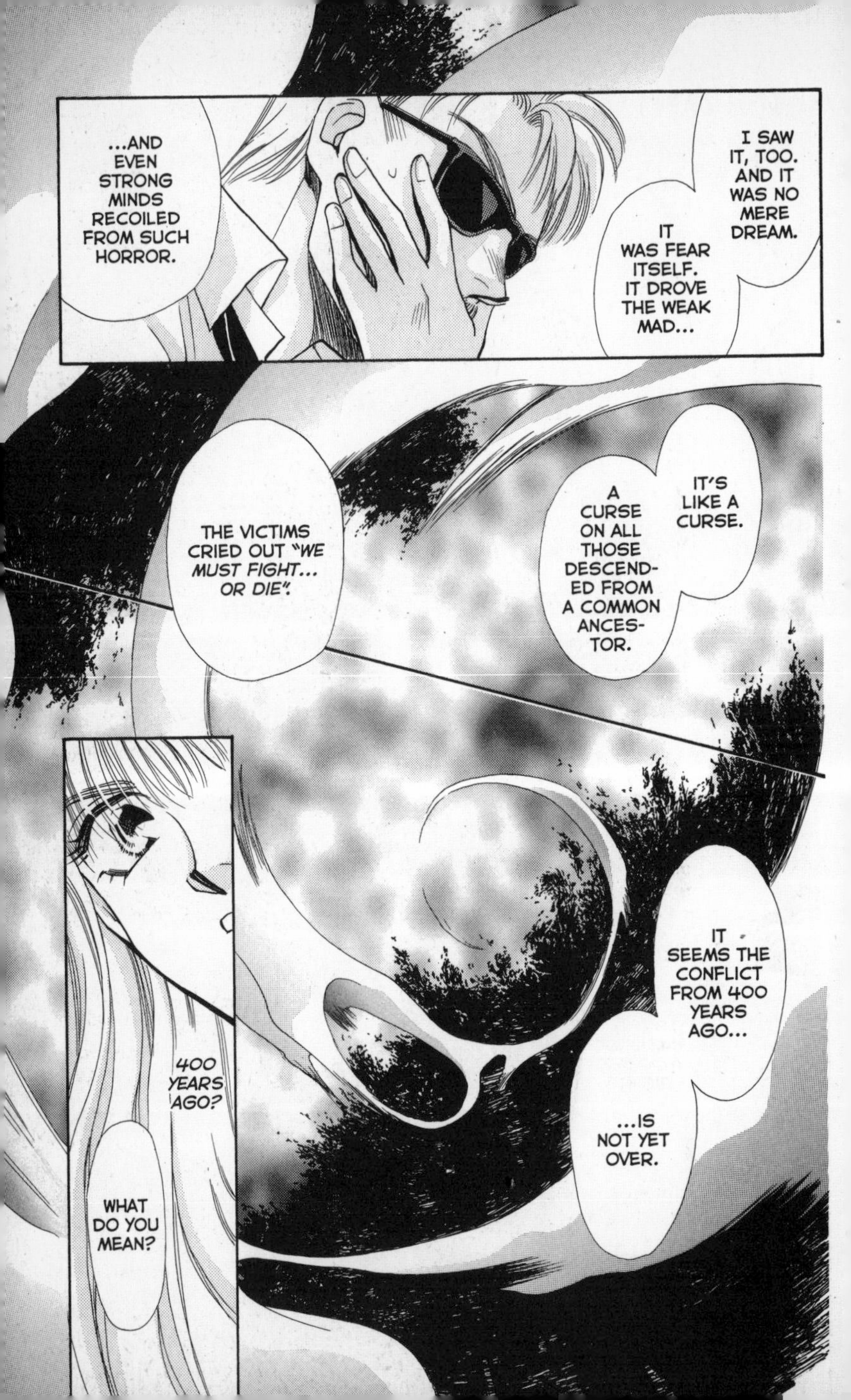
I SAW IT, TOO. AND IT WAS NO MERE DREAM.
IT WAS FEAR ITSELF. IT DROVE THE WEAK MAD...
...AND EVEN STRONG MINDS RECOILED FROM SUCH HORROR.
IT'S LIKE A CURSE.
A CURSE ON ALL THOSE DESCENDED FROM A COMMON ANCESTOR.
THE VICTIMS CRIED OUT "*WE MUST FIGHT... OR DIE*".
IT SEEMS THE CONFLICT FROM 400 YEARS AGO...
...IS NOT YET OVER.
400 YEARS AGO?
WHAT DO YOU MEAN?

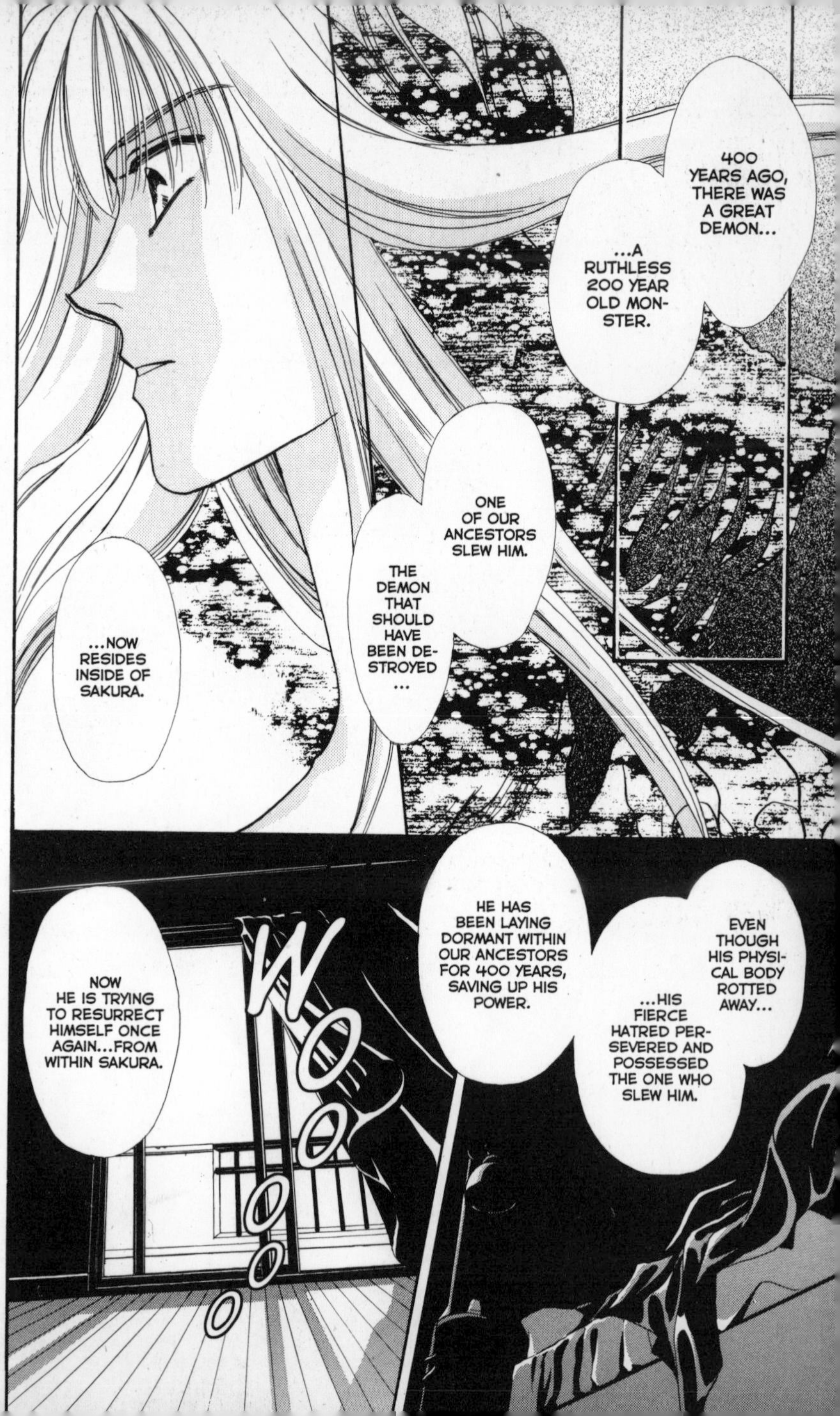
400 YEARS AGO, THERE WAS A GREAT DEMON...
...A RUTHLESS 200 YEAR OLD MON-STER.
ONE OF OUR ANCESTORS SLEW HIM.
THE DEMON THAT SHOULD HAVE BEEN DE-STROYED ...
...NOW RESIDES INSIDE OF SAKURA.
EVEN THOUGH HIS PHYSI-CAL BODY ROTTED AWAY...
...HIS FIERCE HATRED PER-SEVERED AND POSSESSED THE ONE WHO SLEW HIM.
HE HAS BEEN LAYING DORMANT WITHIN OUR ANCESTORS FOR 400 YEARS, SAVING UP HIS POWER.
WOOOOOO
NOW HE IS TRYING TO RESURRECT HIMSELF ONCE AGAIN...FROM WITHIN SAKURA.

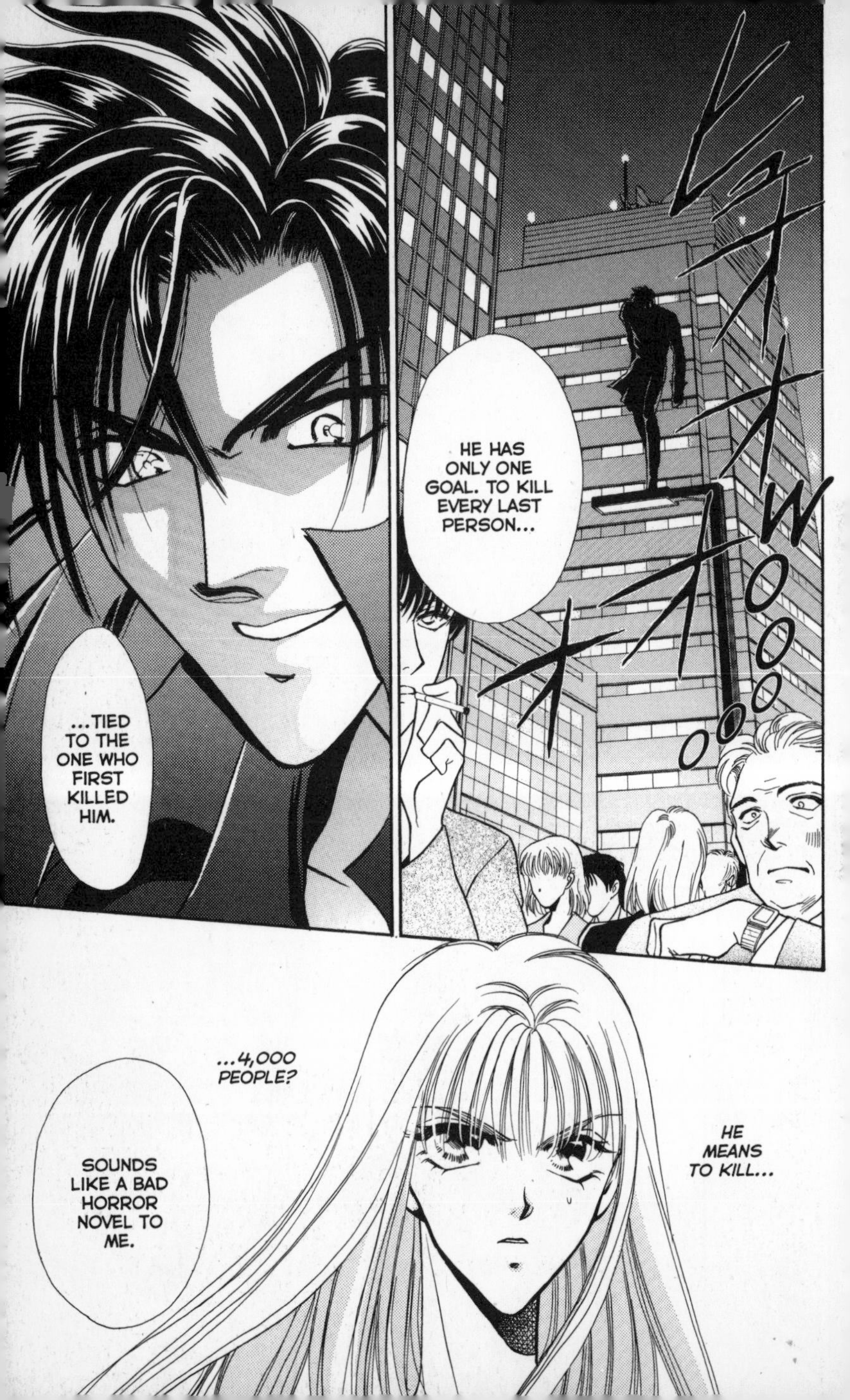
HE HAS ONLY ONE GOAL. TO KILL EVERY LAST PERSON...
WOOOOOOO
...TIED TO THE ONE WHO FIRST KILLED HIM.
HE MEANS TO KILL...
...4,000 PEOPLE?
SOUNDS LIKE A BAD HORROR NOVEL TO ME.

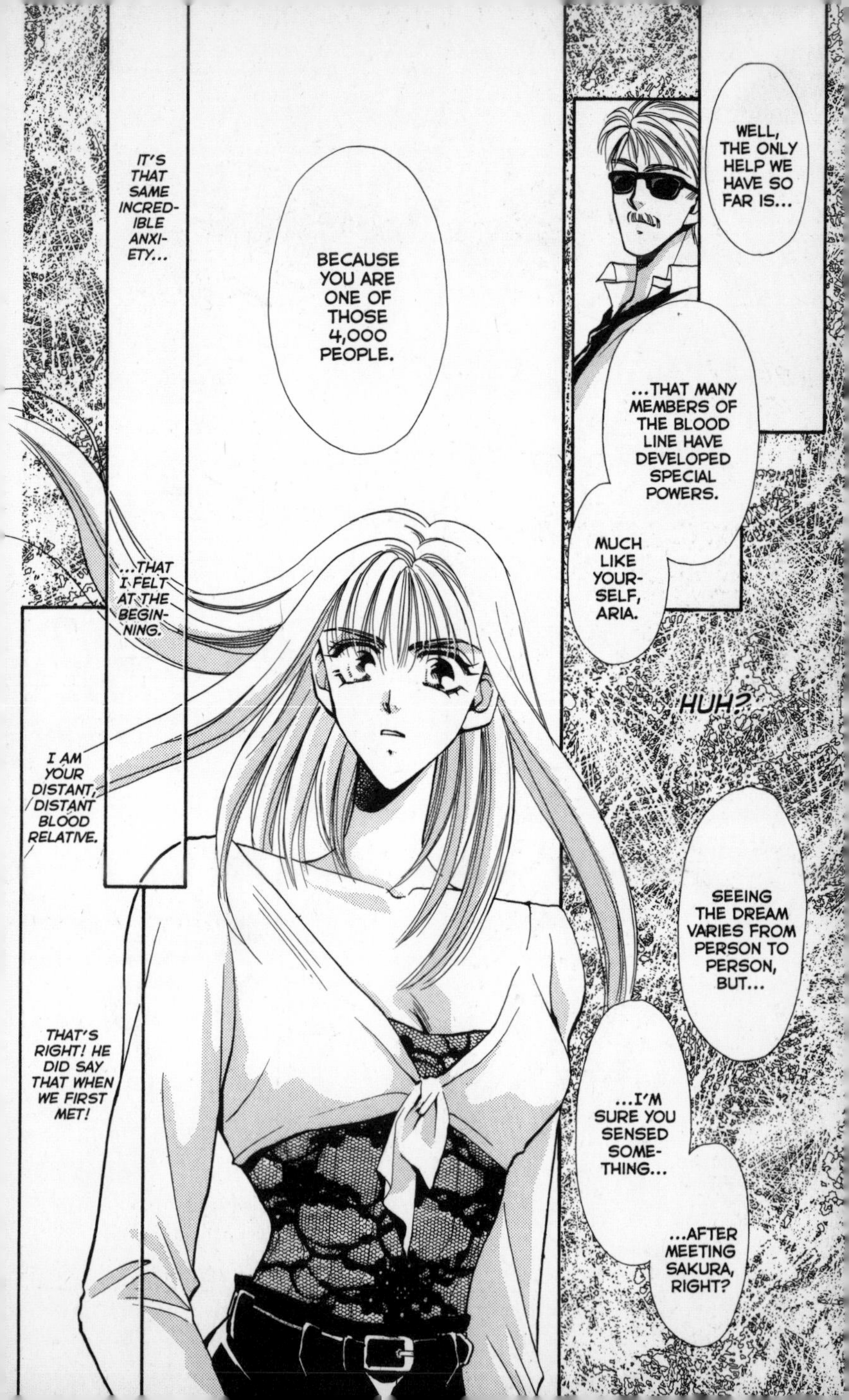
WELL, THE ONLY HELP WE HAVE SO FAR IS...
...THAT MANY MEMBERS OF THE BLOOD LINE HAVE DEVELOPED SPECIAL POWERS.
MUCH LIKE YOURSELF, ARIA.
HUH?
SEEING THE DREAM VARIES FROM PERSON TO PERSON, BUT...
...I'M SURE YOU SENSED SOMETHING...
...AFTER MEETING SAKURA, RIGHT?
BECAUSE YOU ARE ONE OF THOSE 4,000 PEOPLE.
IT'S THAT SAME INCREDIBLE ANXIETY...
...THAT I FELT AT THE BEGINNING.
I AM YOUR DISTANT, DISTANT BLOOD RELATIVE.
THAT'S RIGHT! HE DID SAY THAT WHEN WE FIRST MET!

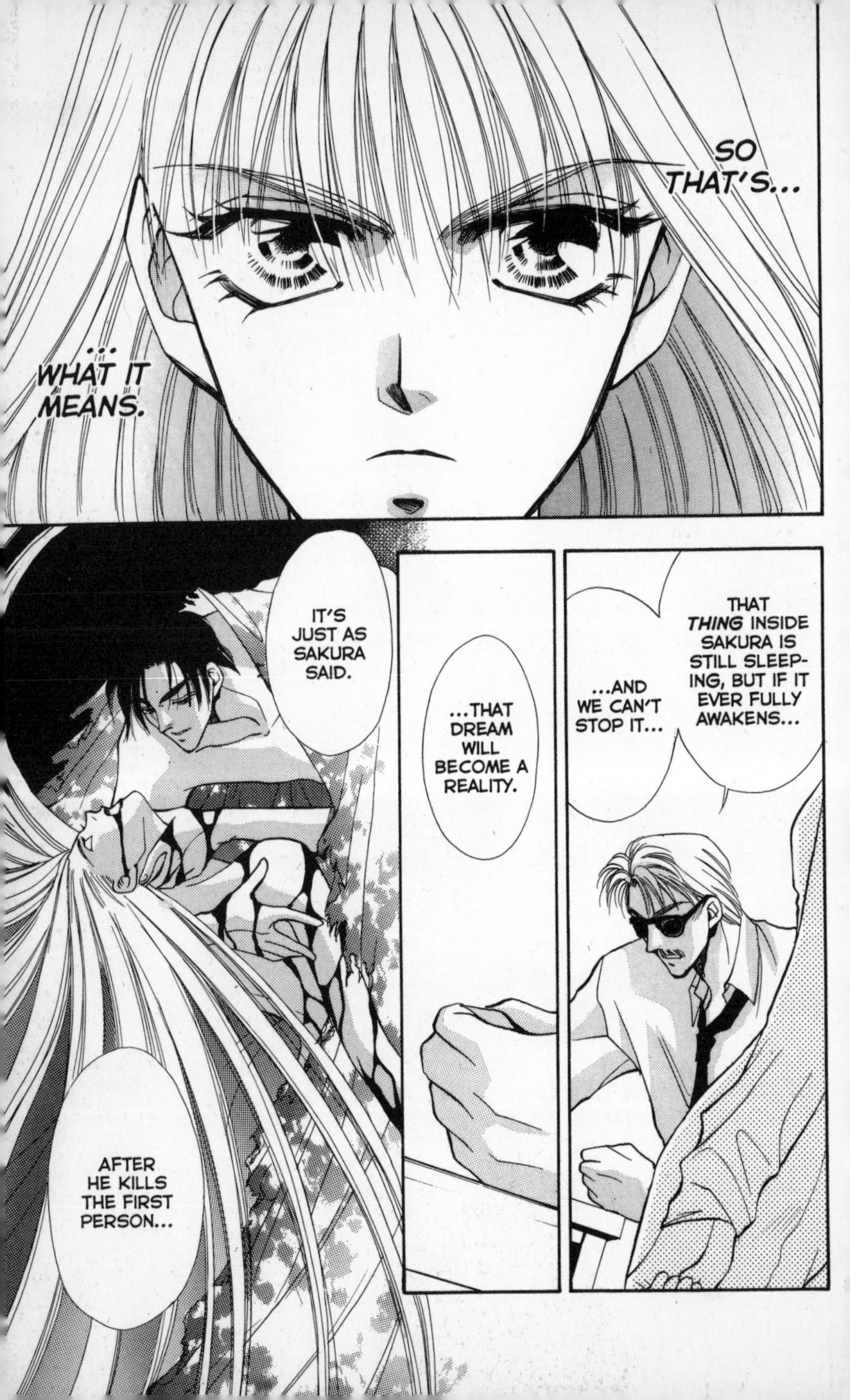
SO THAT'S...
...WHAT IT MEANS.
THAT *THING* INSIDE SAKURA IS STILL SLEEPING, BUT IF IT EVER FULLY AWAKENS...
...AND WE CAN'T STOP IT...
...THAT DREAM WILL BECOME A REALITY.
IT'S JUST AS SAKURA SAID.
AFTER HE KILLS THE FIRST PERSON...

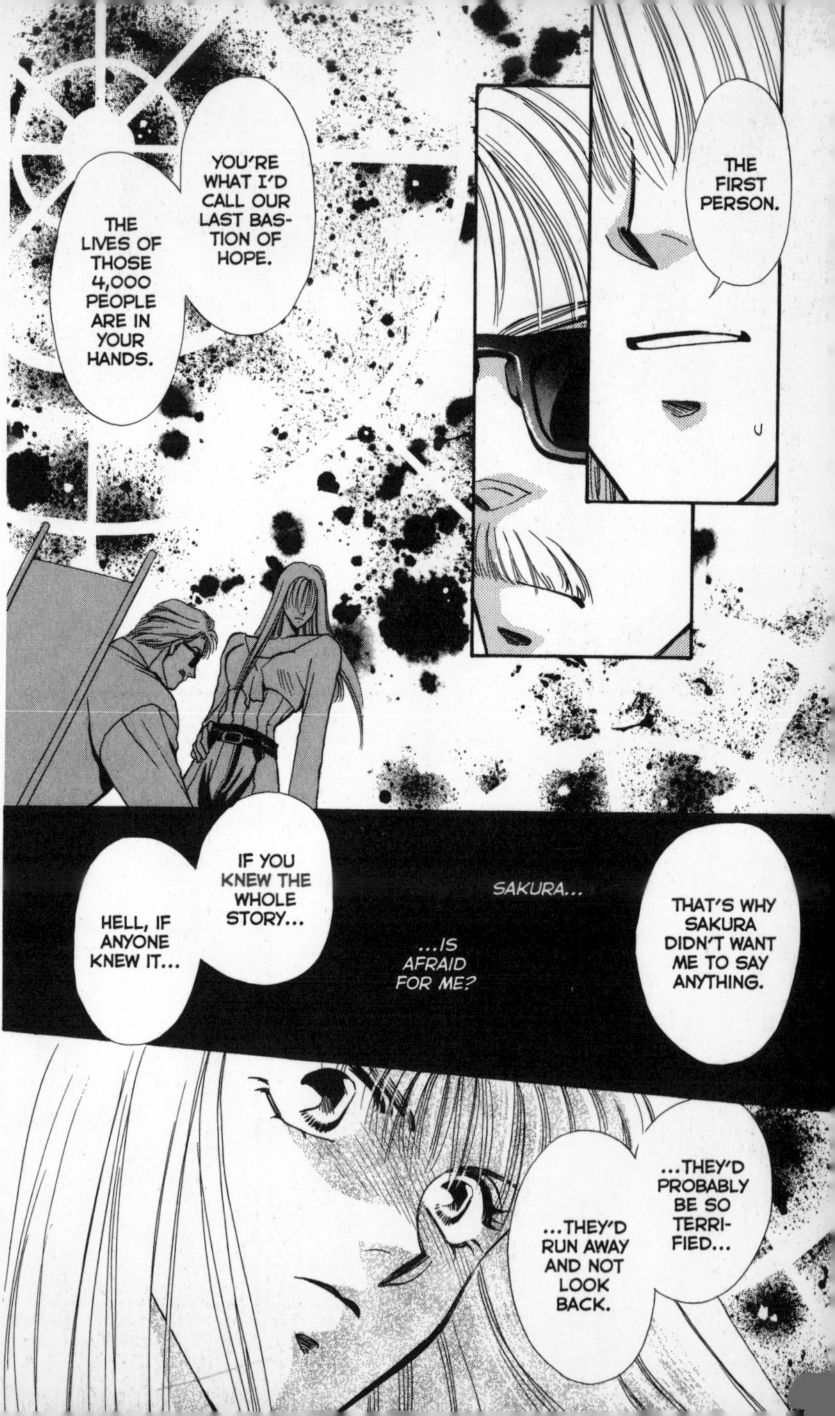
THE FIRST PERSON.
YOU'RE WHAT I'D CALL OUR LAST BAS-TION OF HOPE.
THE LIVES OF THOSE 4,000 PEOPLE ARE IN YOUR HANDS.
THAT'S WHY SAKURA DIDN'T WANT ME TO SAY ANYTHING.
SAKURA...
...IS AFRAID FOR ME?
IF YOU KNEW THE WHOLE STORY...
HELL, IF ANYONE KNEW IT...
...THEY'D PROBABLY BE SO TERRI-FIED...
...THEY'D RUN AWAY AND NOT LOOK BACK.

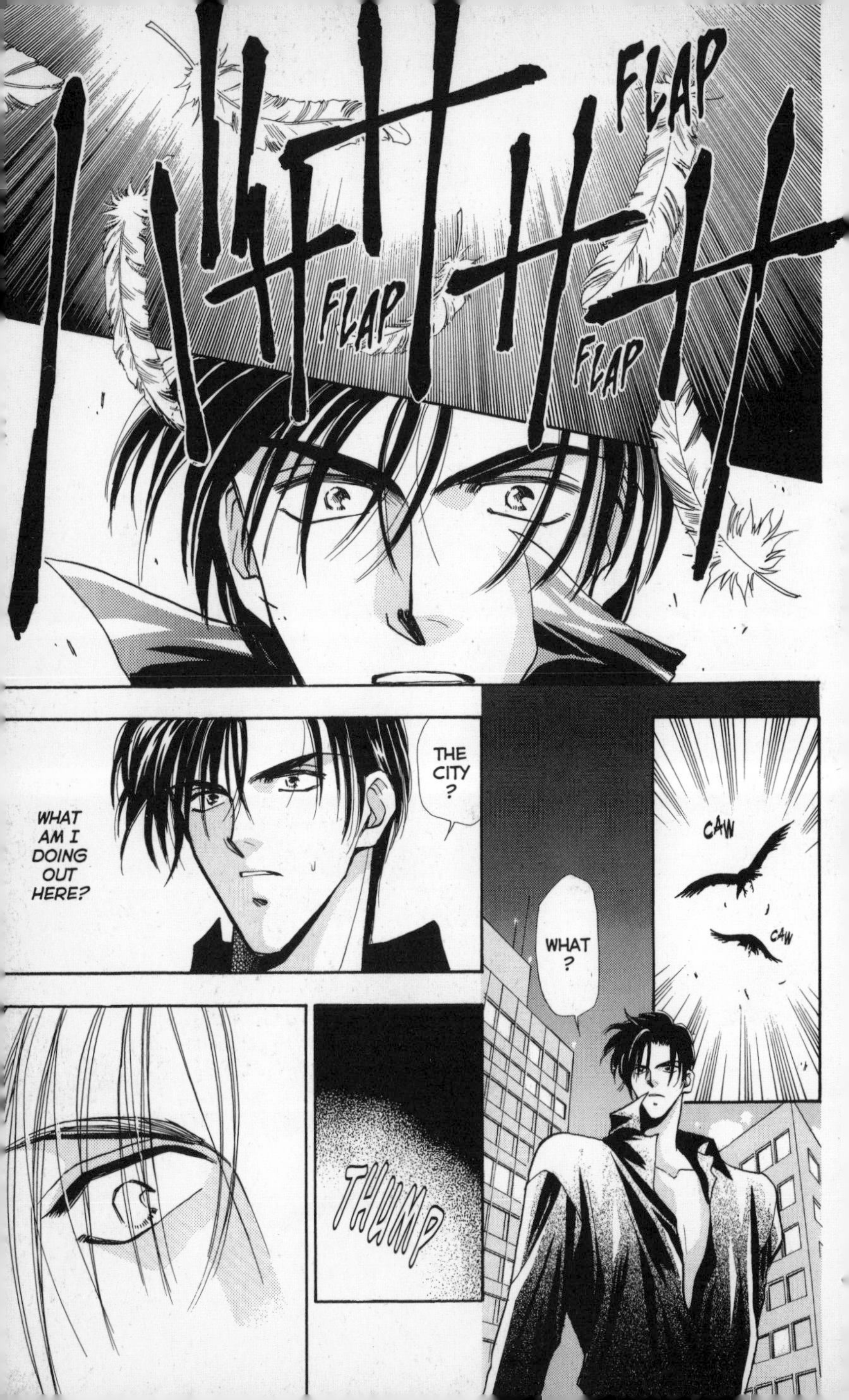
FLAP
FLAP
FLAP
CAW
CAW
WHAT ?
THE CITY ?
WHAT AM I DOING OUT HERE?
THUMP

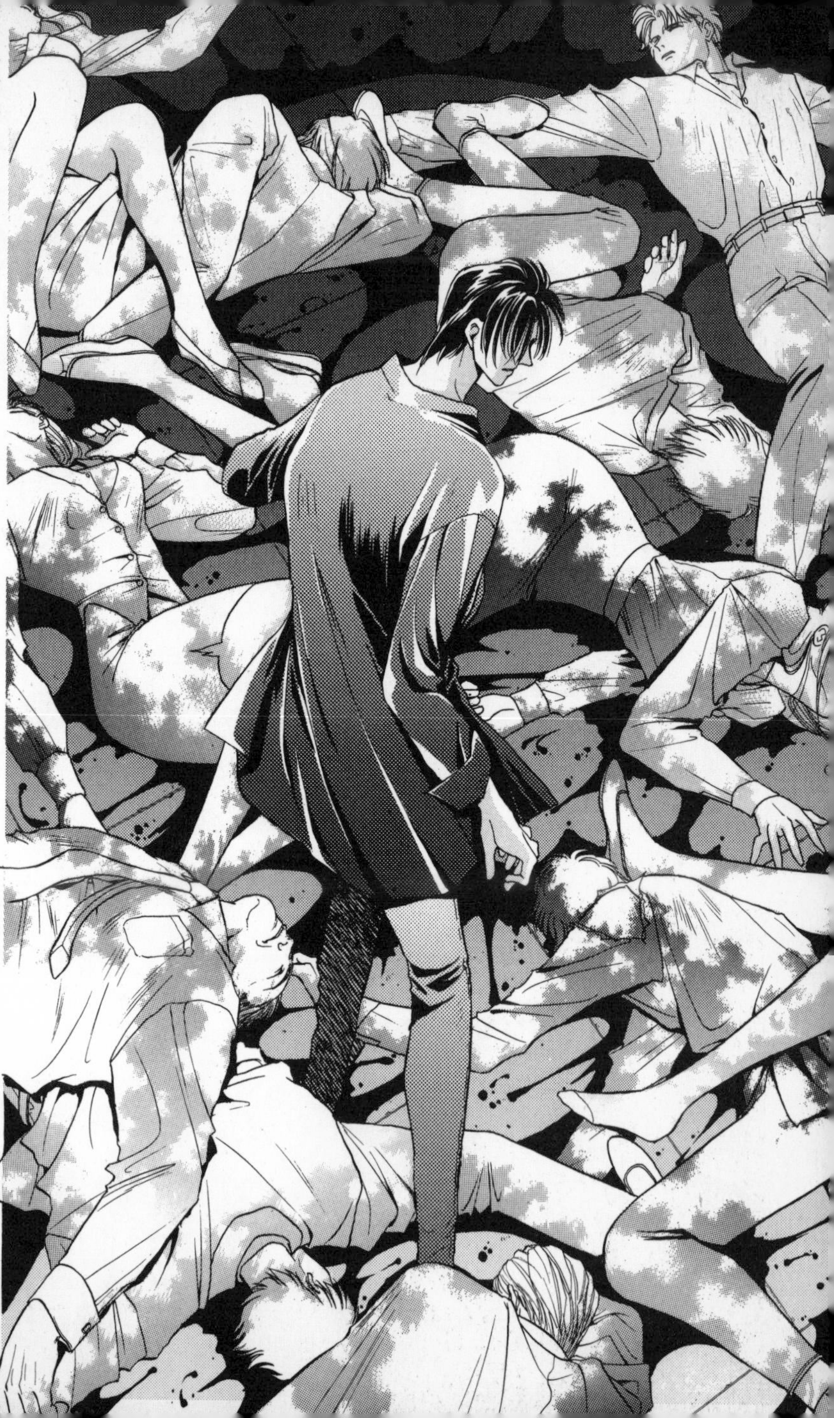

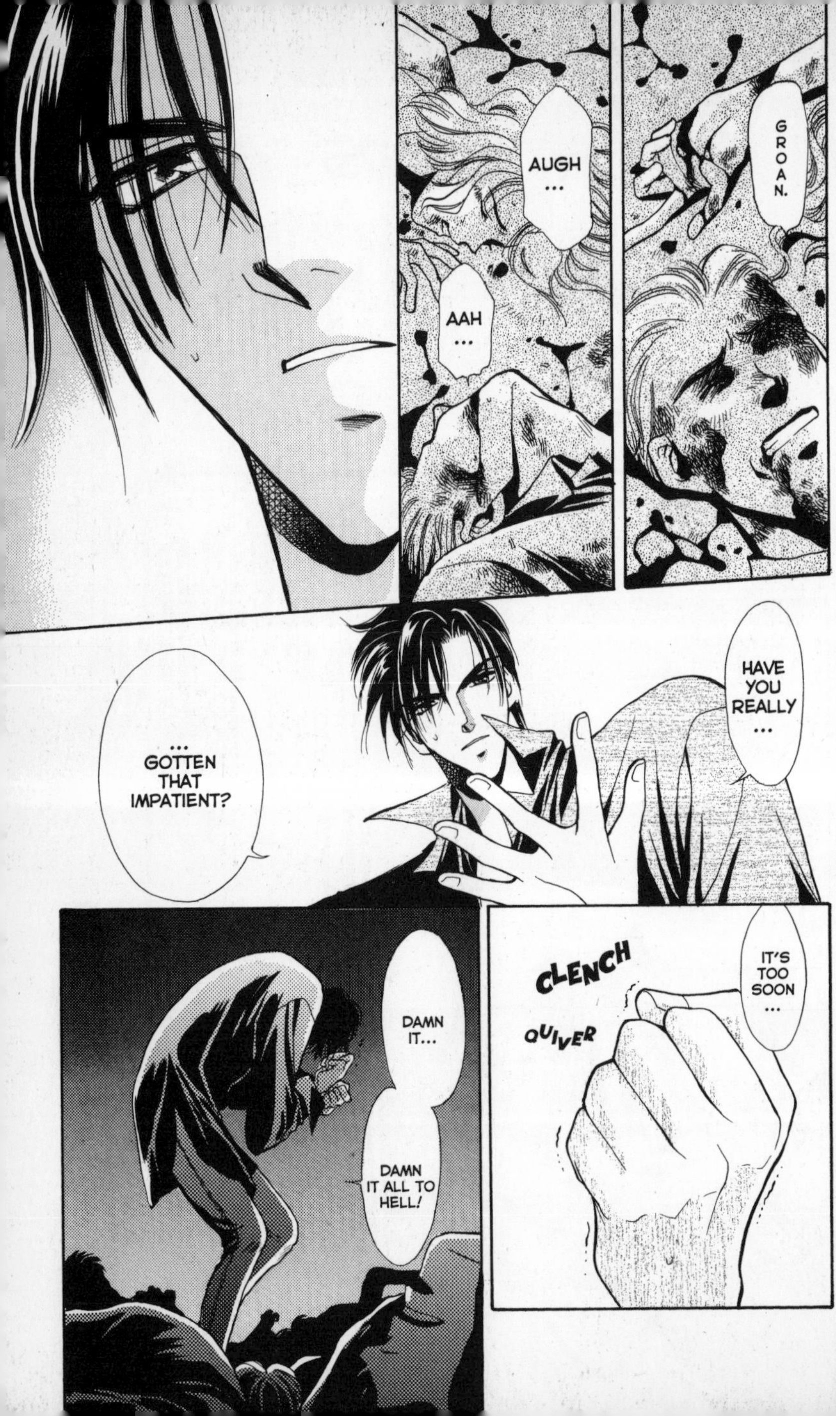
GROAN.
AUGH ...
AAH ...
HAVE YOU REALLY ...
... GOTTEN THAT IMPATIENT?
IT'S TOO SOON ...
CLENCH
QUIVER
DAMN IT...
DAMN IT ALL TO HELL!

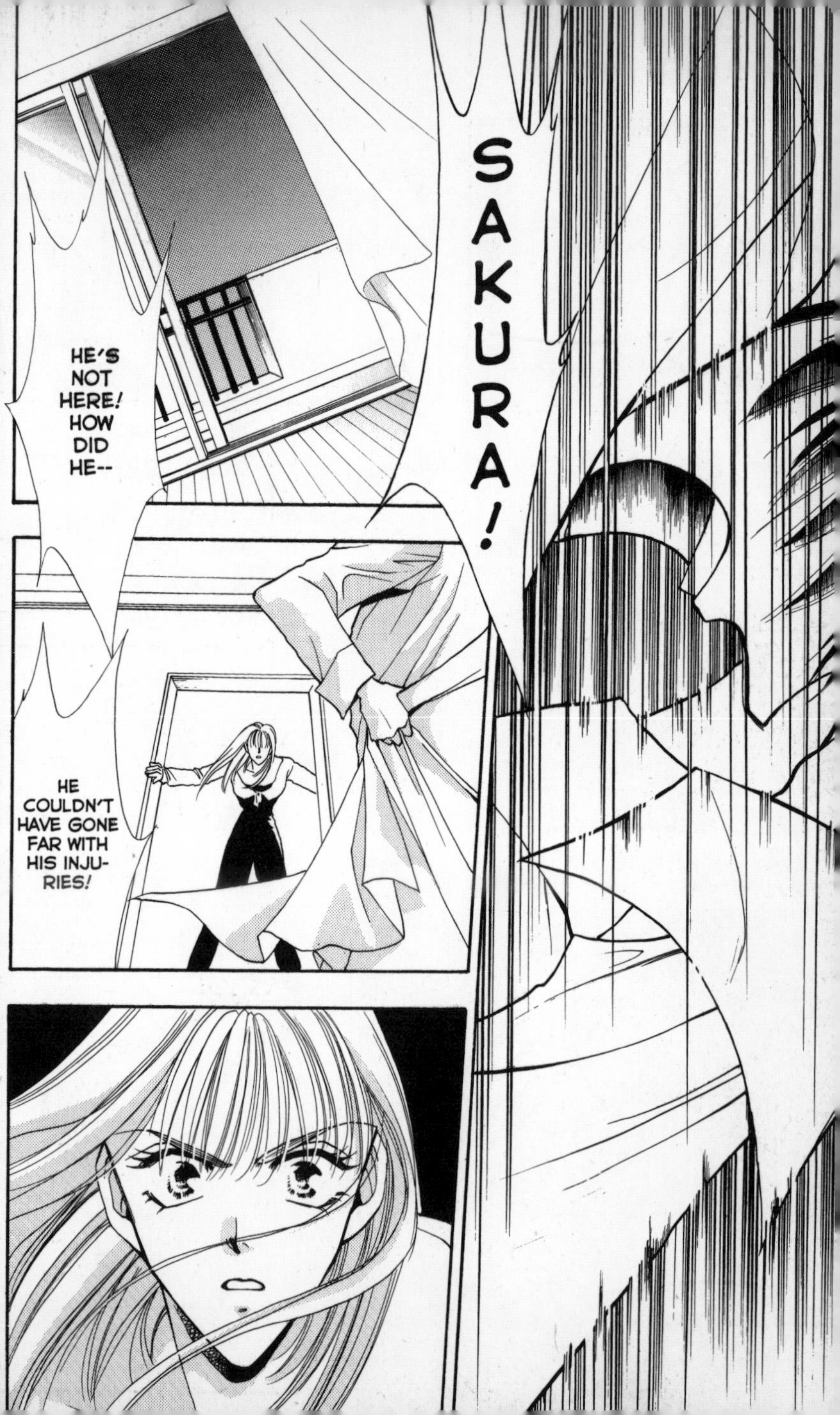
SAKURA!
HE'S NOT HERE! HOW DID HE--
HE COULDN'T HAVE GONE FAR WITH HIS INJU-RIES!

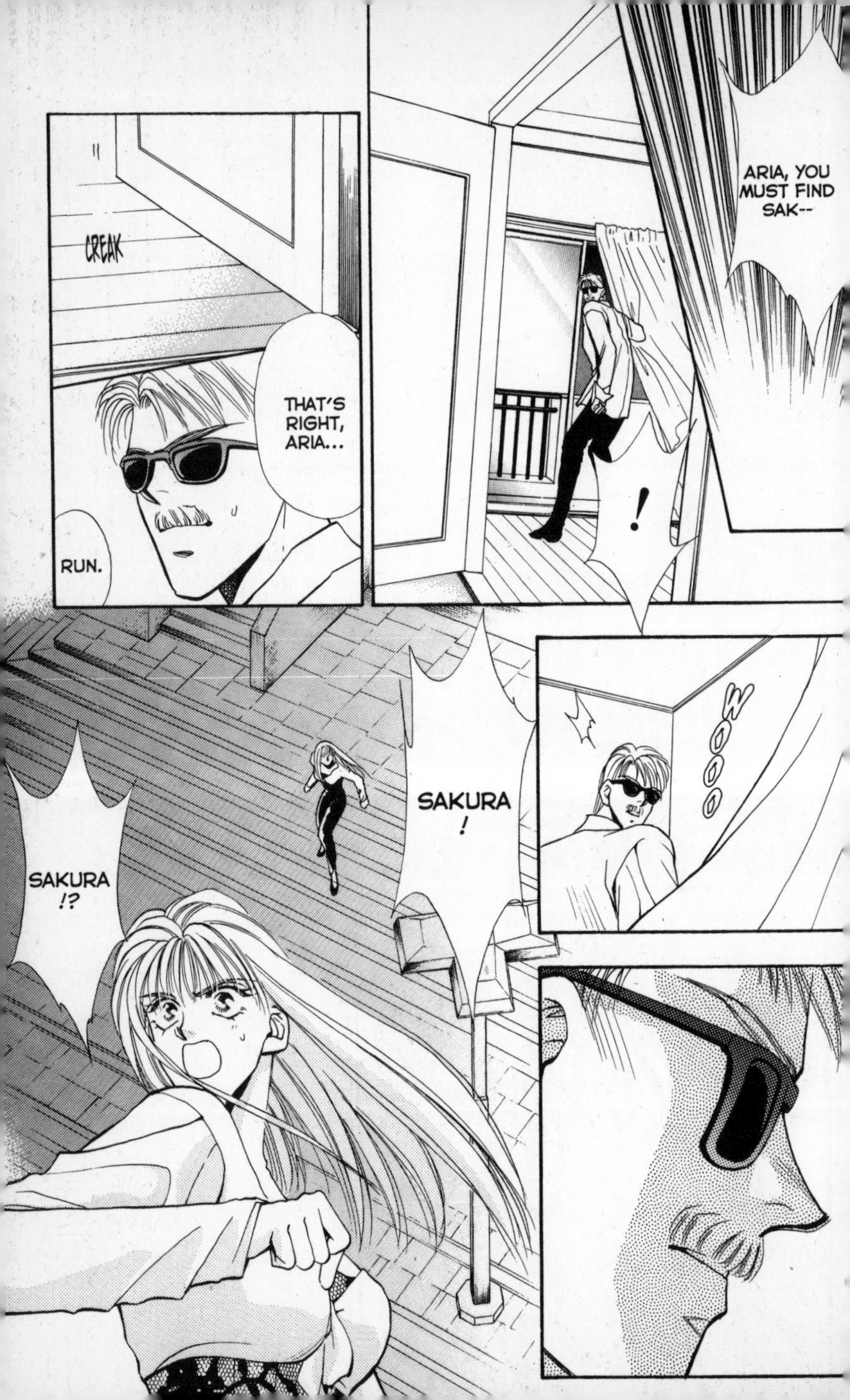
ARIA, YOU MUST FIND SAK--
!
CREAK
THAT'S RIGHT, ARIA...
RUN.
WOOOO
SAKURA!
SAKURA!?

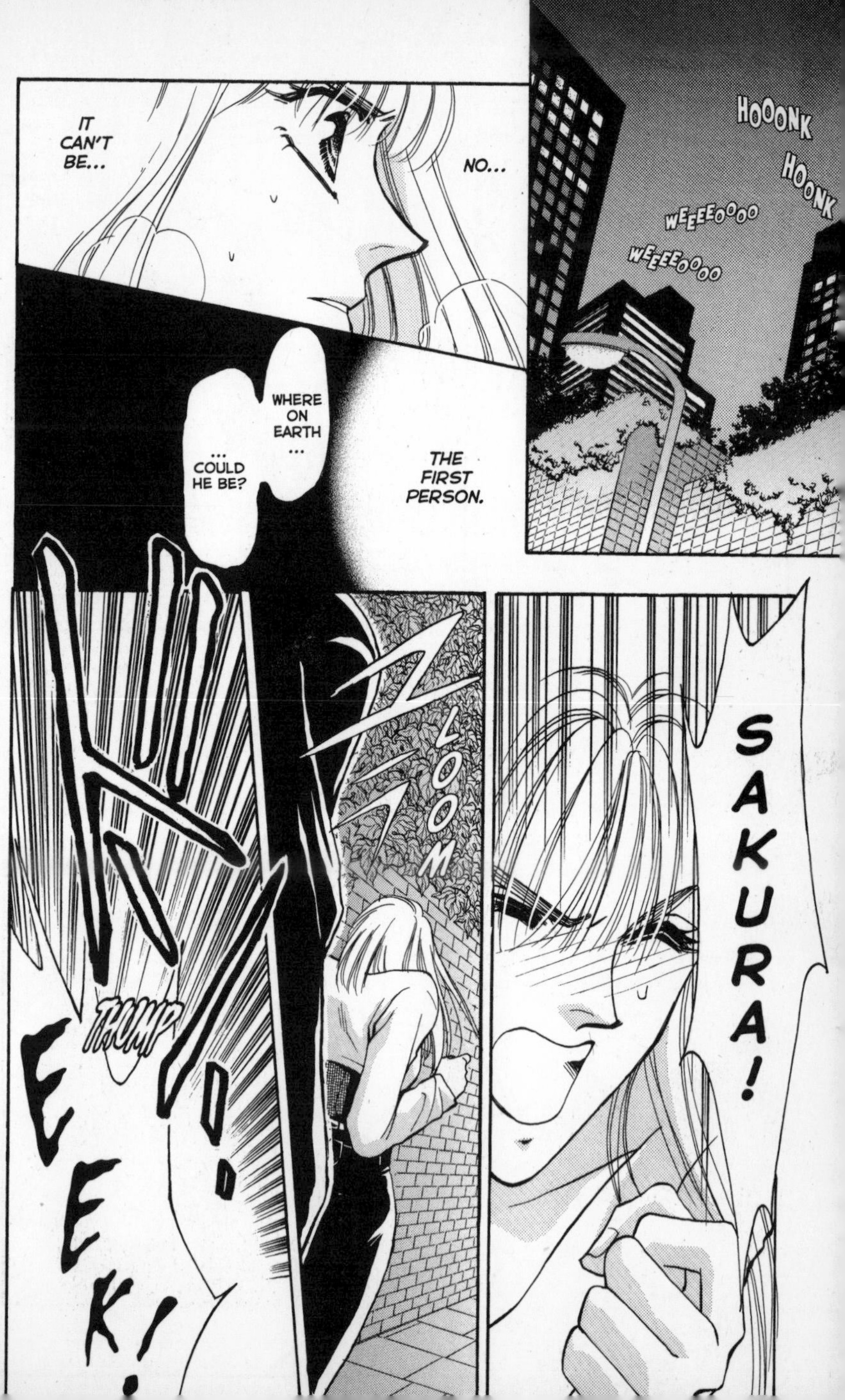
HOOONK
HOOONK
WEEEEOOOO
WEEEEOOOO
NO...
IT CAN'T BE...
THE FIRST PERSON.
WHERE ON EARTH ...
... COULD HE BE?
SAKURA!
ZLOOM
THOMP
EEEK!

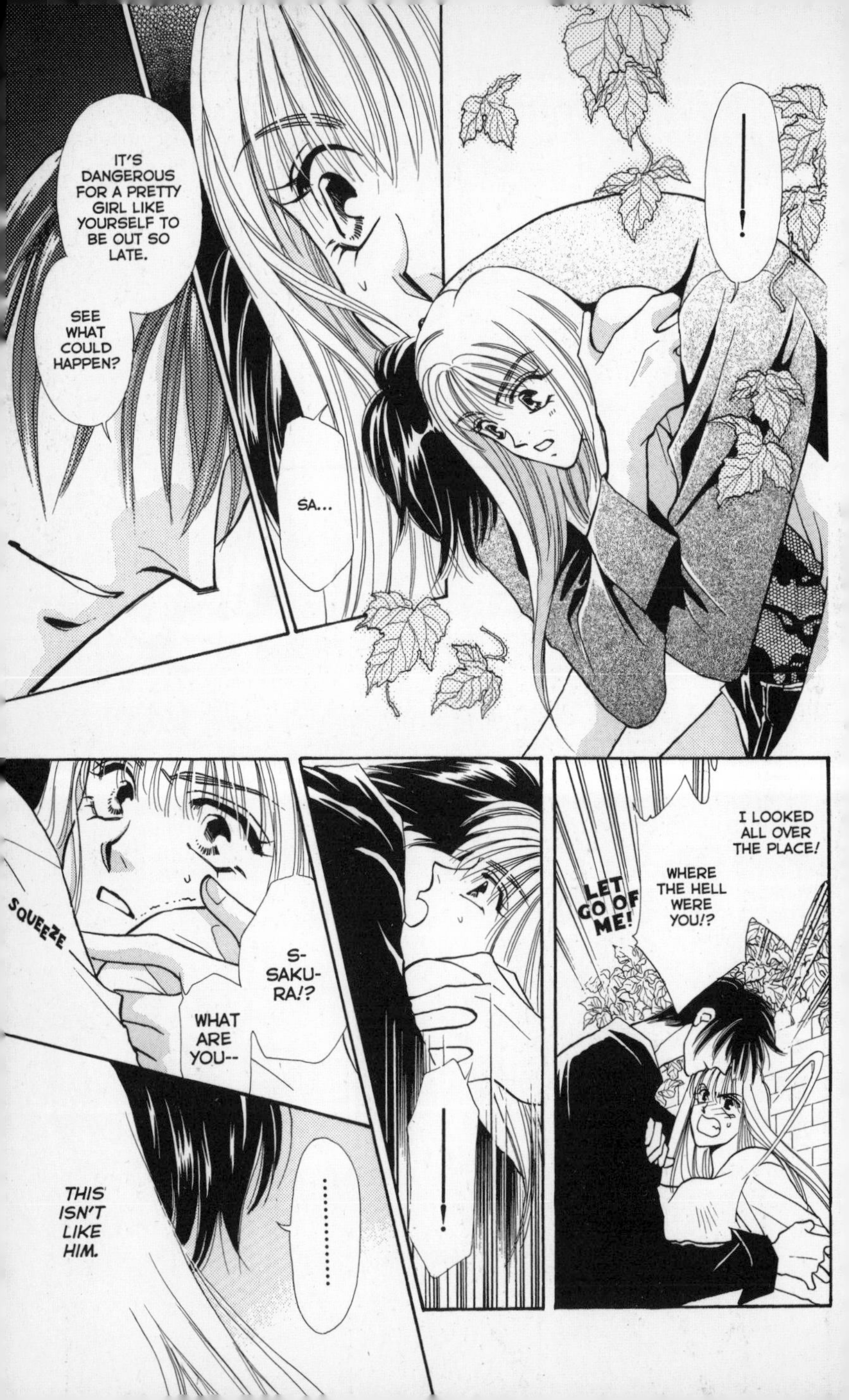
!
SA...
IT'S DANGEROUS FOR A PRETTY GIRL LIKE YOURSELF TO BE OUT SO LATE.
SEE WHAT COULD HAPPEN?
I LOOKED ALL OVER THE PLACE!
WHERE THE HELL WERE YOU!?
LET GO OF ME!
!
......
S-SAKU-RA!?
WHAT ARE YOU--
SQUEEZE
THIS ISN'T LIKE HIM.

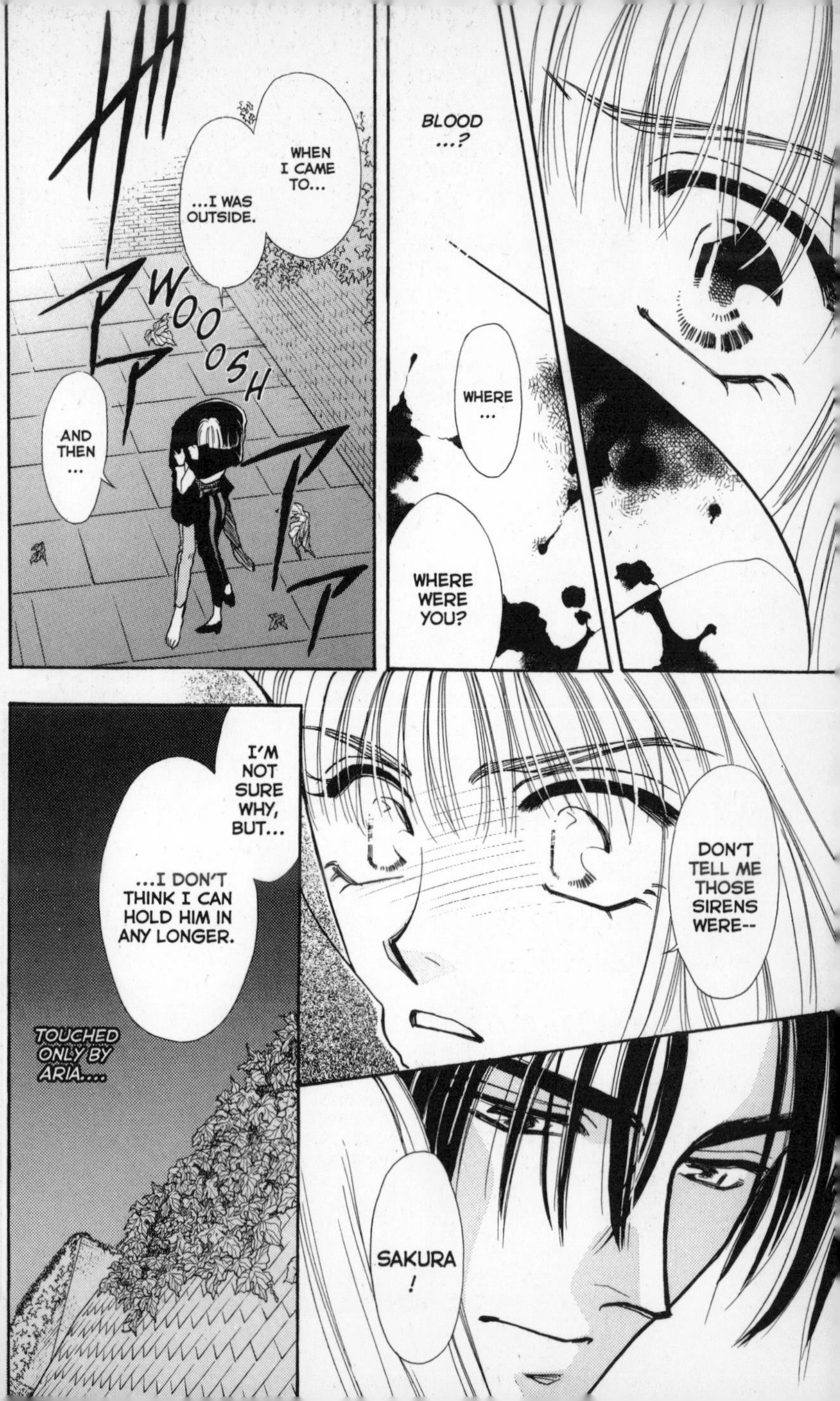
BLOOD ...?
WHERE ...
WHERE WERE YOU?
WHEN I CAME TO...
...I WAS OUTSIDE.
WOOSH
AND THEN ...
DON'T TELL ME THOSE SIRENS WERE--
SAKURA !
I'M NOT SURE WHY, BUT...
...I DON'T THINK I CAN HOLD HIM IN ANY LONGER.
TOUCHED ONLY BY ARIA....

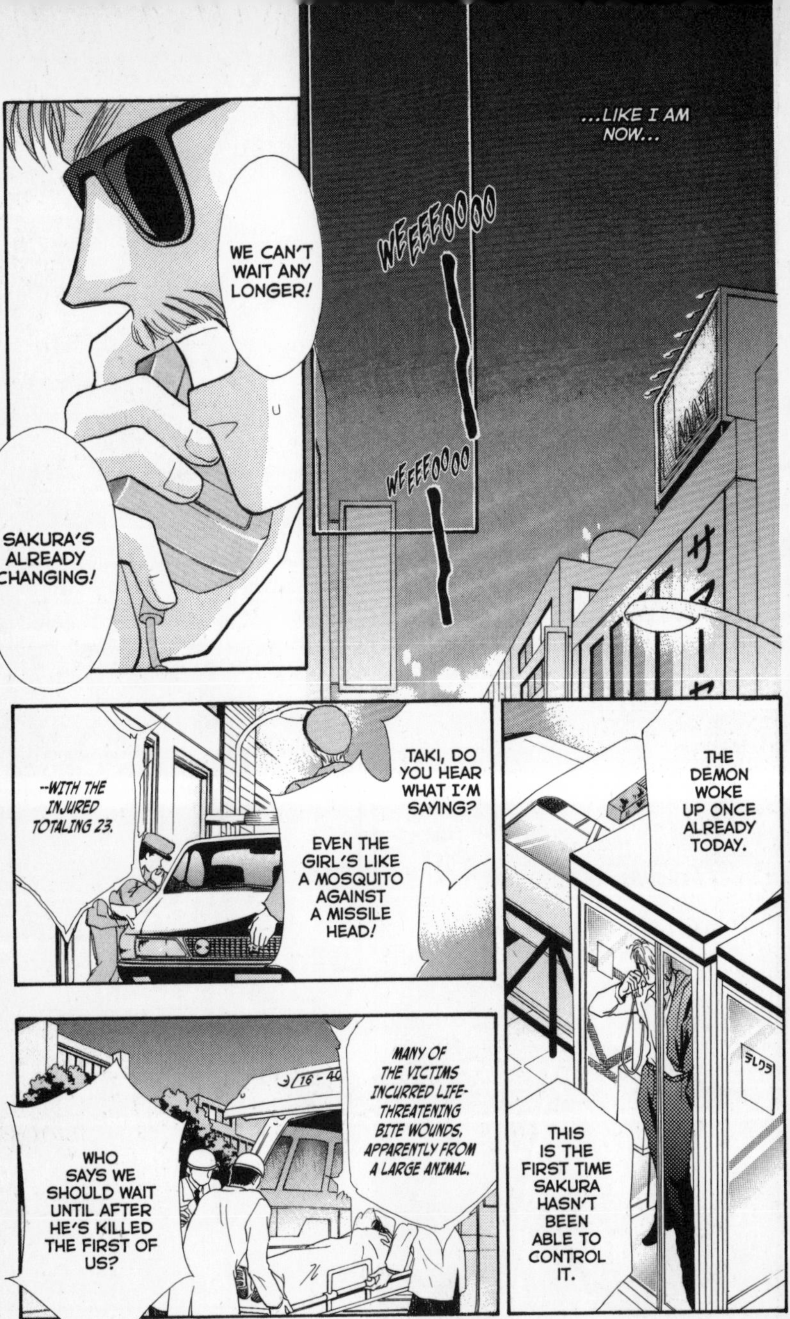
...LIKE I AM NOW...
WEEEOOOO
WEEEOOO
WE CAN'T WAIT ANY LONGER!
SAKURA'S ALREADY CHANGING!
THE DEMON WOKE UP ONCE ALREADY TODAY.
THIS IS THE FIRST TIME SAKURA HASN'T BEEN ABLE TO CONTROL IT.
TAKI, DO YOU HEAR WHAT I'M SAYING?
EVEN THE GIRL'S LIKE A MOSQUITO AGAINST A MISSILE HEAD!
--WITH THE INJURED TOTALING 23.
MANY OF THE VICTIMS INCURRED LIFE-THREATENING BITE WOUNDS, APPARENTLY FROM A LARGE ANIMAL.
WHO SAYS WE SHOULD WAIT UNTIL AFTER HE'S KILLED THE FIRST OF US?

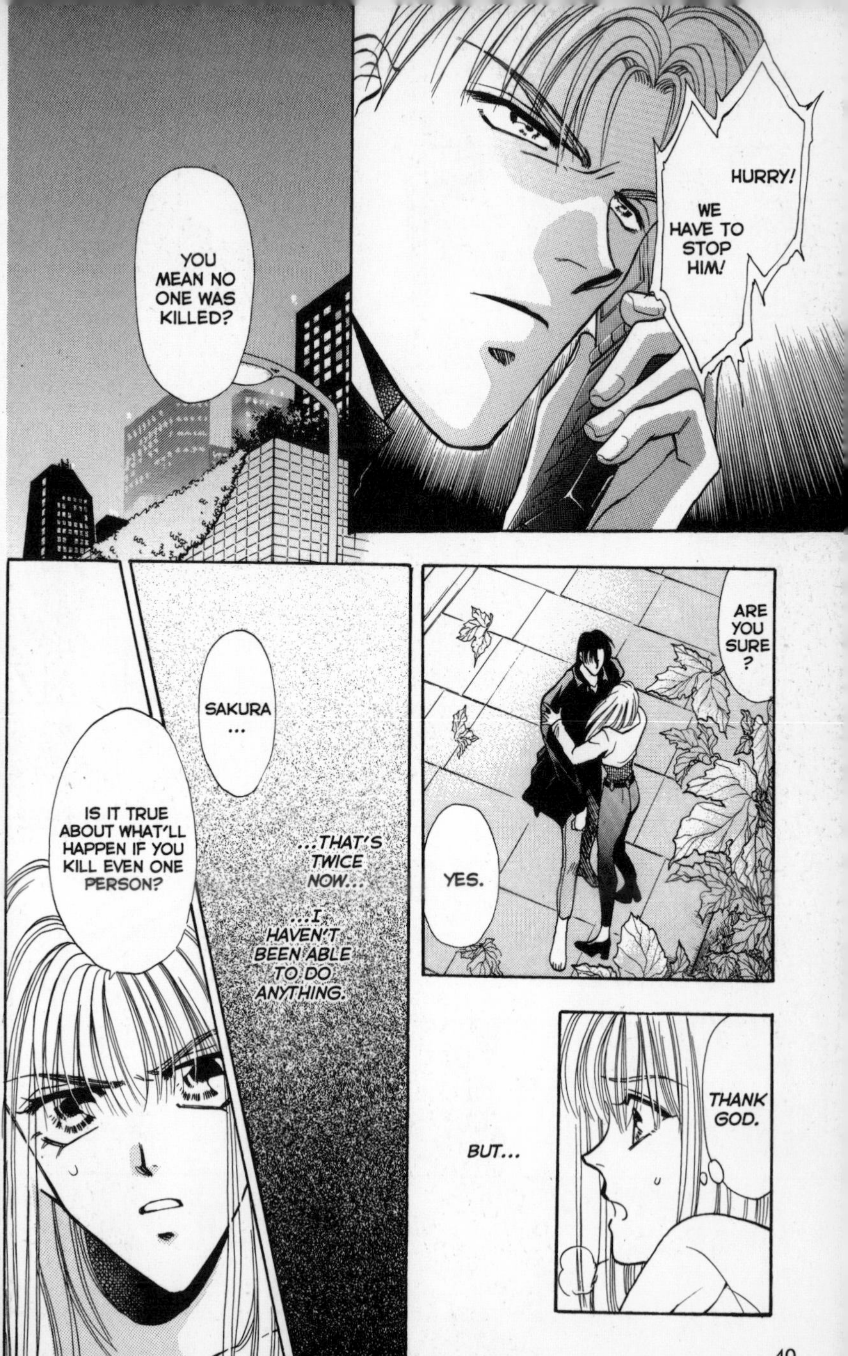
HURRY!
WE HAVE TO STOP HIM!
YOU MEAN NO ONE WAS KILLED?
ARE YOU SURE?
YES.
THANK GOD.
BUT...
SAKURA...
IS IT TRUE ABOUT WHAT'LL HAPPEN IF YOU KILL EVEN ONE PERSON?
...THAT'S TWICE NOW...
...I HAVEN'T BEEN ABLE TO DO ANYTHING.

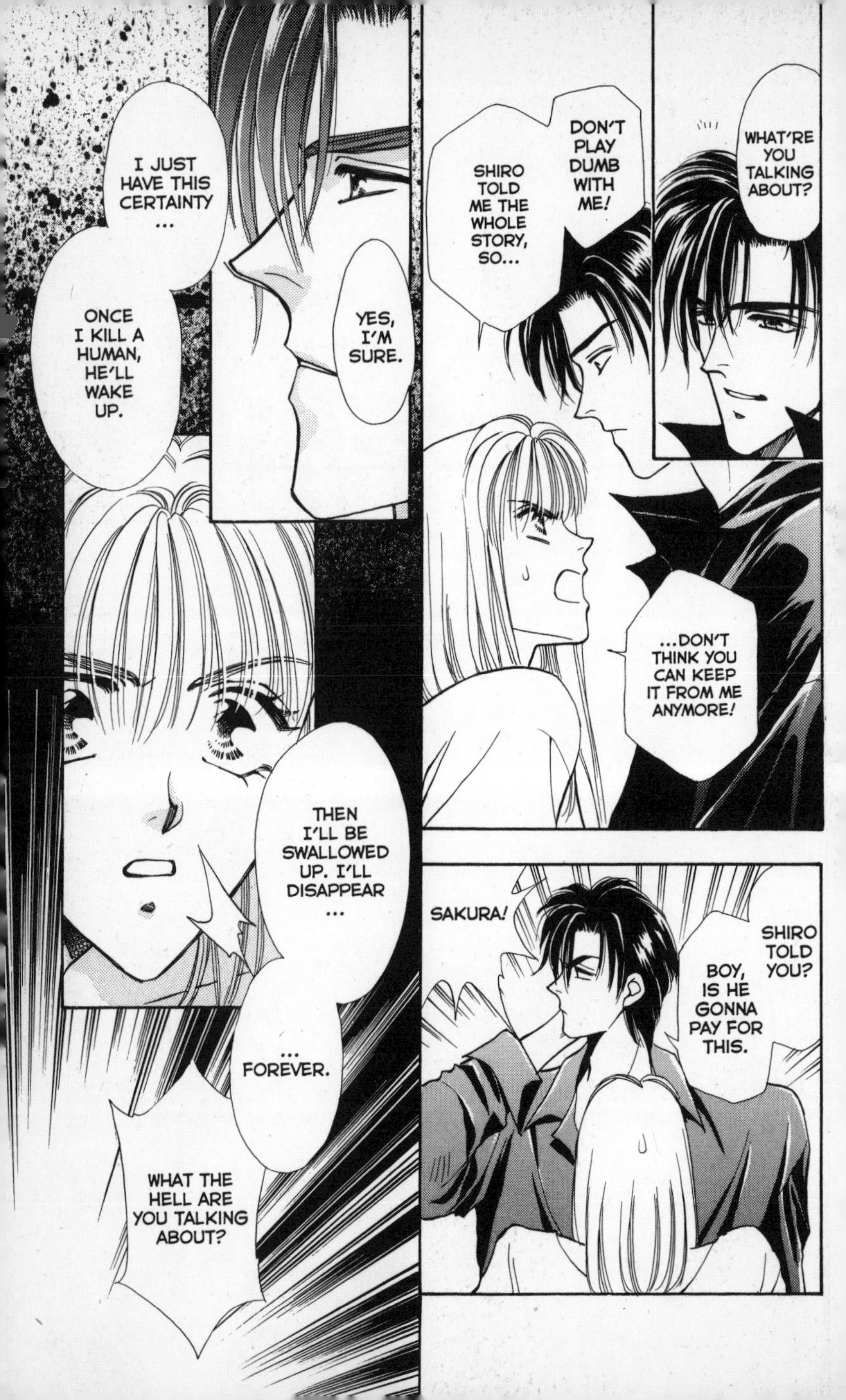
WHAT'RE YOU TALKING ABOUT?
DON'T PLAY DUMB WITH ME!
SHIRO TOLD ME THE WHOLE STORY, SO...
...DON'T THINK YOU CAN KEEP IT FROM ME ANYMORE!
SHIRO TOLD YOU?
BOY, IS HE GONNA PAY FOR THIS.
SAKURA!
YES, I'M SURE.
I JUST HAVE THIS CERTAINTY...
ONCE I KILL A HUMAN, HE'LL WAKE UP.
THEN I'LL BE SWALLOWED UP. I'LL DISAPPEAR...
...FOREVER.
WHAT THE HELL ARE YOU TALKING ABOUT?

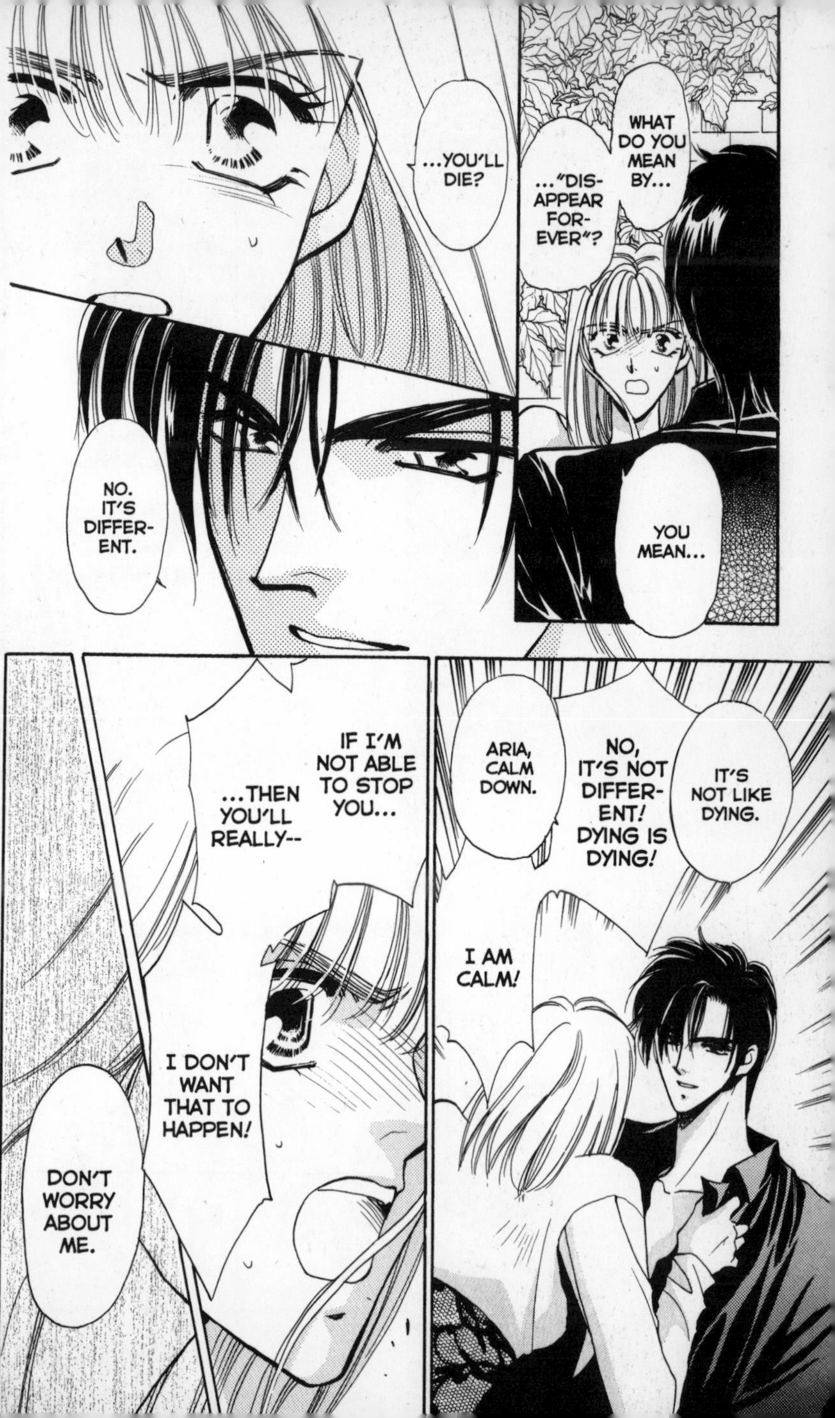
WHAT DO YOU MEAN BY...
..."DIS-APPEAR FOR-EVER"?
YOU MEAN...
...YOU'LL DIE?
NO. IT'S DIFFER-ENT.
IT'S NOT LIKE DYING.
NO, IT'S NOT DIFFER-ENT! DYING IS DYING!
ARIA, CALM DOWN.
I AM CALM!
IF I'M NOT ABLE TO STOP YOU...
...THEN YOU'LL REALLY--
I DON'T WANT THAT TO HAPPEN!
DON'T WORRY ABOUT ME.

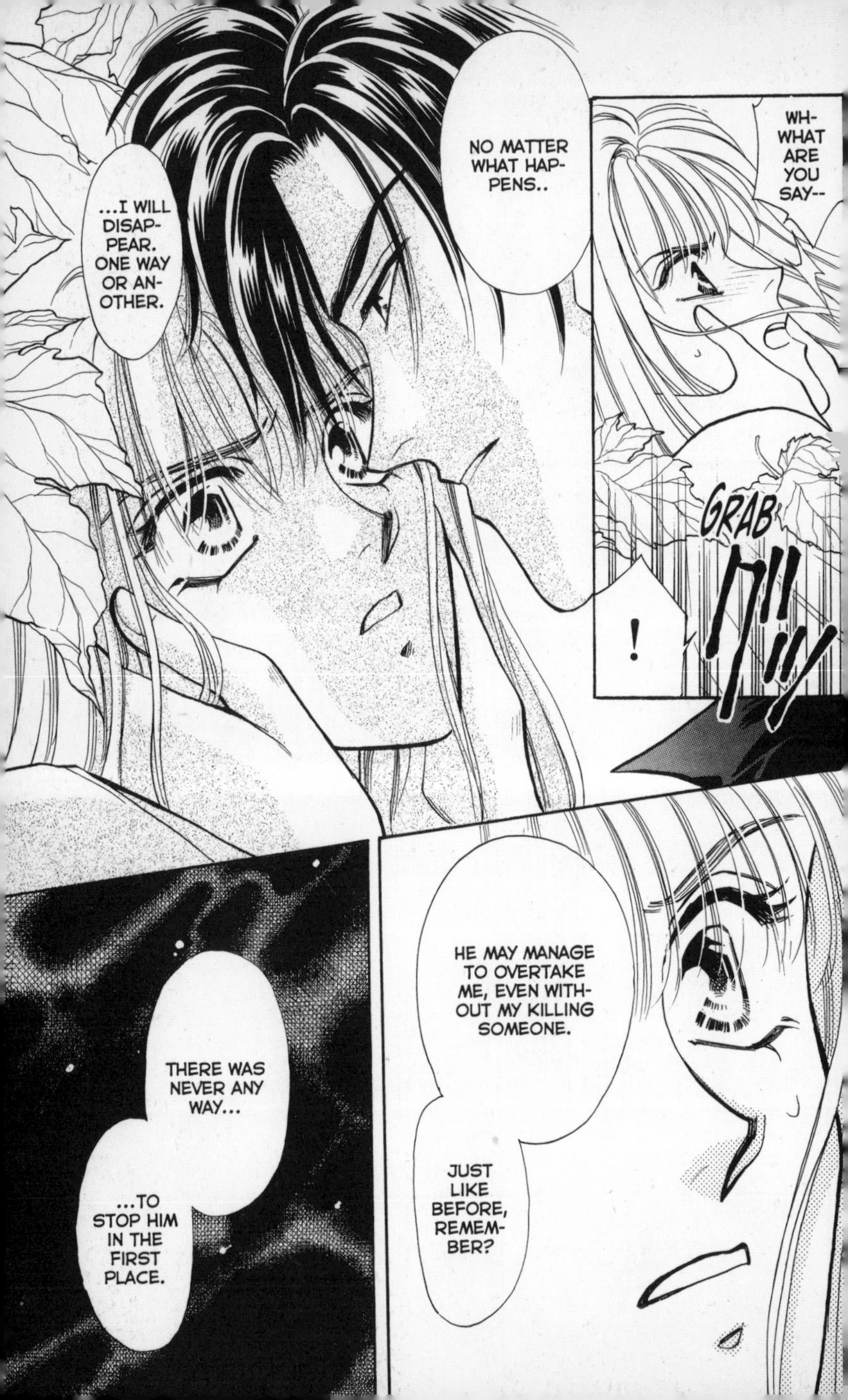
NO MATTER WHAT HAP-PENS..
...I WILL DISAP-PEAR. ONE WAY OR AN-OTHER.
WH-WHAT ARE YOU SAY--
!
GRAB
HE MAY MANAGE TO OVERTAKE ME, EVEN WITH-OUT MY KILLING SOMEONE.
JUST LIKE BEFORE, REMEM-BER?
THERE WAS NEVER ANY WAY...
...TO STOP HIM IN THE FIRST PLACE.

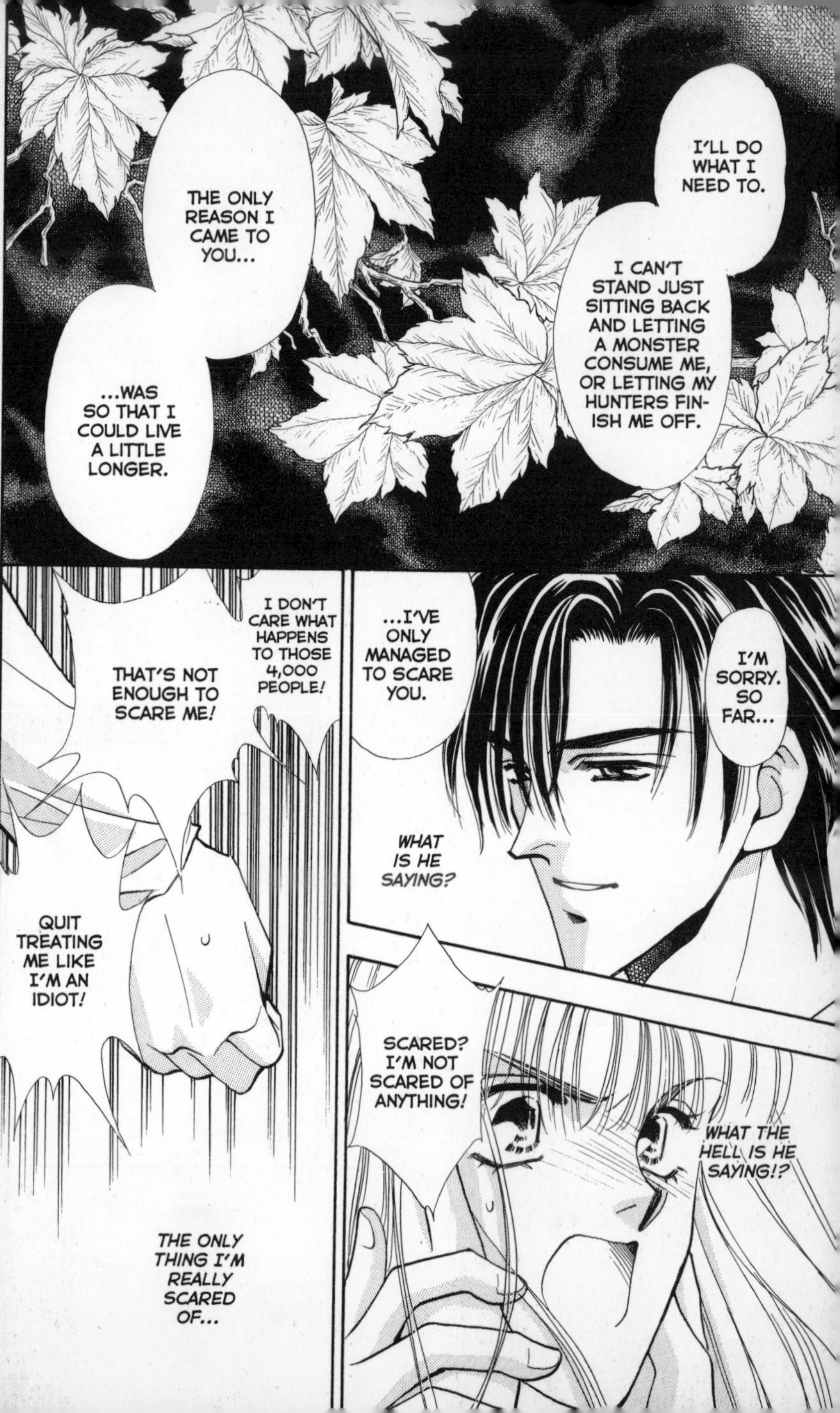
I'LL DO WHAT I NEED TO.
I CAN'T STAND JUST SITTING BACK AND LETTING A MONSTER CONSUME ME, OR LETTING MY HUNTERS FIN-ISH ME OFF.
THE ONLY REASON I CAME TO YOU...
...WAS SO THAT I COULD LIVE A LITTLE LONGER.
I'M SORRY. SO FAR...
...I'VE ONLY MANAGED TO SCARE YOU.
WHAT IS HE SAYING?
SCARED? I'M NOT SCARED OF ANYTHING!
WHAT THE HELL IS HE SAYING!?
I DON'T CARE WHAT HAPPENS TO THOSE 4,000 PEOPLE!
THAT'S NOT ENOUGH TO SCARE ME!
QUIT TREATING ME LIKE I'M AN IDIOT!
THE ONLY THING I'M REALLY SCARED OF...

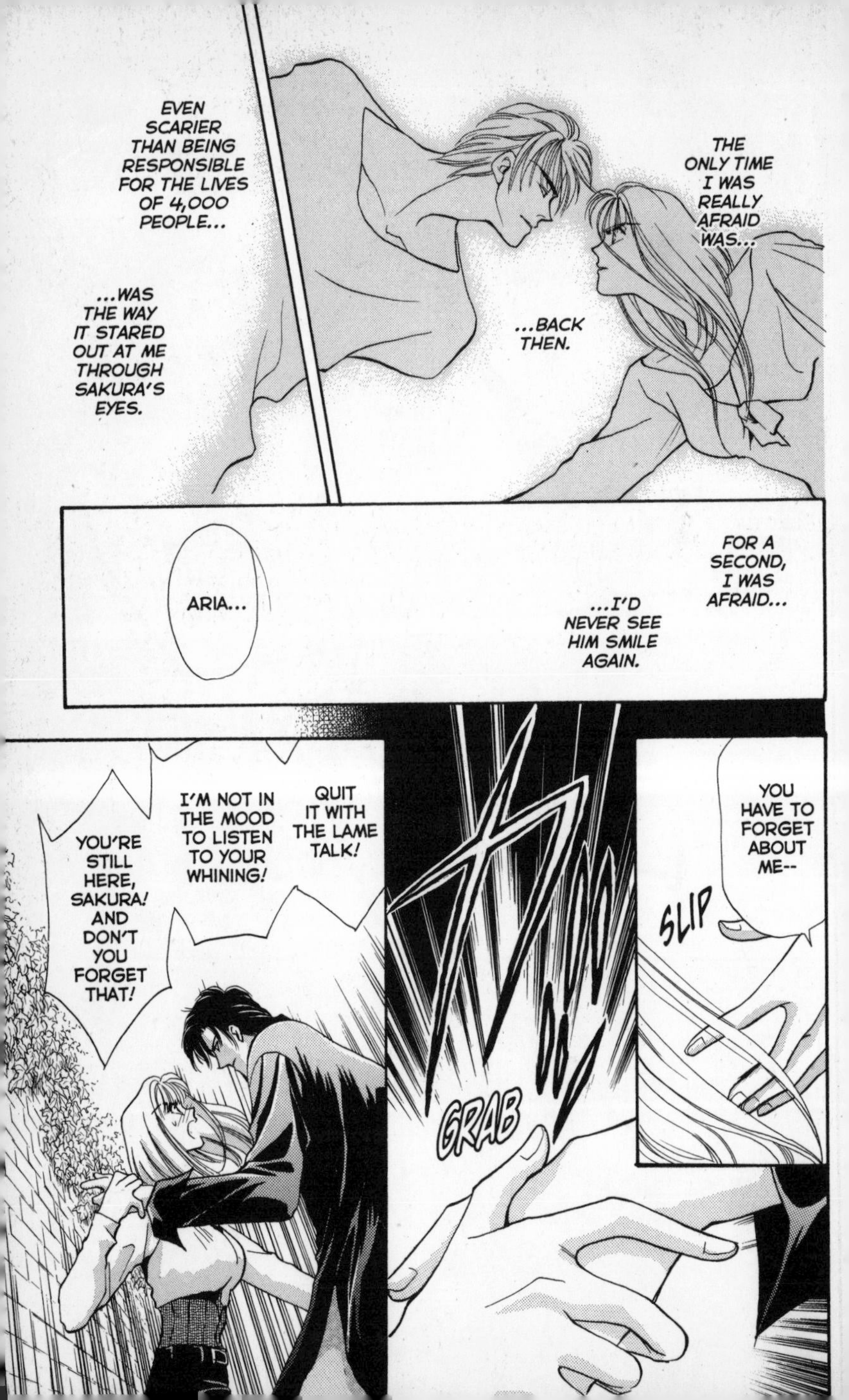
THE ONLY TIME I WAS REALLY AFRAID WAS...
...BACK THEN.
EVEN SCARIER THAN BEING RESPONSIBLE FOR THE LIVES OF 4,000 PEOPLE...
...WAS THE WAY IT STARED OUT AT ME THROUGH SAKURA'S EYES.
FOR A SECOND, I WAS AFRAID...
...I'D NEVER SEE HIM SMILE AGAIN.
ARIA...
YOU HAVE TO FORGET ABOUT ME--
SLIP
GRAB
QUIT IT WITH THE LAME TALK!
I'M NOT IN THE MOOD TO LISTEN TO YOUR WHINING!
YOU'RE STILL HERE, SAKURA! AND DON'T YOU FORGET THAT!

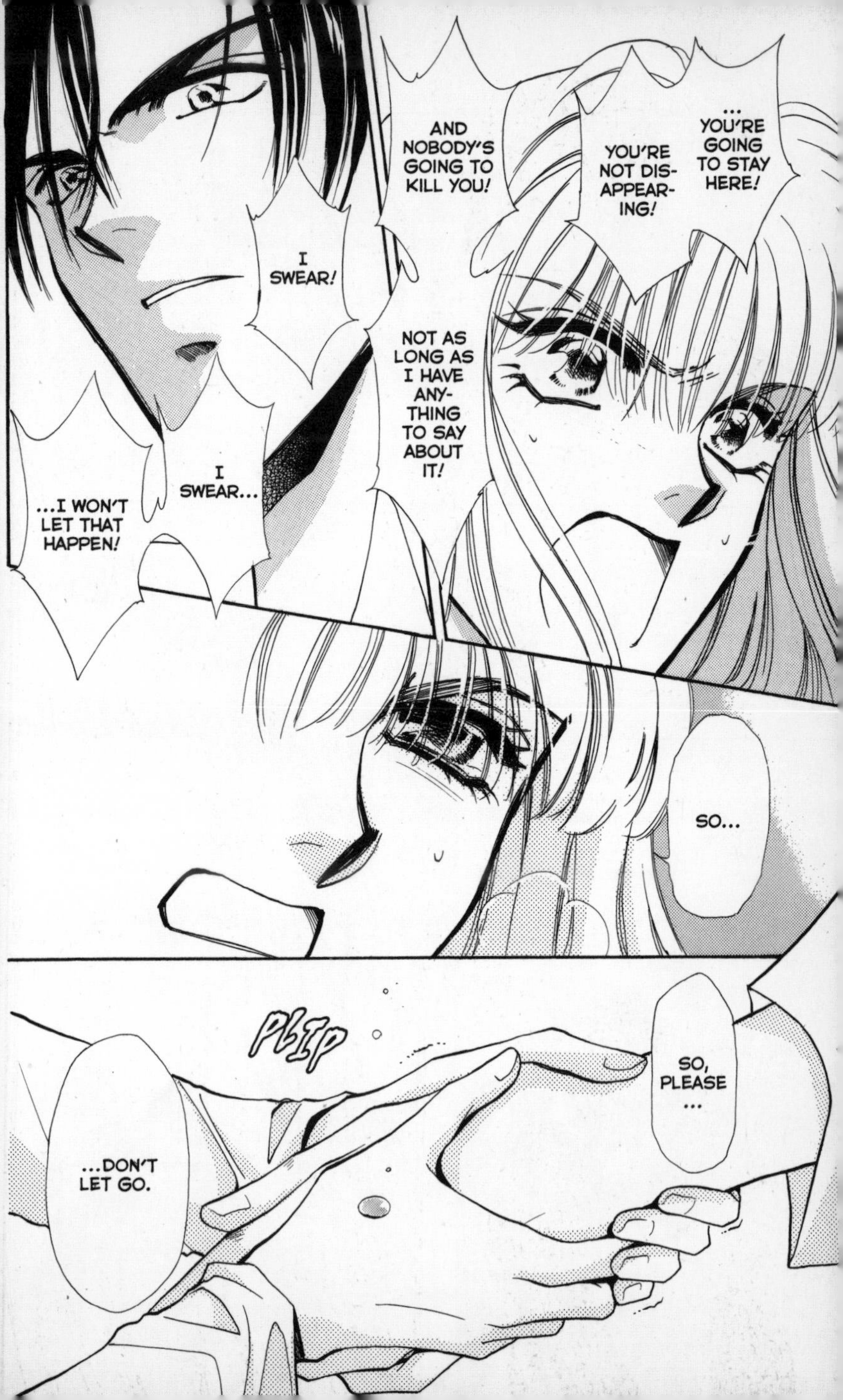
... YOU'RE GOING TO STAY HERE!
YOU'RE NOT DISAPPEARING!
AND NOBODY'S GOING TO KILL YOU!
NOT AS LONG AS I HAVE ANYTHING TO SAY ABOUT IT!
I SWEAR!
I SWEAR...
...I WON'T LET THAT HAPPEN!
SO...
SO, PLEASE ...
PLIP
...DON'T LET GO.

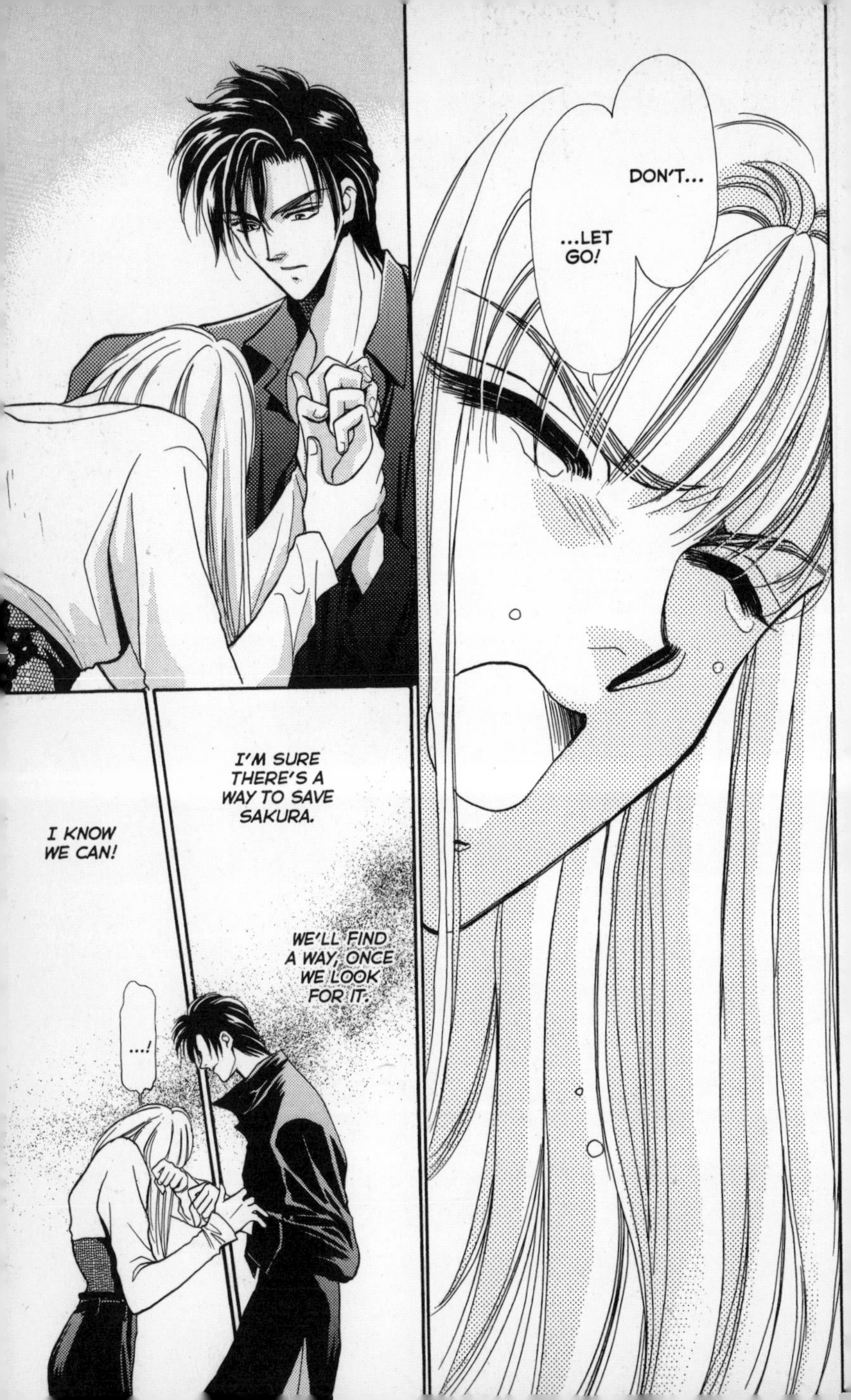
DON'T...
...LET GO!
I'M SURE THERE'S A WAY TO SAVE SAKURA.
I KNOW WE CAN!
WE'LL FIND A WAY, ONCE WE LOOK FOR IT.
...!

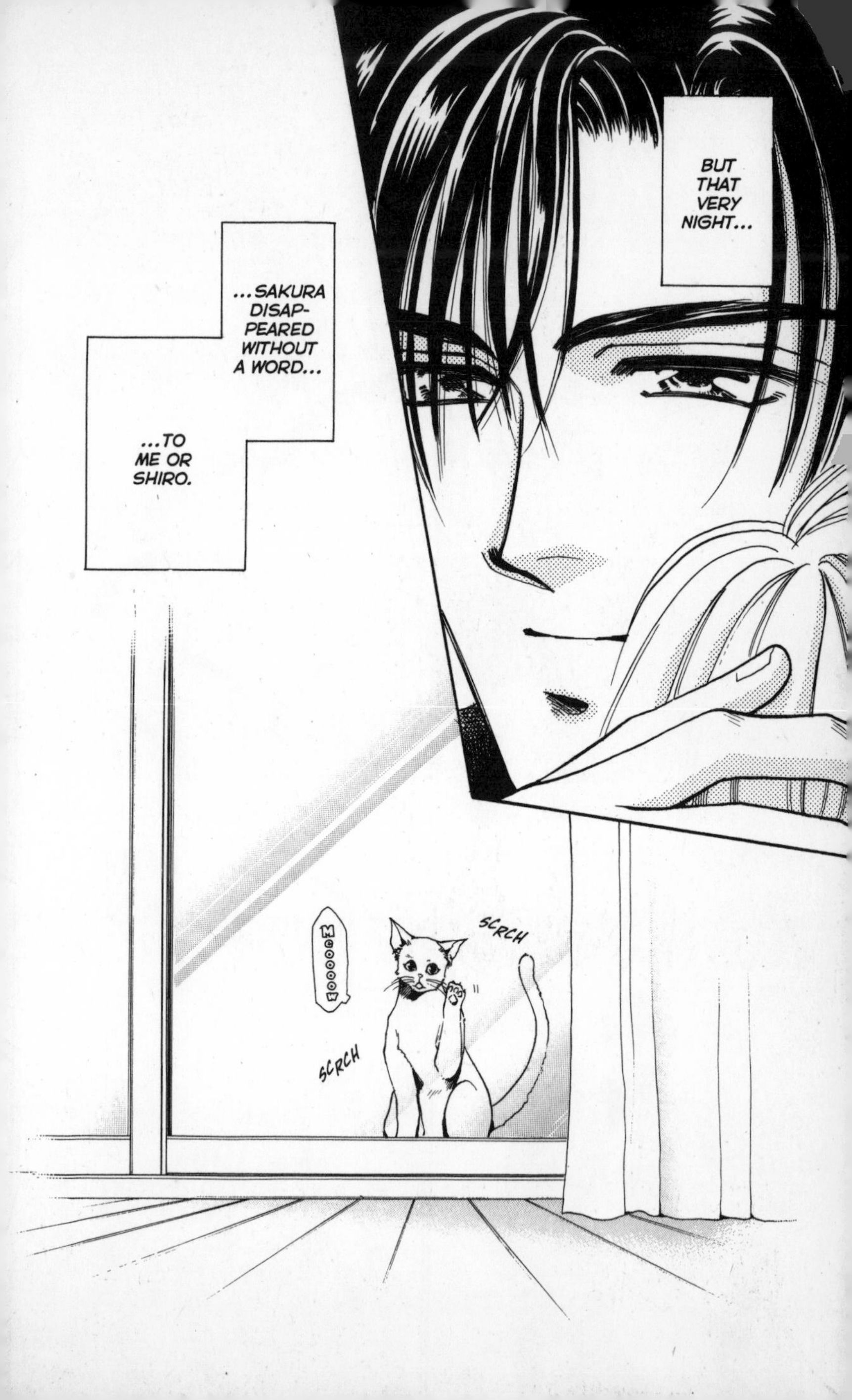
BUT THAT VERY NIGHT...
...SAKURA DISAP-PEARED WITHOUT A WORD...
...TO ME OR SHIRO.
SCRCH
MEOOOOOW
SCRCH

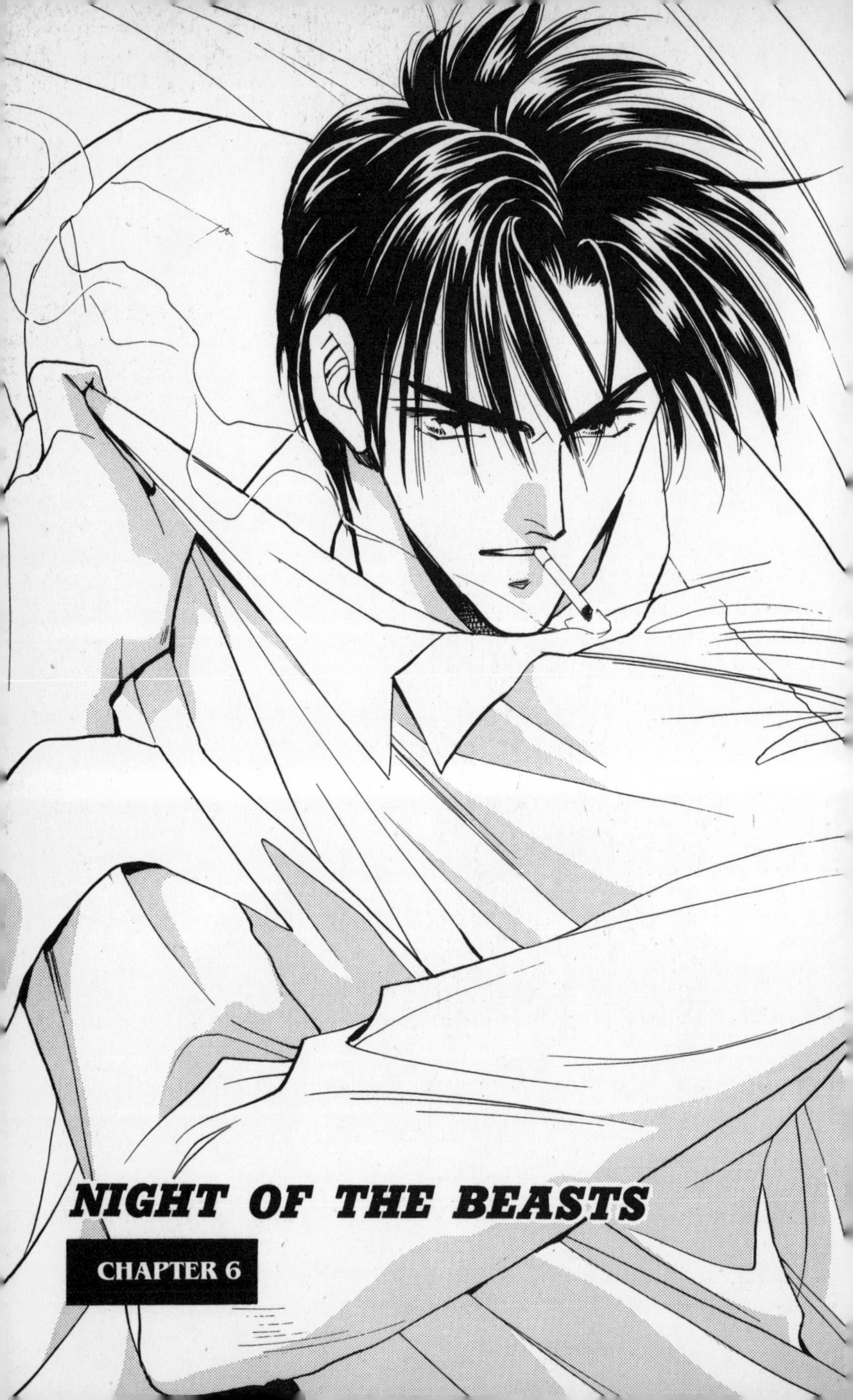
NIGHT OF THE BEASTS
CHAPTER 6

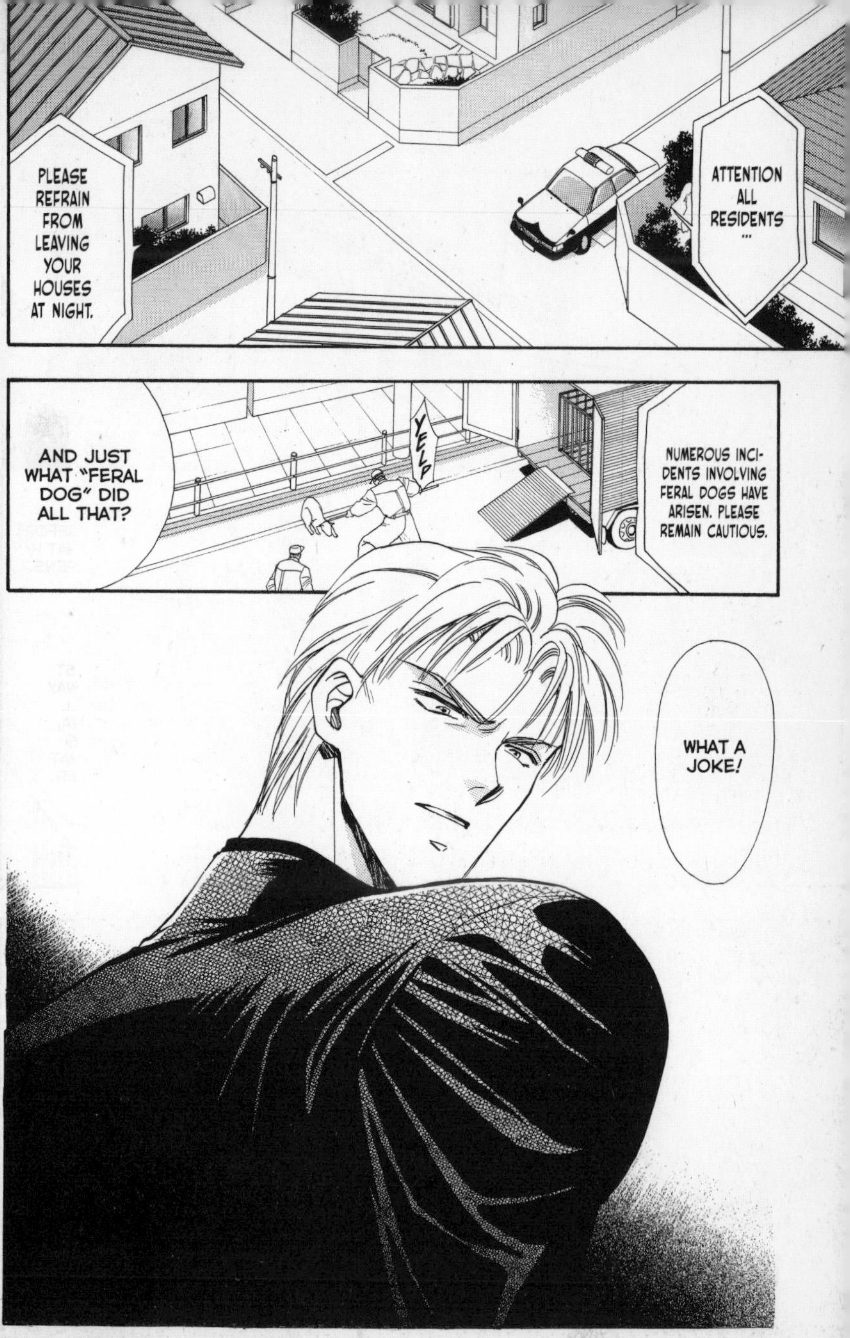
ATTENTION ALL RESIDENTS ...
PLEASE REFRAIN FROM LEAVING YOUR HOUSES AT NIGHT.
NUMEROUS INCIDENTS INVOLVING FERAL DOGS HAVE ARISEN. PLEASE REMAIN CAUTIOUS.
YELP
AND JUST WHAT "FERAL DOG" DID ALL THAT?
WHAT A JOKE!

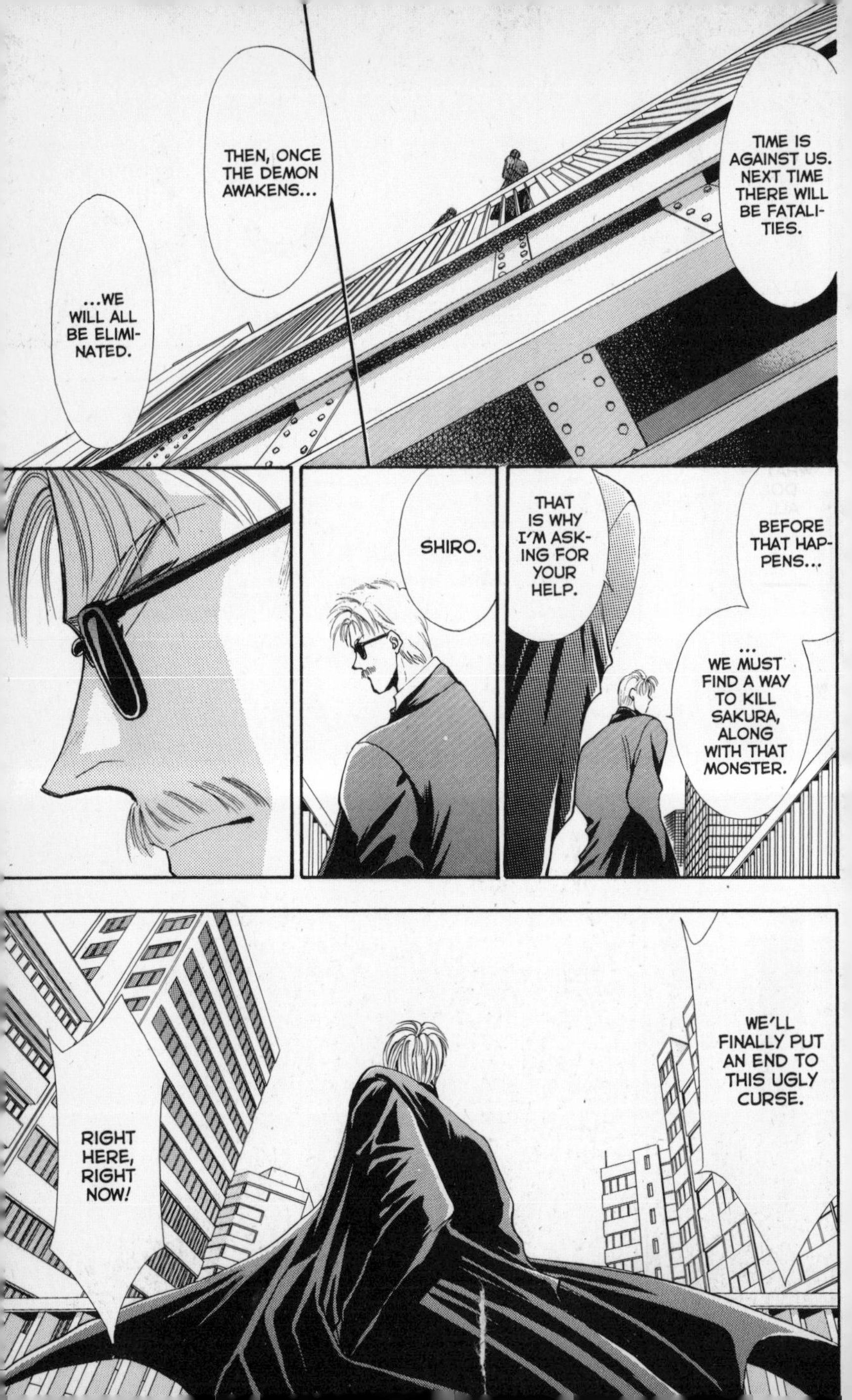
TIME IS AGAINST US. NEXT TIME THERE WILL BE FATALI-TIES.
THEN, ONCE THE DEMON AWAKENS...
...WE WILL ALL BE ELIMI-NATED.
BEFORE THAT HAP-PENS...
...WE MUST FIND A WAY TO KILL SAKURA, ALONG WITH THAT MONSTER.
THAT IS WHY I'M ASK-ING FOR YOUR HELP.
SHIRO.
WE'LL FINALLY PUT AN END TO THIS UGLY CURSE.
RIGHT HERE, RIGHT NOW!

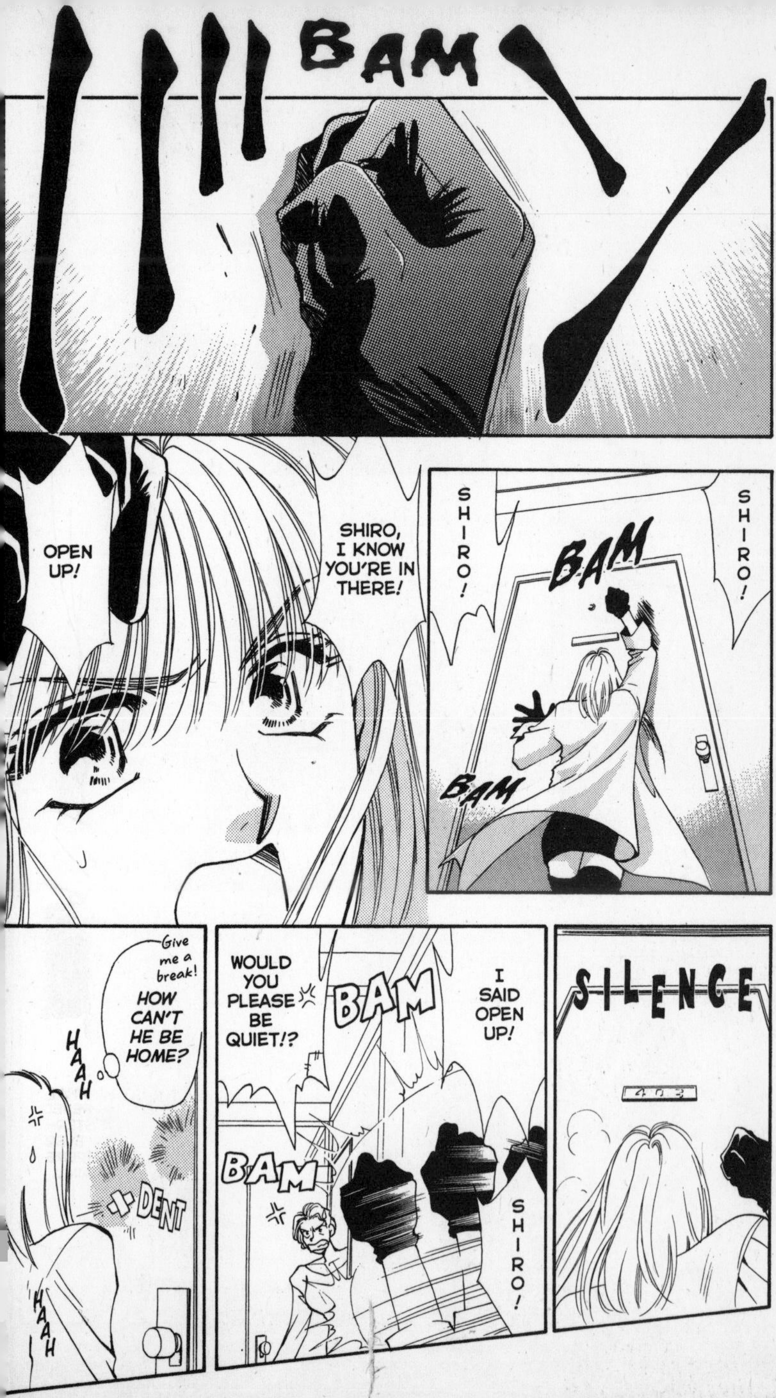
BAM
SHIRO!
SHIRO!
BAM
BAM
SHIRO, I KNOW YOU'RE IN THERE!
OPEN UP!
SILENCE
I SAID OPEN UP!
BAM
WOULD YOU PLEASE BE QUIET!?
SHIRO!
BAM
HOW CAN'T HE BE HOME?
Give me a break!
HAAAH
DENT
HAAAH

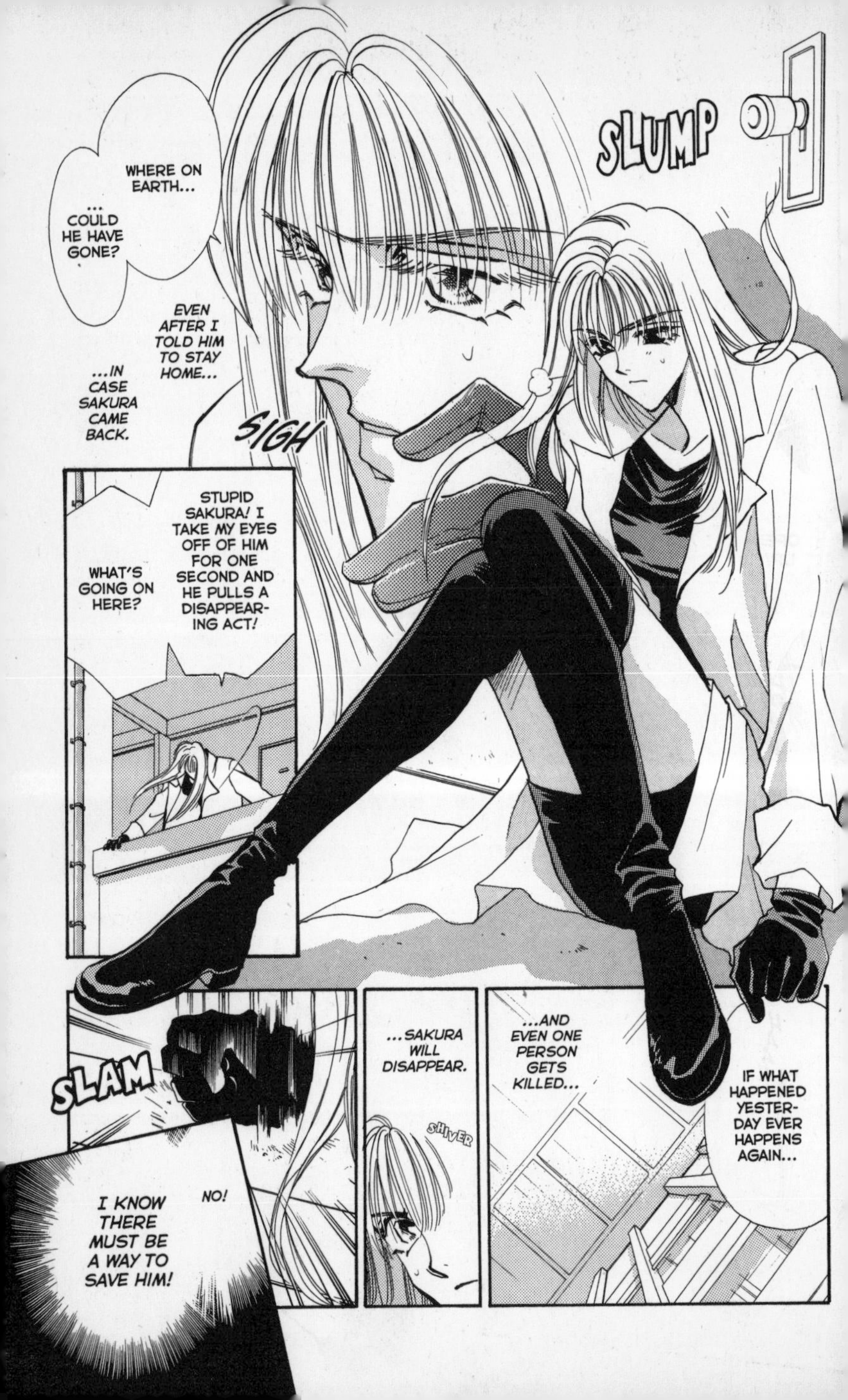
SLUMP
WHERE ON EARTH...
...COULD HE HAVE GONE?
EVEN AFTER I TOLD HIM TO STAY HOME...
...IN CASE SAKURA CAME BACK.
SIGH
STUPID SAKURA! I TAKE MY EYES OFF OF HIM FOR ONE SECOND AND HE PULLS A DISAPPEARING ACT!
WHAT'S GOING ON HERE?
IF WHAT HAPPENED YESTERDAY EVER HAPPENS AGAIN...
...AND EVEN ONE PERSON GETS KILLED...
...SAKURA WILL DISAPPEAR.
SHIVER
SLAM
NO!
I KNOW THERE MUST BE A WAY TO SAVE HIM!

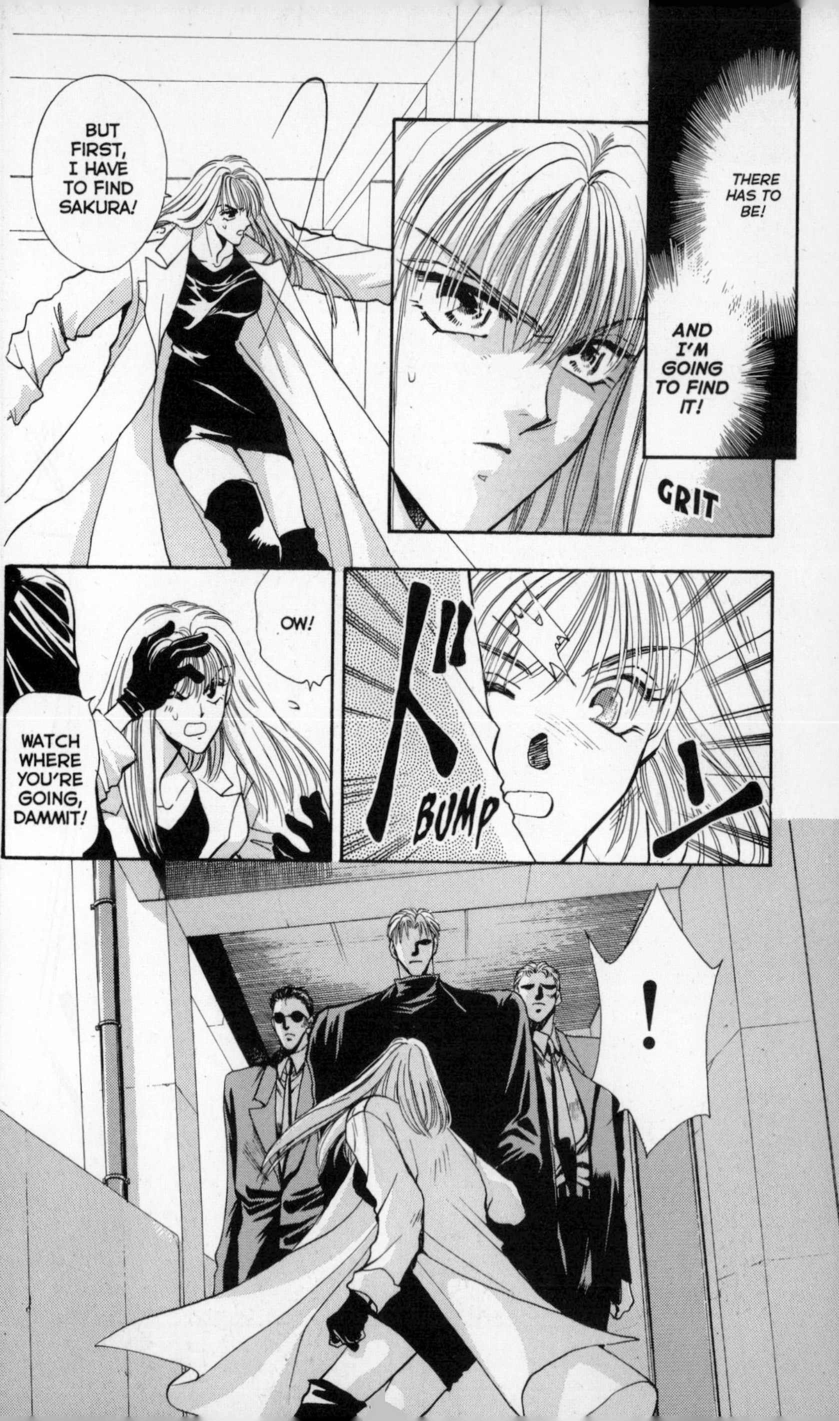
THERE HAS TO BE!
AND I'M GOING TO FIND IT!
GRIT
BUT FIRST, I HAVE TO FIND SAKURA!
BUMP
OW!
WATCH WHERE YOU'RE GOING, DAMMIT!
!

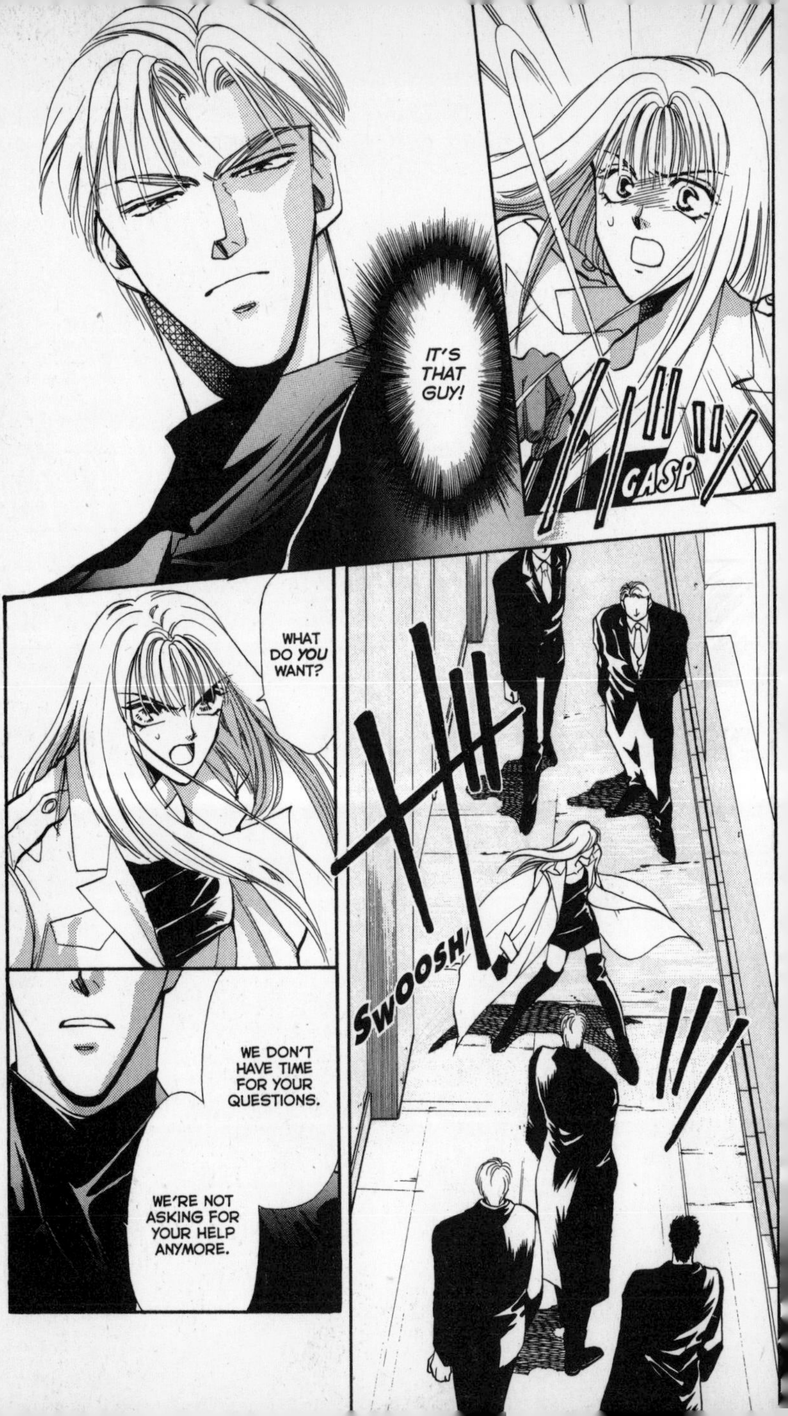
GASP
IT'S THAT GUY!
SWOOSH
WHAT DO YOU WANT?
WE DON'T HAVE TIME FOR YOUR QUESTIONS.
WE'RE NOT ASKING FOR YOUR HELP ANYMORE.

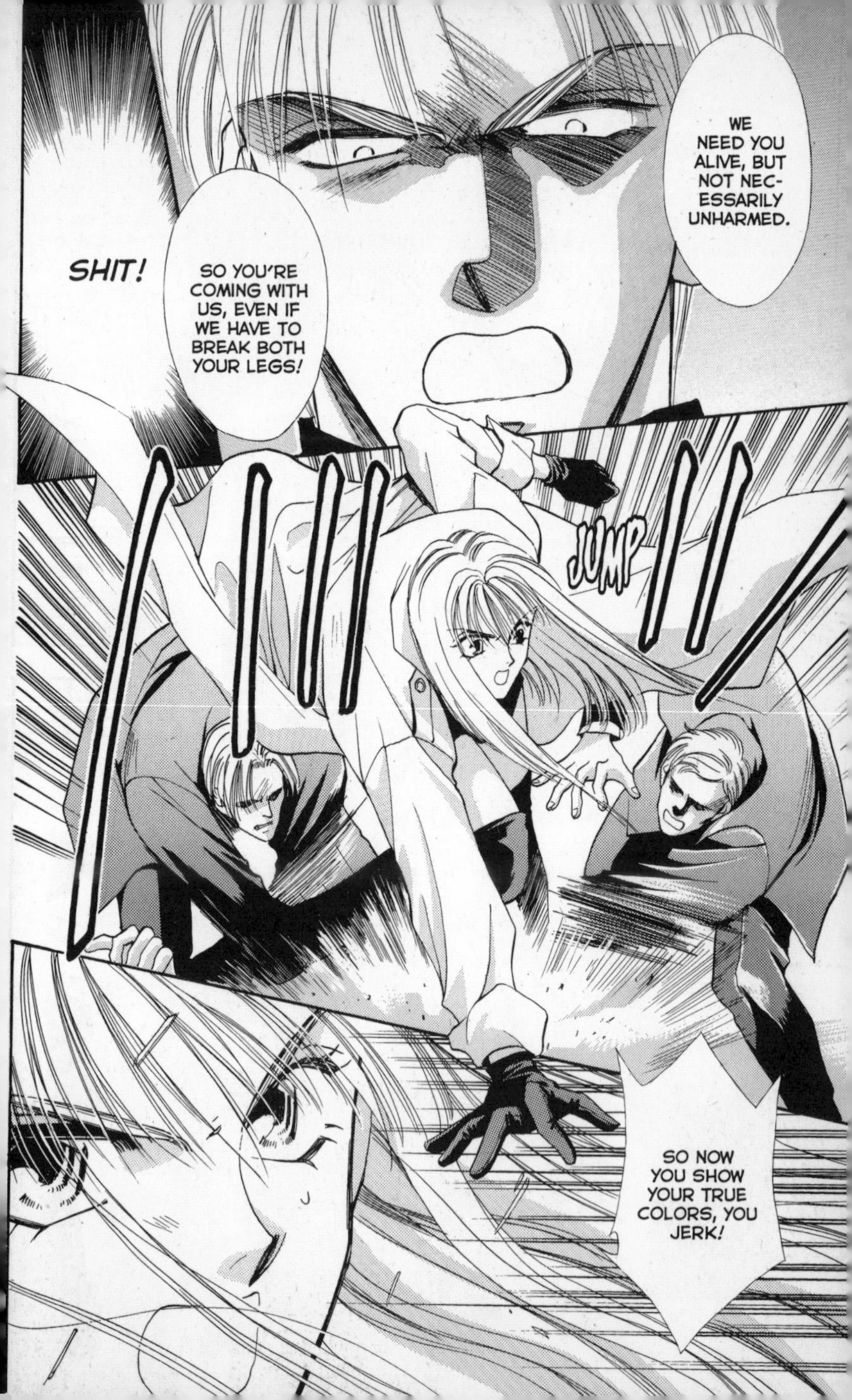
WE NEED YOU ALIVE, BUT NOT NECESSARILY UNHARMED.
SO YOU'RE COMING WITH US, EVEN IF WE HAVE TO BREAK BOTH YOUR LEGS!
SHIT!
JUMP
SO NOW YOU SHOW YOUR TRUE COLORS, YOU JERK!

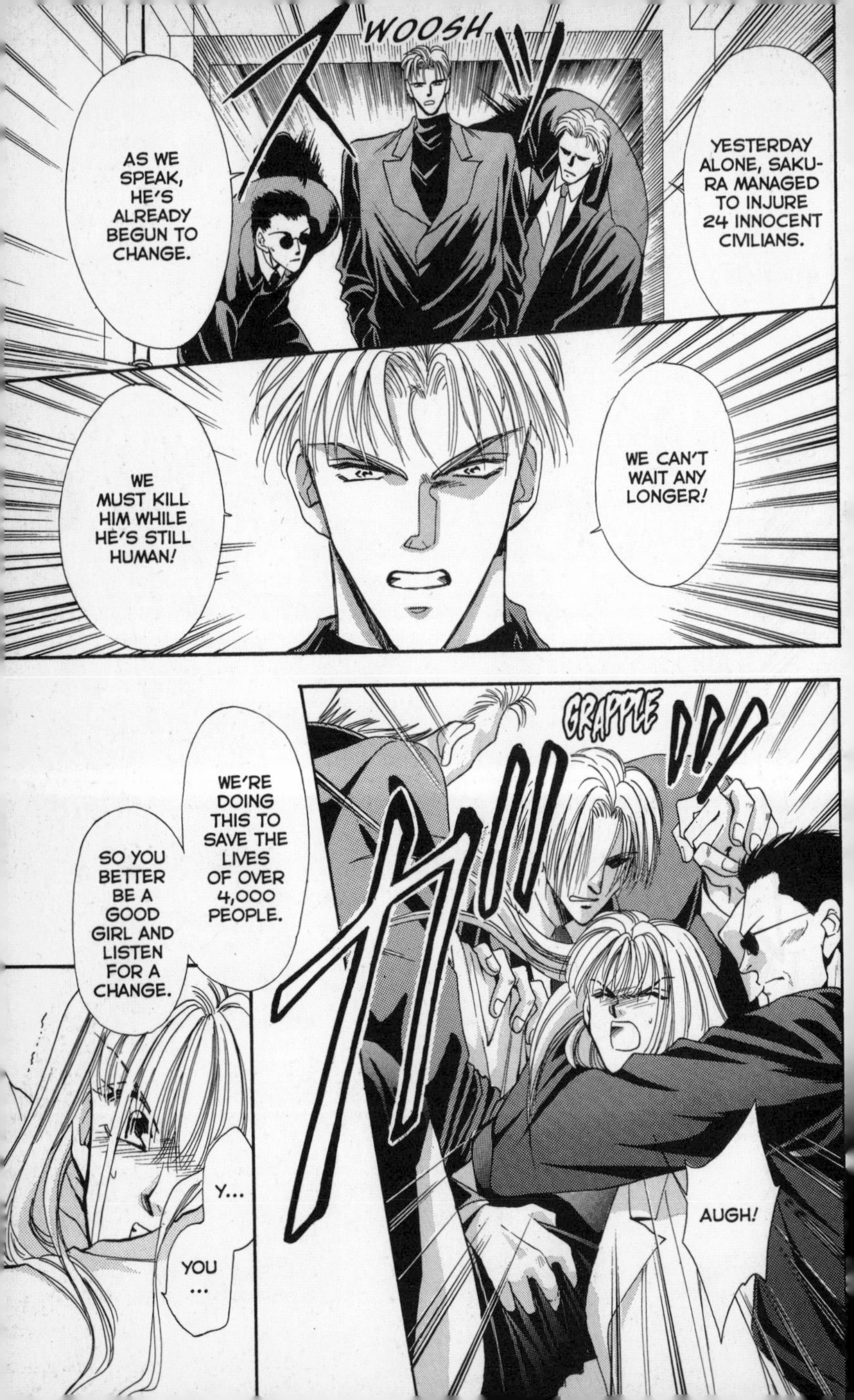
YESTERDAY ALONE, SAKU-RA MANAGED TO INJURE 24 INNOCENT CIVILIANS.
WOOSH
AS WE SPEAK, HE'S ALREADY BEGUN TO CHANGE.
WE CAN'T WAIT ANY LONGER!
WE MUST KILL HIM WHILE HE'S STILL HUMAN!
GRAPPLE
AUGH!
WE'RE DOING THIS TO SAVE THE LIVES OF OVER 4,000 PEOPLE.
SO YOU BETTER BE A GOOD GIRL AND LISTEN FOR A CHANGE.
Y...
YOU ...

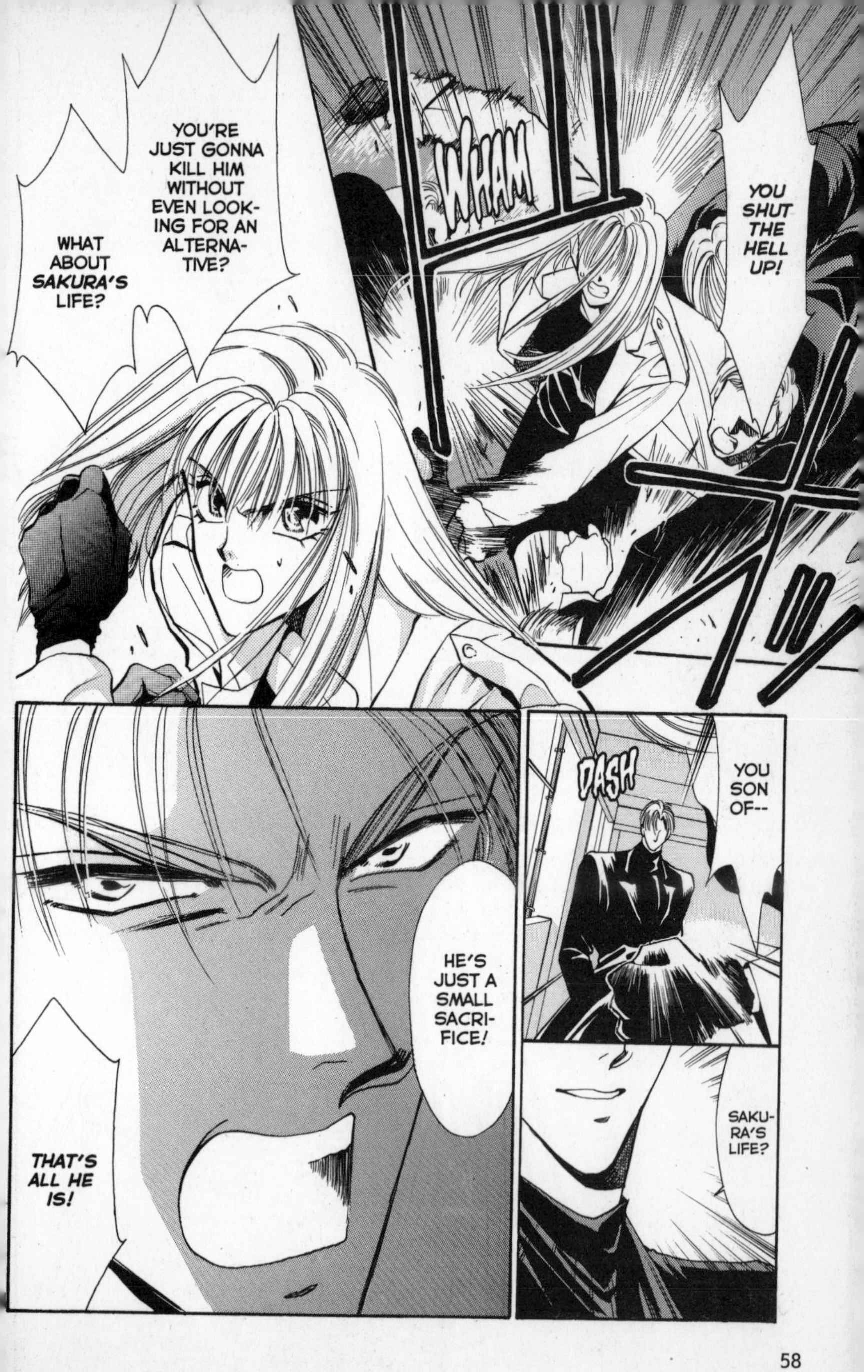
YOU'RE JUST GONNA KILL HIM WITHOUT EVEN LOOKING FOR AN ALTERNATIVE?
WHAT ABOUT SAKURA'S LIFE?
YOU SHUT THE HELL UP!
WHAM
DASH
YOU SON OF--
SAKURA'S LIFE?
HE'S JUST A SMALL SACRIFICE!
THAT'S ALL HE IS!

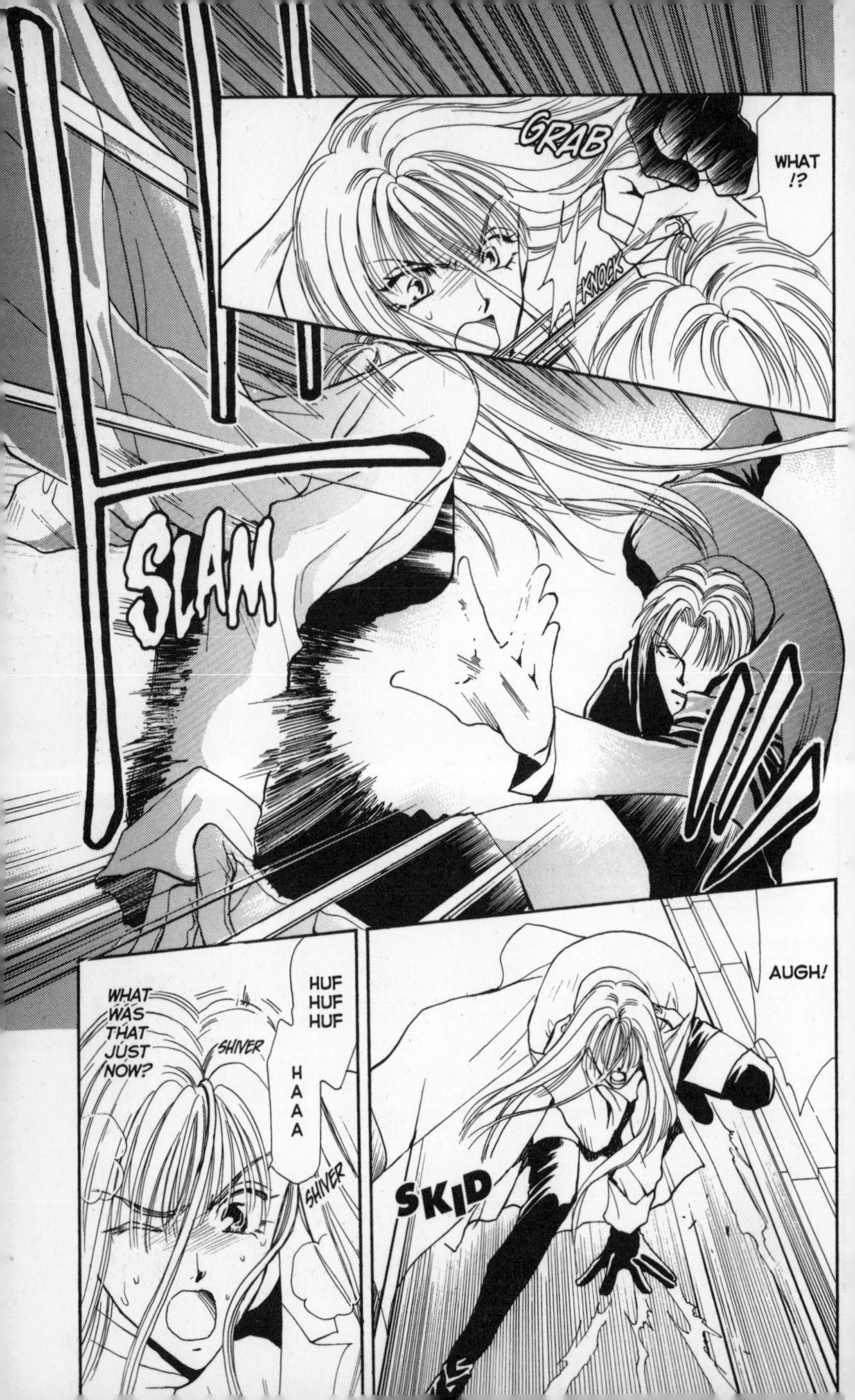
WHAT !?
GRAB
KNOCK
SLAM
AUGH!
SKID
HUF HUF HUF
WHAT WAS THAT JUST NOW?
SHIVER
HAAA
SHIVER

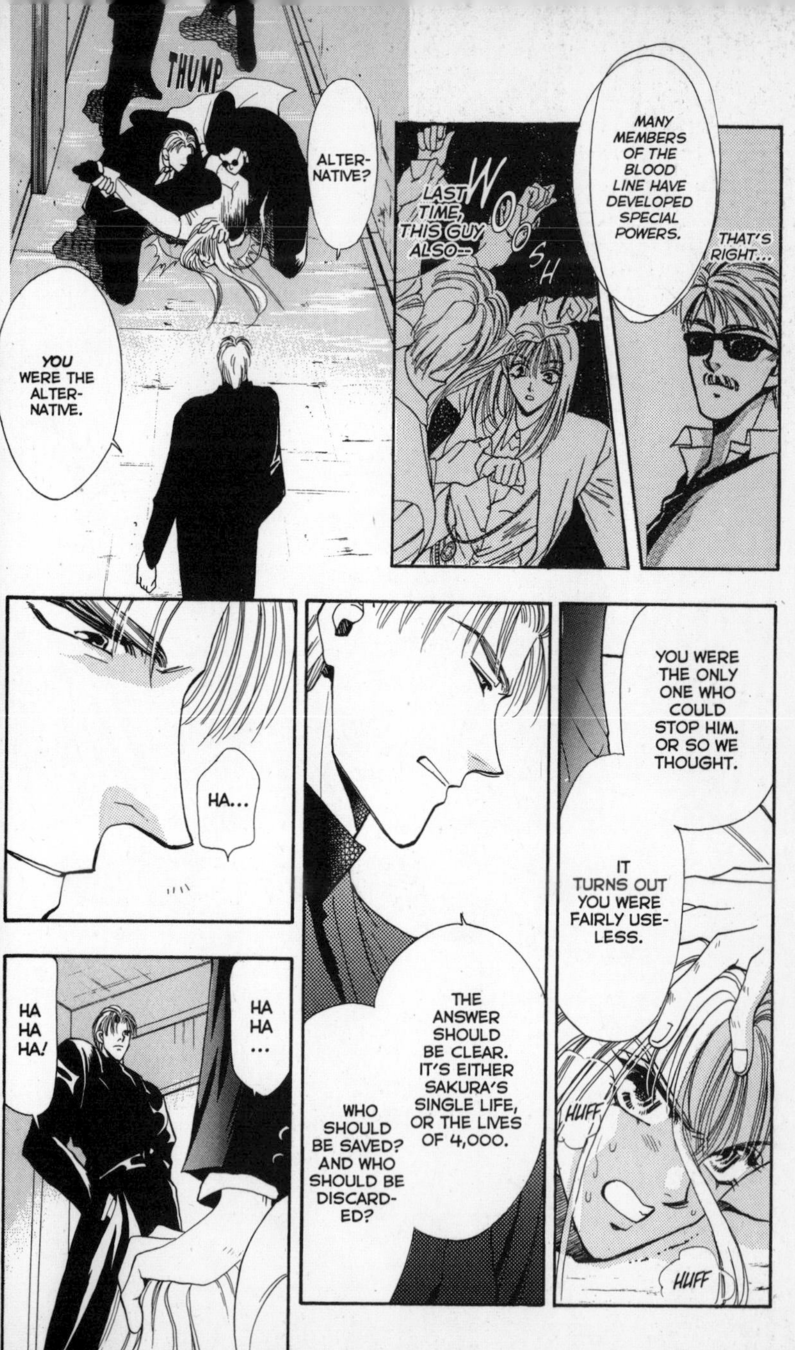
MANY MEMBERS OF THE BLOOD LINE HAVE DEVELOPED SPECIAL POWERS.
THAT'S RIGHT...
LAST TIME, THIS GUY ALSO--
WOOSH
THUMP
ALTER-NATIVE?
YOU WERE THE ALTER-NATIVE.
YOU WERE THE ONLY ONE WHO COULD STOP HIM. OR SO WE THOUGHT.
IT TURNS OUT YOU WERE FAIRLY USE-LESS.
HUFF
HUFF
THE ANSWER SHOULD BE CLEAR. IT'S EITHER SAKURA'S SINGLE LIFE, OR THE LIVES OF 4,000.
WHO SHOULD BE SAVED? AND WHO SHOULD BE DISCARD-ED?
HA...
HA HA ...
HA HA HA!

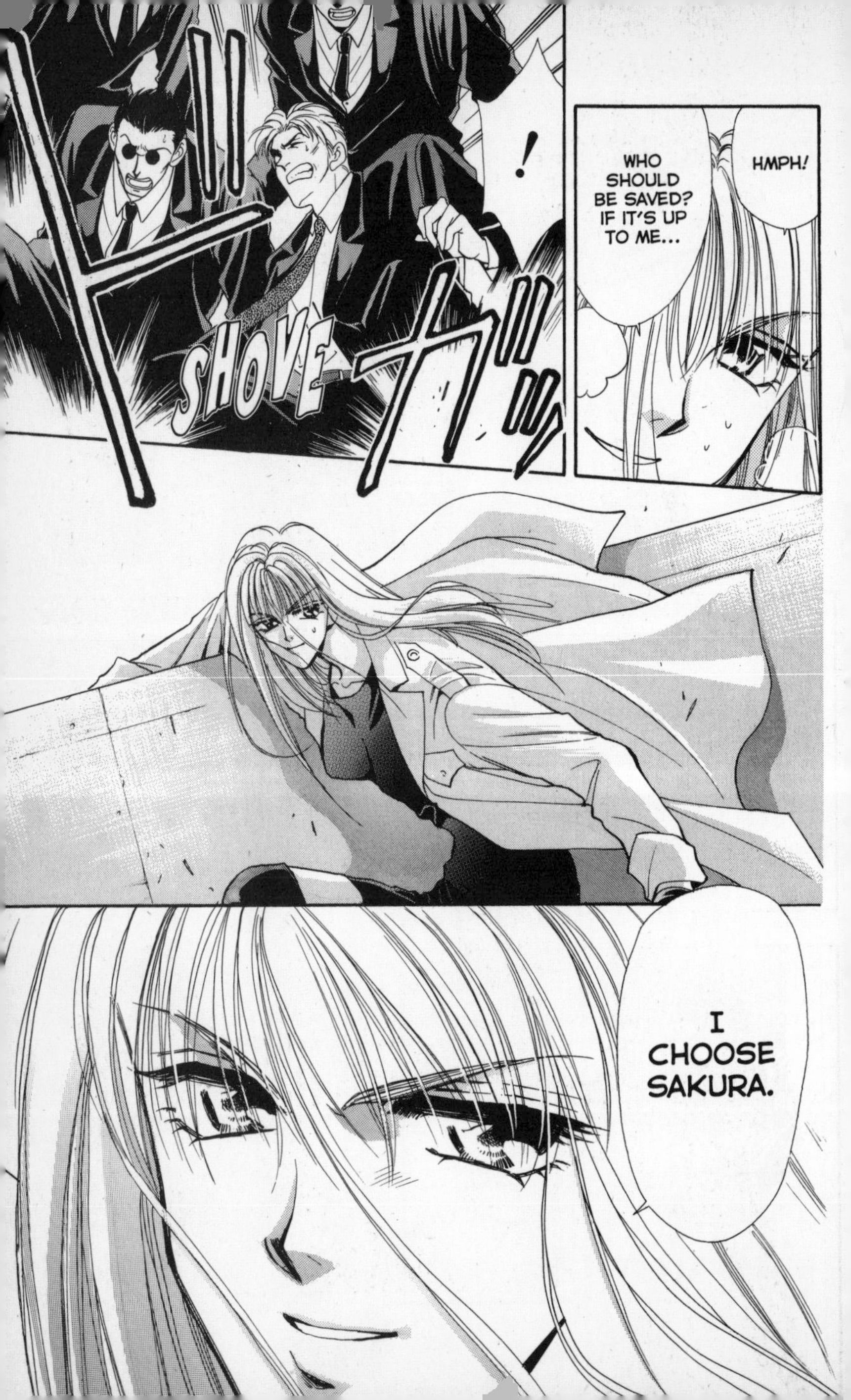
HMPH!
WHO SHOULD BE SAVED? IF IT'S UP TO ME...
!
SHOVE
I CHOOSE SAKURA.

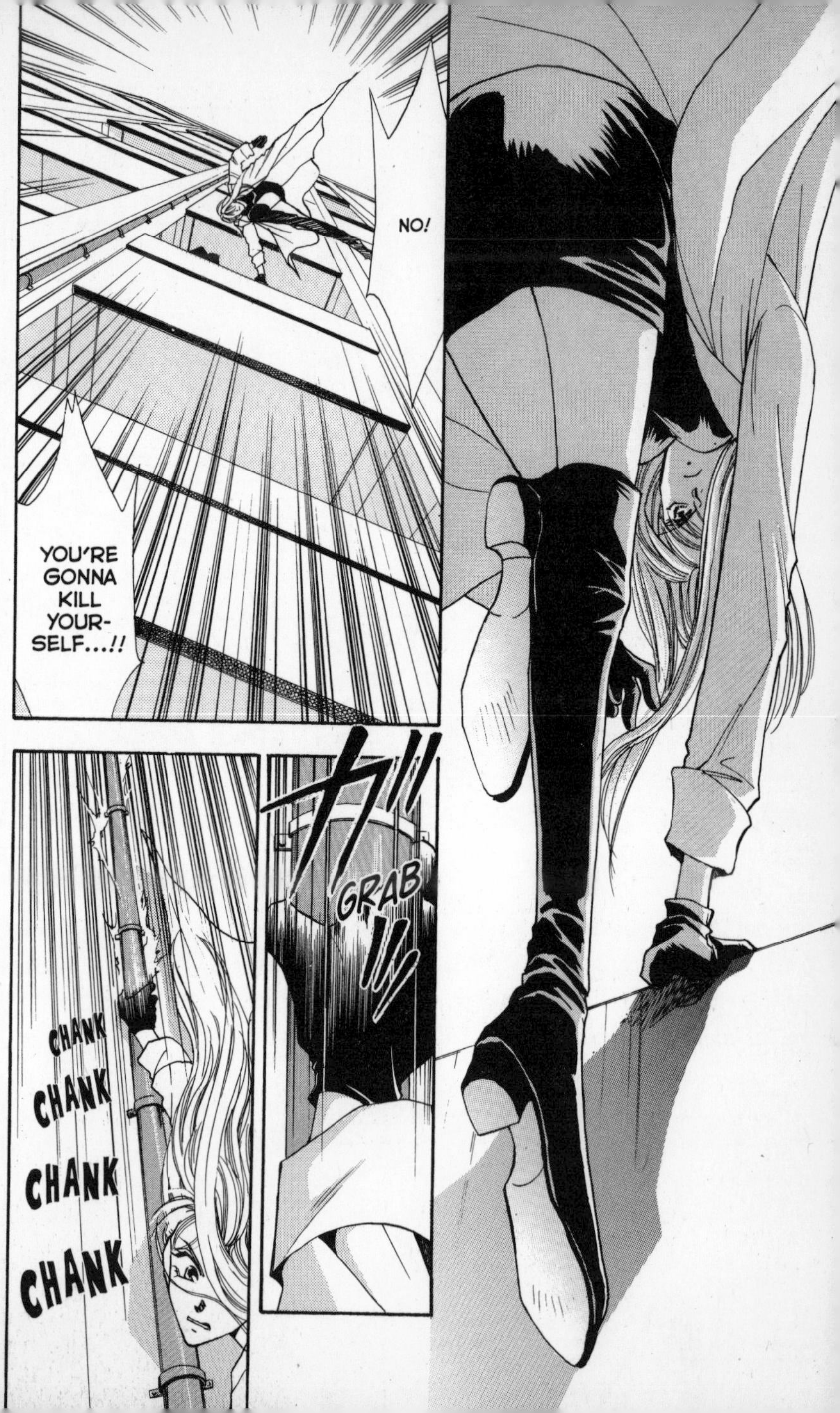
NO!
YOU'RE GONNA KILL YOUR-SELF...!!
GRAB
CHANK
CHANK
CHANK
CHANK

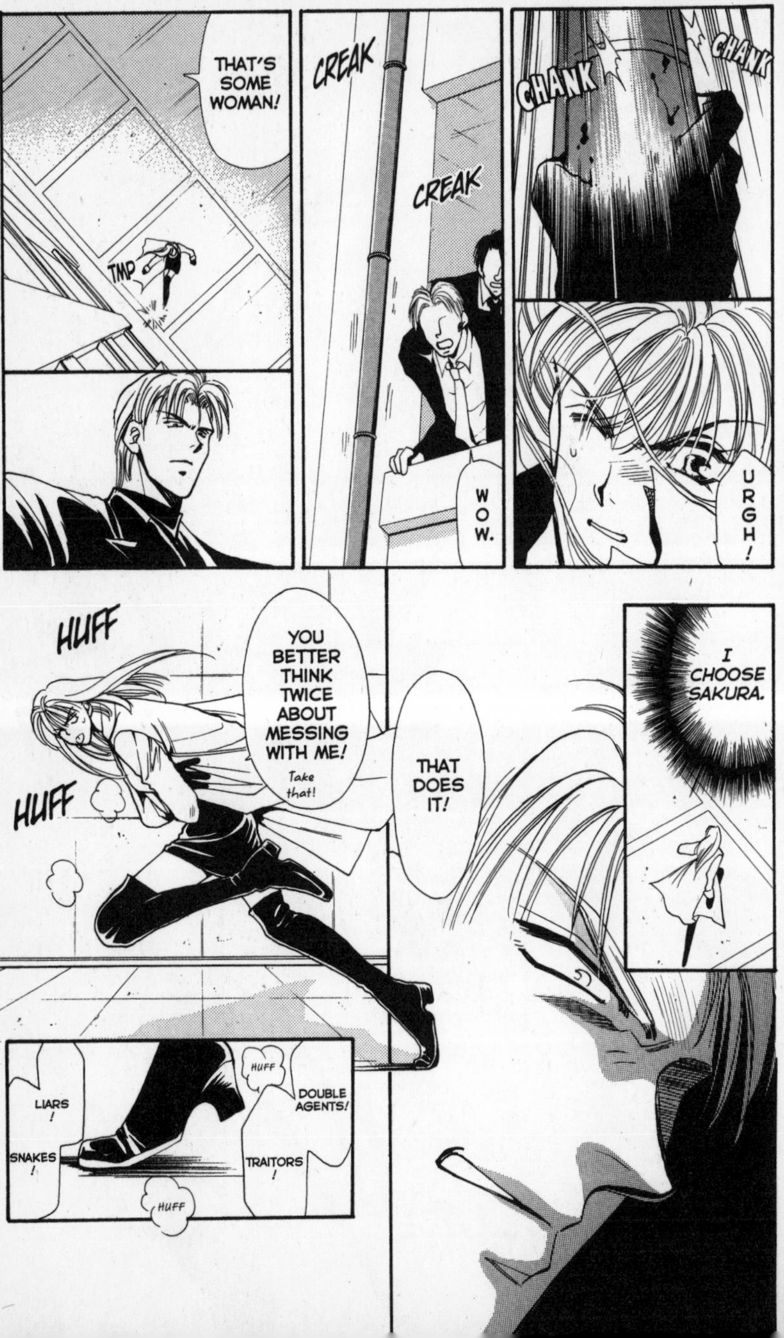
CHANK
CHANK
URGH!
CREAK
CREAK
WOW.
THAT'S SOME WOMAN!
TMP
I CHOOSE SAKURA.
THAT DOES IT!
HUFF
YOU BETTER THINK TWICE ABOUT MESSING WITH ME!
Take that!
HUFF
HUFF
DOUBLE AGENTS!
TRAITORS!
LIARS!
SNAKES!
HUFF

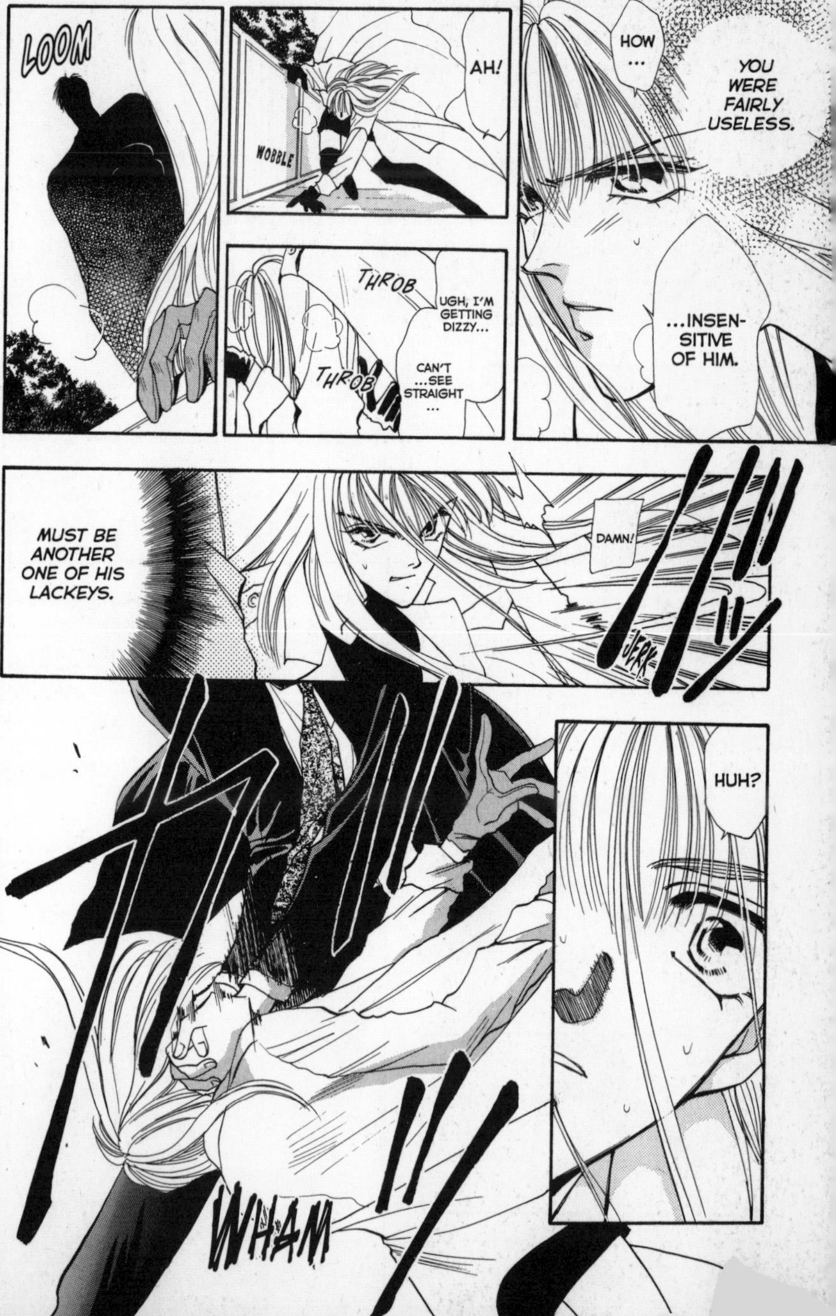
YOU WERE FAIRLY USELESS.
HOW ...
...INSEN-SITIVE OF HIM.
AH!
WOBBLE
THROB
UGH, I'M GETTING DIZZY...
CAN'T ...SEE STRAIGHT ...
THROB
LOOM
DAMN!
JERK
MUST BE ANOTHER ONE OF HIS LACKEYS.
HUH?
WHAM

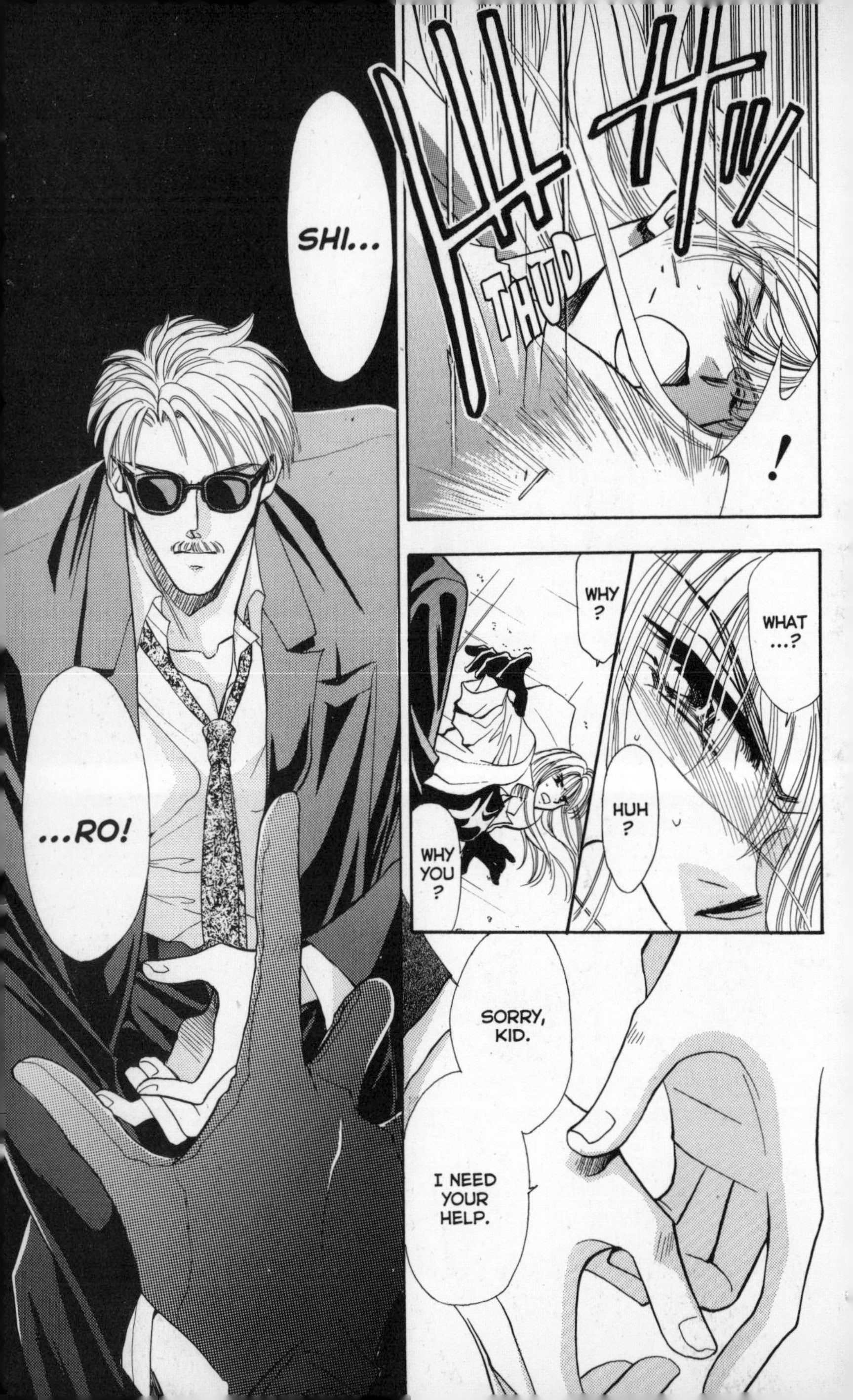
THUD
!
WHAT ...?
HUH ?
WHY ?
WHY YOU ?
SORRY, KID.
I NEED YOUR HELP.
SHI...
...RO!

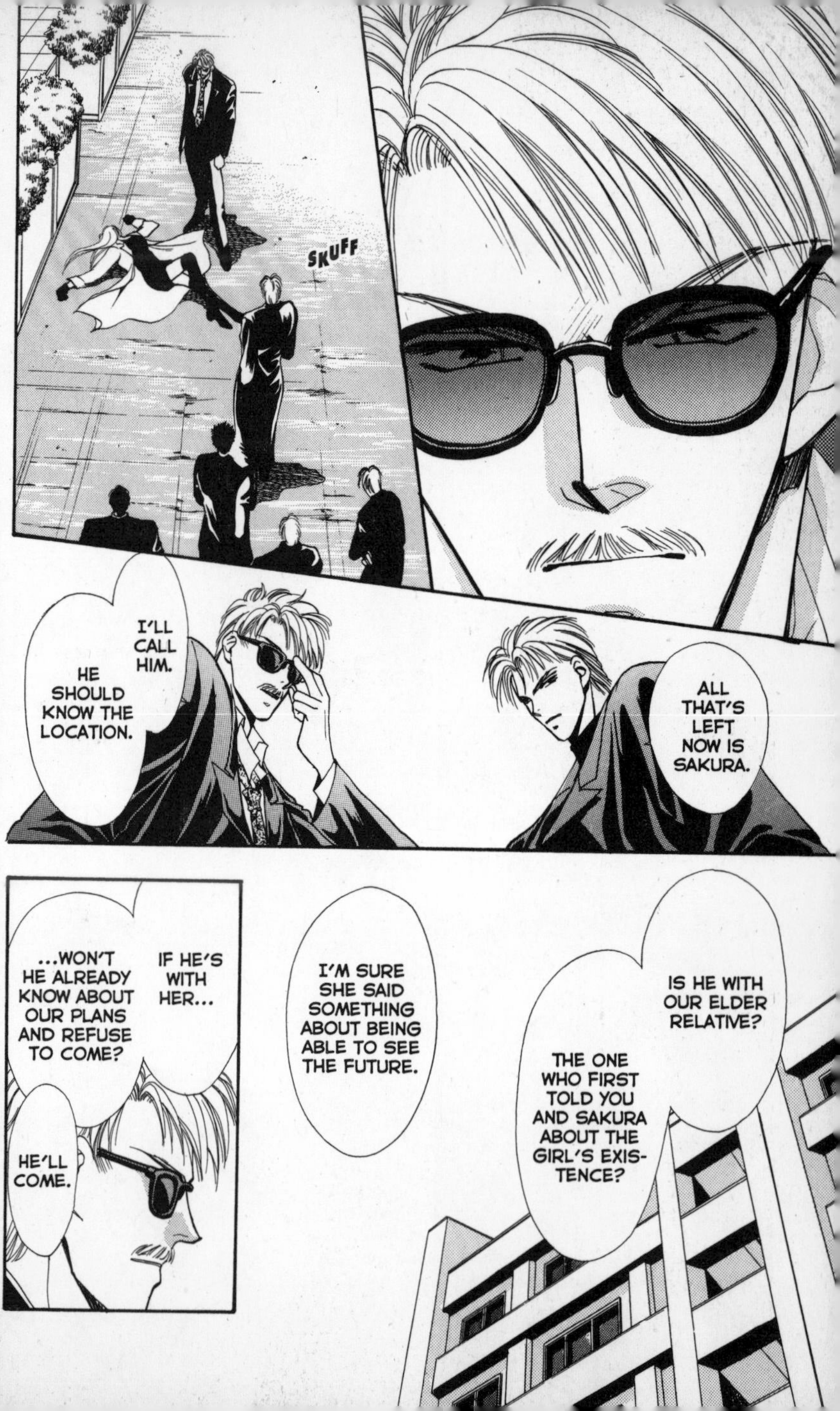
SKUFF
ALL THAT'S LEFT NOW IS SAKURA.
I'LL CALL HIM.
HE SHOULD KNOW THE LOCATION.
IS HE WITH OUR ELDER RELATIVE?
THE ONE WHO FIRST TOLD YOU AND SAKURA ABOUT THE GIRL'S EXISTENCE?
I'M SURE SHE SAID SOMETHING ABOUT BEING ABLE TO SEE THE FUTURE.
IF HE'S WITH HER...
...WON'T HE ALREADY KNOW ABOUT OUR PLANS AND REFUSE TO COME?
HE'LL COME.

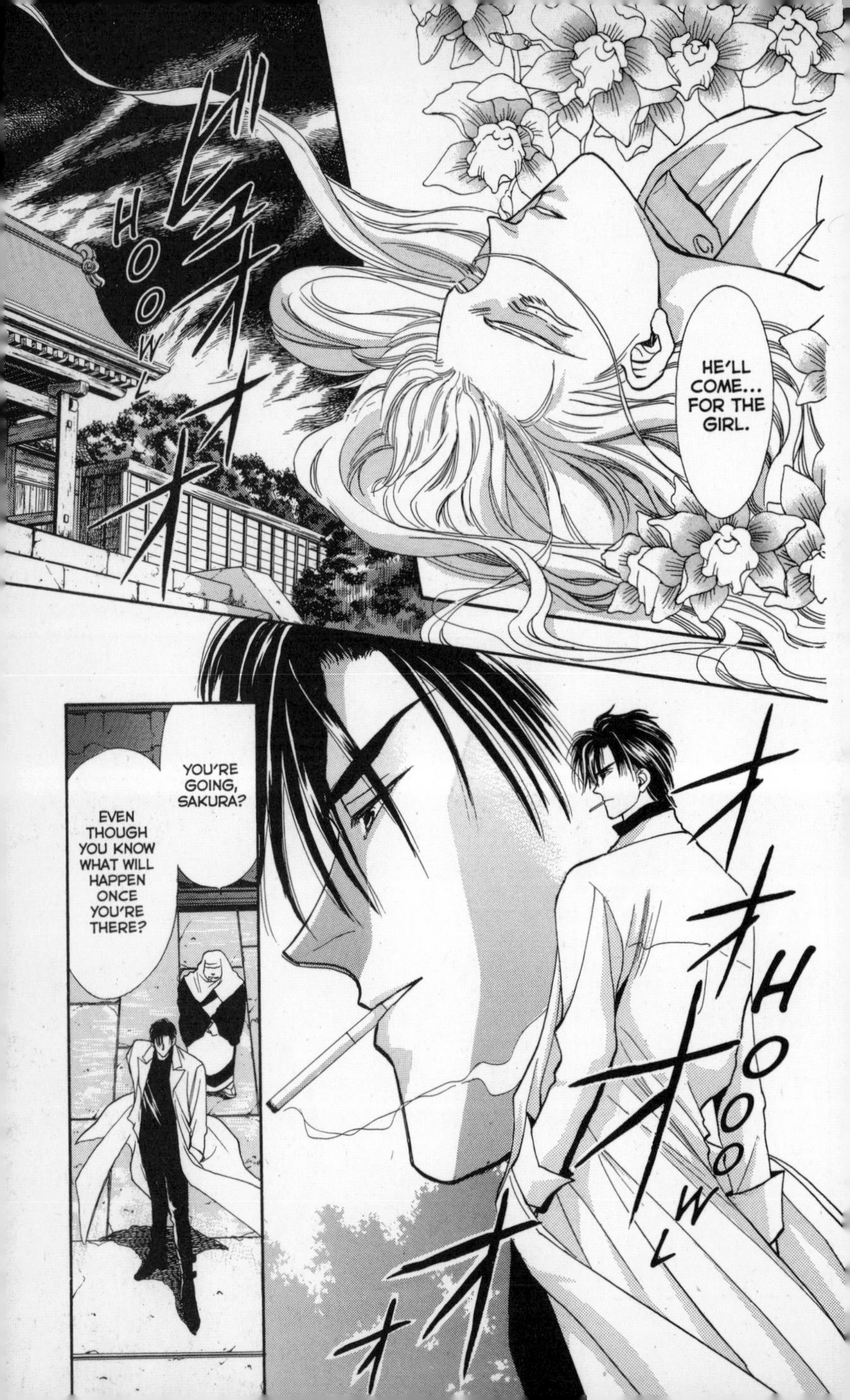
HOOWL
HE'LL COME... FOR THE GIRL.
HOOOWL
YOU'RE GOING, SAKURA?
EVEN THOUGH YOU KNOW WHAT WILL HAPPEN ONCE YOU'RE THERE?

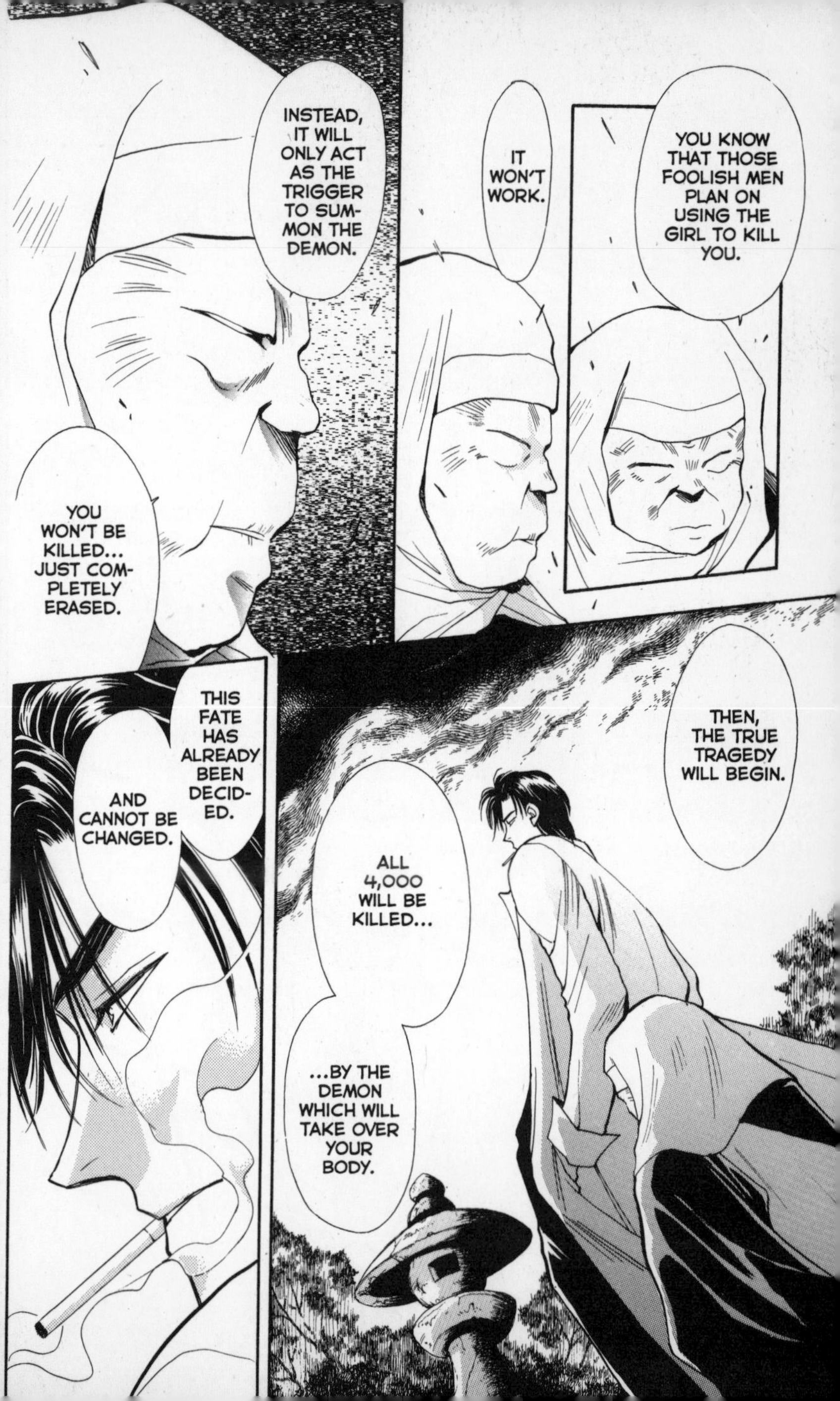
YOU KNOW THAT THOSE FOOLISH MEN PLAN ON USING THE GIRL TO KILL YOU.
IT WON'T WORK.
INSTEAD, IT WILL ONLY ACT AS THE TRIGGER TO SUMMON THE DEMON.
YOU WON'T BE KILLED... JUST COMPLETELY ERASED.
THEN, THE TRUE TRAGEDY WILL BEGIN.
ALL 4,000 WILL BE KILLED...
...BY THE DEMON WHICH WILL TAKE OVER YOUR BODY.
THIS FATE HAS ALREADY BEEN DECIDED.
AND CANNOT BE CHANGED.

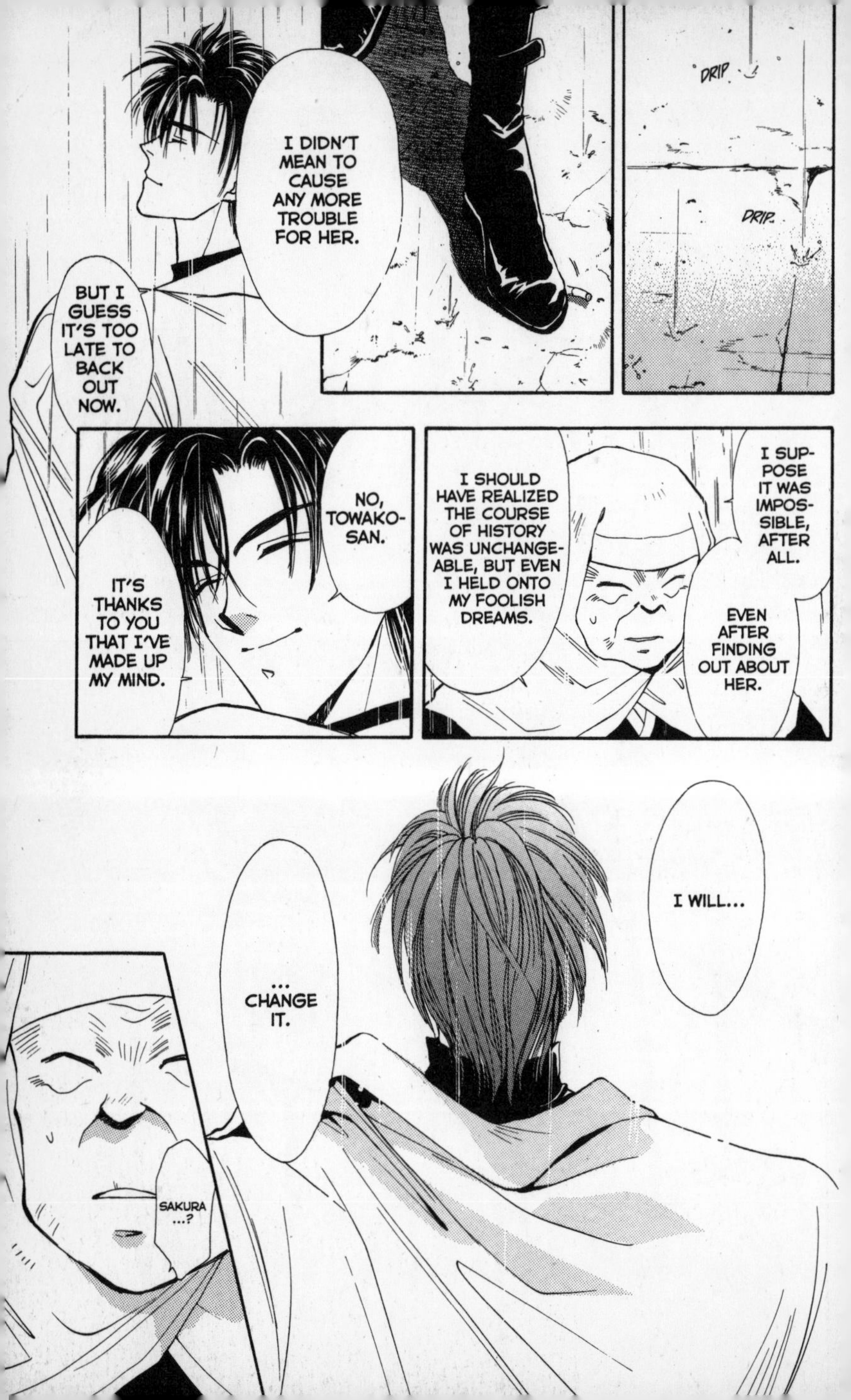
DRIP
DRIP
I DIDN'T MEAN TO CAUSE ANY MORE TROUBLE FOR HER.
BUT I GUESS IT'S TOO LATE TO BACK OUT NOW.
I SUPPOSE IT WAS IMPOSSIBLE, AFTER ALL.
EVEN AFTER FINDING OUT ABOUT HER.
I SHOULD HAVE REALIZED THE COURSE OF HISTORY WAS UNCHANGEABLE, BUT EVEN I HELD ONTO MY FOOLISH DREAMS.
NO, TOWAKO-SAN.
IT'S THANKS TO YOU THAT I'VE MADE UP MY MIND.
I WILL...
...CHANGE IT.
SAKURA ...?

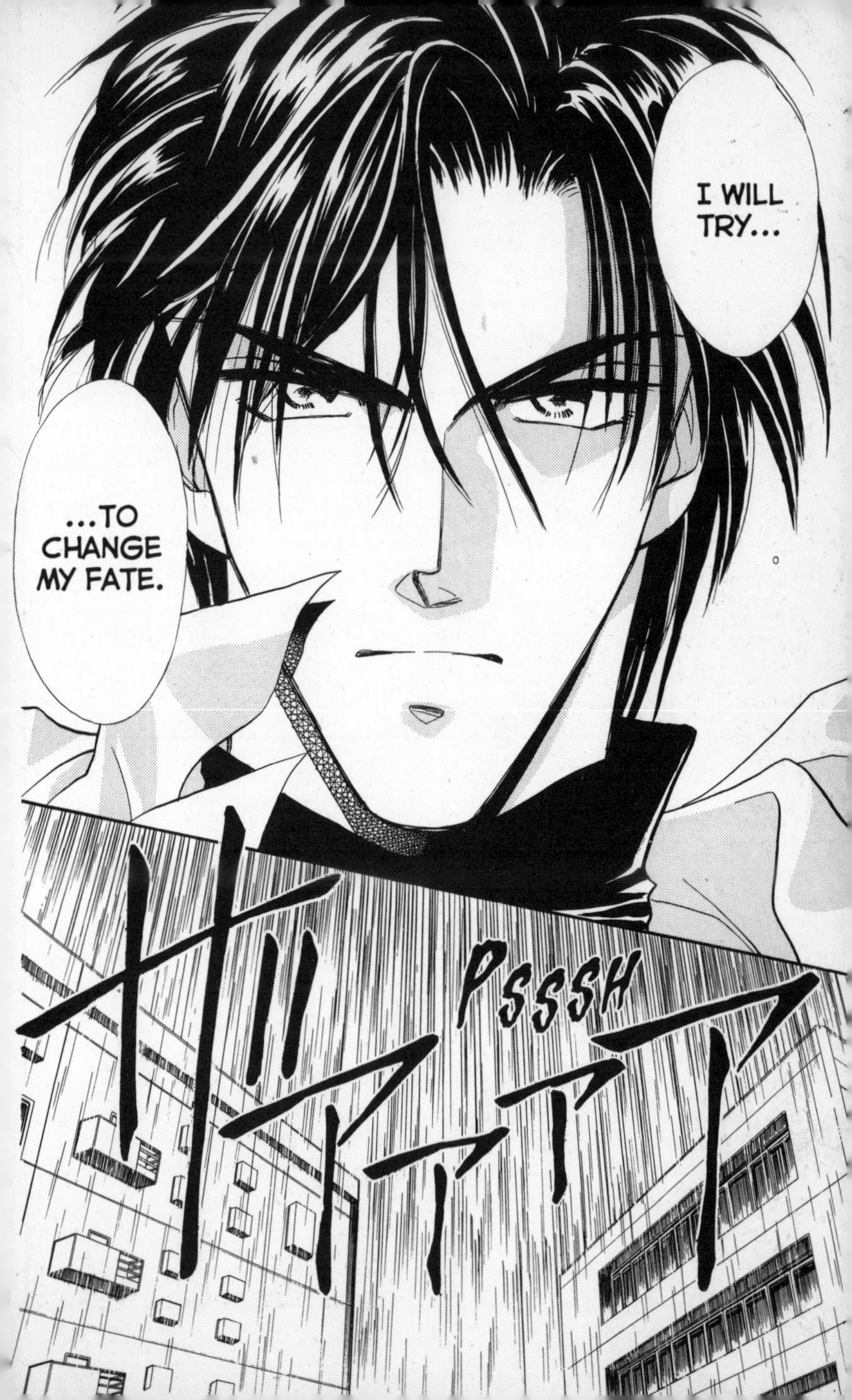
I WILL TRY...
...TO CHANGE MY FATE.
PSSSH

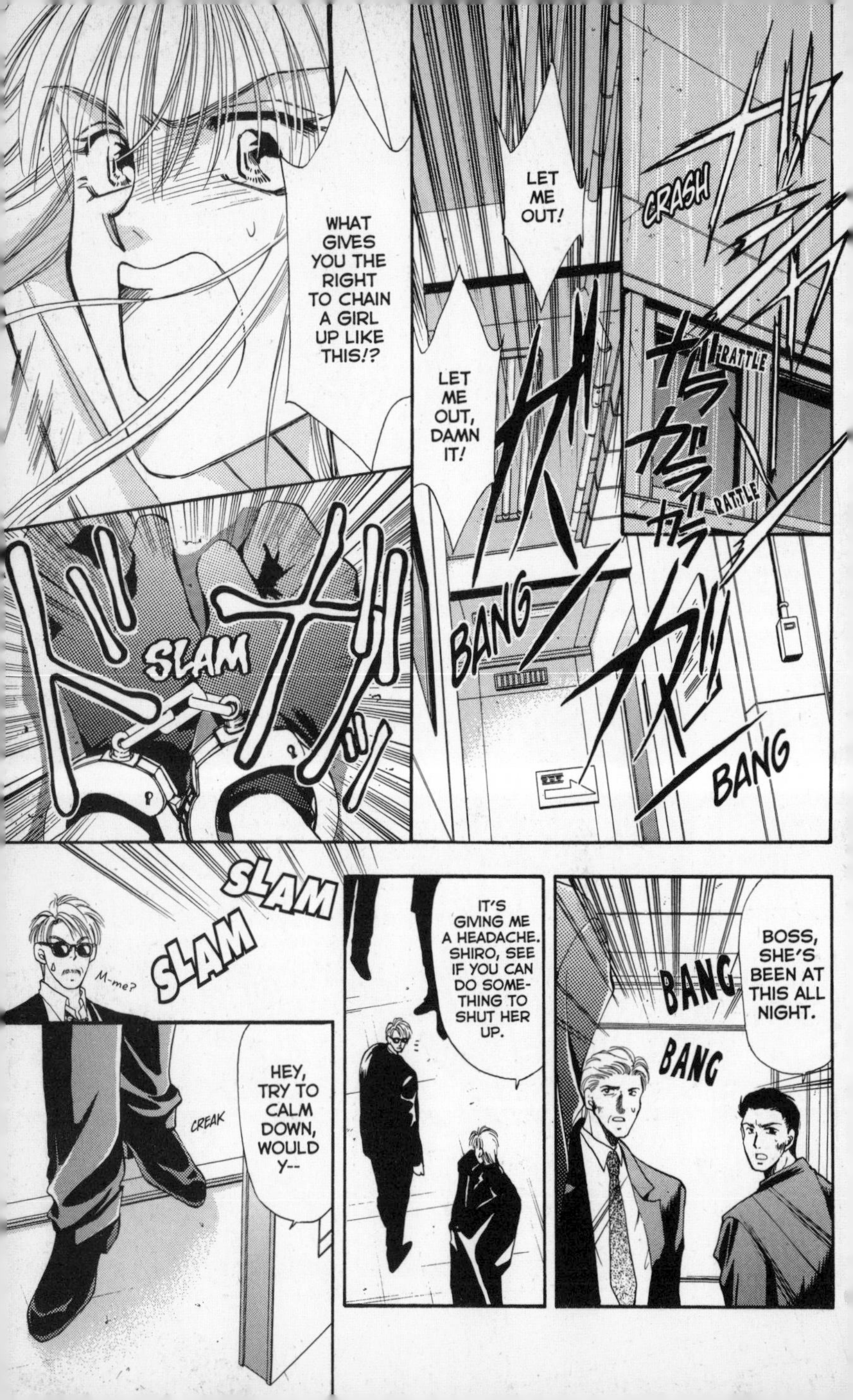
CRASH
RATTLE
RATTLE
LET ME OUT!
LET ME OUT, DAMN IT!
BANG
BANG
WHAT GIVES YOU THE RIGHT TO CHAIN A GIRL UP LIKE THIS!?
SLAM
BOSS, SHE'S BEEN AT THIS ALL NIGHT.
BANG
BANG
IT'S GIVING ME A HEADACHE. SHIRO, SEE IF YOU CAN DO SOME-THING TO SHUT HER UP.
SLAM
SLAM
M-me?
HEY, TRY TO CALM DOWN, WOULD Y--
CREAK

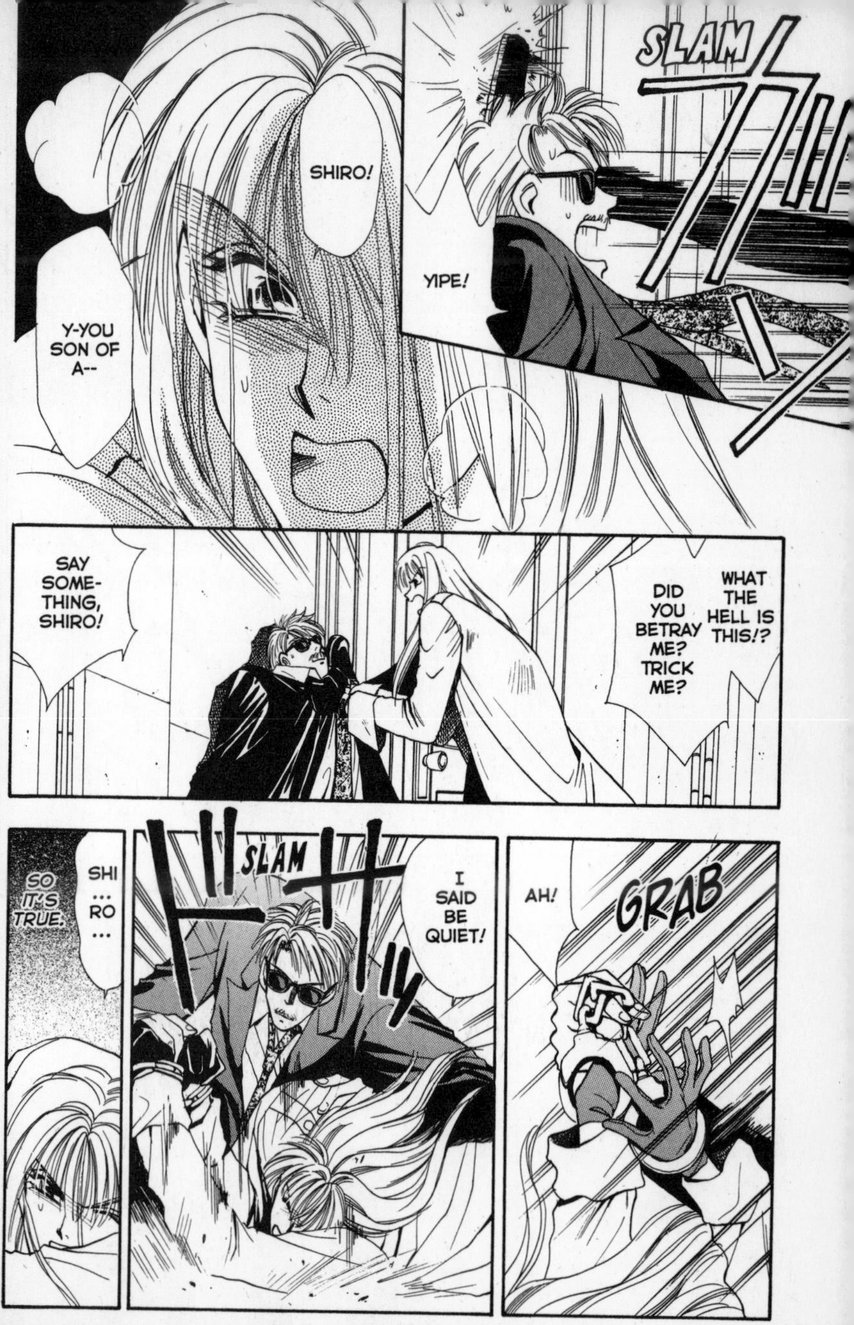
SLAM
YIPE!
SHIRO!
Y-YOU SON OF A--
WHAT THE HELL IS THIS!?
DID YOU BETRAY ME? TRICK ME?
SAY SOME-THING, SHIRO!
GRAB
AH!
I SAID BE QUIET!
SLAM
SHI ... RO ...
SO IT'S TRUE.

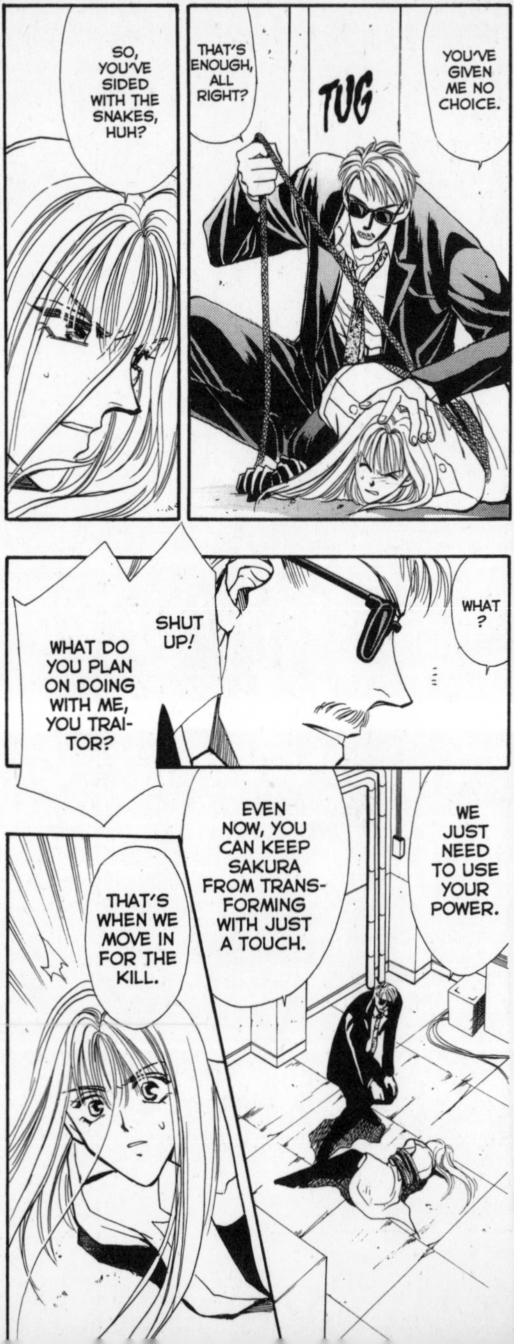
YOU'VE GIVEN ME NO CHOICE.
TUG
THAT'S ENOUGH, ALL RIGHT?
SO, YOU'VE SIDED WITH THE SNAKES, HUH?
WHAT?
SHUT UP!
WHAT DO YOU PLAN ON DOING WITH ME, YOU TRAITOR?
WE JUST NEED TO USE YOUR POWER.
EVEN NOW, YOU CAN KEEP SAKURA FROM TRANSFORMING WITH JUST A TOUCH.
THAT'S WHEN WE MOVE IN FOR THE KILL.

■ Work Diary ■
Eraser Part 1

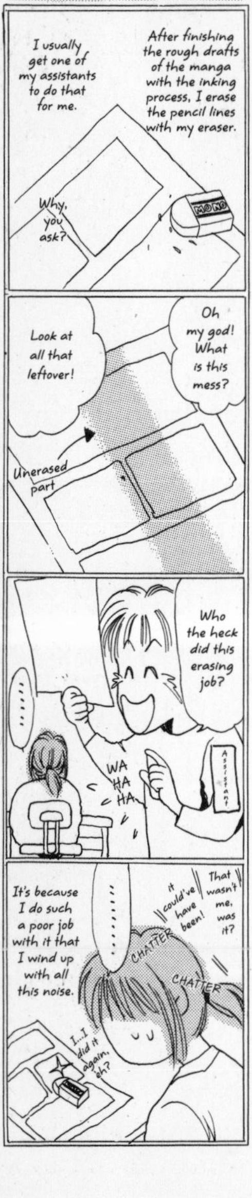
After finishing the rough drafts of the manga with the inking process, I erase the pencil lines with my eraser.
I usually get one of my assistants to do that for me.
Why, you ask?
MONO
Oh my god! What is this mess?
Look at all that leftover!
Unerased part
Who the heck did this erasing job?
WA HA HA
......
Assistant
That wasn't me, was it?
it could've have been!
It's because I do such a poor job with it that I wind up with all this noise.
......
CHATTER
CHATTER
I...I did it again, eh?

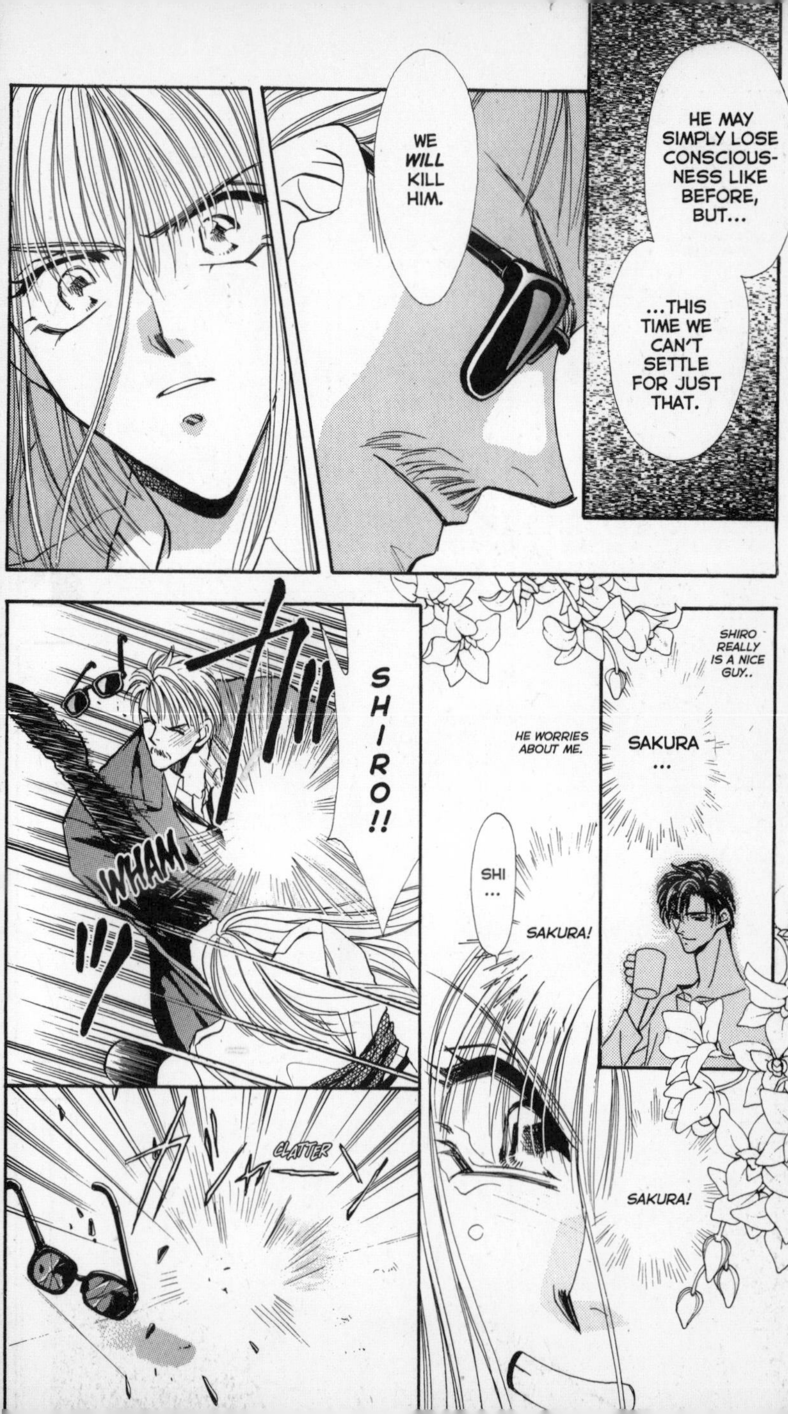
HE MAY SIMPLY LOSE CONSCIOUS-NESS LIKE BEFORE, BUT...
...THIS TIME WE CAN'T SETTLE FOR JUST THAT.
WE *WILL* KILL HIM.
SHIRO REALLY IS A NICE GUY..
SAKURA ...
HE WORRIES ABOUT ME.
SHI ...
SAKURA!
SAKURA!
SHIRO!!
WHAM
CLATTER

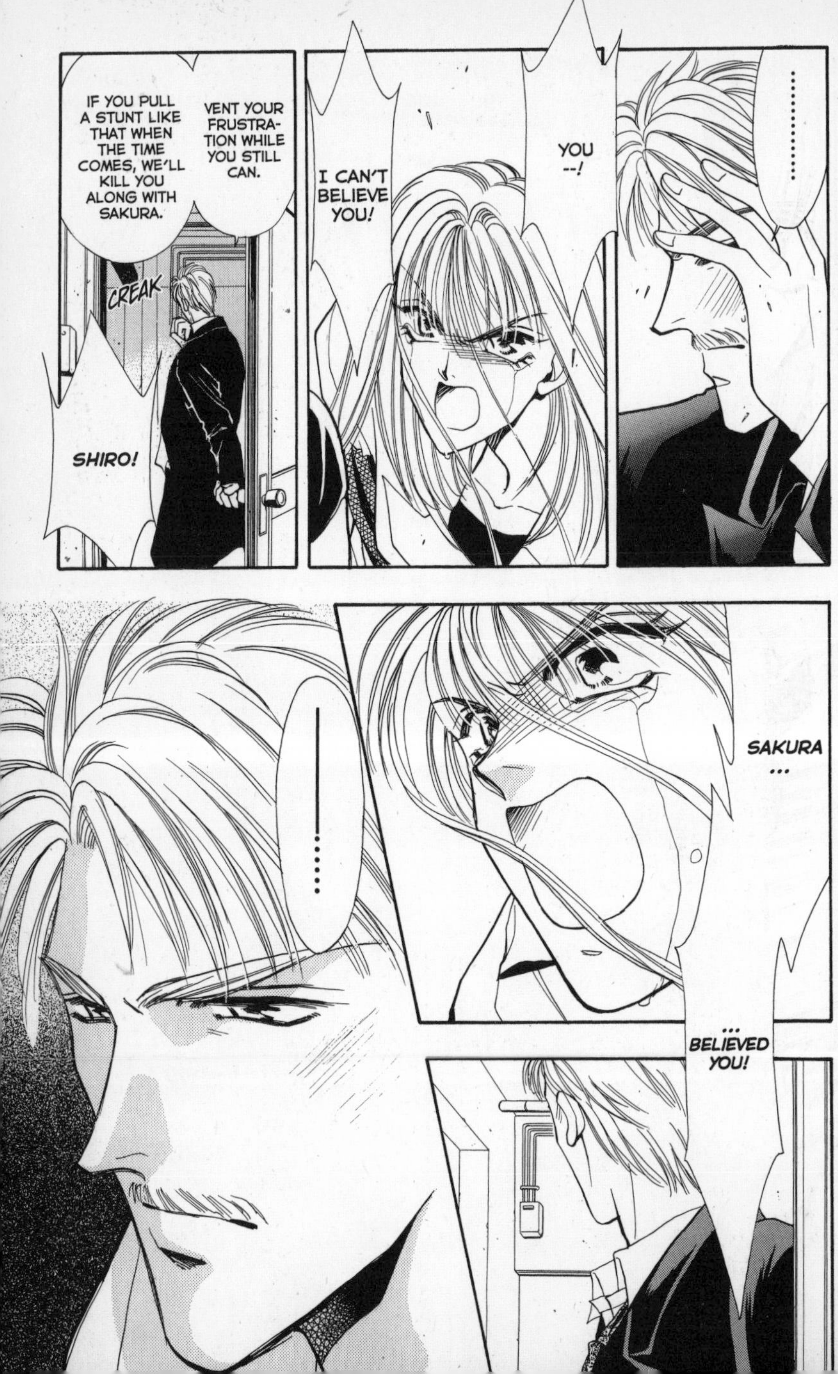
......
YOU --!
I CAN'T BELIEVE YOU!
VENT YOUR FRUSTRATION WHILE YOU STILL CAN.
IF YOU PULL A STUNT LIKE THAT WHEN THE TIME COMES, WE'LL KILL YOU ALONG WITH SAKURA.
CREAK
SHIRO!
SAKURA ...
... BELIEVED YOU!
......

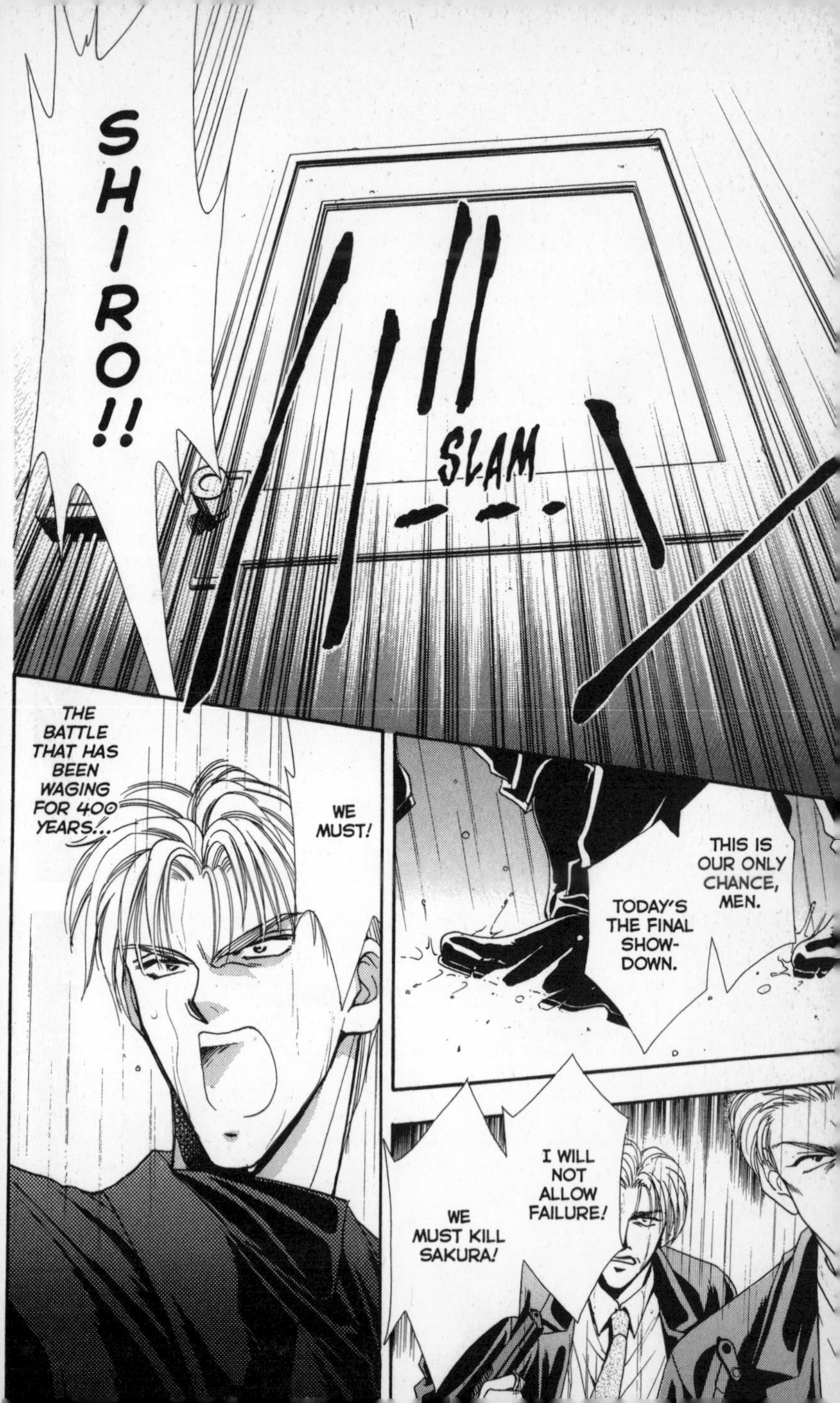
SHIRO!!
SLAM
THIS IS OUR ONLY CHANCE, MEN.
TODAY'S THE FINAL SHOW-DOWN.
I WILL NOT ALLOW FAILURE!
WE MUST KILL SAKURA!
WE MUST!
THE BATTLE THAT HAS BEEN WAGING FOR 400 YEARS...

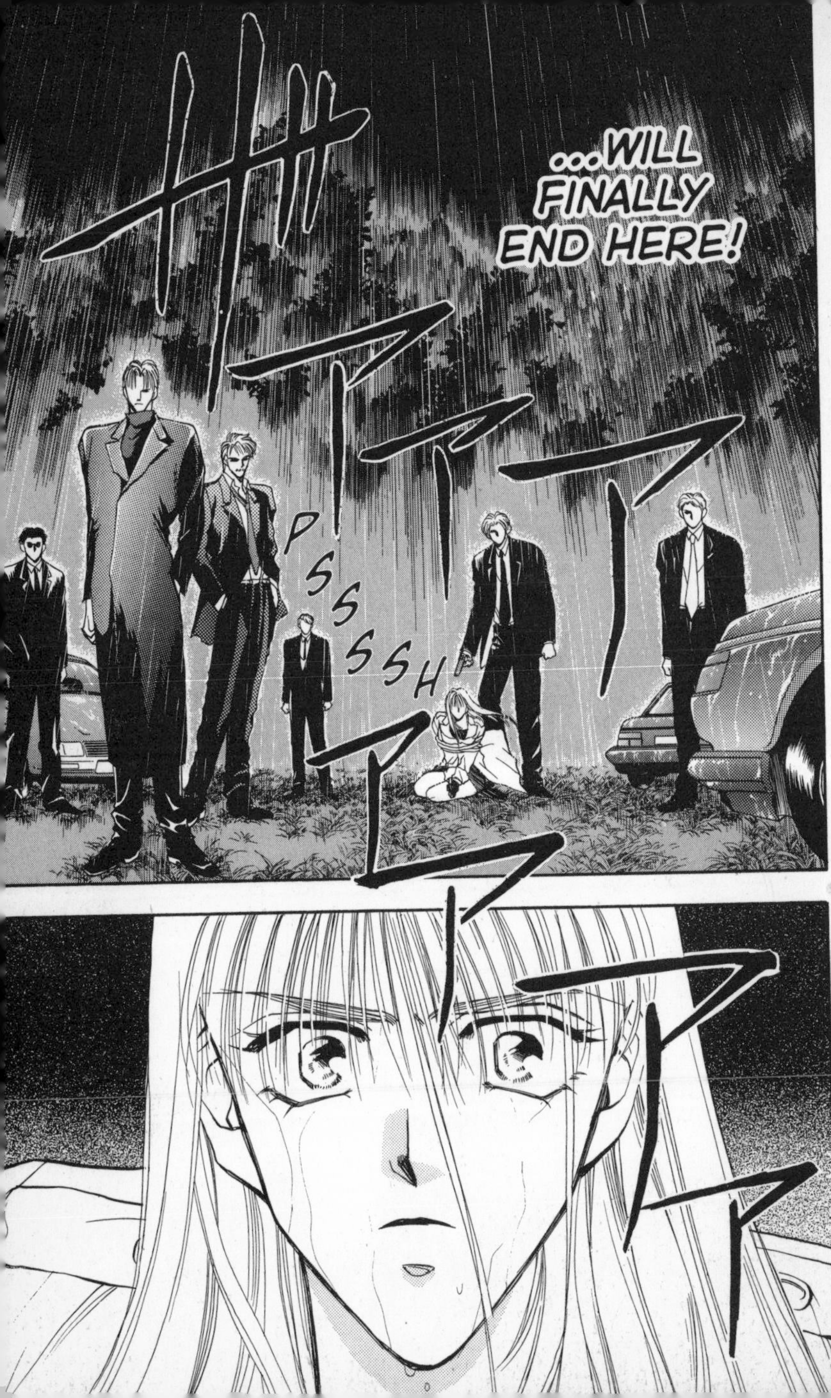
...WILL FINALLY END HERE!
PSSSSH

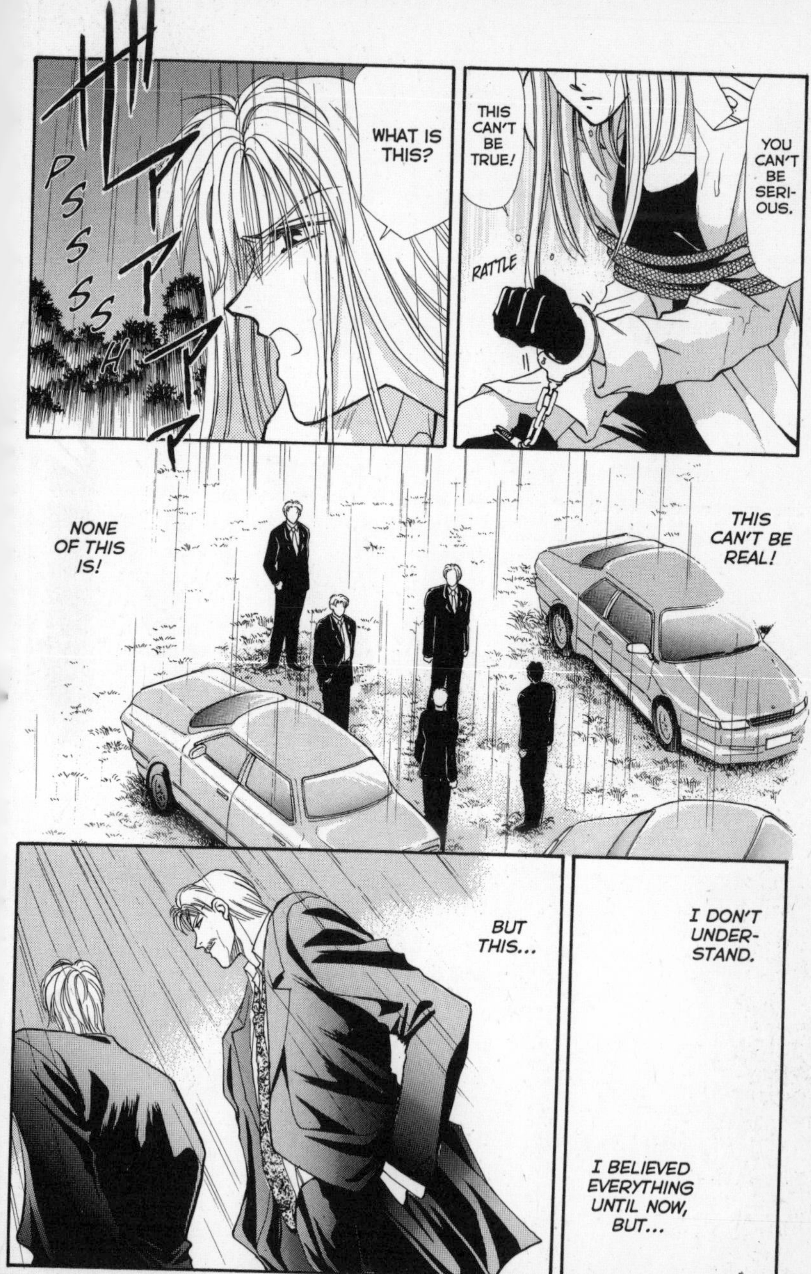
YOU CAN'T BE SERI-OUS.
THIS CAN'T BE TRUE!
RATTLE
WHAT IS THIS?
PSSSSH
THIS CAN'T BE REAL!
NONE OF THIS IS!
I DON'T UNDER-STAND.
I BELIEVED EVERYTHING UNTIL NOW, BUT...
BUT THIS...

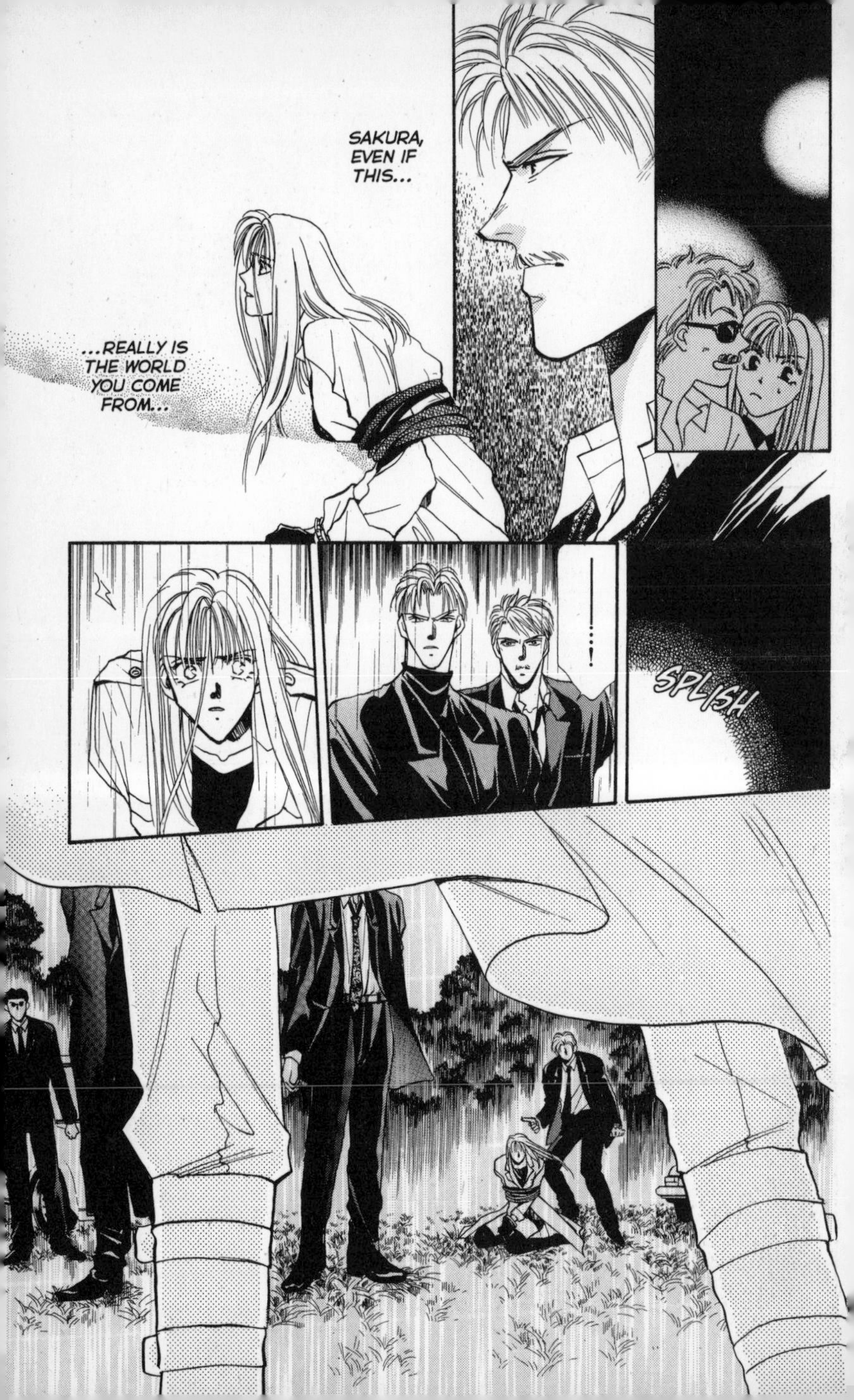
SAKURA, EVEN IF THIS...
...REALLY IS THE WORLD YOU COME FROM...
SPLISH
...!

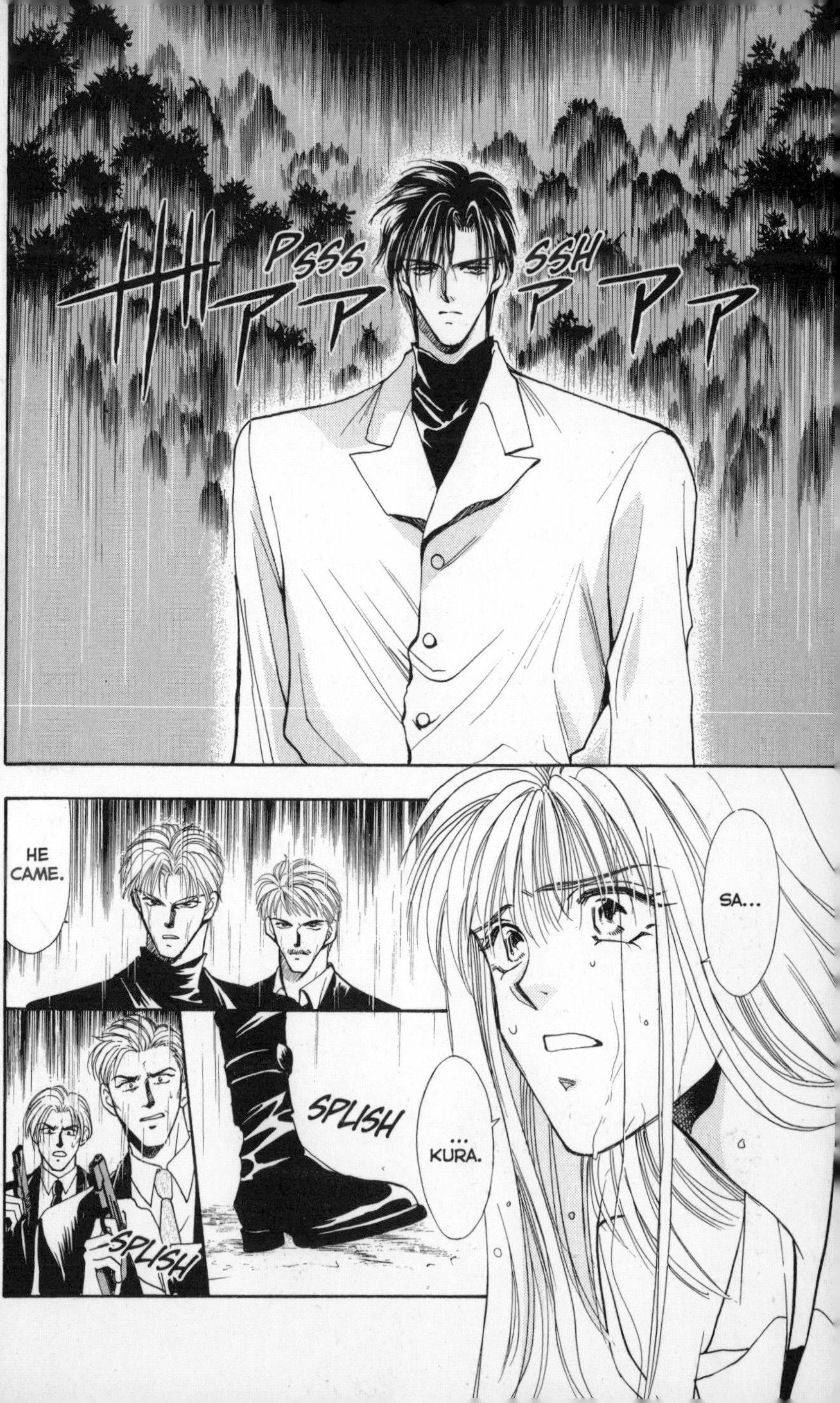

PSSS
SSH
SA...
...KURA.
HE CAME.
SPLISH
SPLISH

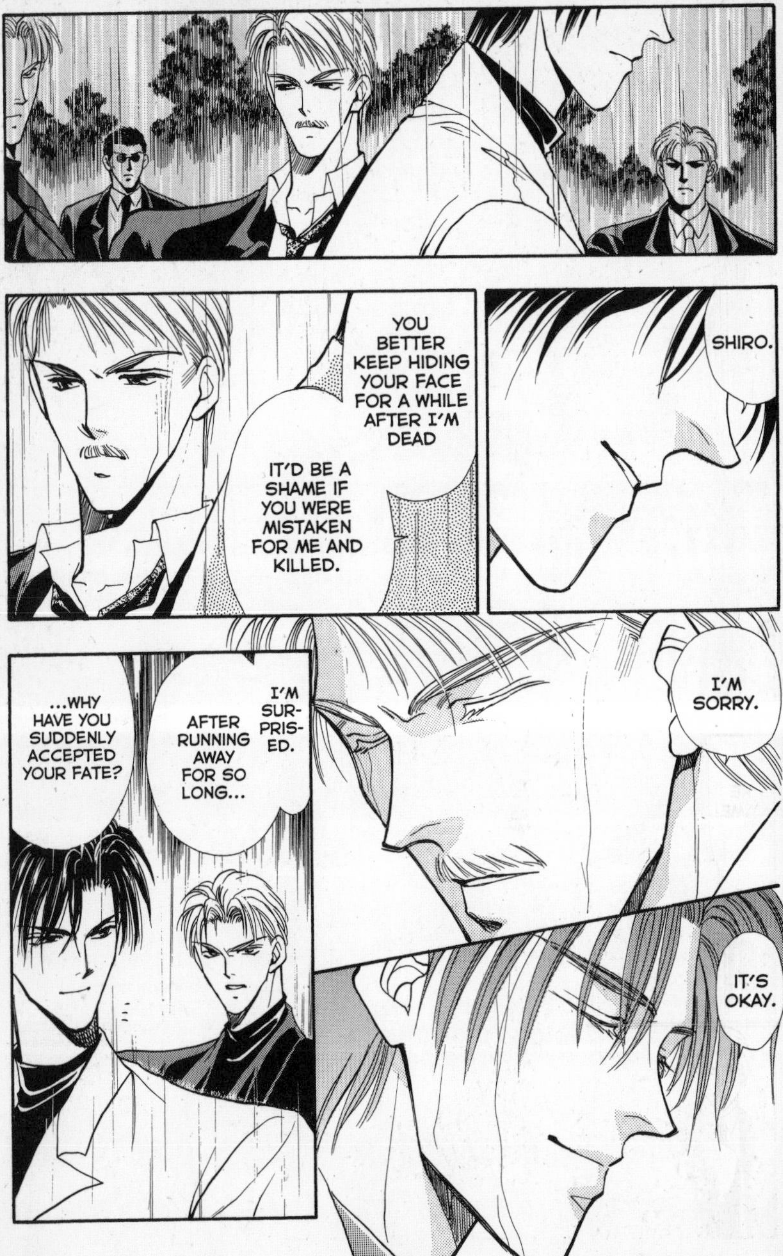
SHIRO.
YOU BETTER KEEP HIDING YOUR FACE FOR A WHILE AFTER I'M DEAD
IT'D BE A SHAME IF YOU WERE MISTAKEN FOR ME AND KILLED.
I'M SORRY.
IT'S OKAY.
I'M SUR-PRIS-ED.
AFTER RUNNING AWAY FOR SO LONG...
...WHY HAVE YOU SUDDENLY ACCEPTED YOUR FATE?

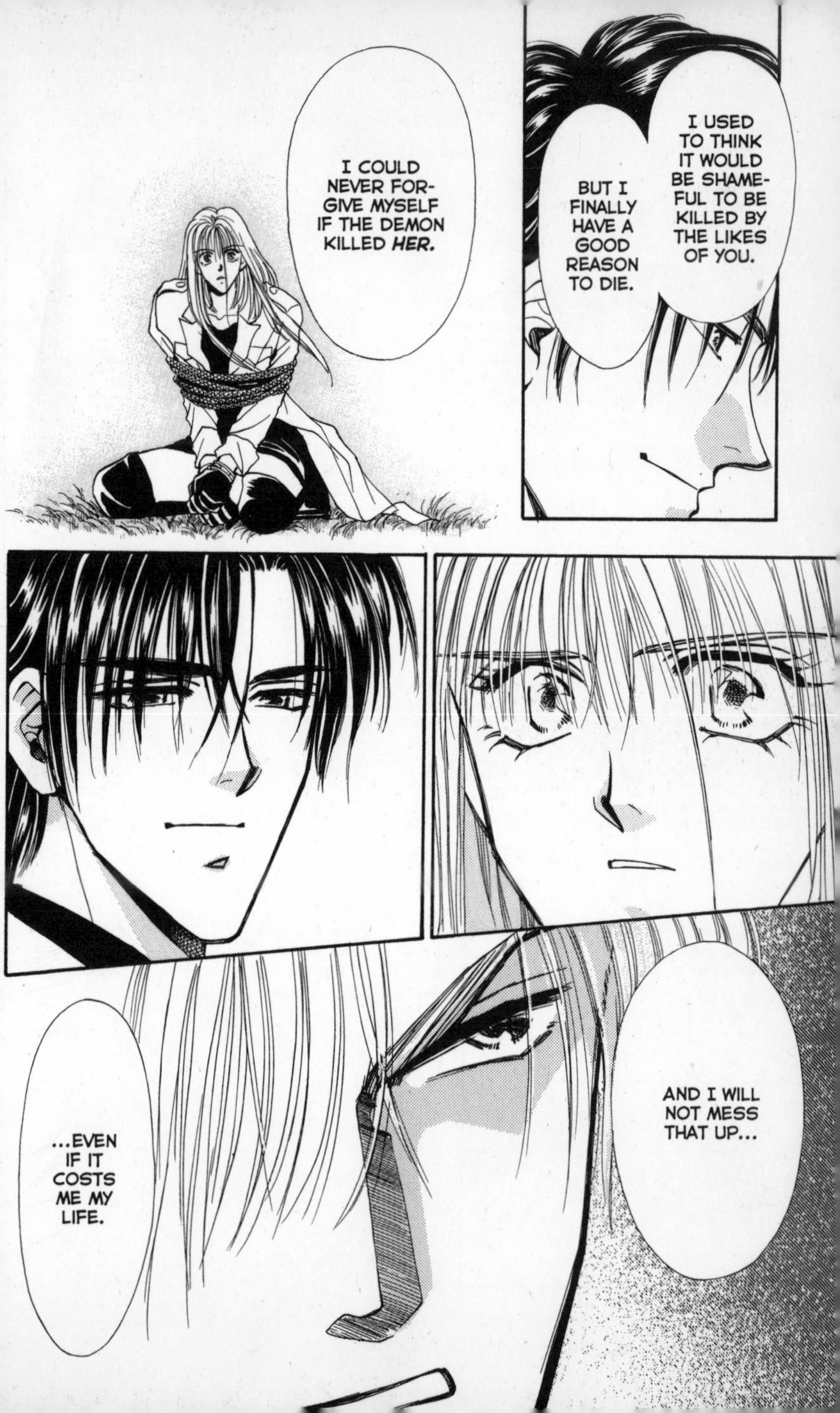
I USED TO THINK IT WOULD BE SHAMEFUL TO BE KILLED BY THE LIKES OF YOU.
BUT I FINALLY HAVE A GOOD REASON TO DIE.
I COULD NEVER FORGIVE MYSELF IF THE DEMON KILLED *HER*.
AND I WILL NOT MESS THAT UP...
...EVEN IF IT COSTS ME MY LIFE.

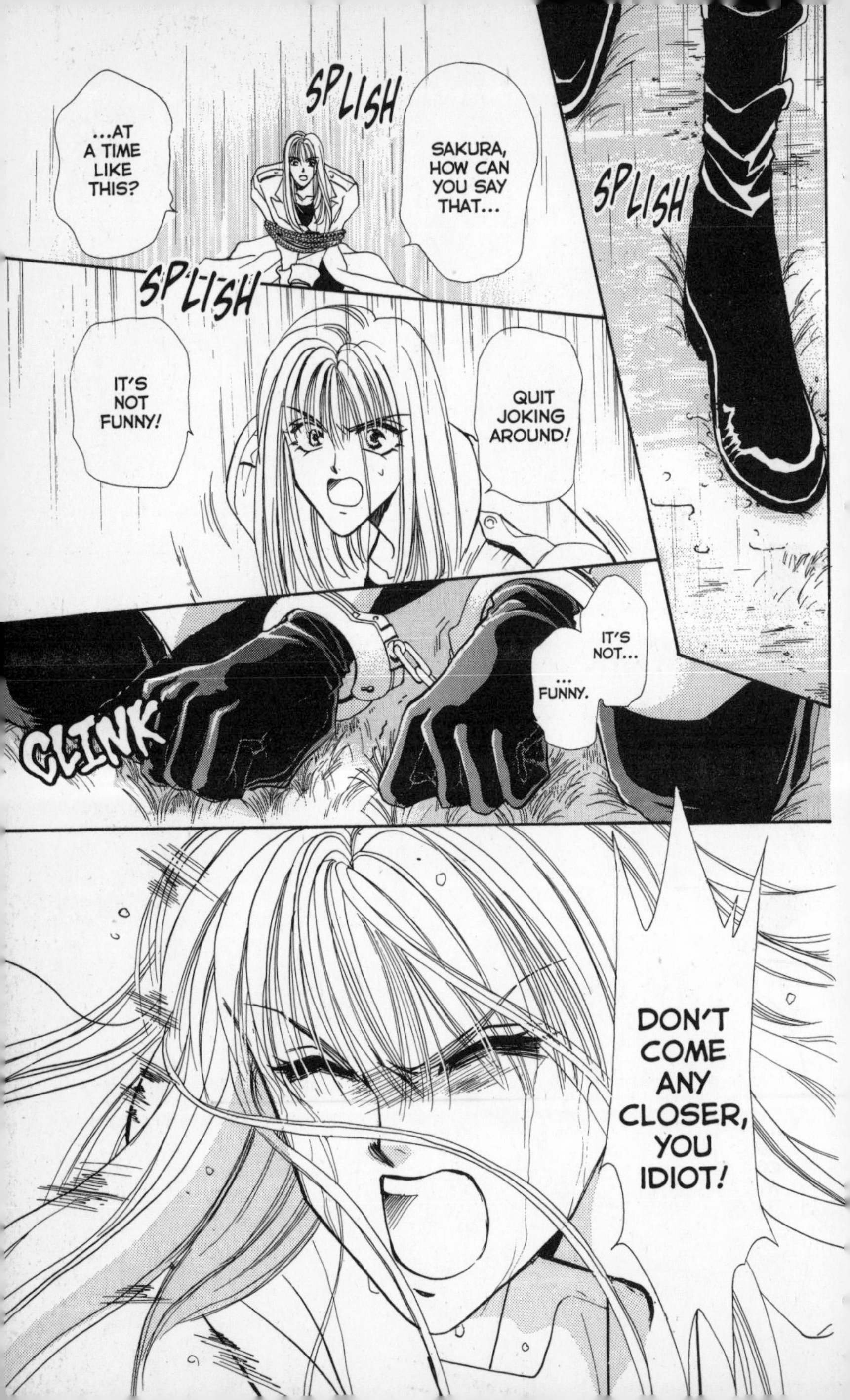

SPLISH
SPLISH
SAKURA, HOW CAN YOU SAY THAT...
...AT A TIME LIKE THIS?
SPLISH
QUIT JOKING AROUND!
IT'S NOT FUNNY!
IT'S NOT...
...FUNNY.
CLINK
DON'T COME ANY CLOSER, YOU IDIOT!

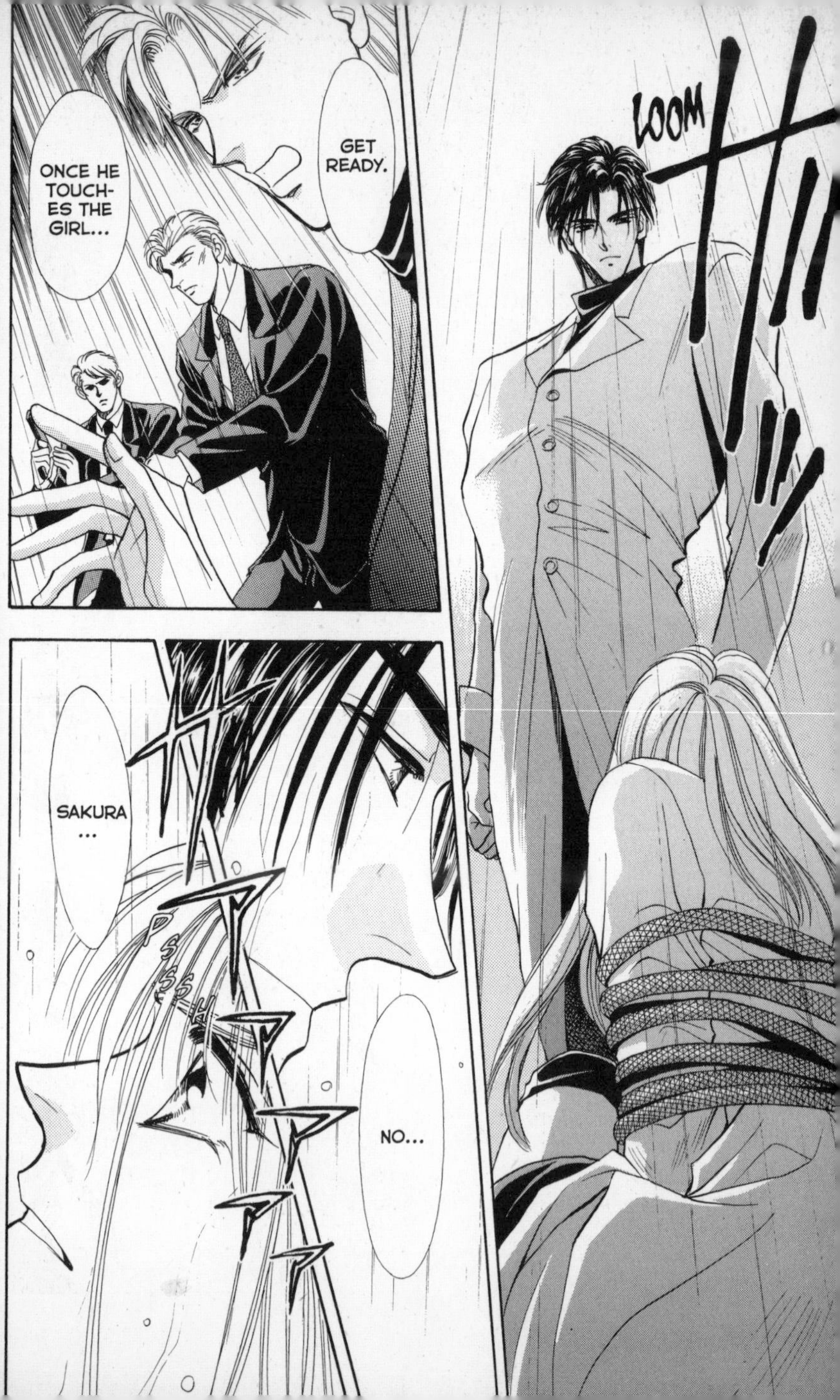
LOOM
GET READY.
ONCE HE TOUCHES THE GIRL...
NO...
SAKURA...
PSSSH

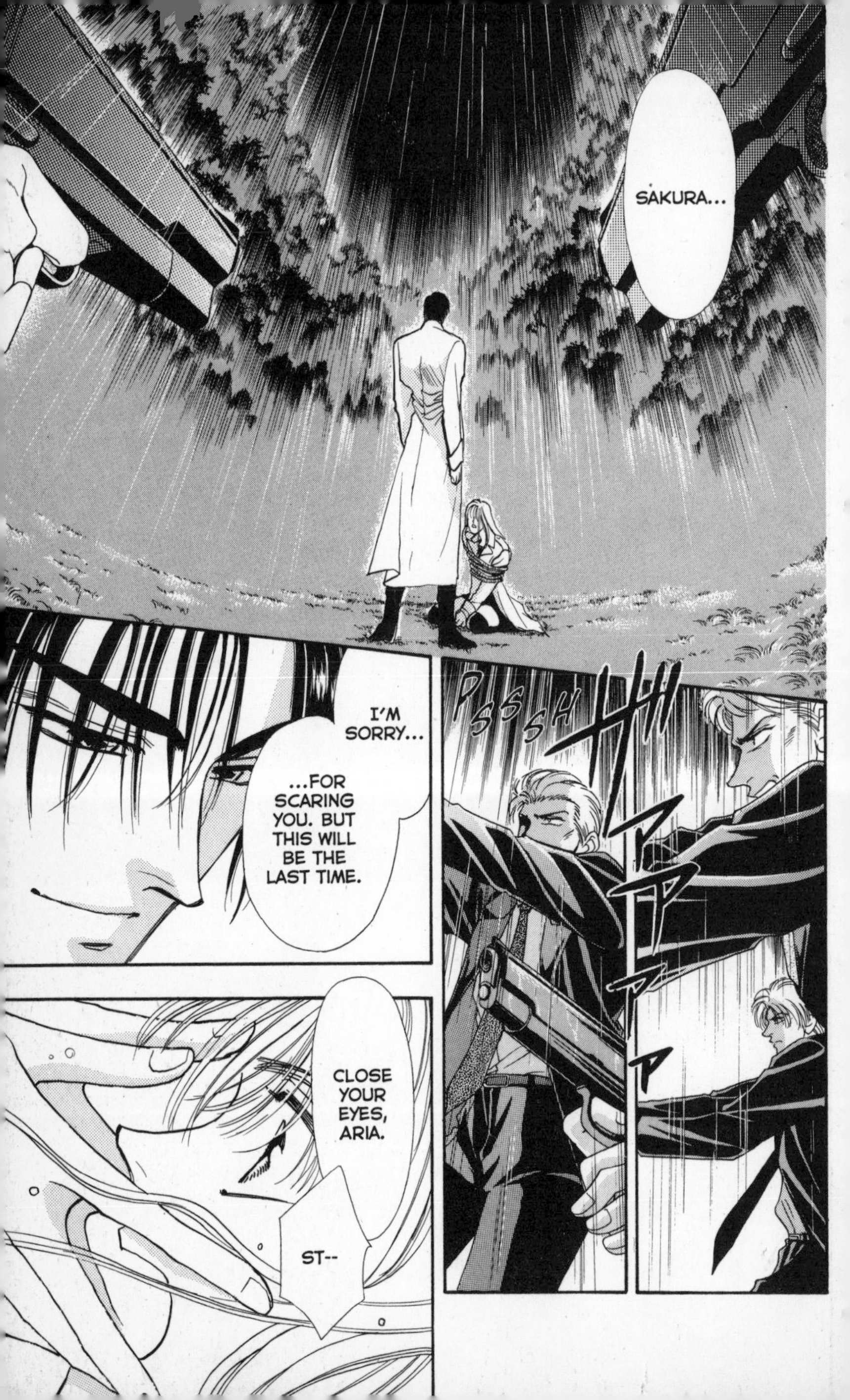
SAKURA...
PSSSHHH
I'M SORRY...
...FOR SCARING YOU. BUT THIS WILL BE THE LAST TIME.
CLOSE YOUR EYES, ARIA.
ST--

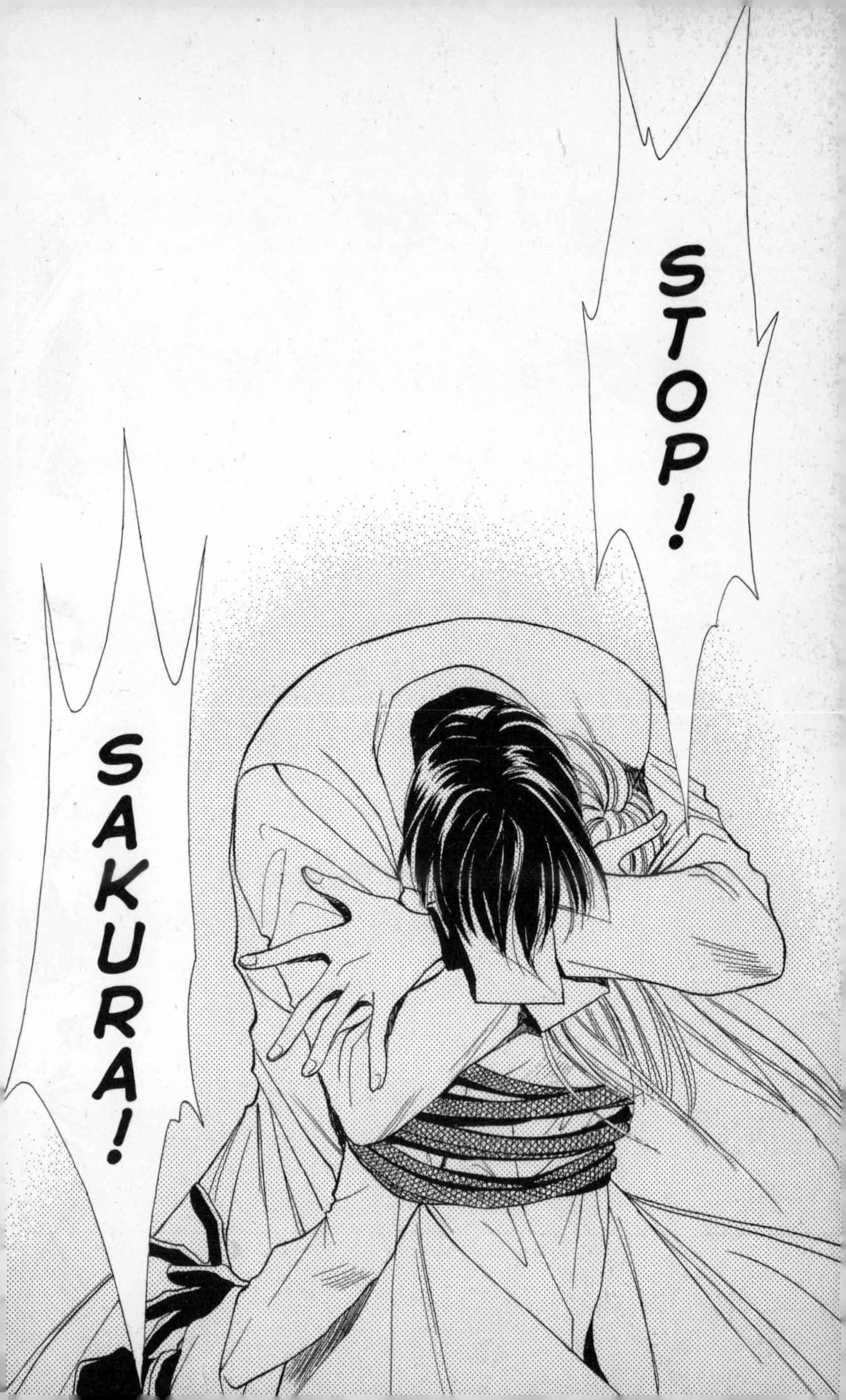
STOP!
SAKURA!

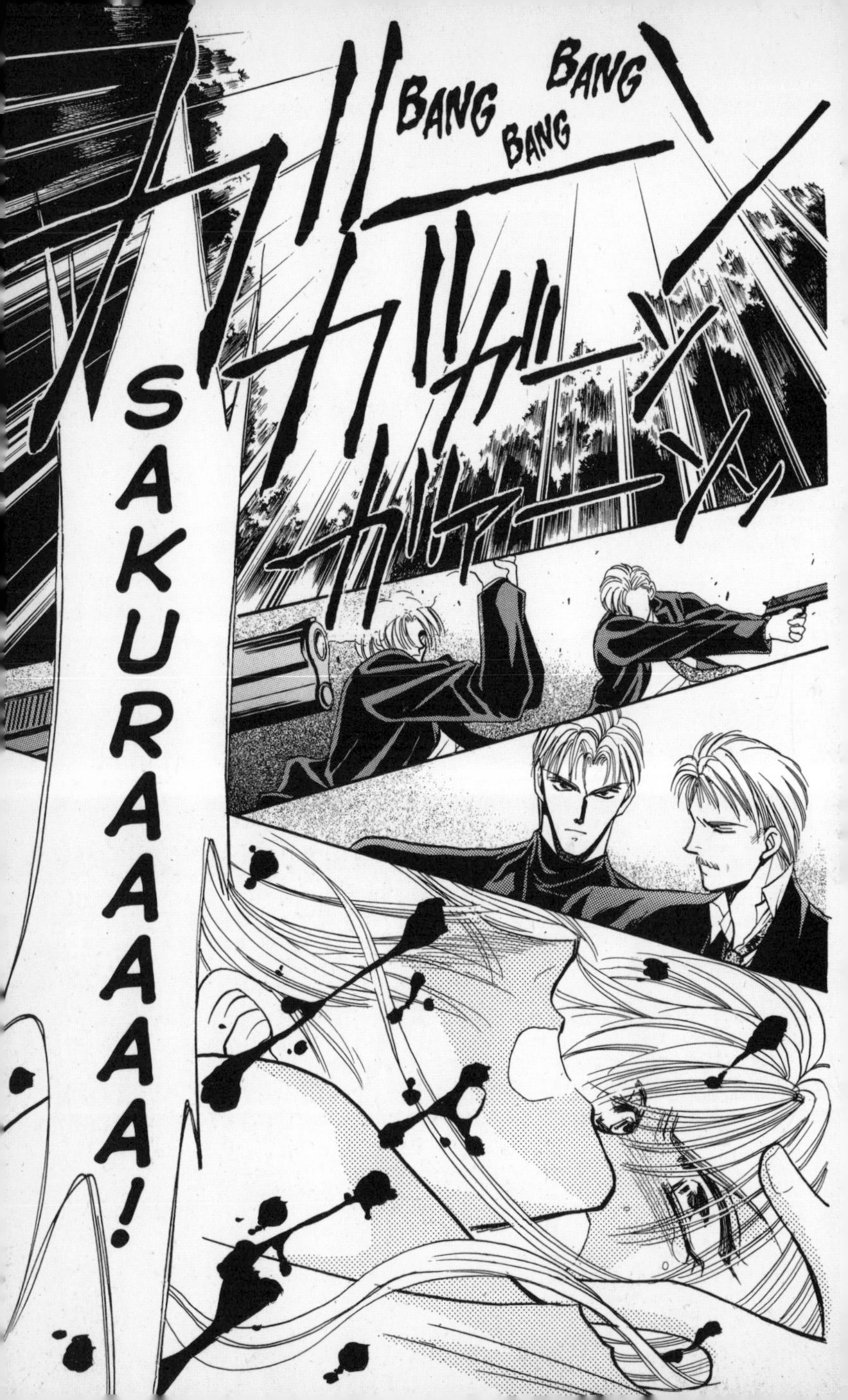
BANG
BANG
BANG
SAKURAAAAAA!

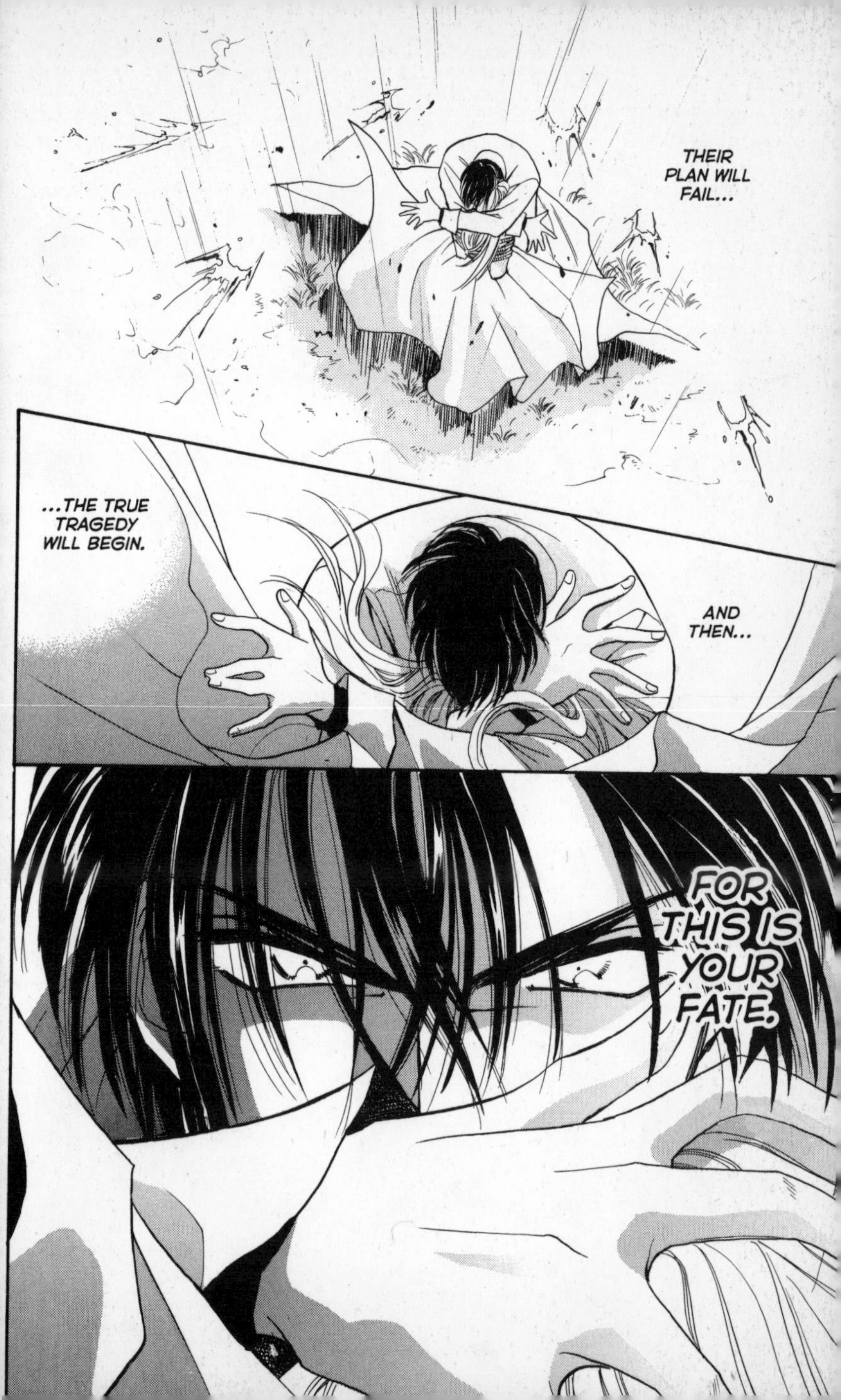
THEIR PLAN WILL FAIL...
AND THEN...
...THE TRUE TRAGEDY WILL BEGIN.
FOR THIS IS YOUR FATE.

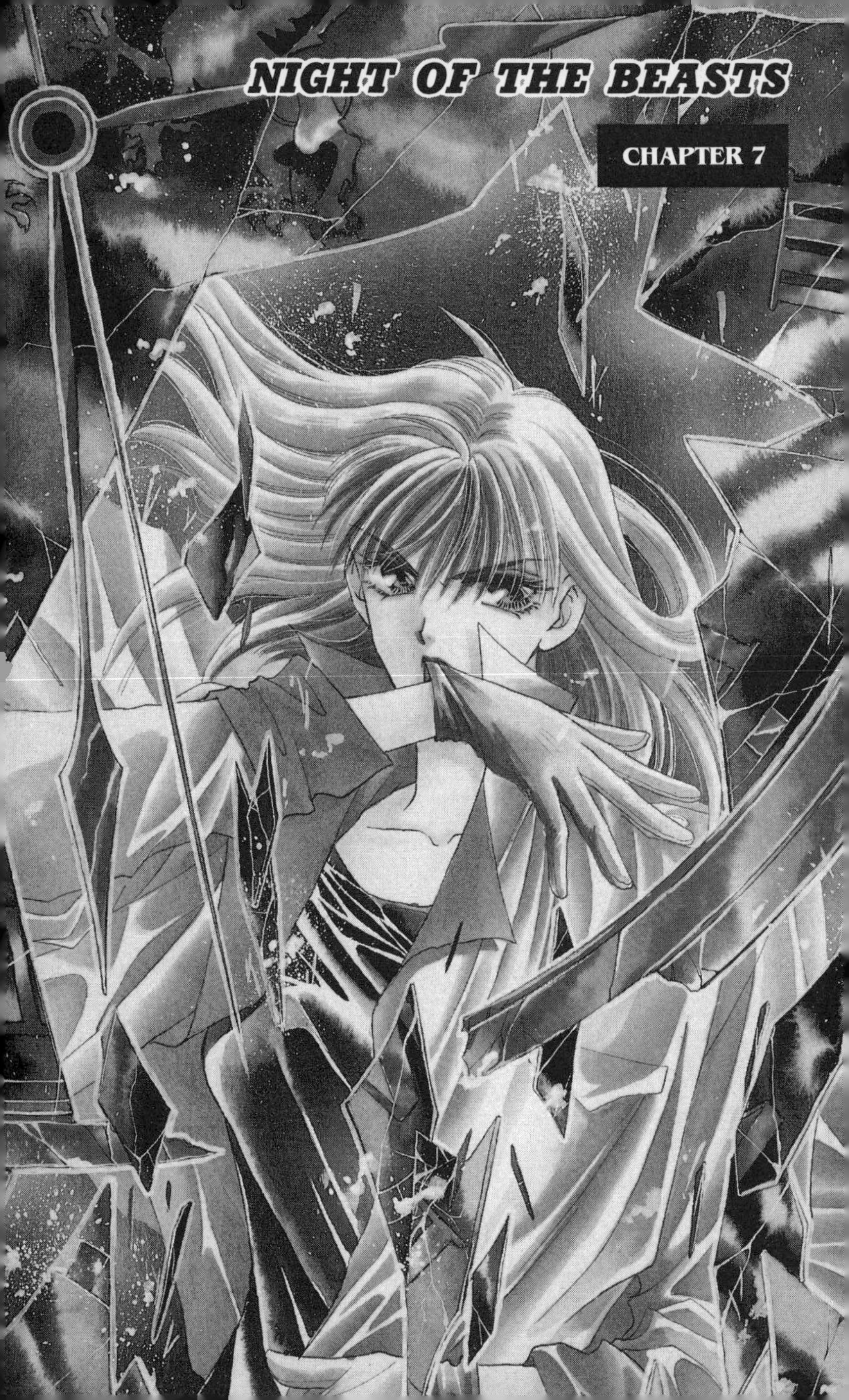
NIGHT OF THE BEASTS
CHAPTER 7

獣たちの夜

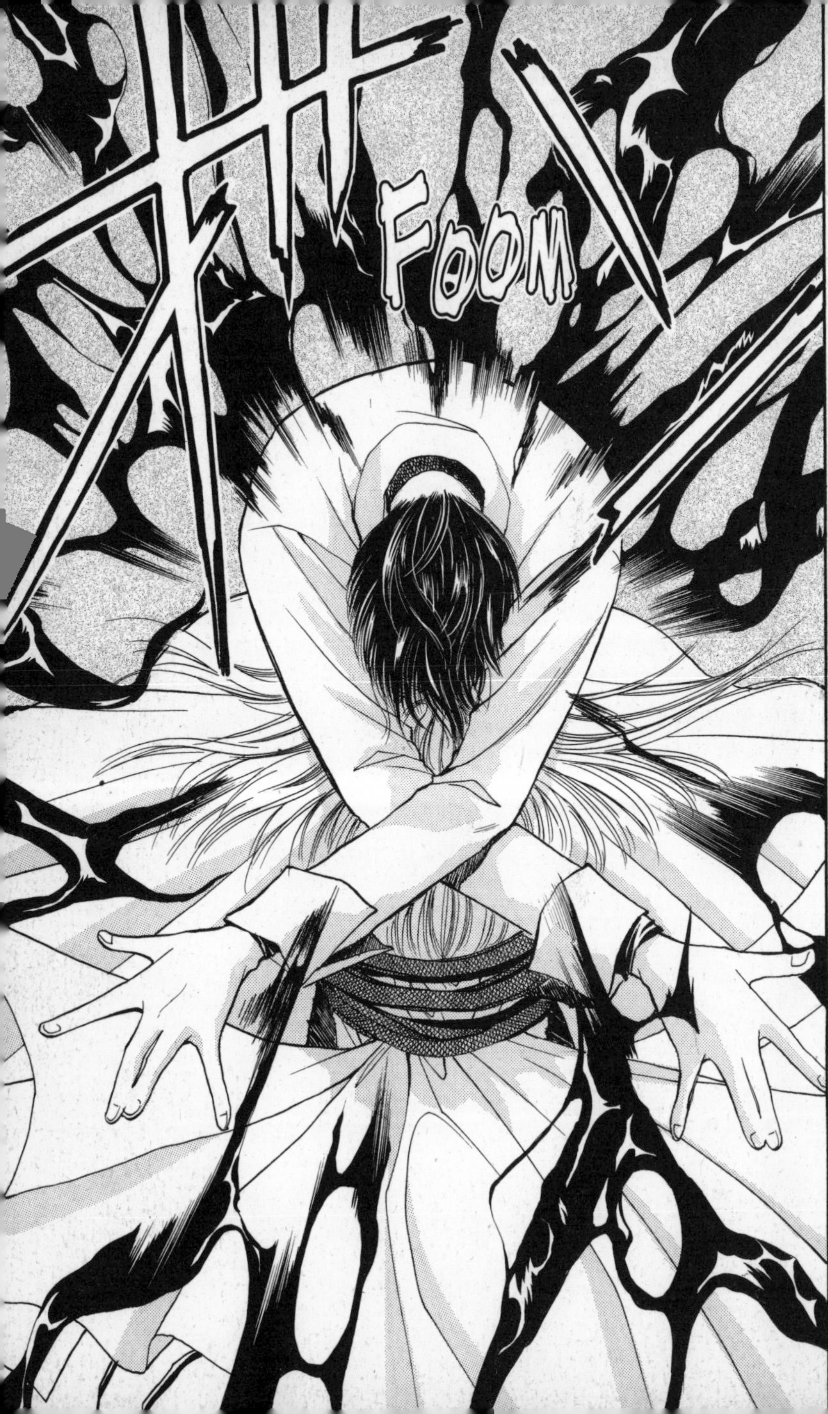
FOOM

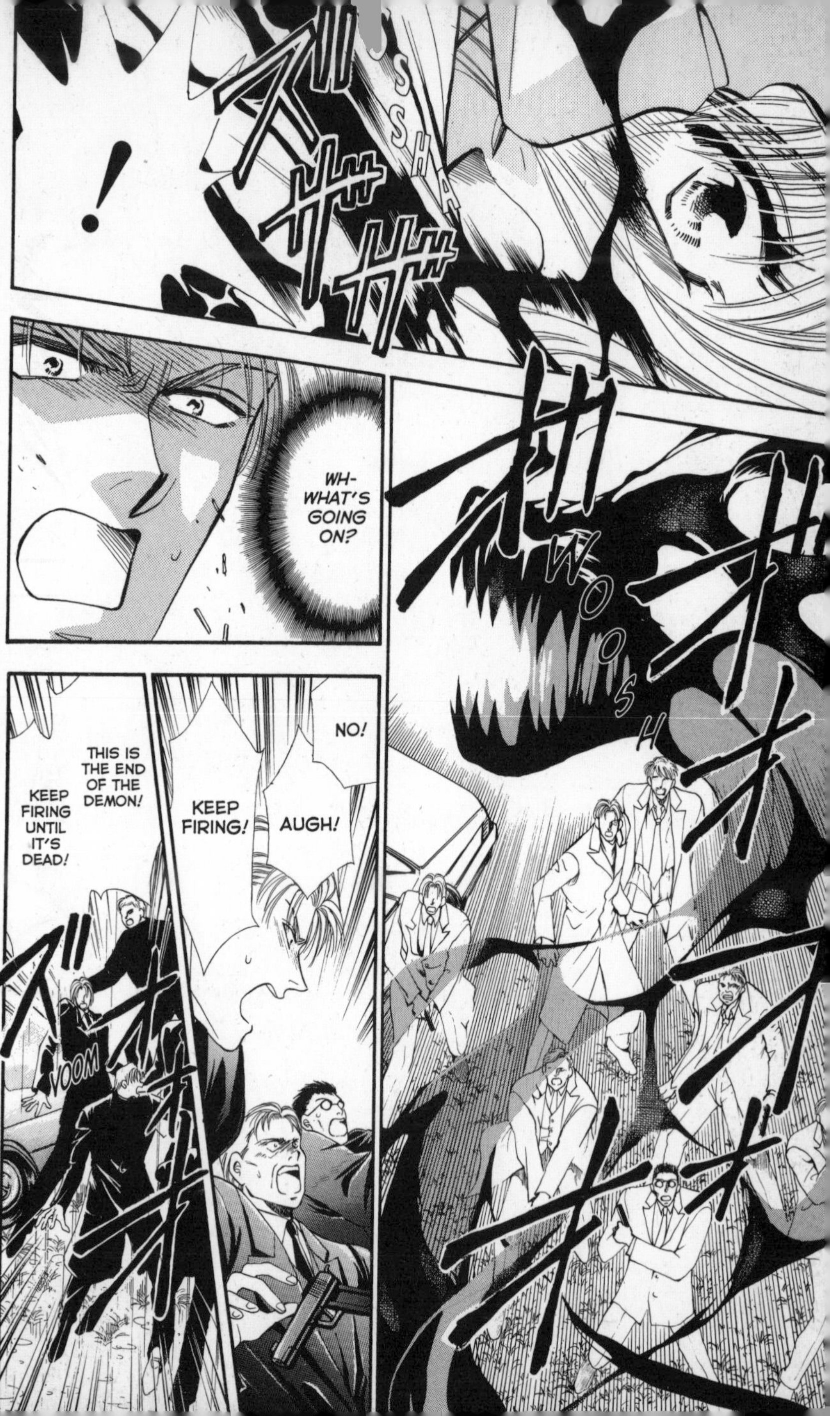
SHA
!
WOOSH
WH- WHAT'S GOING ON?
NO!
AUGH!
KEEP FIRING!
THIS IS THE END OF THE DEMON!
KEEP FIRING UNTIL IT'S DEAD!
VOOM

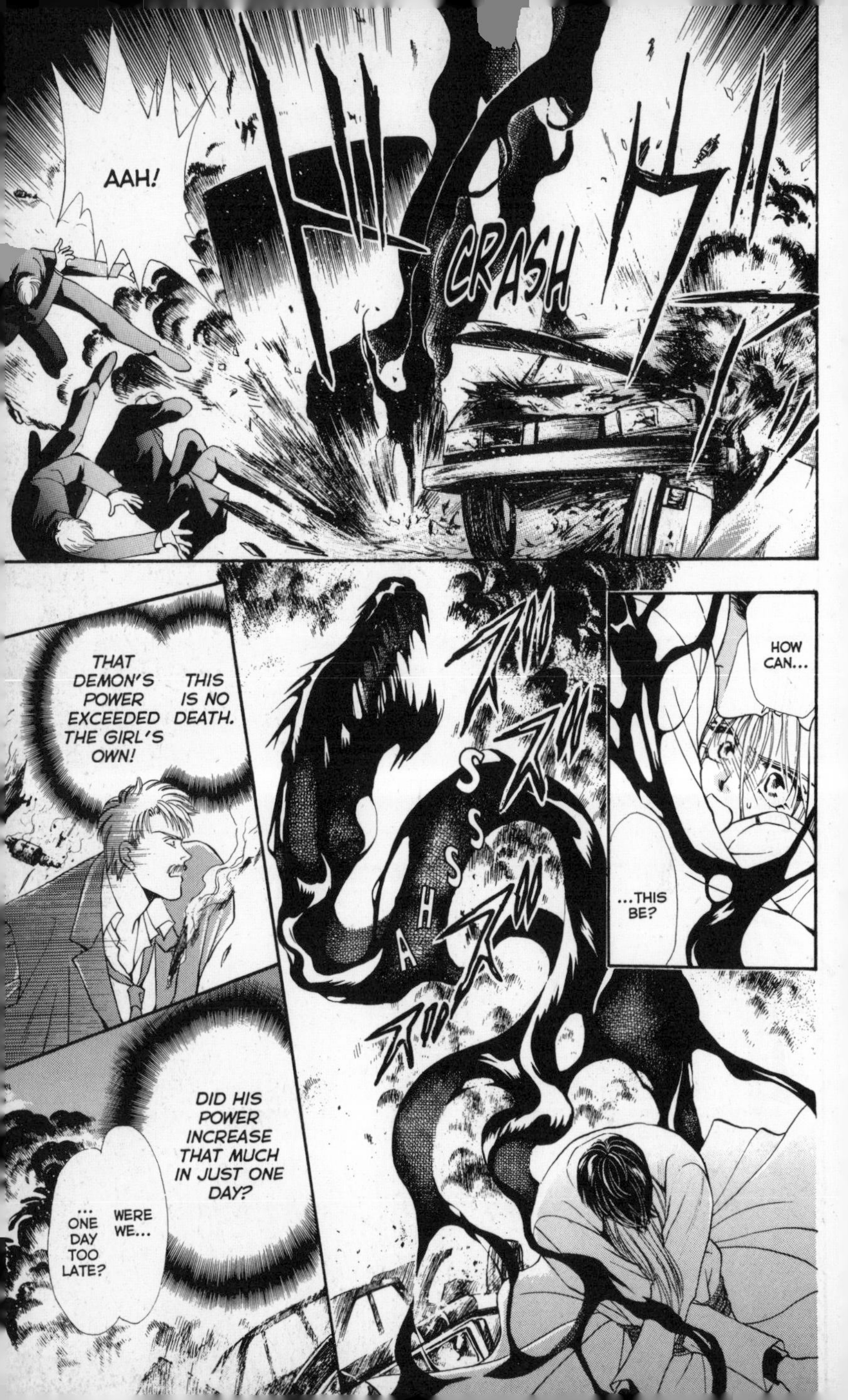
AAH!
CRASH
HOW CAN...
...THIS BE?
SSSHA
THIS IS NO DEATH.
THAT DEMON'S POWER EXCEEDED THE GIRL'S OWN!
DID HIS POWER INCREASE THAT MUCH IN JUST ONE DAY?
WERE WE...
...ONE DAY TOO LATE?

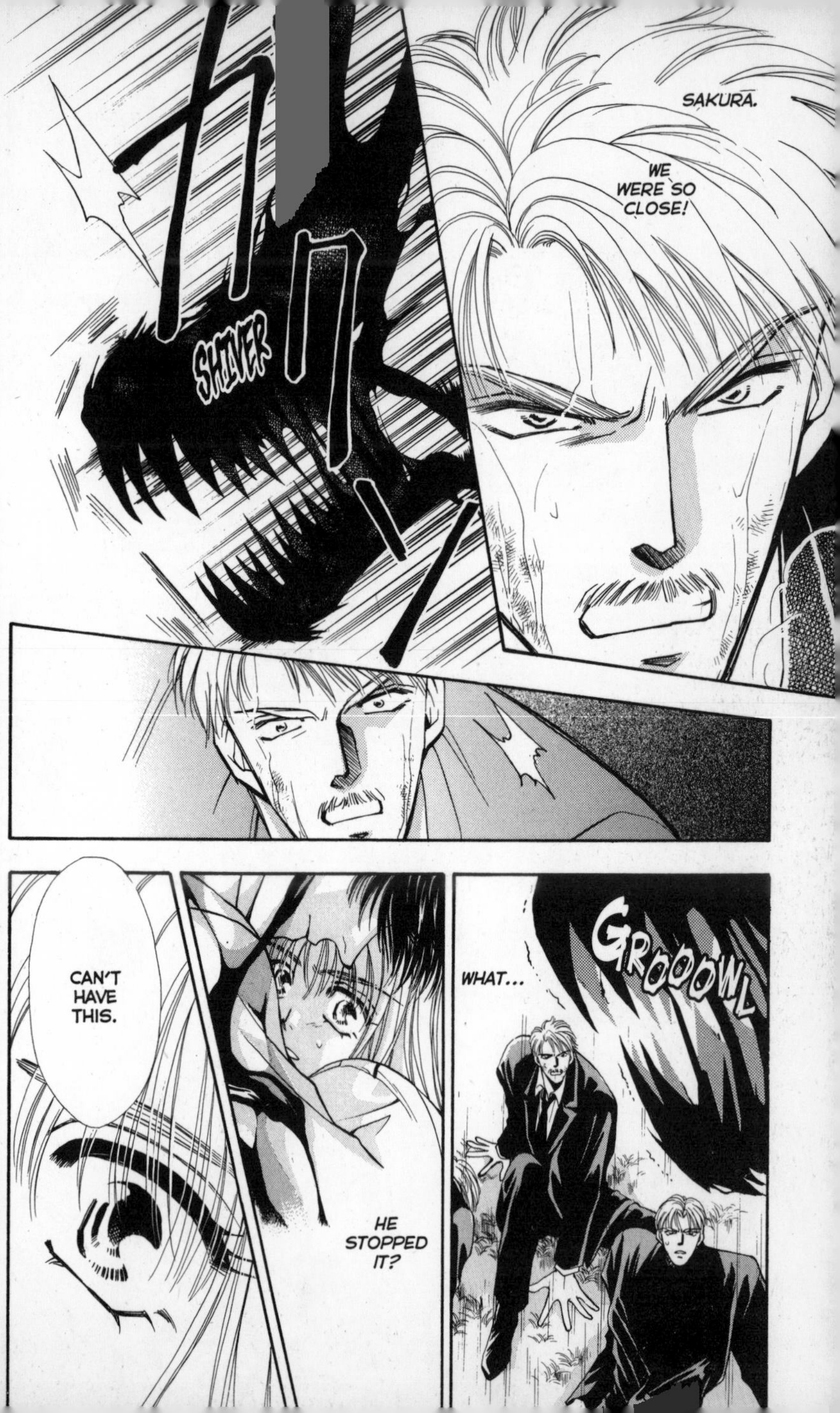
SAKURA.
WE WERE SO CLOSE!
SHIVER
WHAT...
GROOOWL
HE STOPPED IT?
CAN'T HAVE THIS.

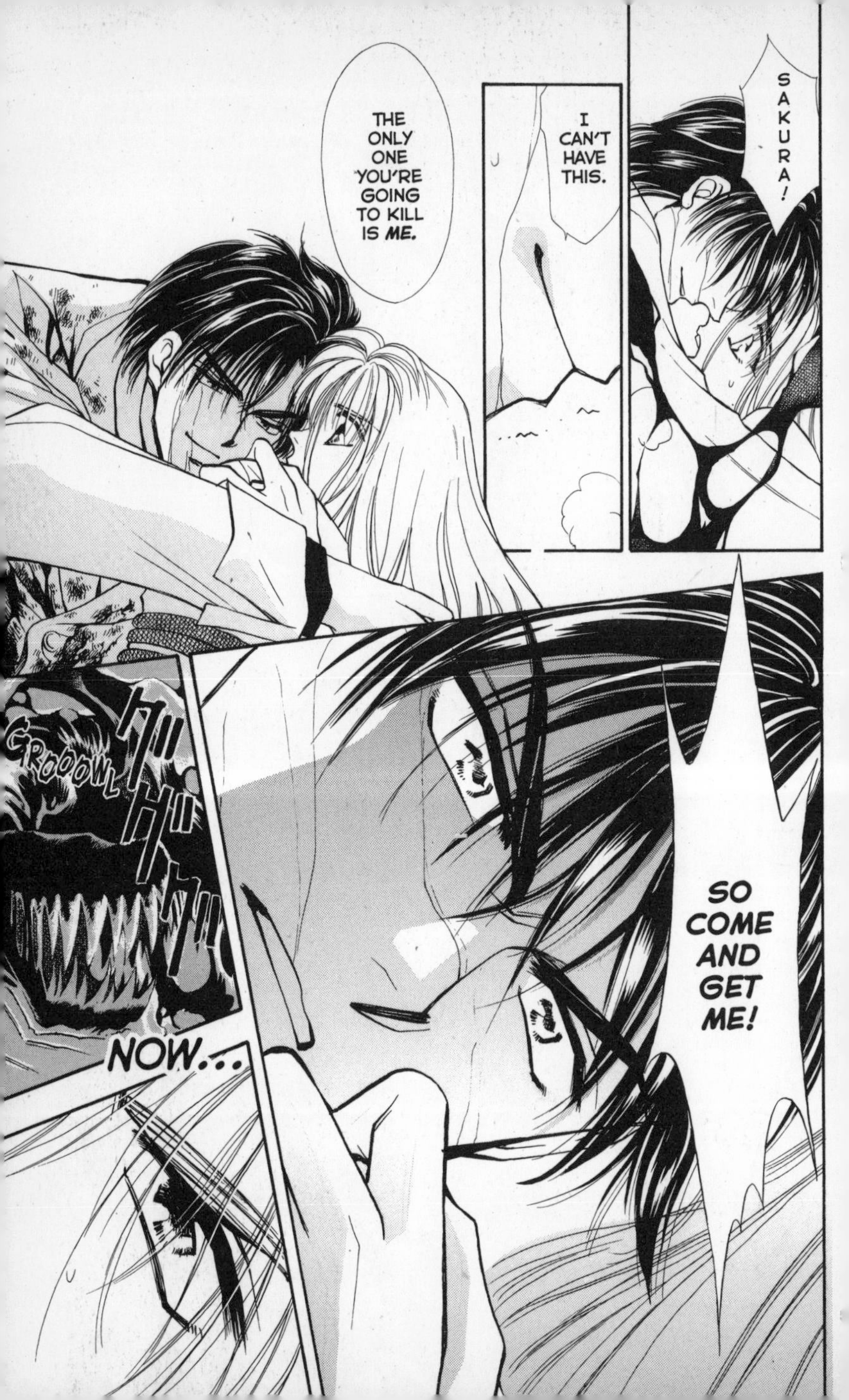
SAKURA!
I CAN'T HAVE THIS.
THE ONLY ONE YOU'RE GOING TO KILL IS *ME.*
SO COME AND GET ME!
GROOOWL
NOW...

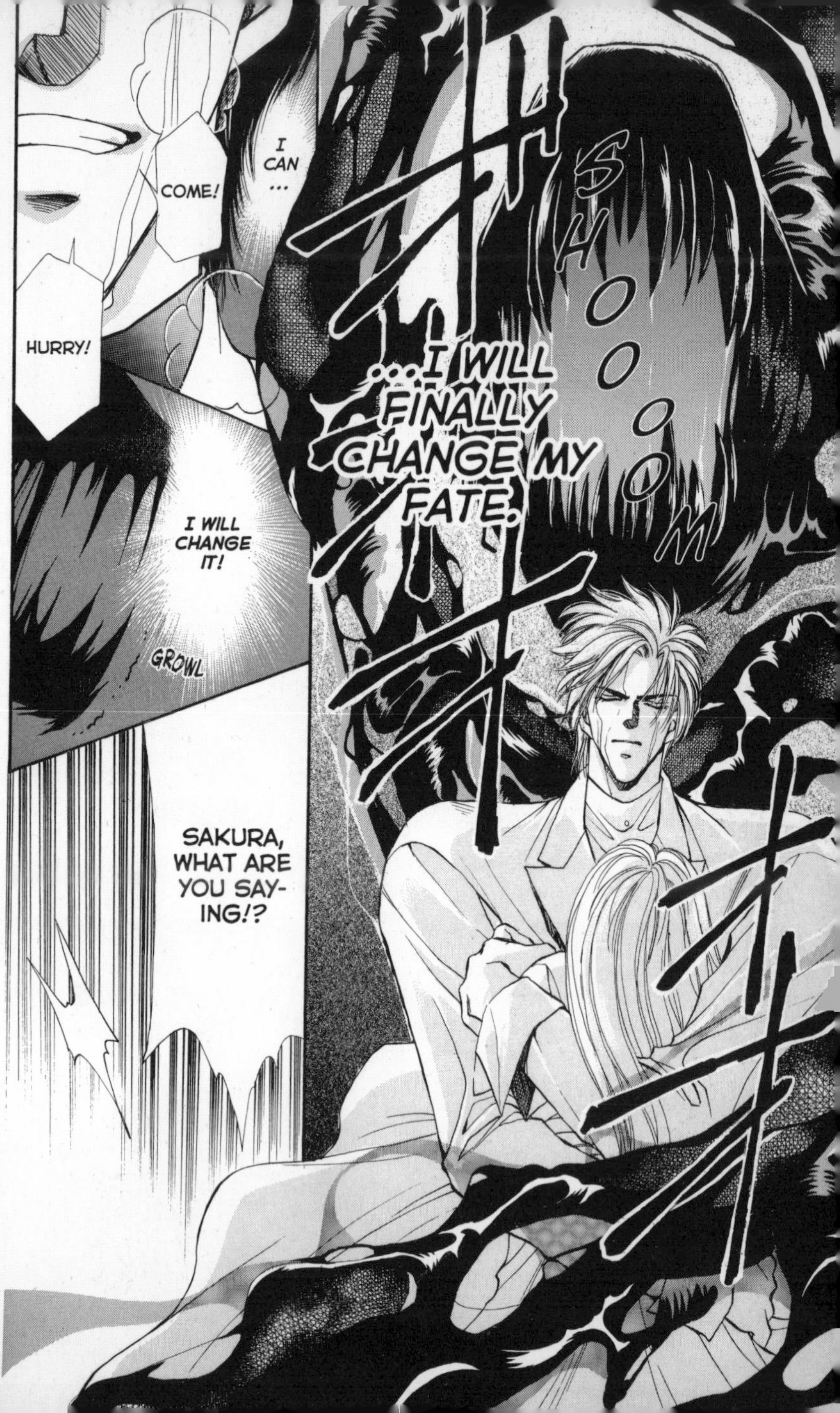
SHOOOOOM
...I WILL FINALLY CHANGE MY FATE.
I CAN ...
COME!
HURRY!
I WILL CHANGE IT!
GROWL
SAKURA, WHAT ARE YOU SAY-ING!?

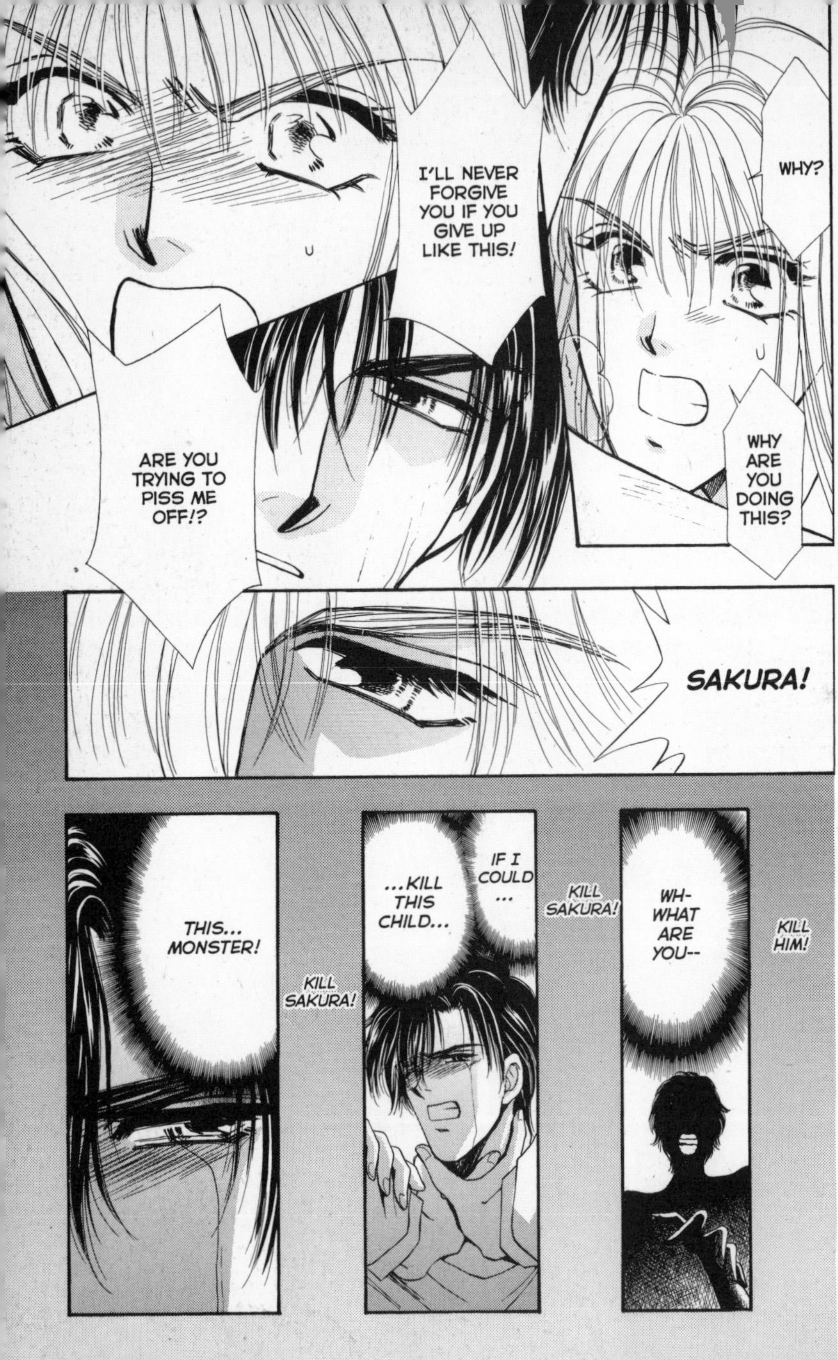
WHY?
WHY ARE YOU DOING THIS?
I'LL NEVER FORGIVE YOU IF YOU GIVE UP LIKE THIS!
ARE YOU TRYING TO PISS ME OFF!?
SAKURA!
KILL HIM!
WH- WHAT ARE YOU--
KILL SAKURA!
IF I COULD...
...KILL THIS CHILD...
KILL SAKURA!
THIS... MONSTER!

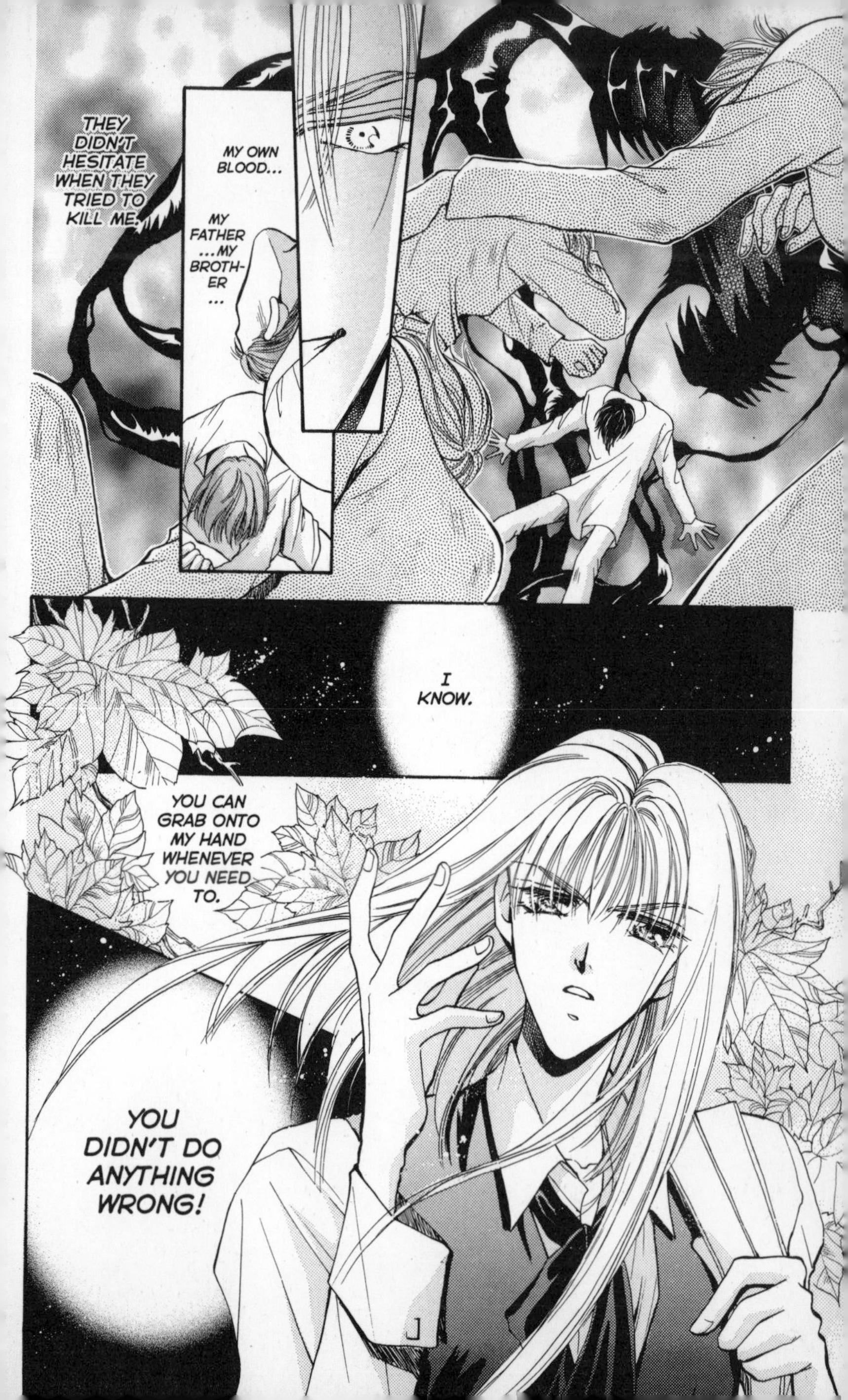
MY OWN BLOOD...
MY FATHER ...MY BROTHER- ...
THEY DIDN'T HESITATE WHEN THEY TRIED TO KILL ME.
I KNOW.
YOU CAN GRAB ONTO MY HAND WHENEVER YOU NEED TO.
YOU DIDN'T DO ANYTHING WRONG!

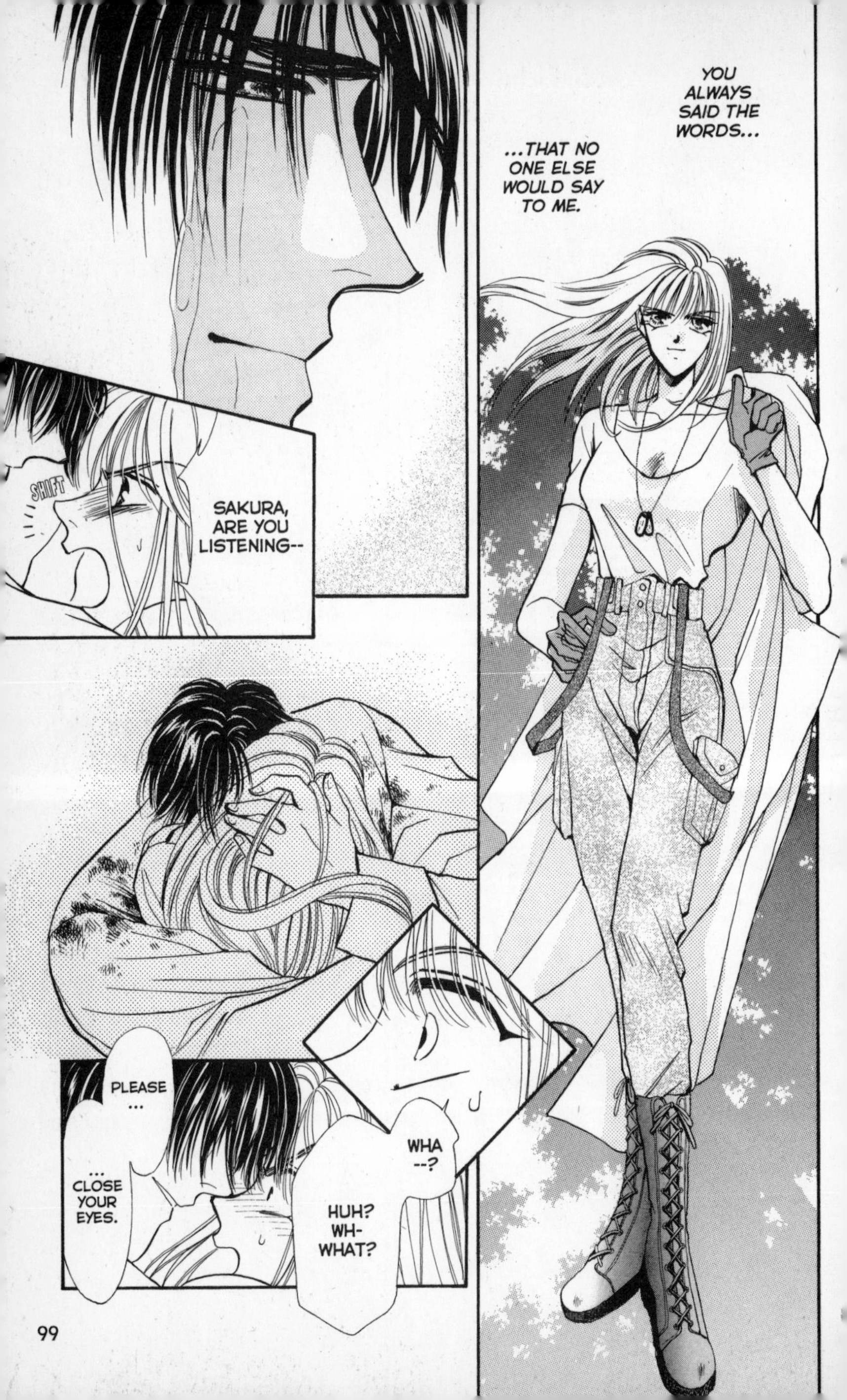
YOU ALWAYS SAID THE WORDS...
...THAT NO ONE ELSE WOULD SAY TO ME.
SHIFT
SAKURA, ARE YOU LISTENING--
WHA --?
HUH? WH- WHAT?
PLEASE ...
... CLOSE YOUR EYES.

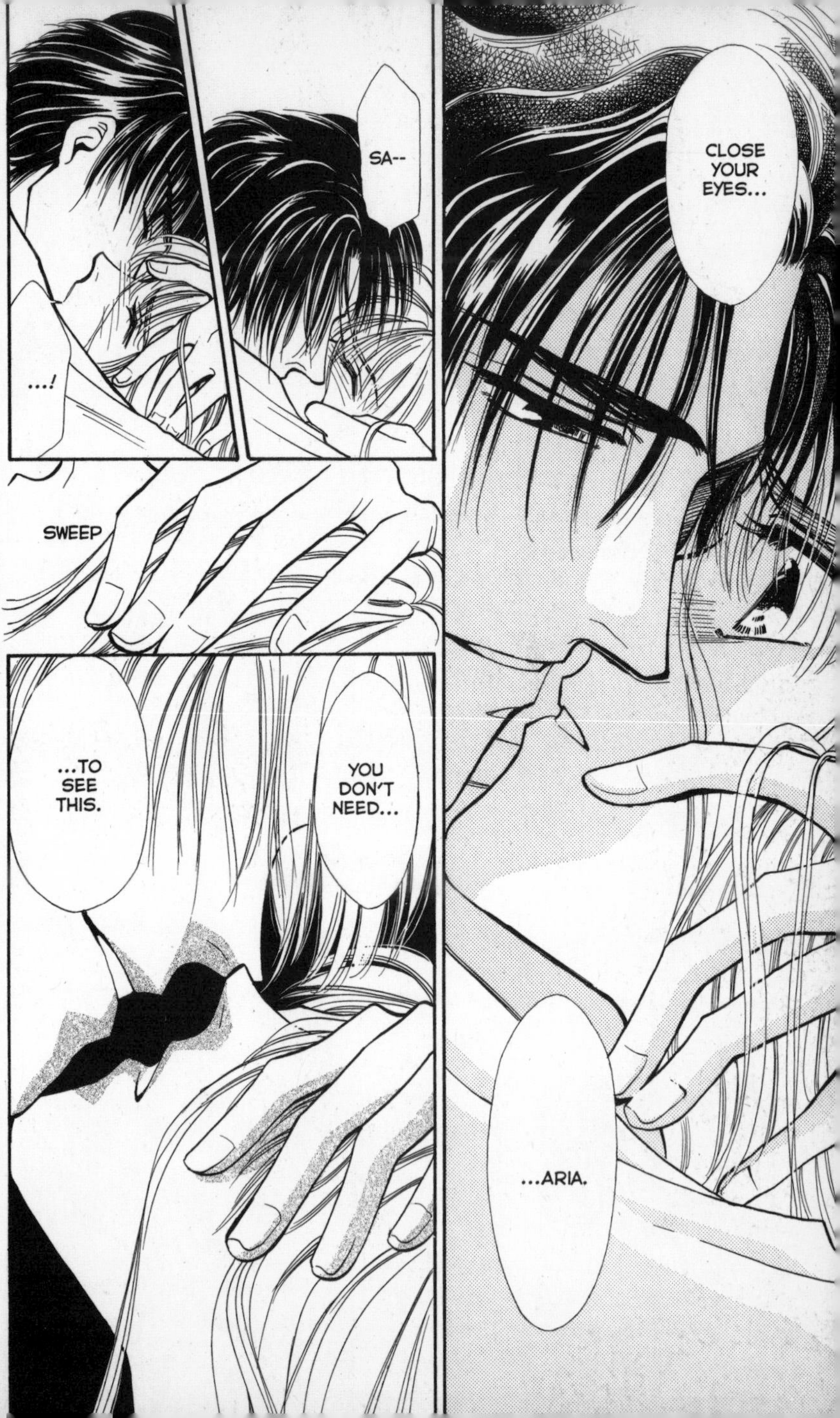
CLOSE YOUR EYES...
...ARIA.
SA--
...!
SWEEP
YOU DON'T NEED...
...TO SEE THIS.

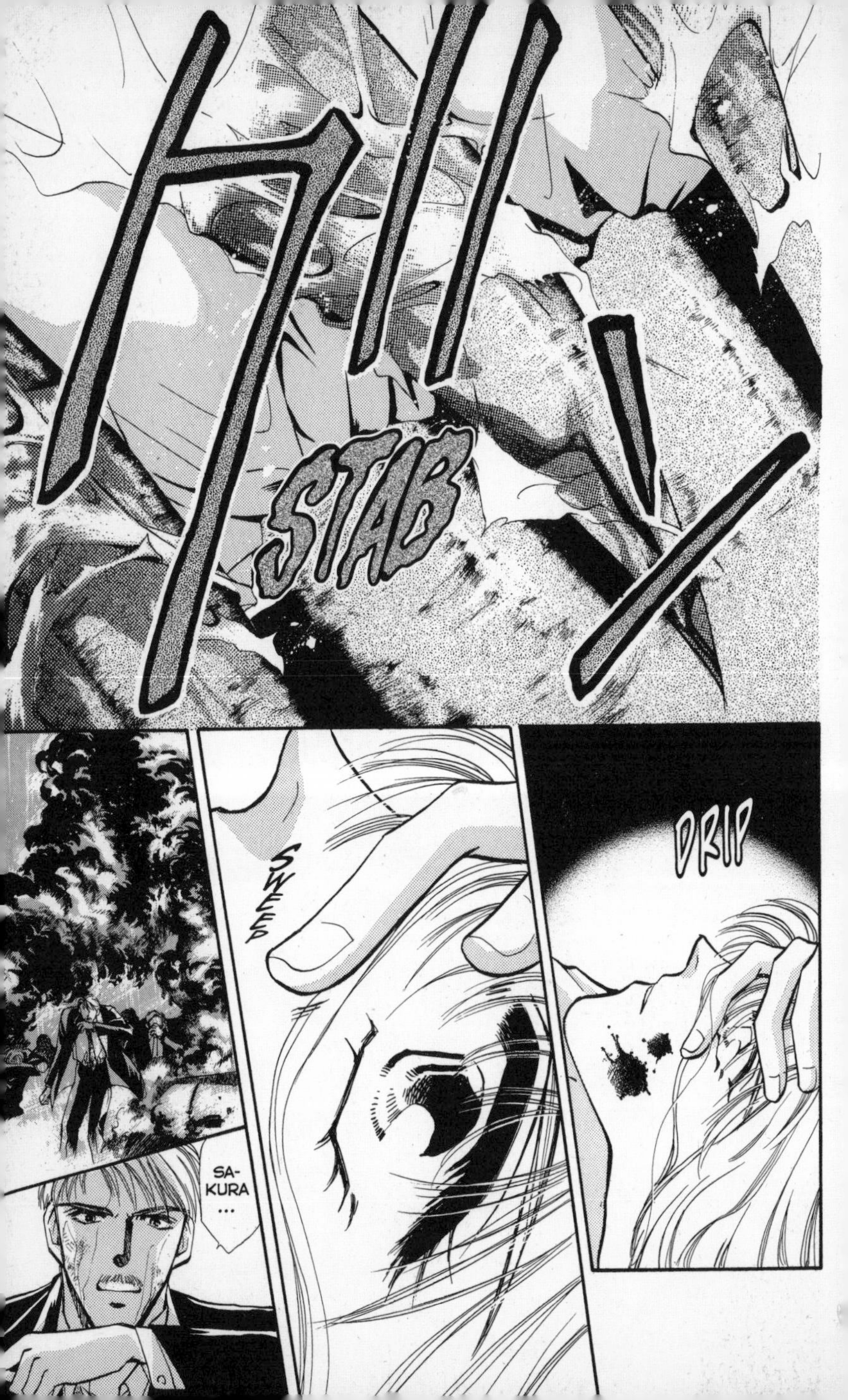
STAB
DRIP
SWEEP
SA-
KURA
...

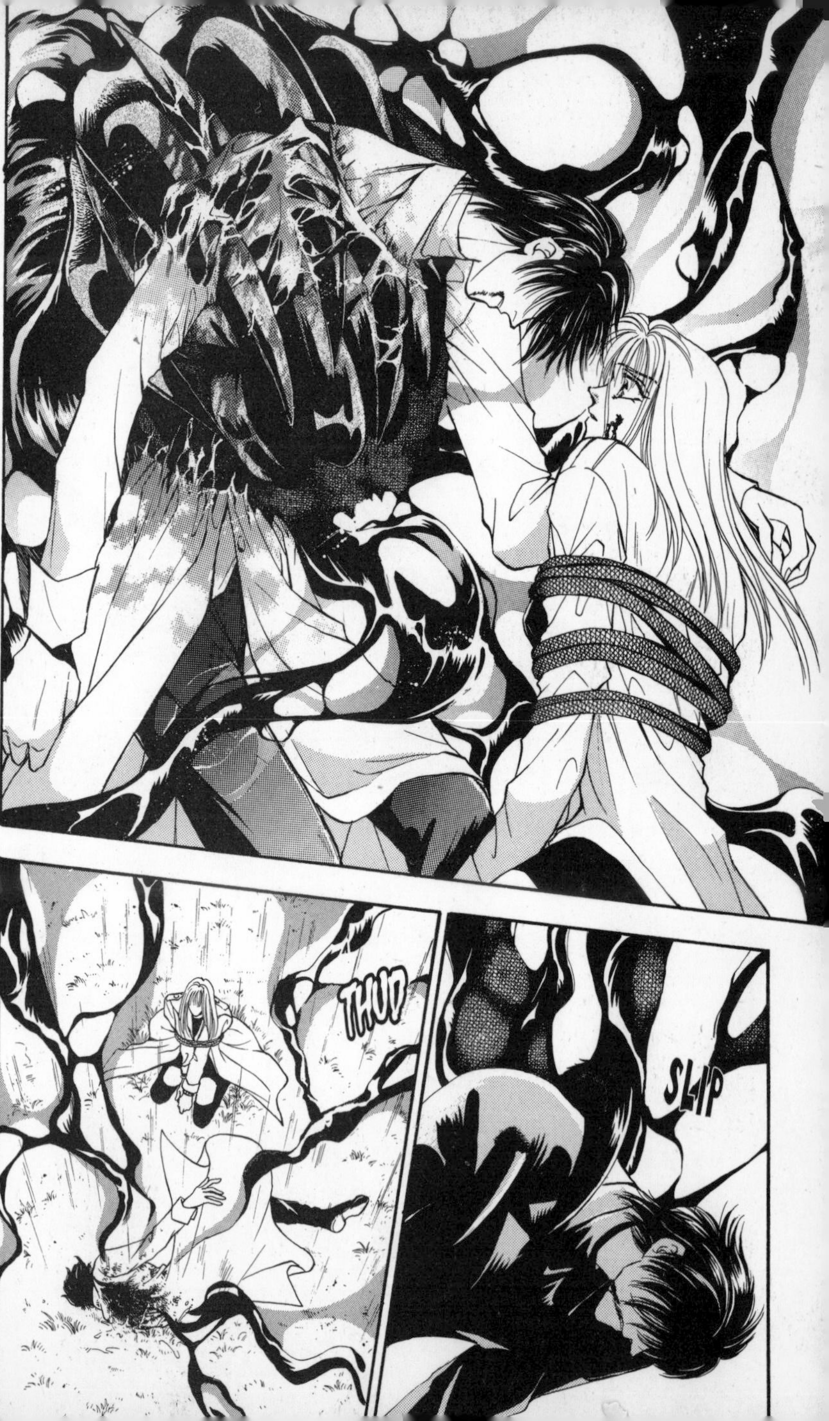
SLIP
THUD

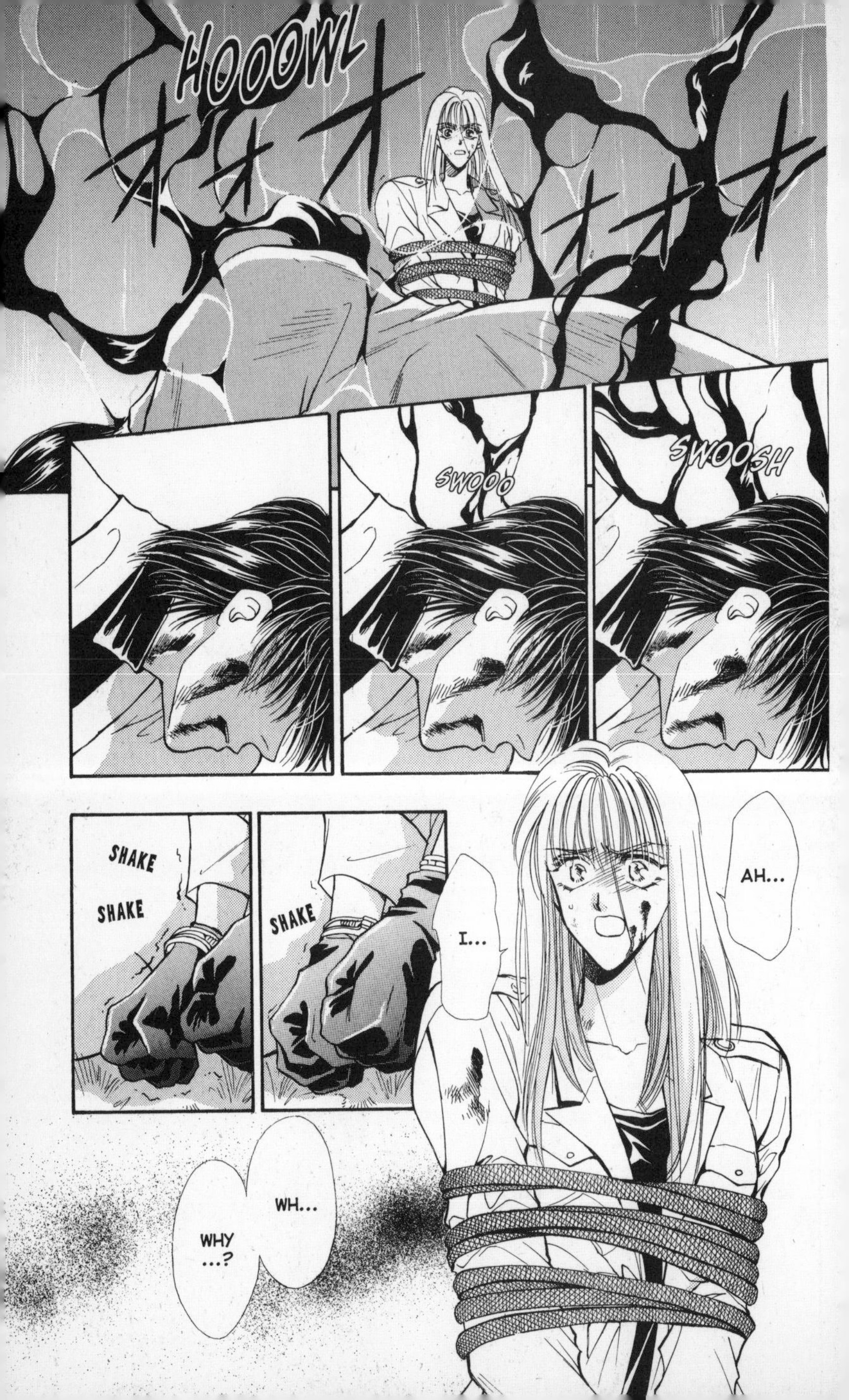
HOOOWL
オォォ
ォォォ
SWOOSH
SWOOO
AH...
I...
WH...
WHY ...?
SHAKE
SHAKE
SHAKE

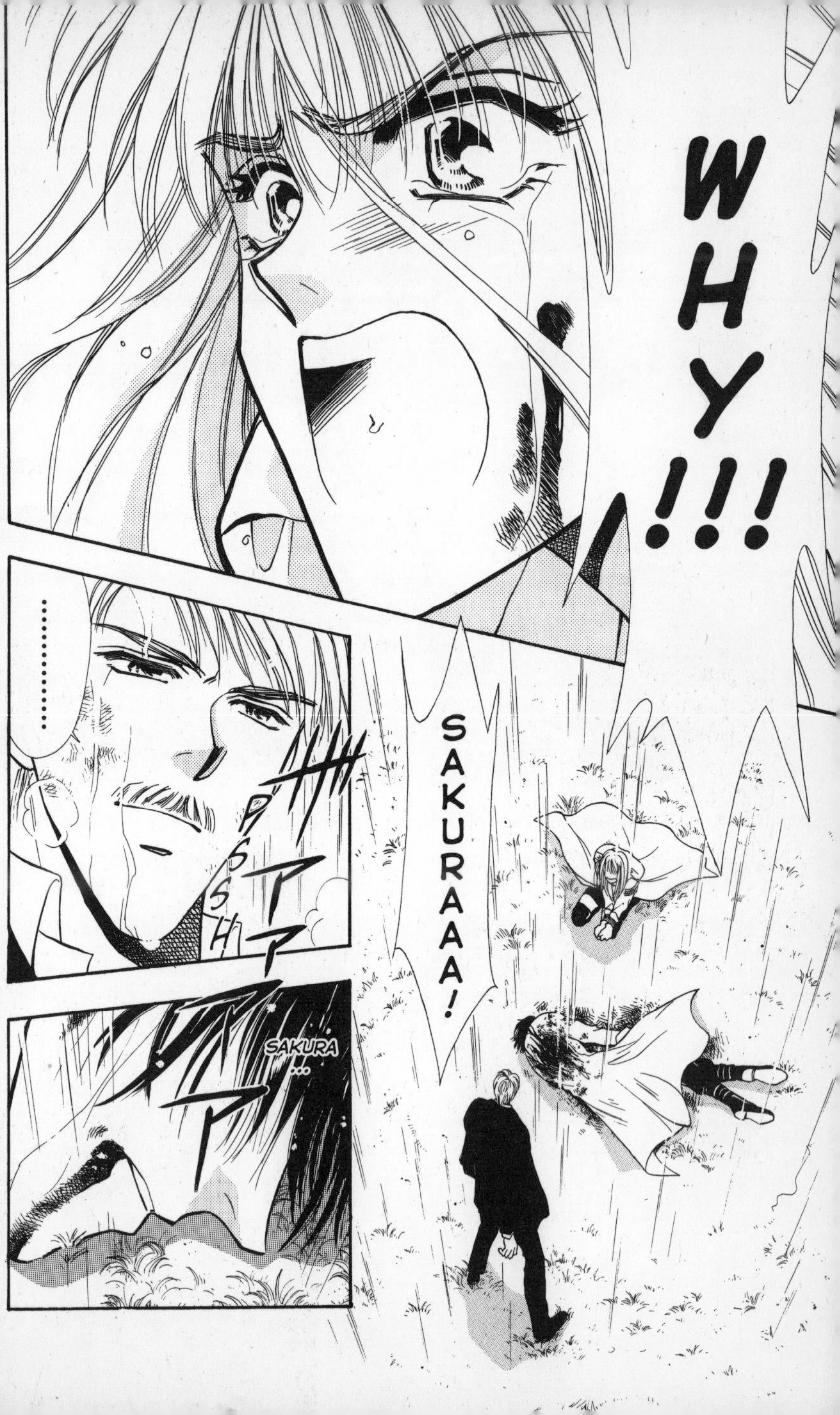
WHY!!!
SAKURAAAA!
......
DASSH
SAKURA ...

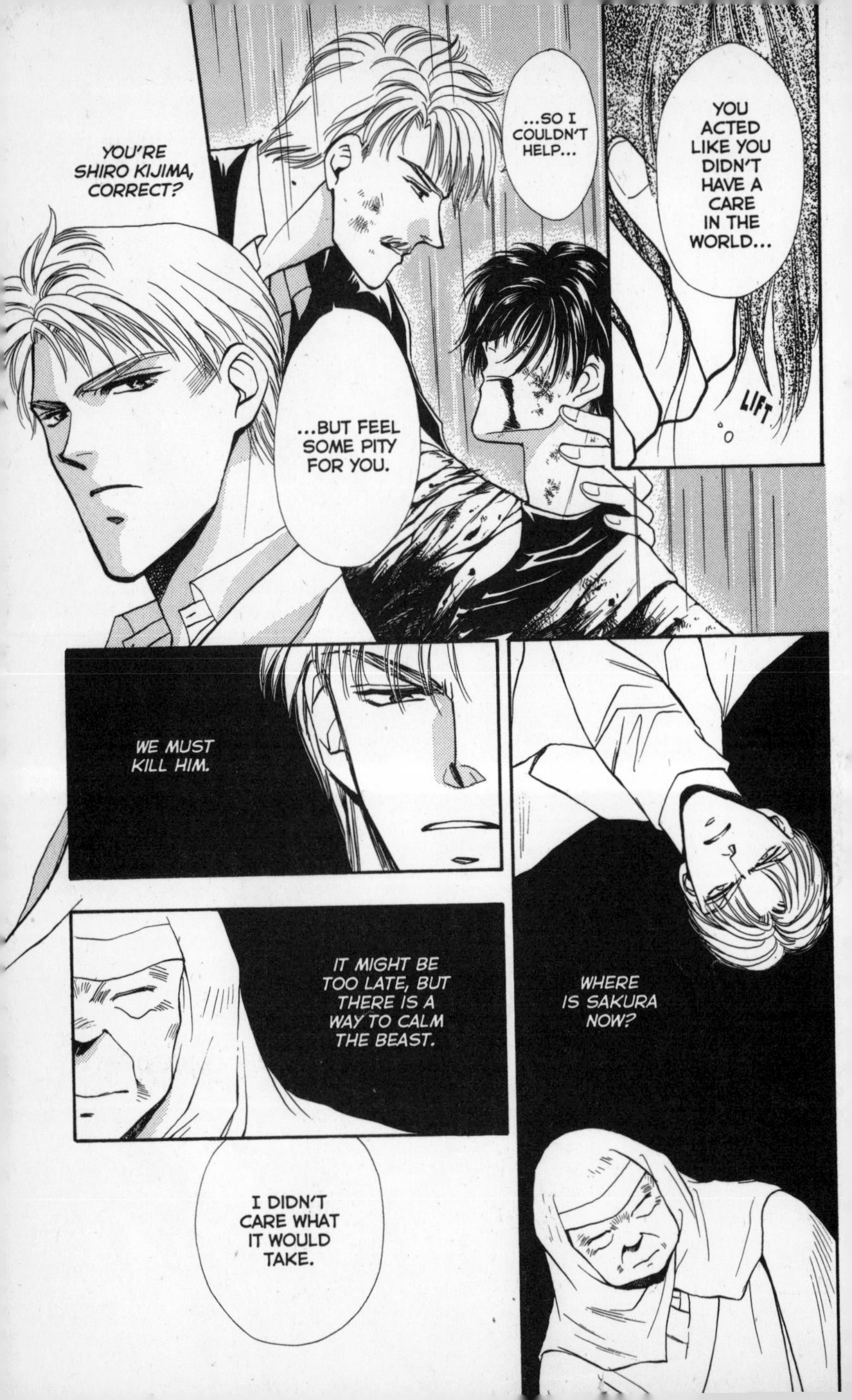
YOU ACTED LIKE YOU DIDN'T HAVE A CARE IN THE WORLD...
LIFT
...SO I COULDN'T HELP...
...BUT FEEL SOME PITY FOR YOU.
YOU'RE SHIRO KIJIMA, CORRECT?
WHERE IS SAKURA NOW?
WE MUST KILL HIM.
IT MIGHT BE TOO LATE, BUT THERE IS A WAY TO CALM THE BEAST.
I DIDN'T CARE WHAT IT WOULD TAKE.

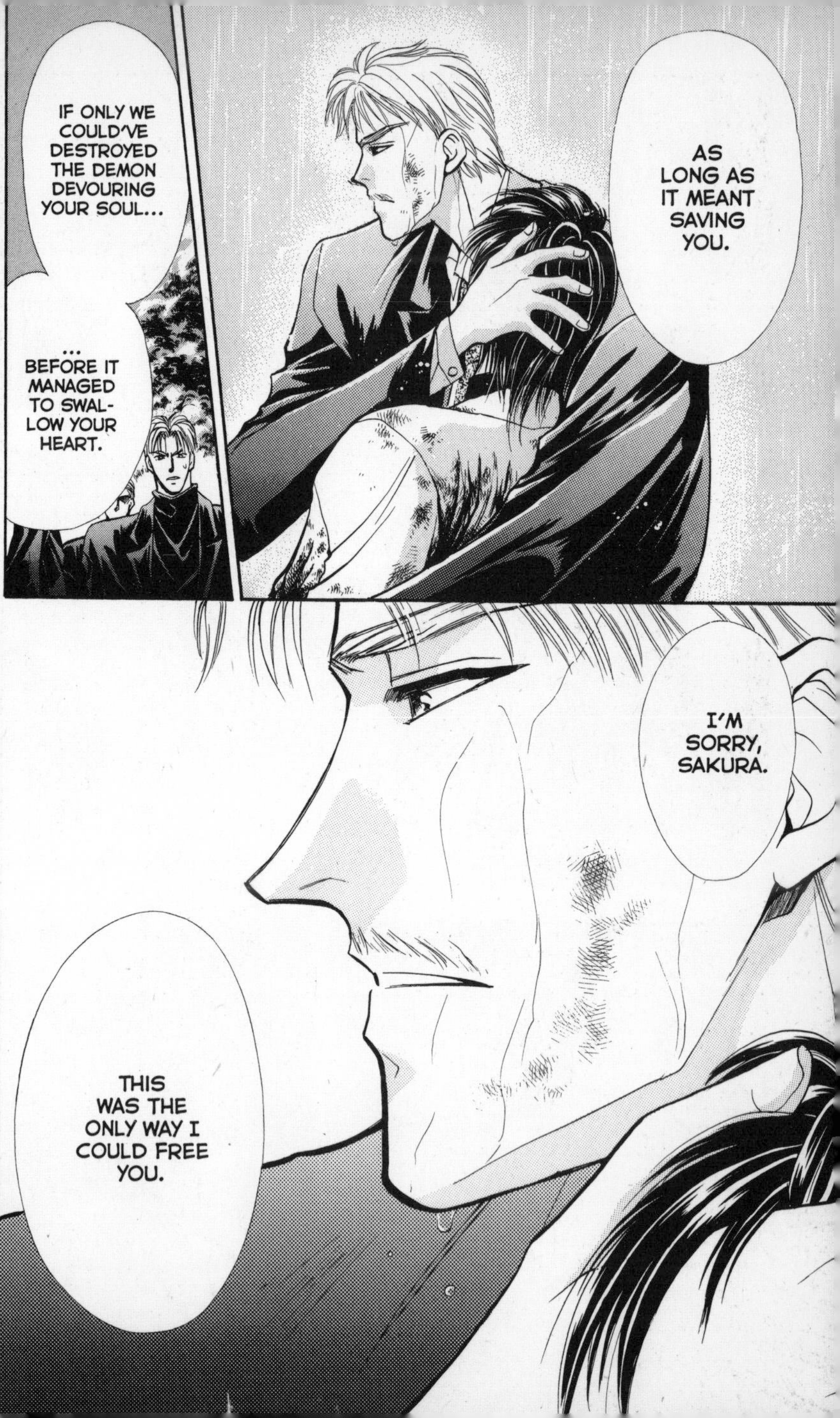
AS LONG AS IT MEANT SAVING YOU.
IF ONLY WE COULD'VE DESTROYED THE DEMON DEVOURING YOUR SOUL...
...BEFORE IT MANAGED TO SWAL-LOW YOUR HEART.
I'M SORRY, SAKURA.
THIS WAS THE ONLY WAY I COULD FREE YOU.

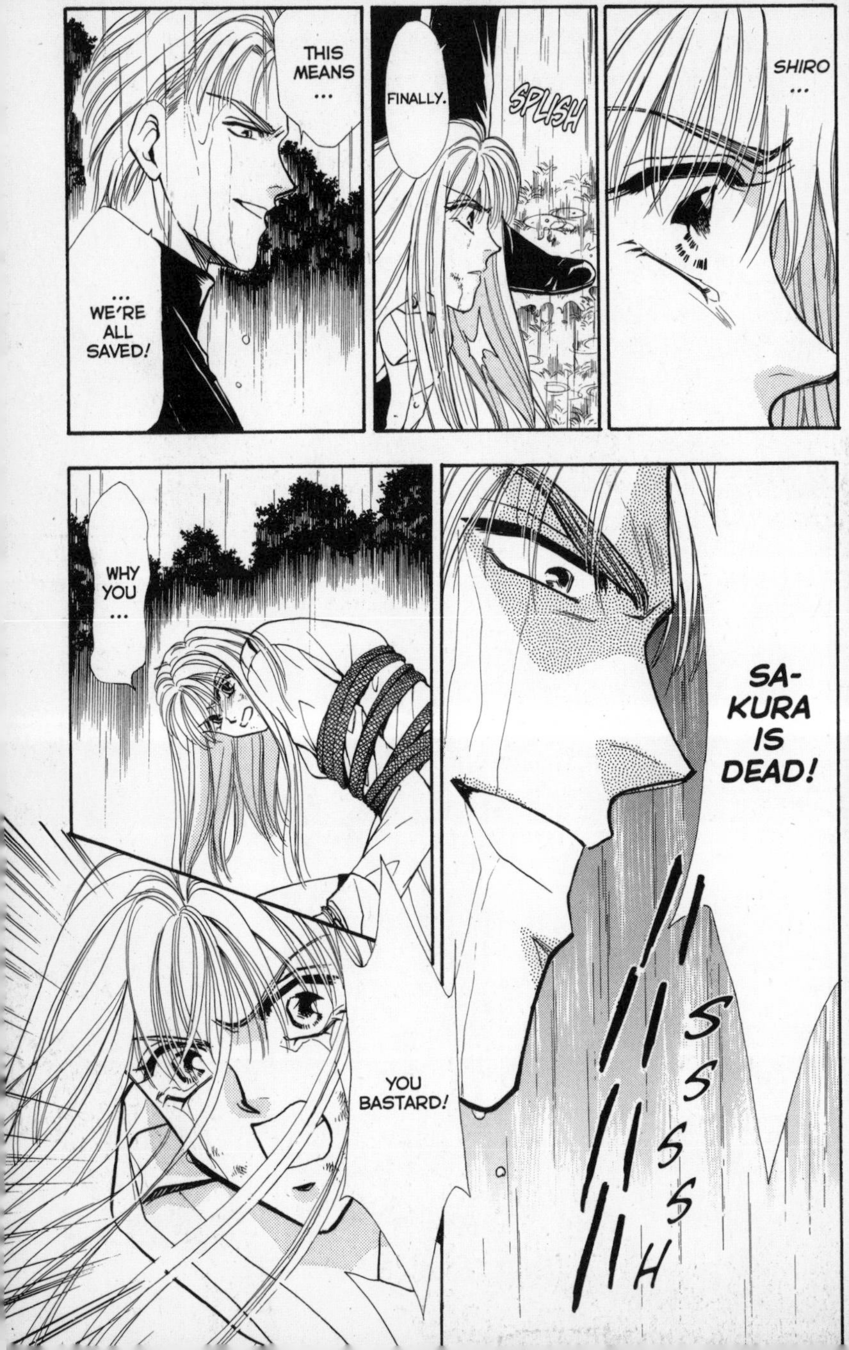
SHIRO ...
FINALLY.
SPLISH
THIS MEANS ...
... WE'RE ALL SAVED!
SA-KURA IS DEAD!
SSSSH
WHY YOU ...
YOU BASTARD!

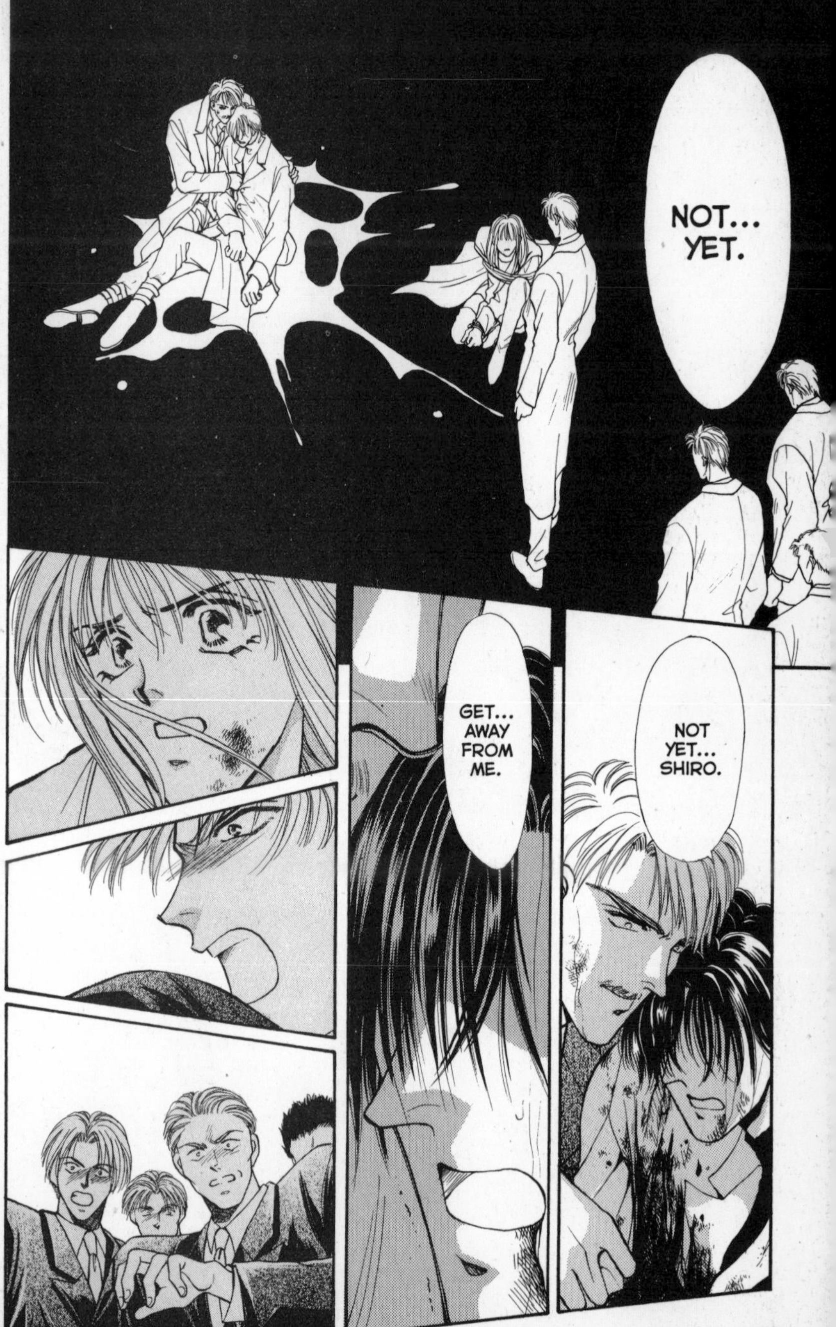
NOT... YET.
NOT YET... SHIRO.
GET... AWAY FROM ME.

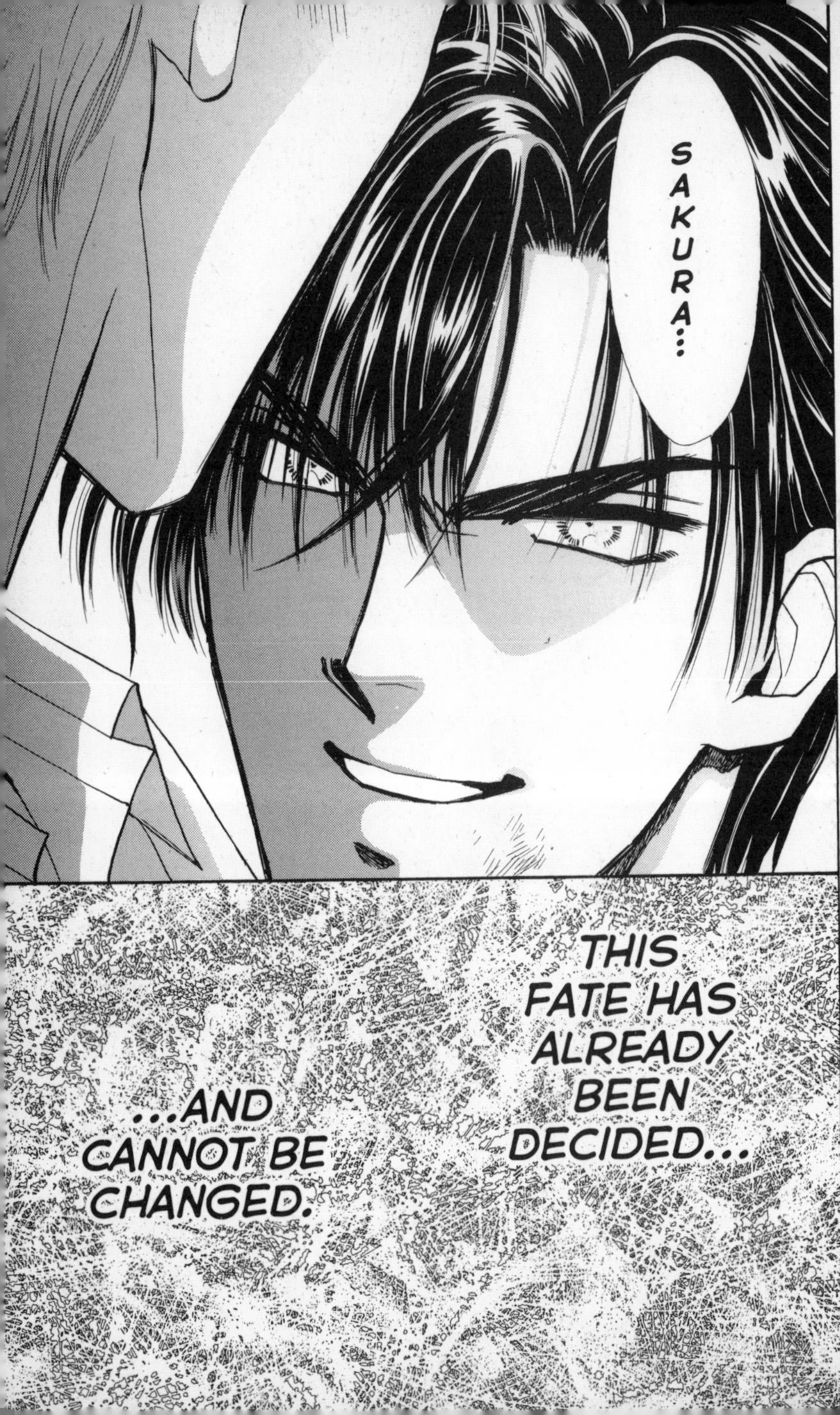
SAKURA...
THIS FATE HAS ALREADY BEEN DECIDED...
...AND CANNOT BE CHANGED.

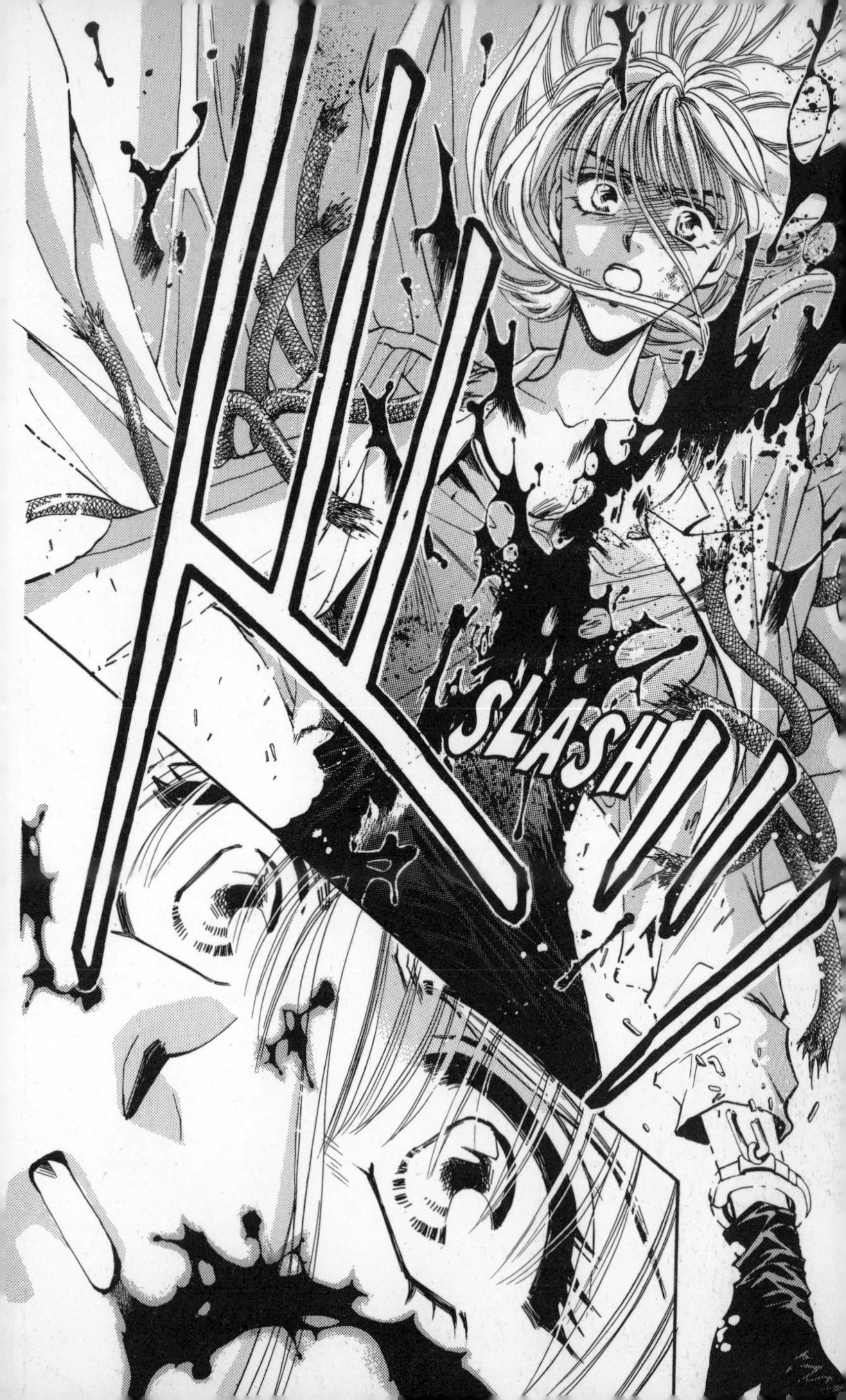
SLASH

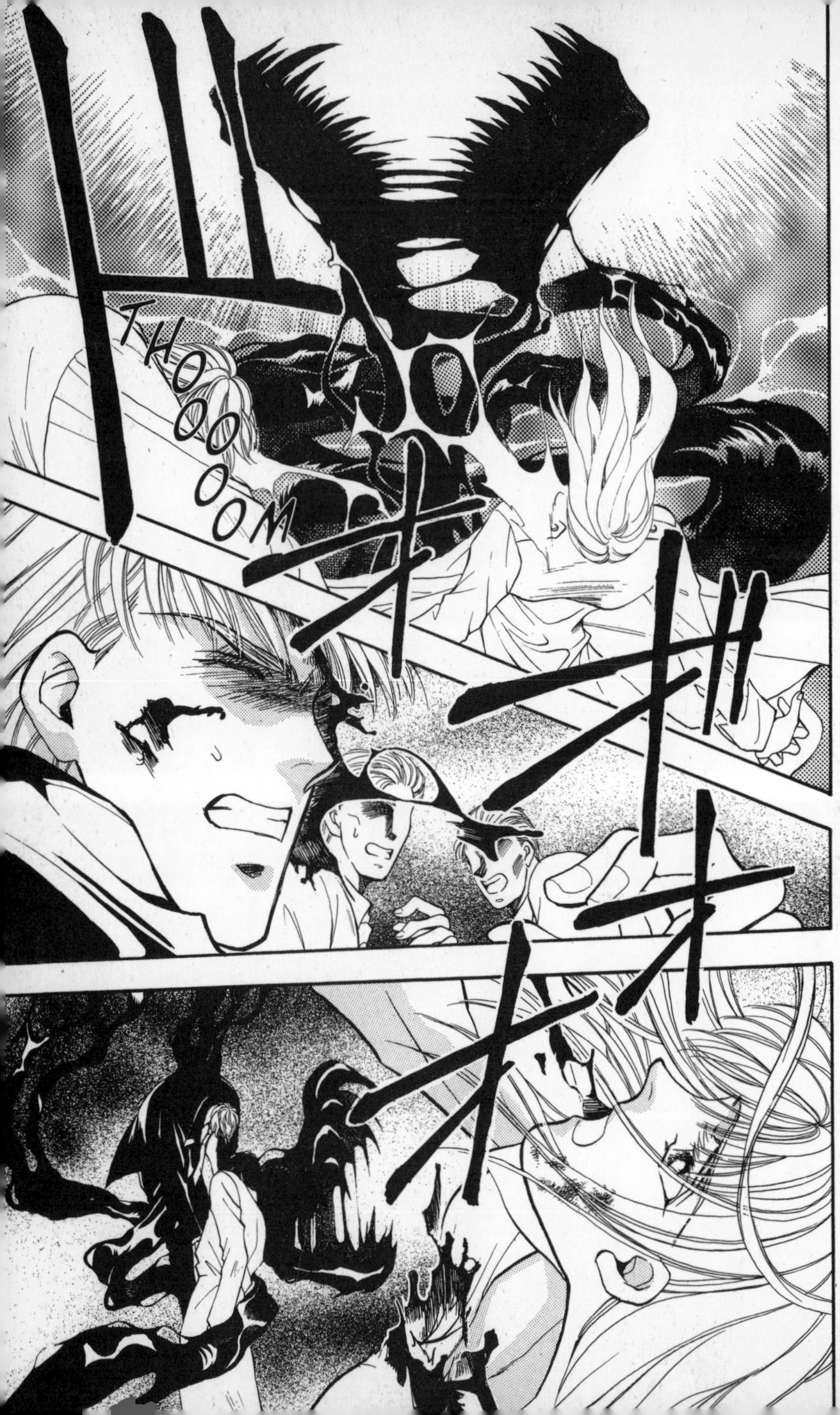
THOOOOOOM

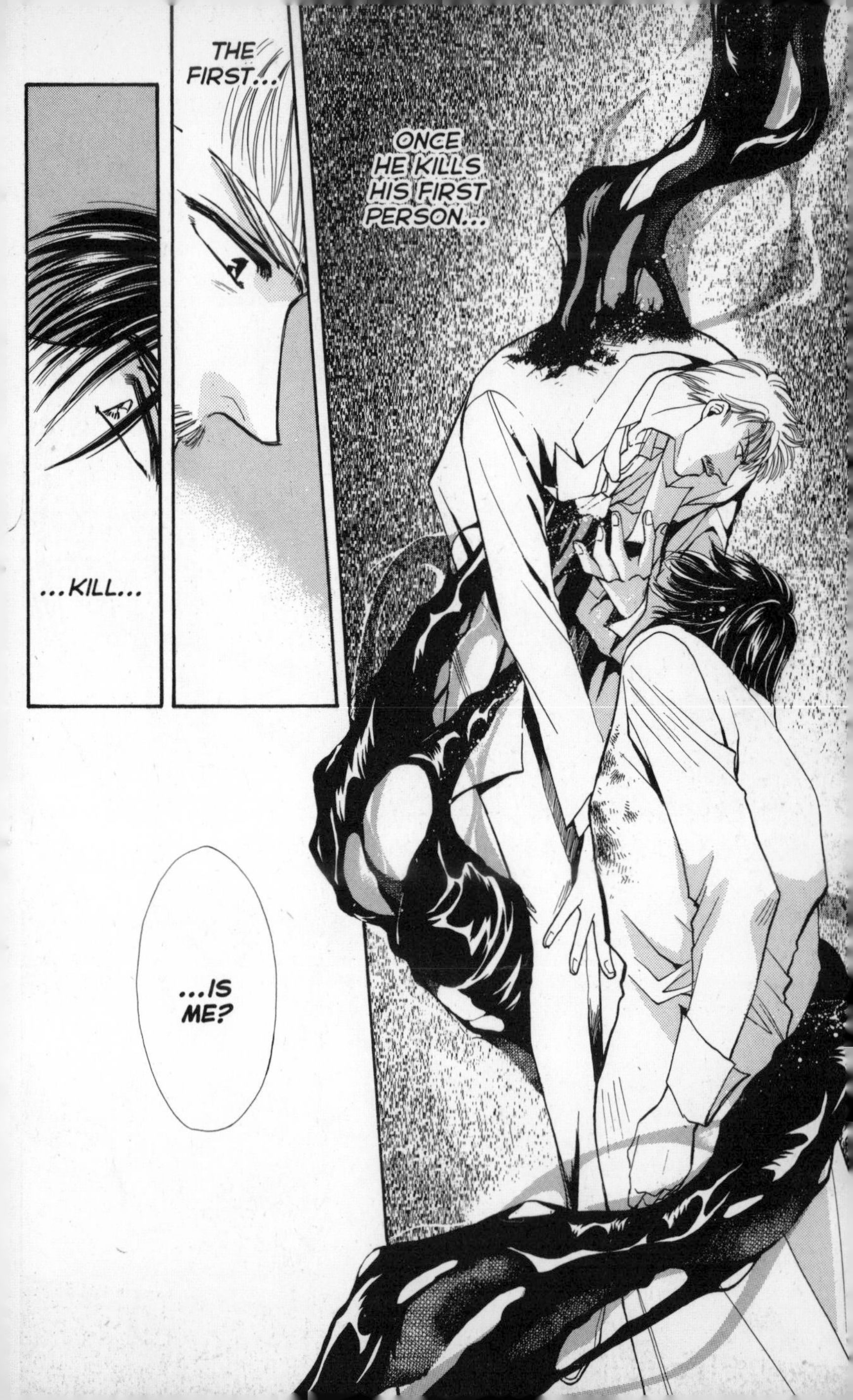
ONCE HE KILLS HIS FIRST PERSON...
THE FIRST...
...KILL...
...IS ME?

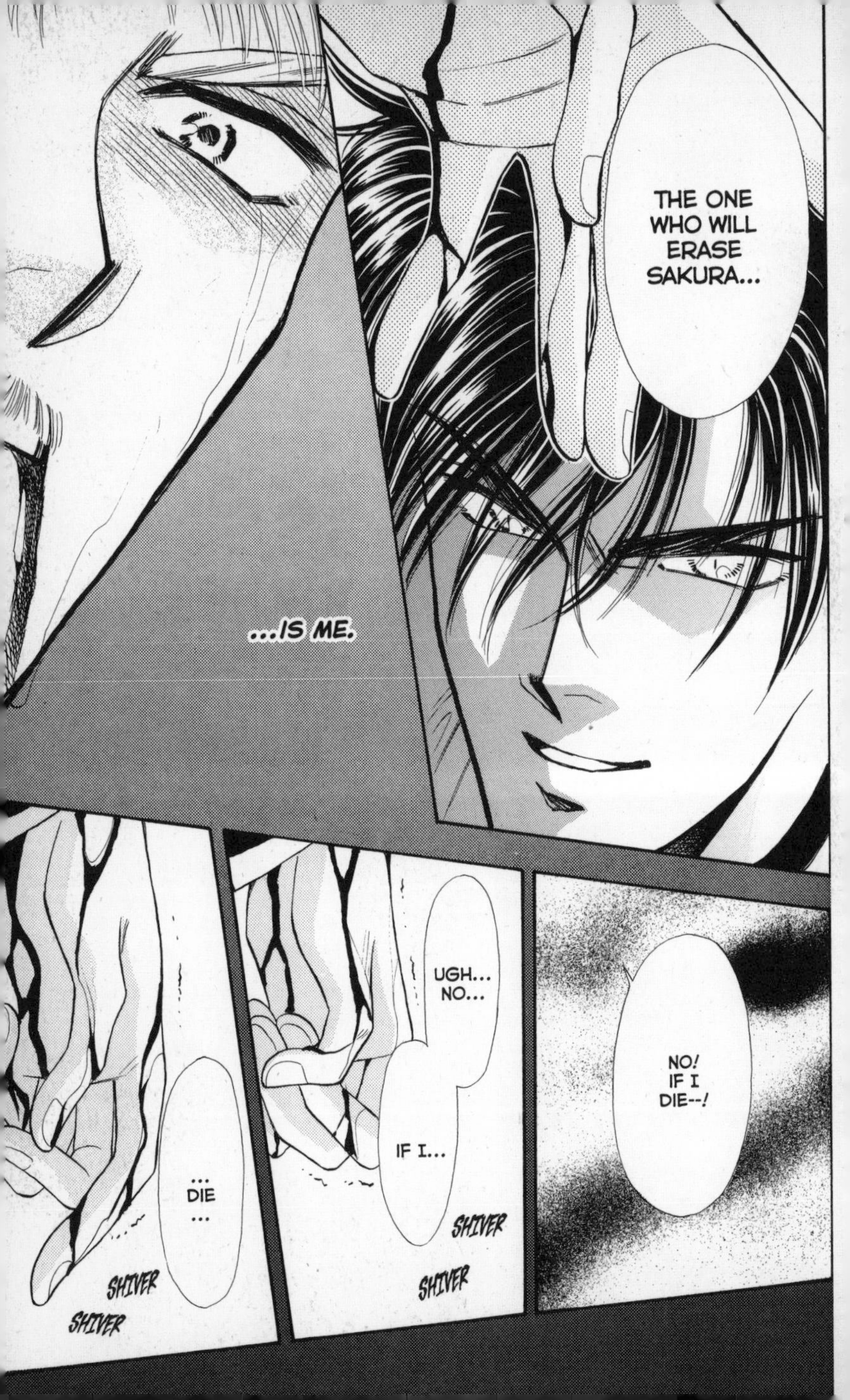
THE ONE WHO WILL ERASE SAKURA...
...IS ME.
NO! IF I DIE--!
UGH... NO...
IF I...
SHIVER
SHIVER
... DIE ...
SHIVER
SHIVER

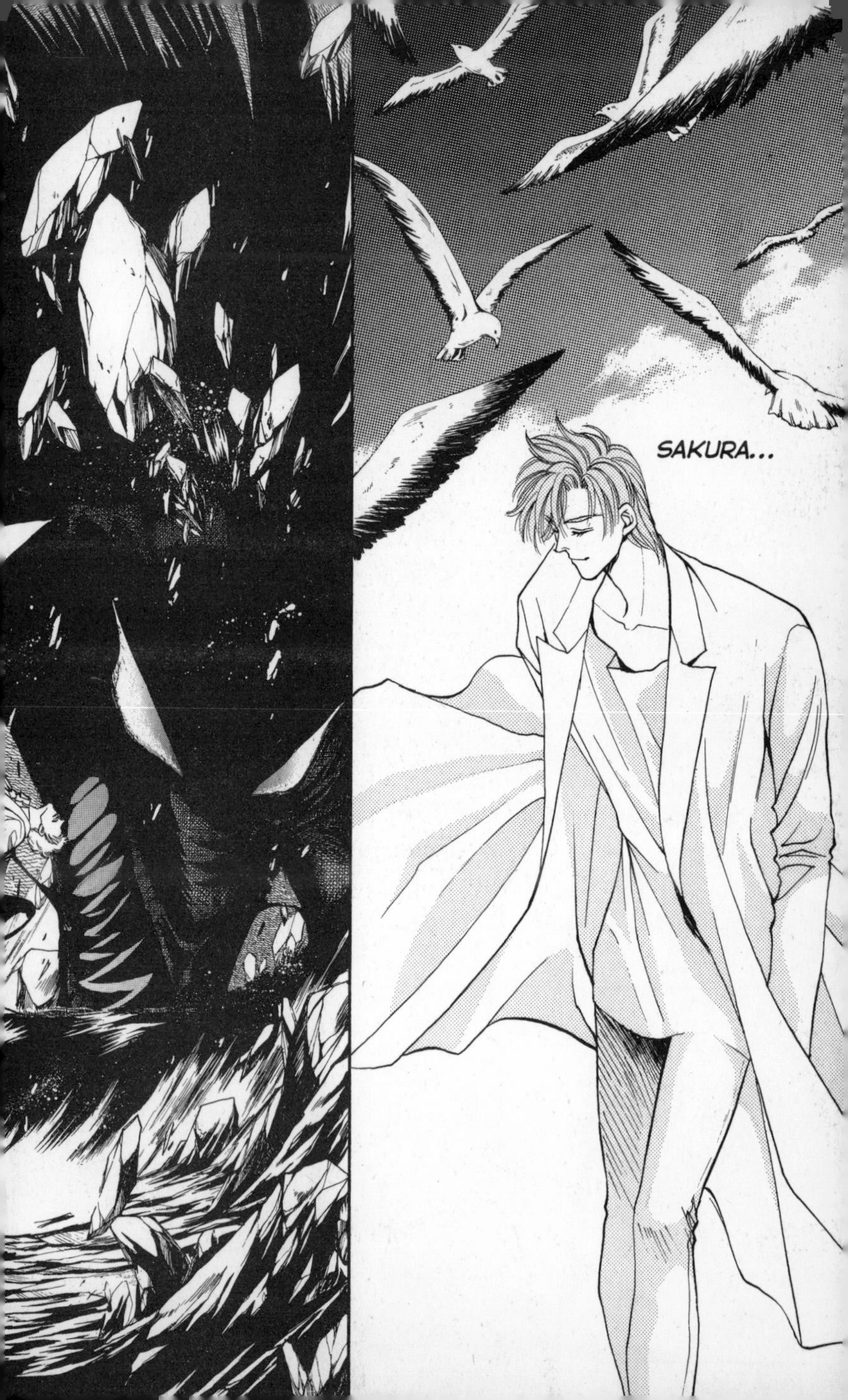
SAKURA...

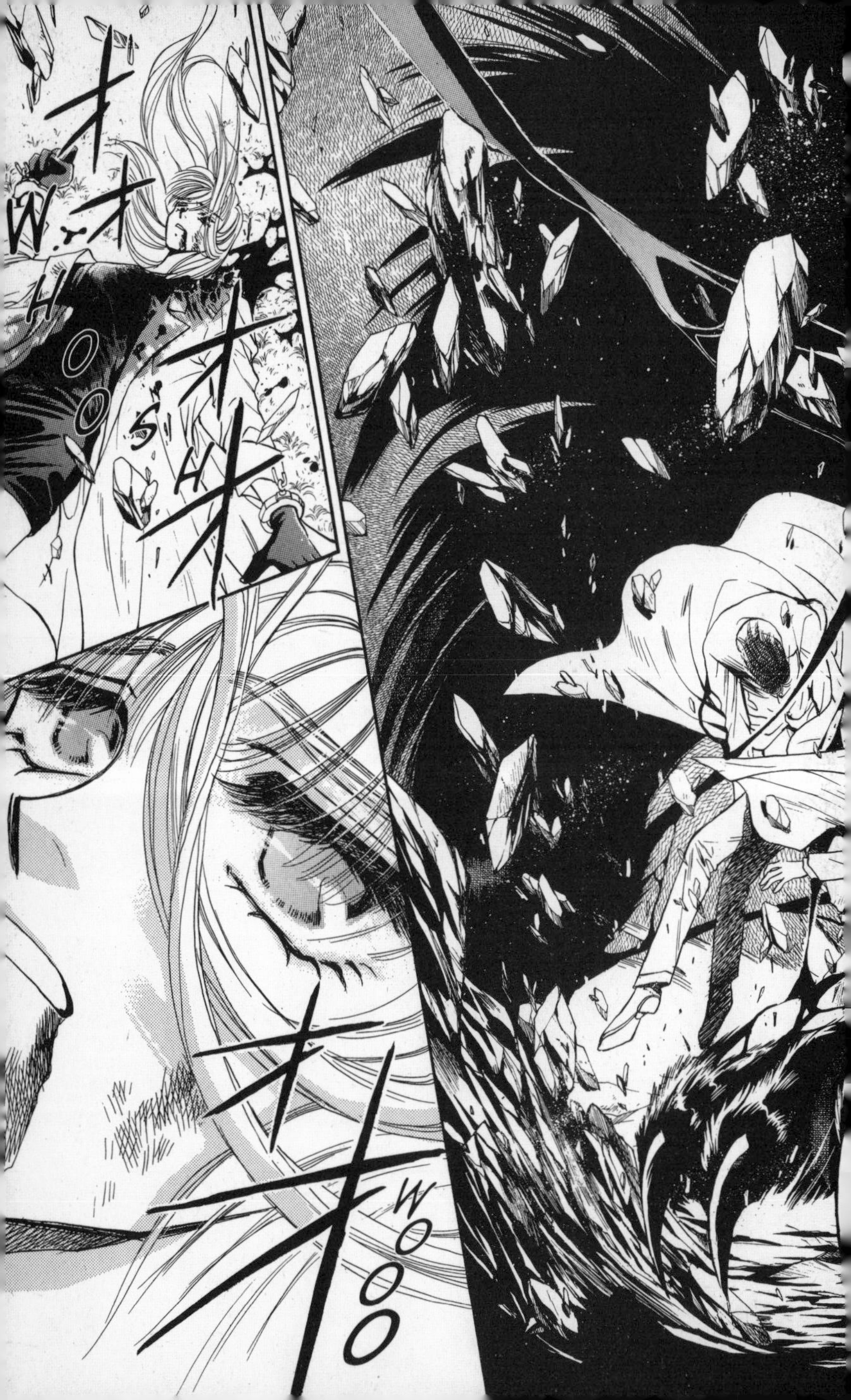
オオオオ
WHOOO
SH
オオ
WOOO

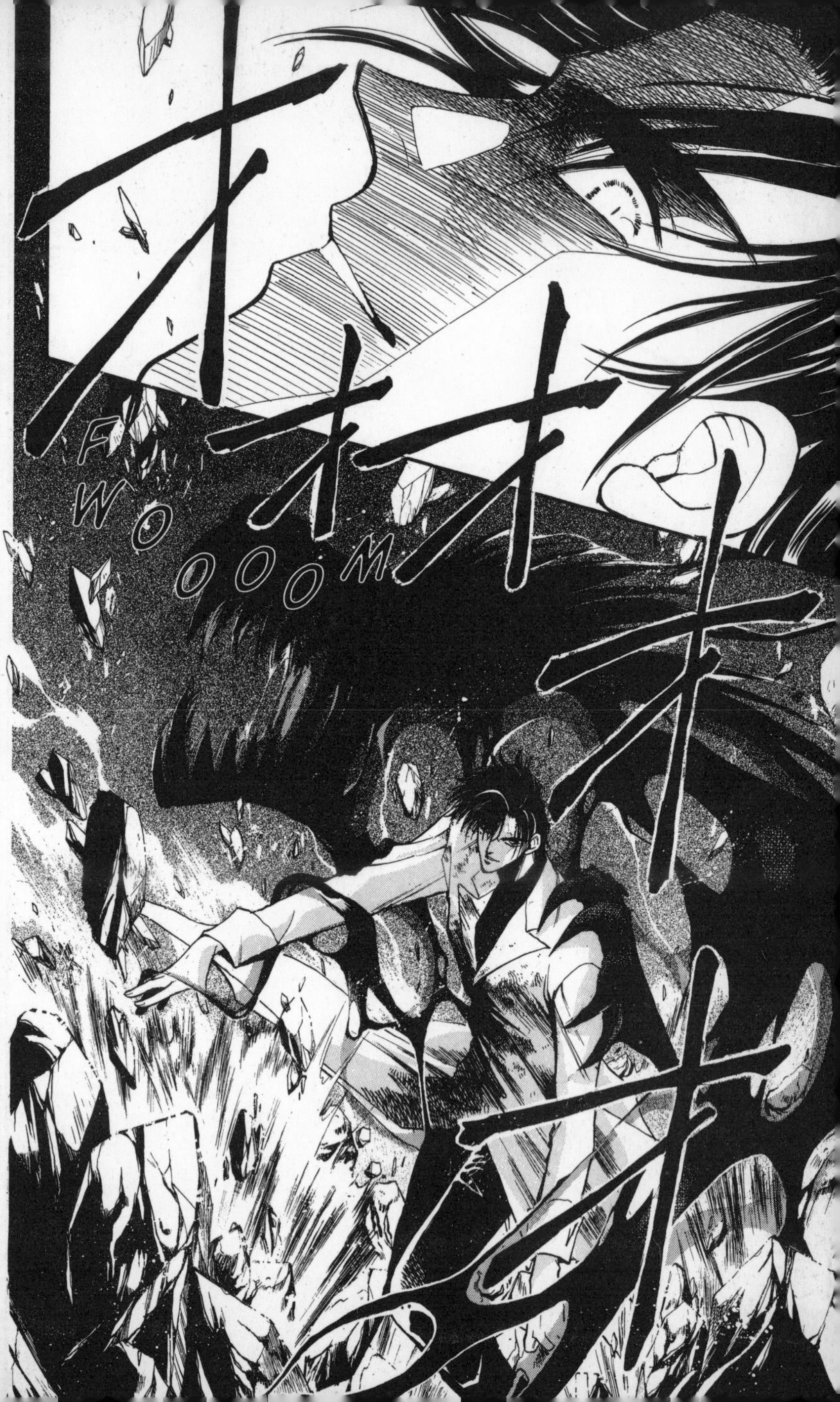
オオオオオ
FWOOOOM

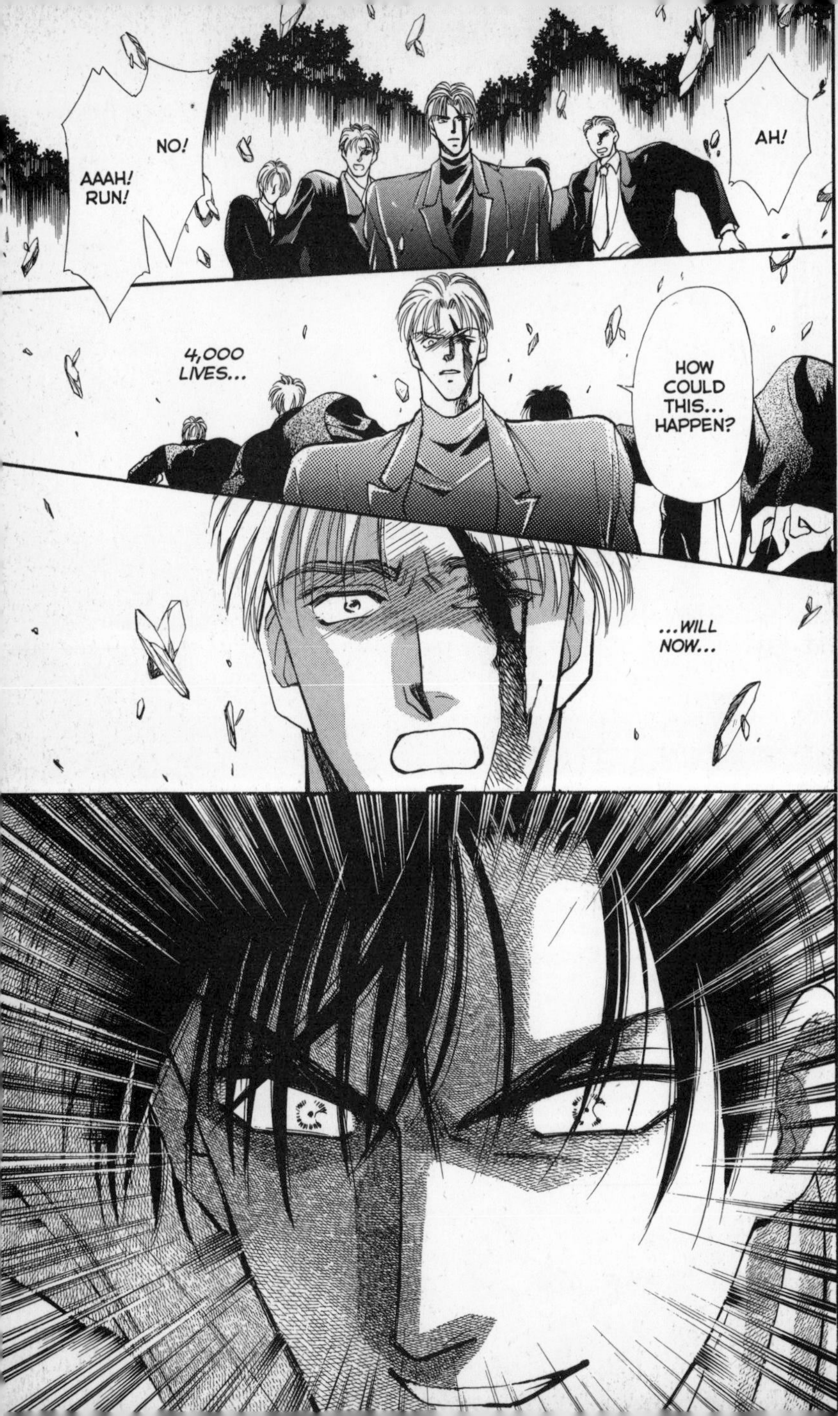
AH!
NO!
AAAH! RUN!
HOW COULD THIS... HAPPEN?
4,000 LIVES...
...WILL NOW...

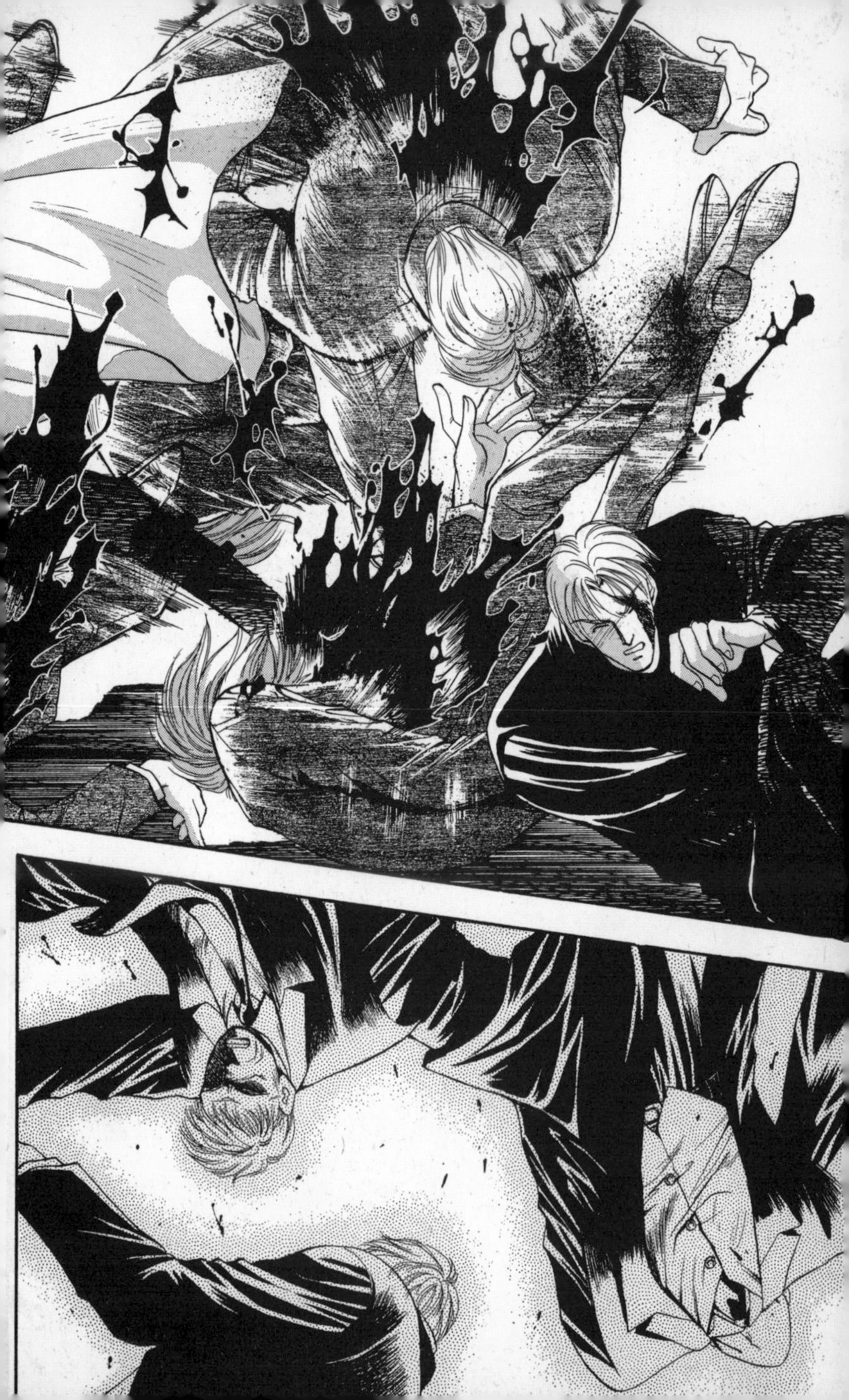

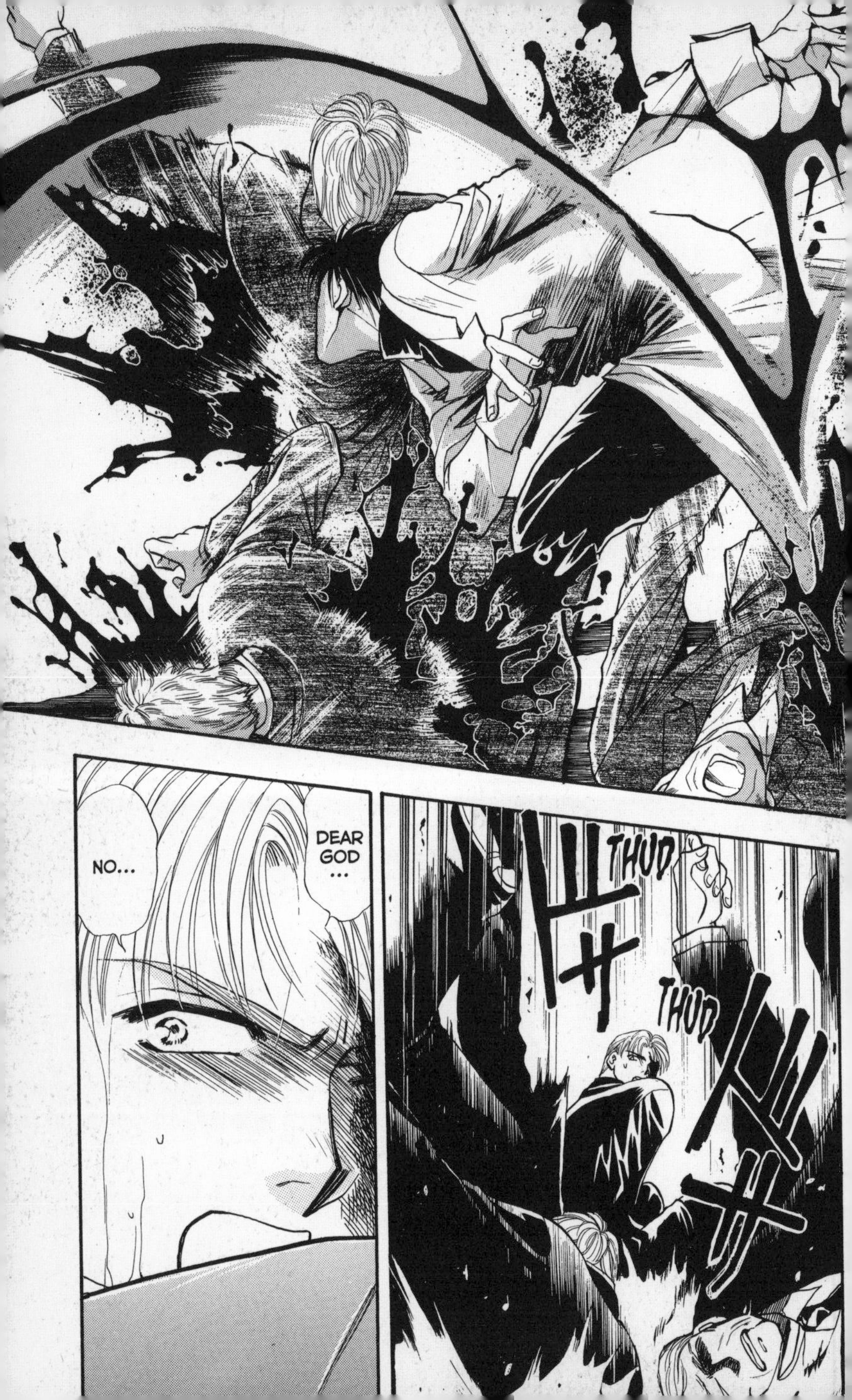
THUD
THUD
DEAR GOD ...
NO...

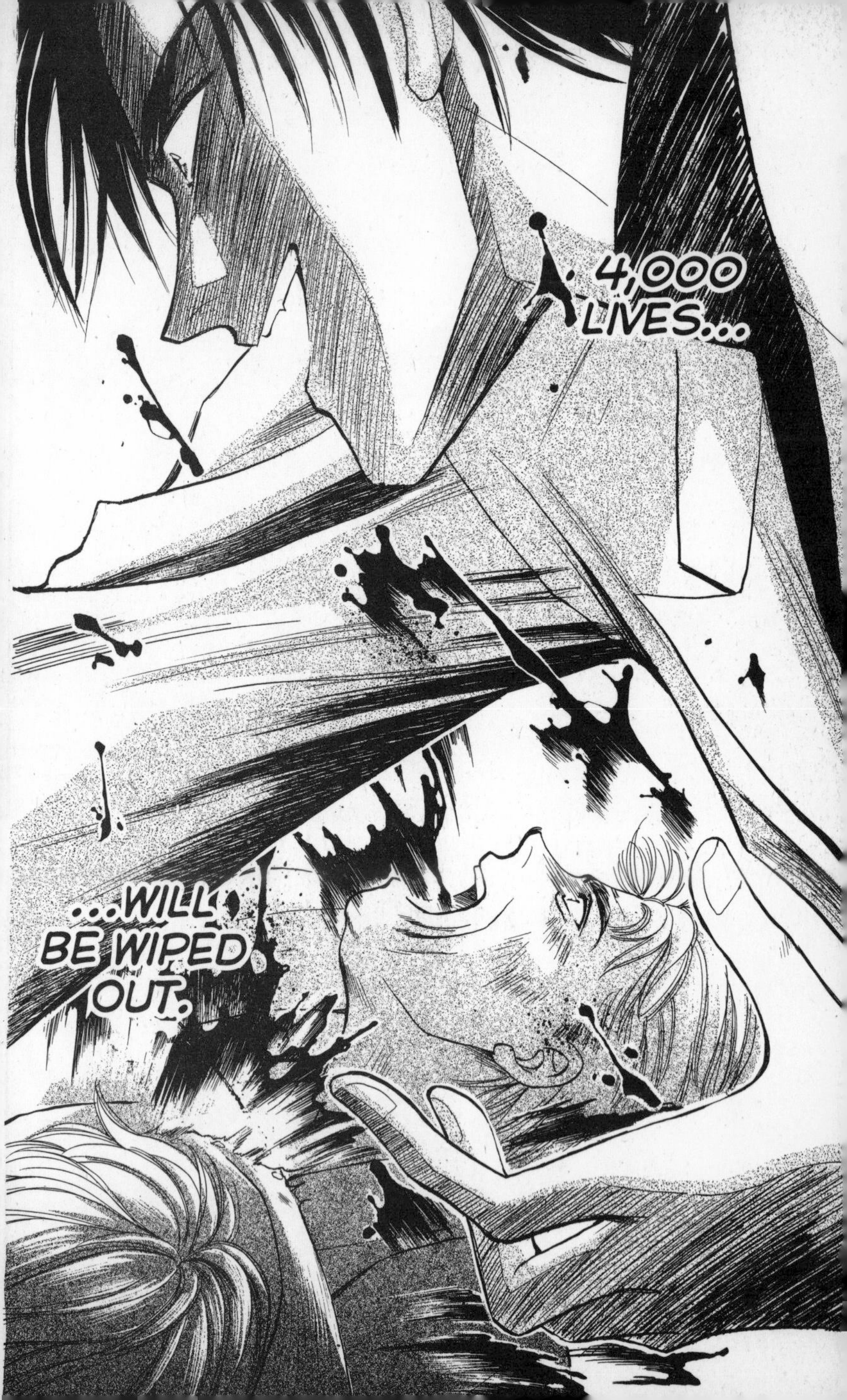

4,000 LIVES...
...WILL BE WIPED OUT.

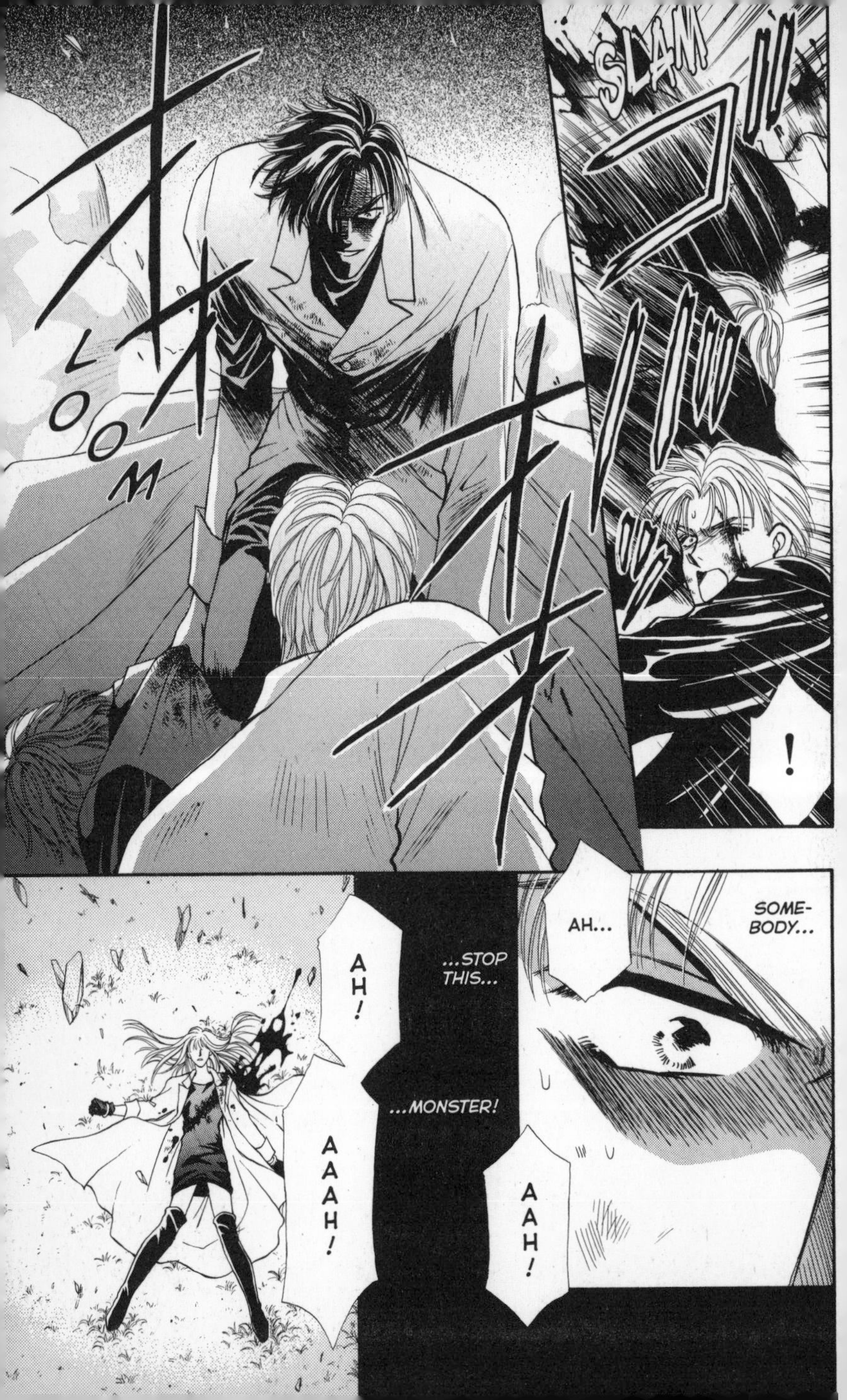
SLAM
!
LOOM
SOME-BODY...
AH...
AAH!
...STOP THIS...
AH!
...MONSTER!
AAAAH!

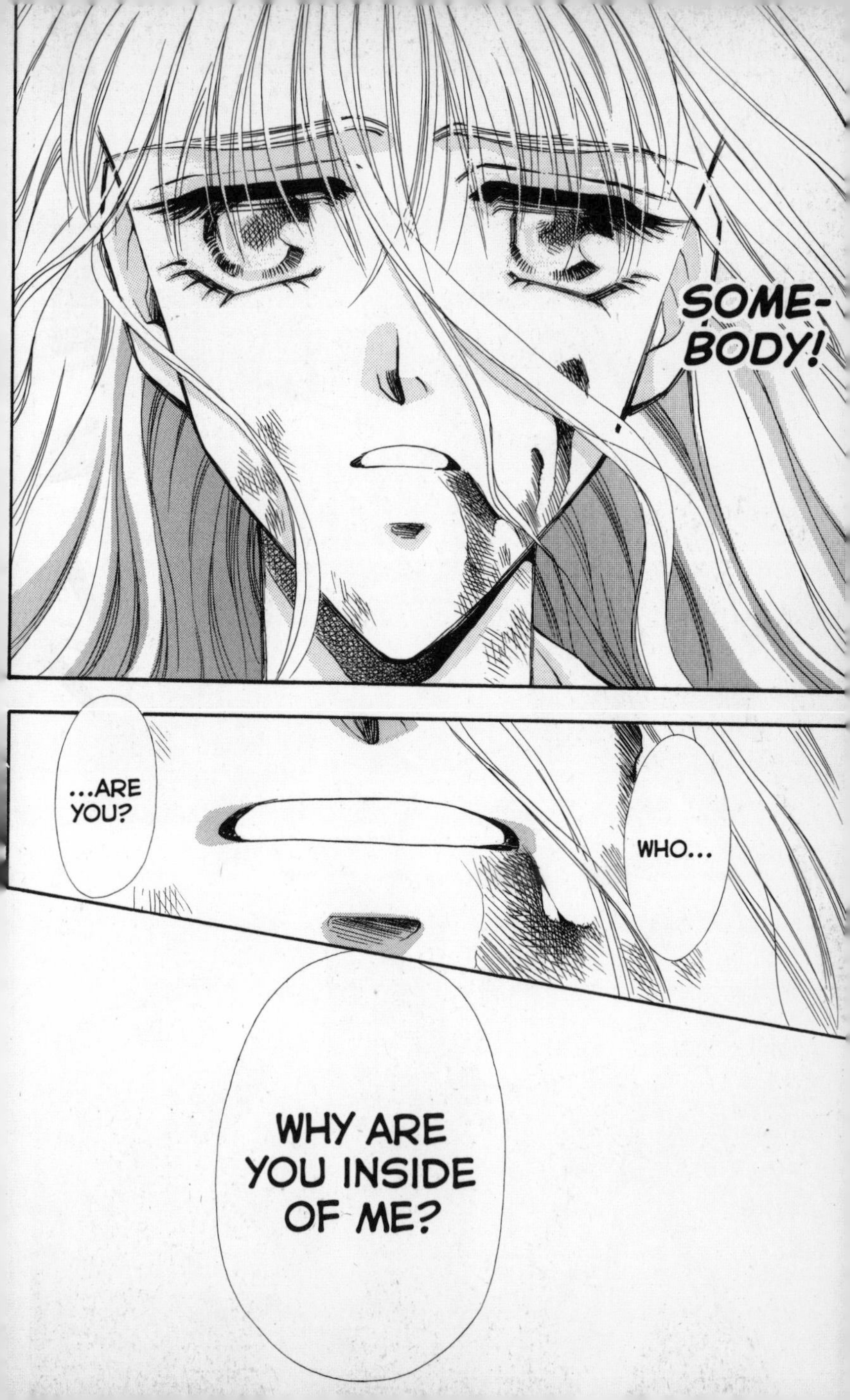
SOME-BODY!
WHO...
...ARE YOU?
WHY ARE YOU INSIDE OF ME?

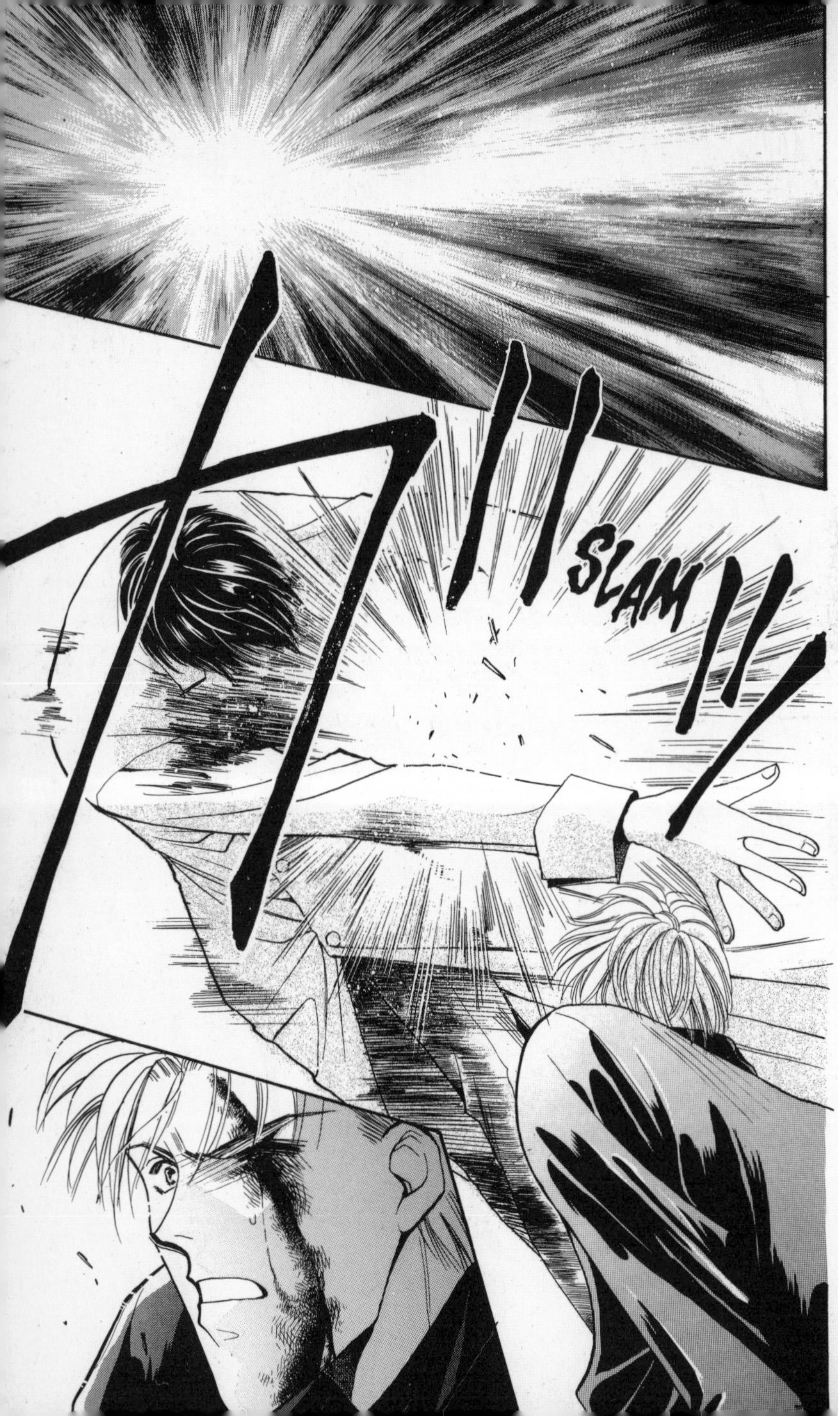
SLAM

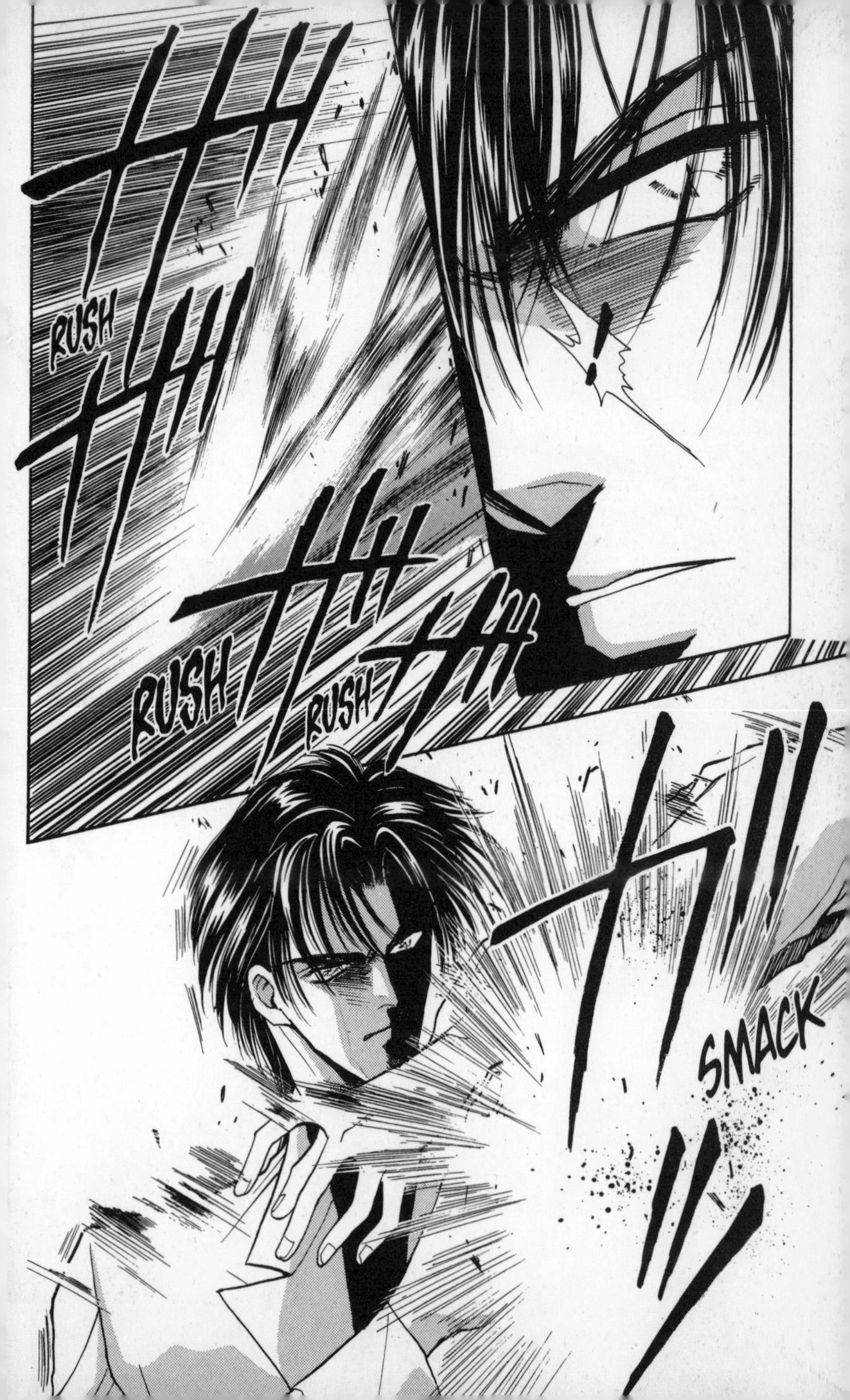
!
RUSH
RUSH
RUSH
SMACK

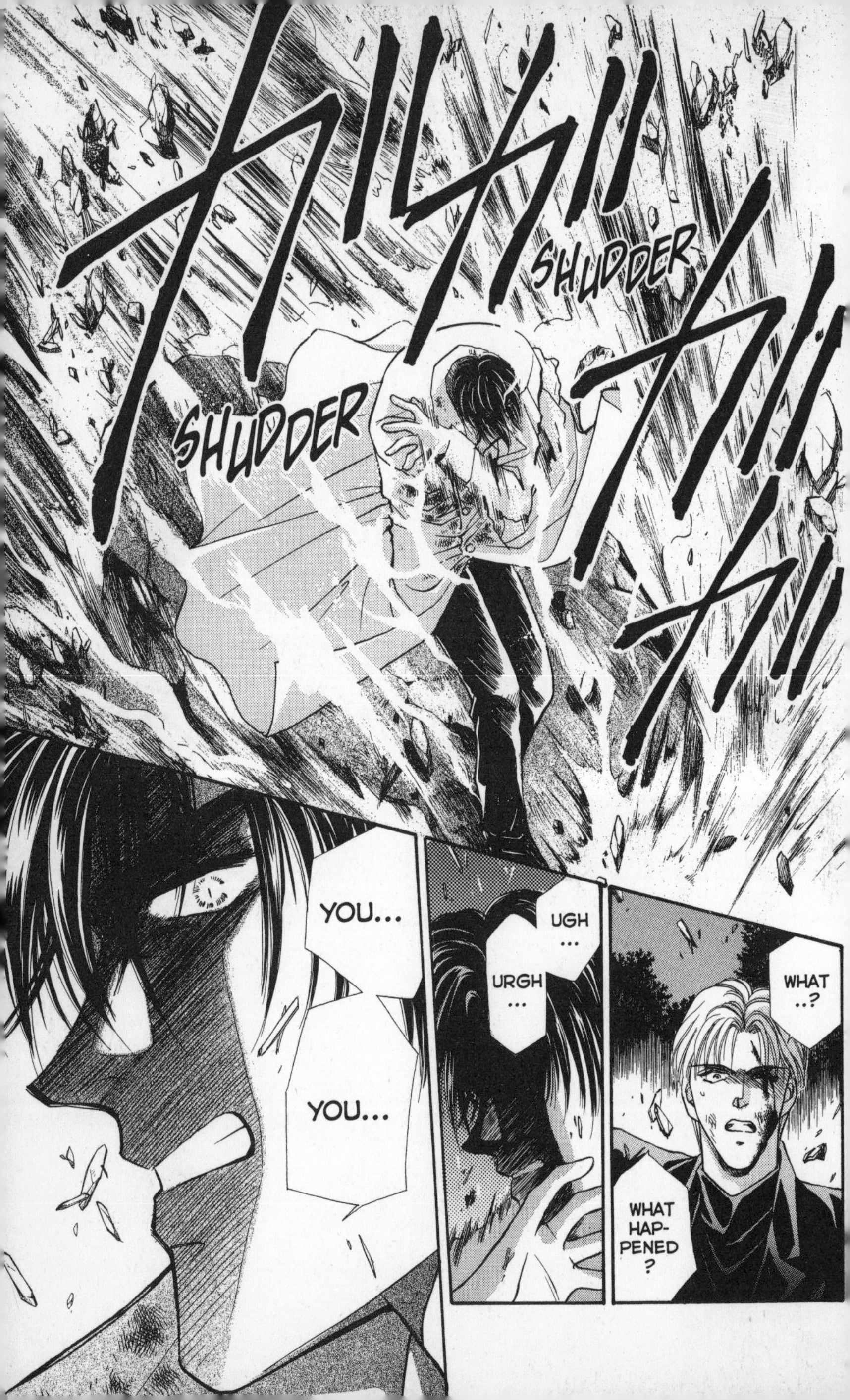
SHUDDER
SHUDDER
WHAT ..?
WHAT HAP-PENED ?
UGH ...
URGH ...
YOU...
YOU...

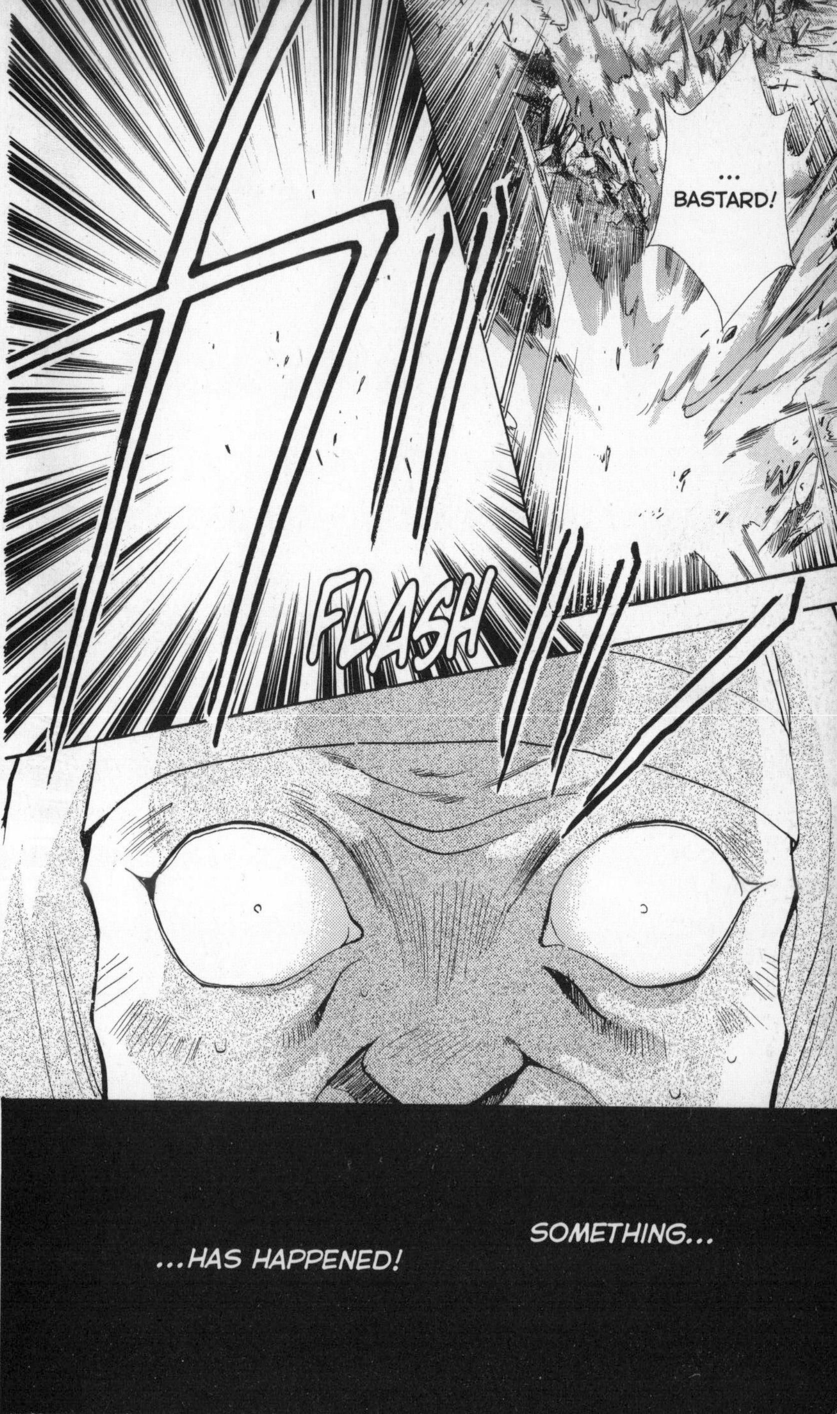
...
BASTARD!
FLASH
SOMETHING...
...HAS HAPPENED!

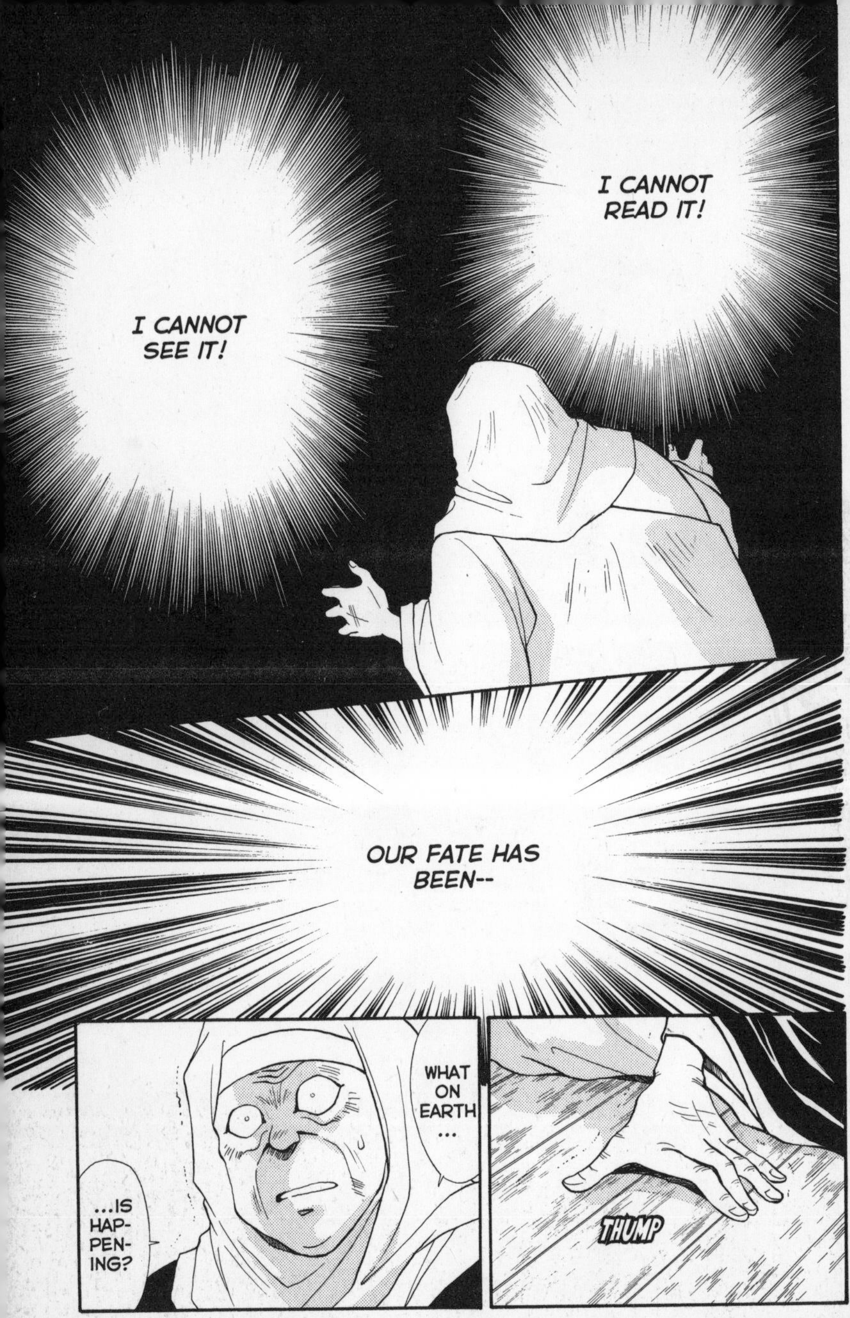
I CANNOT READ IT!
I CANNOT SEE IT!
OUR FATE HAS BEEN--
THUMP
WHAT ON EARTH ...
...IS HAP-PEN-ING?

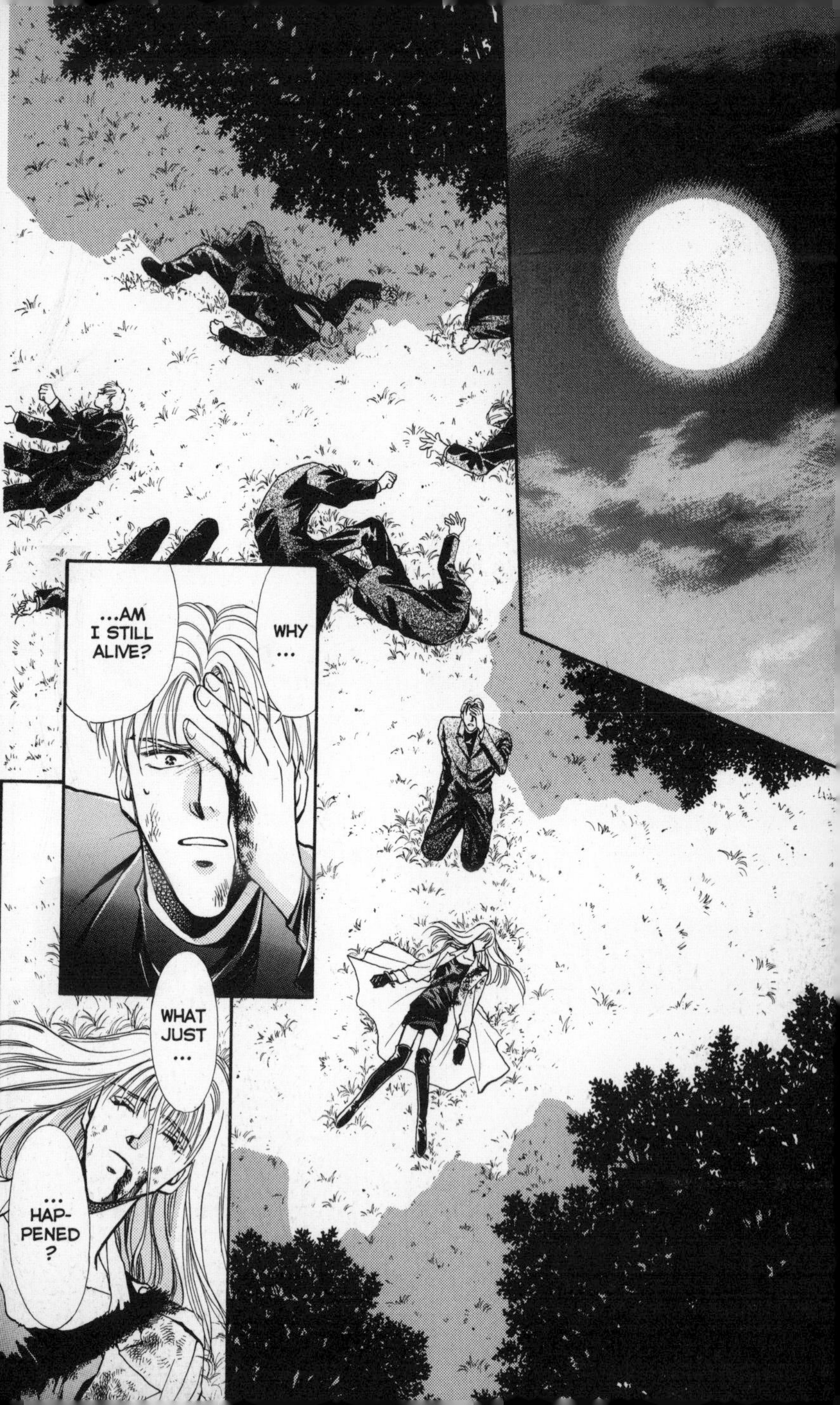
WHY ...
...AM I STILL ALIVE?
WHAT JUST ...
... HAP-PENED ?

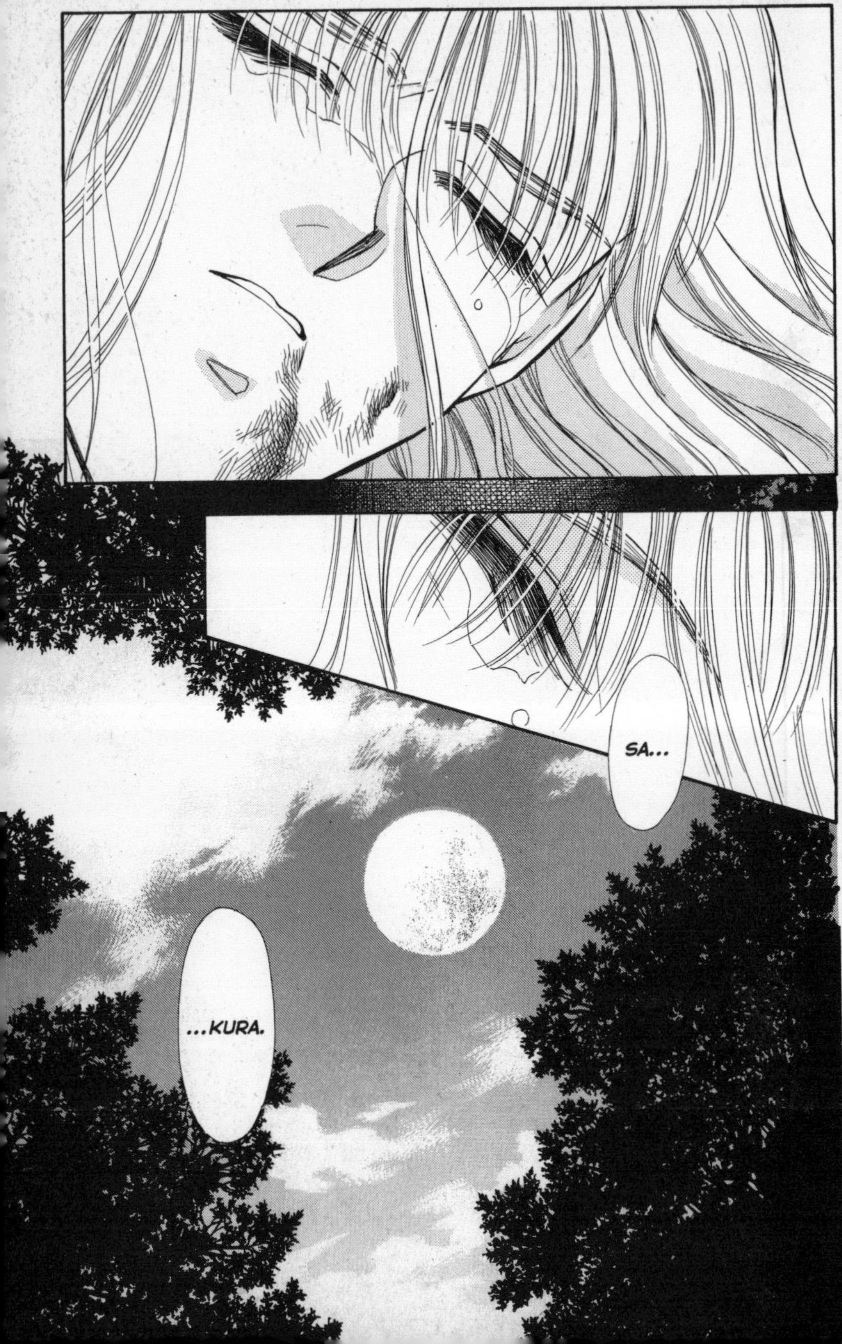
SA...
...KURA.

獣たちの夜

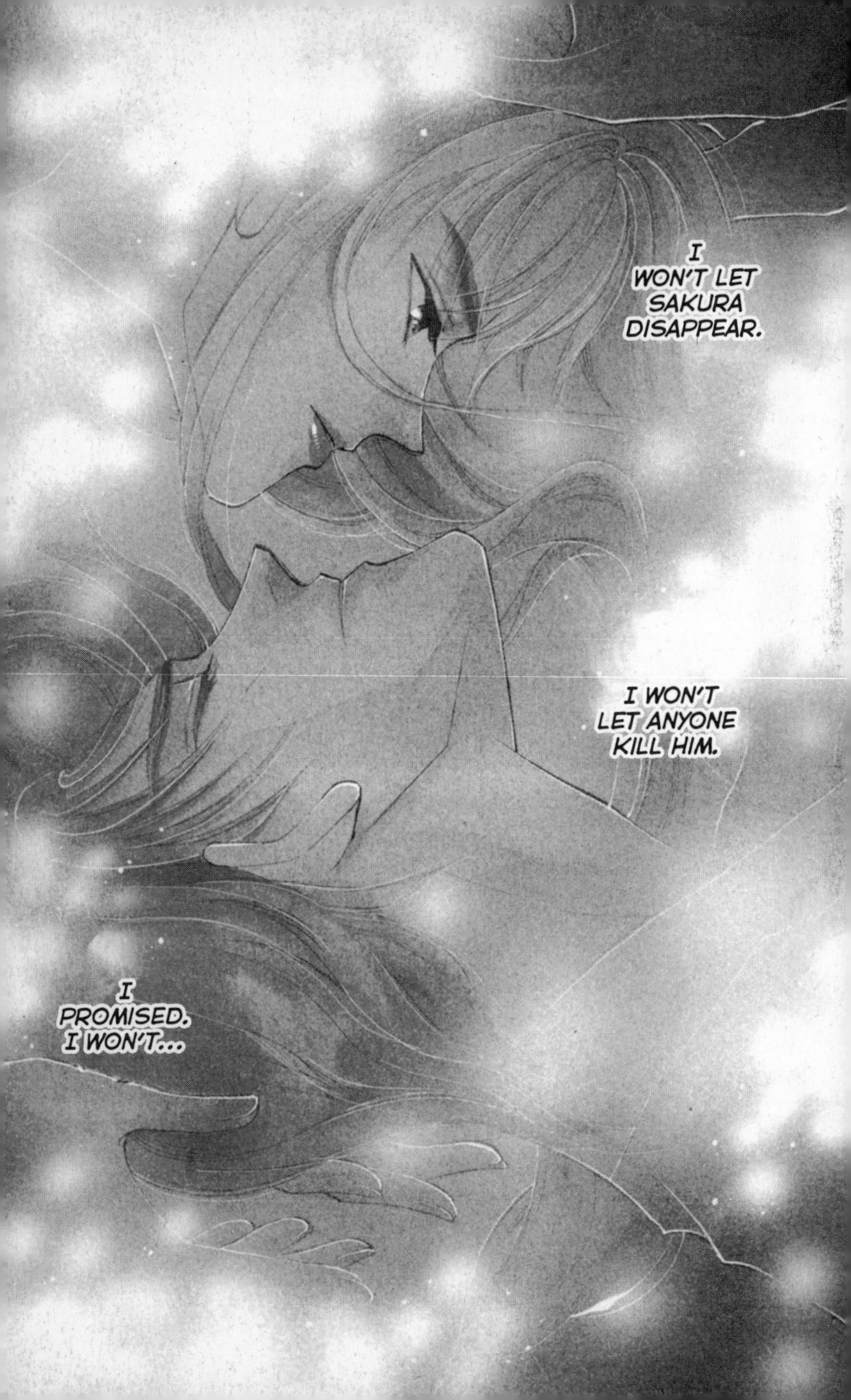
I WON'T LET SAKURA DISAPPEAR.
I WON'T LET ANYONE KILL HIM.
I PROMISED. I WON'T...

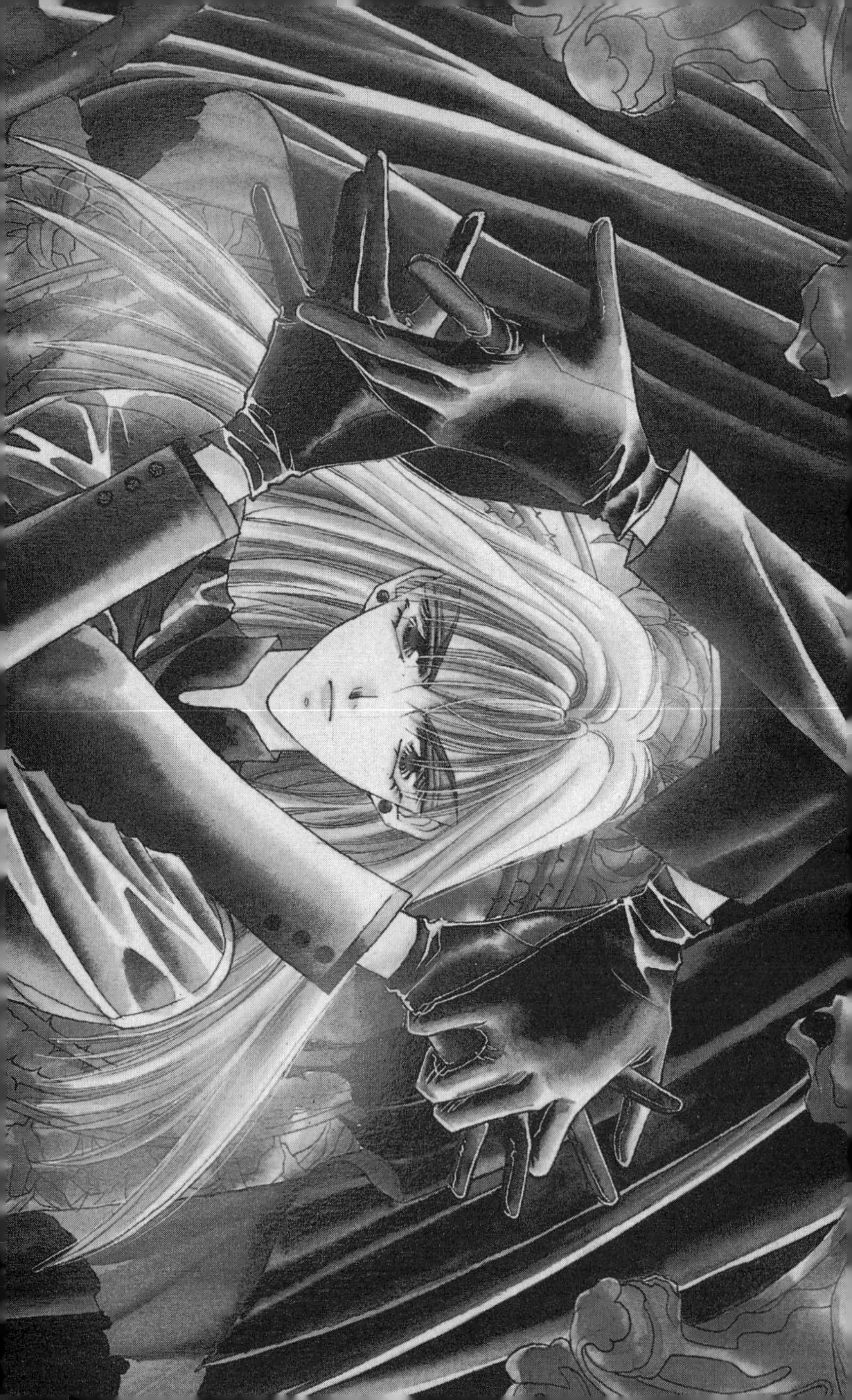

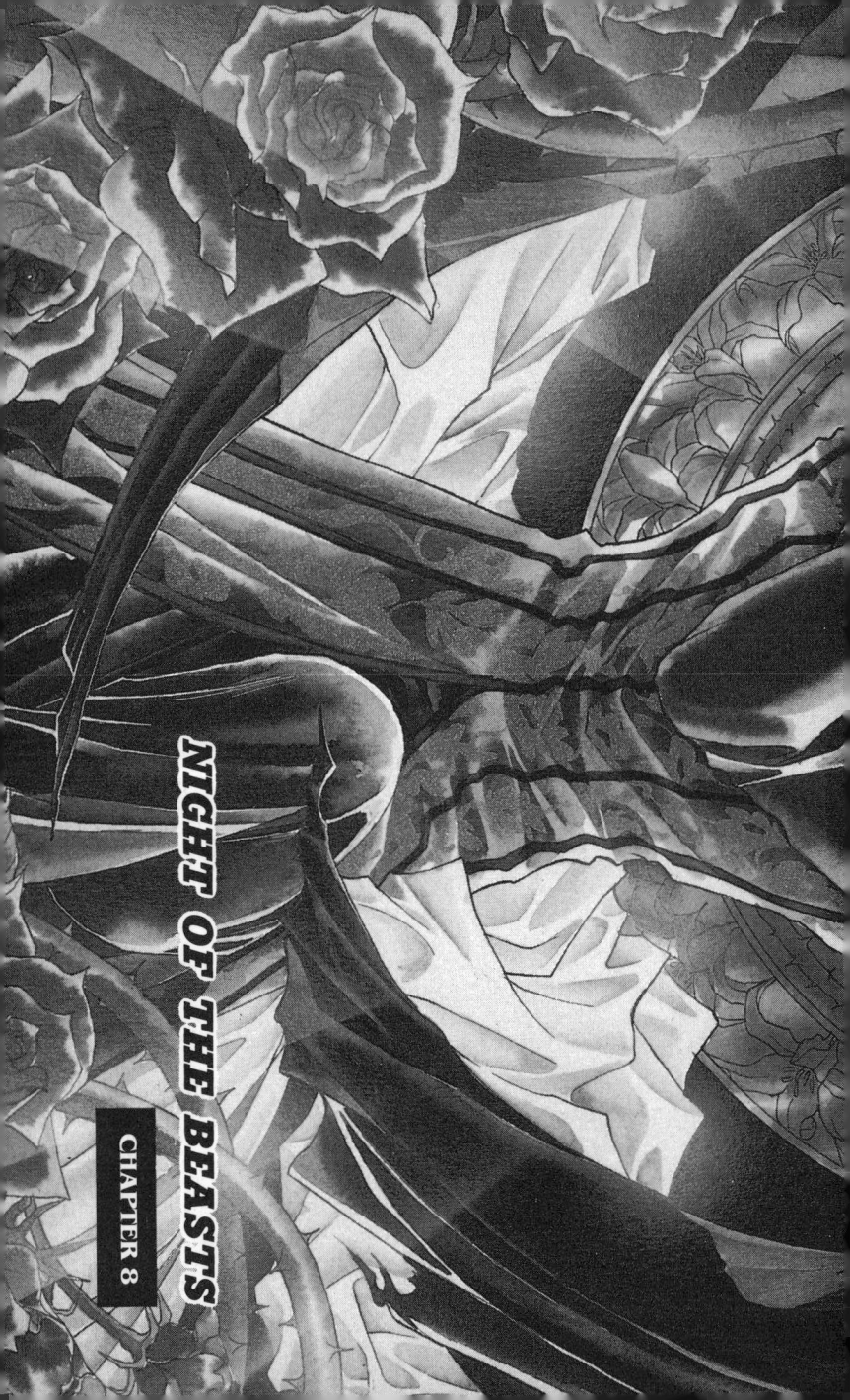

NIGHT OF THE BEASTS

CHAPTER 8

獣たちの夜

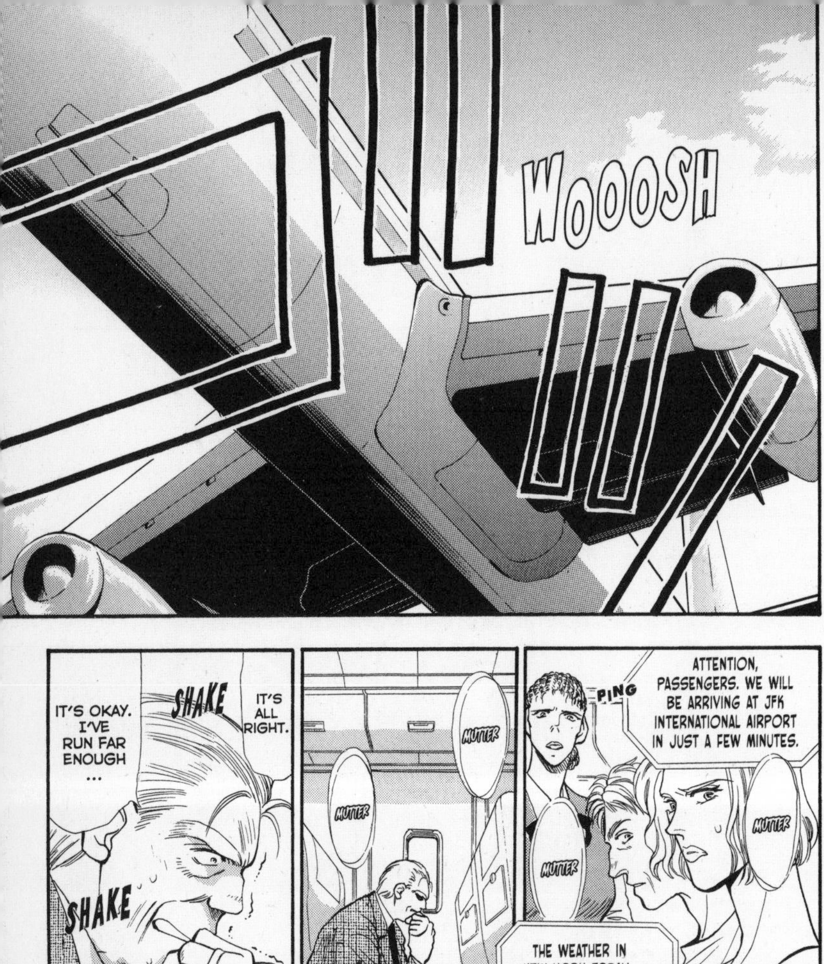
WOOOSH
PING
ATTENTION, PASSENGERS. WE WILL BE ARRIVING AT JFK INTERNATIONAL AIRPORT IN JUST A FEW MINUTES.
MUTTER
MUTTER
THE WEATHER IN NEW YORK TODAY--
MUTTER
MUTTER
IT'S ALL RIGHT.
SHAKE
IT'S OKAY. I'VE RUN FAR ENOUGH ...
SHAKE

■ Sakura Kijima ■

Everyone that heard I'd given my male lead the feminine name "Sakura" gave me a funny look. Originally, I'd planned on giving him Aria's name, but couldn't decide. In the end, I just sort of decided to stick the name "Sakura" on him instead. I don't know about everyone else, but I really like it.

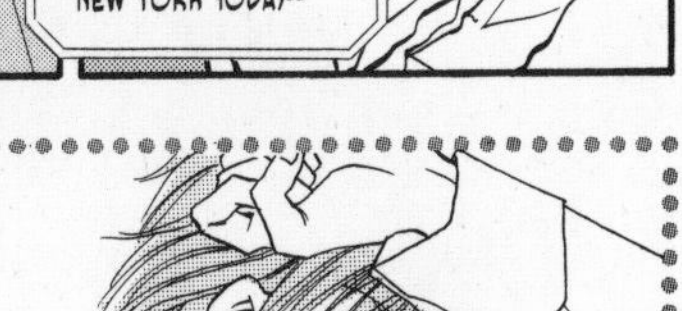

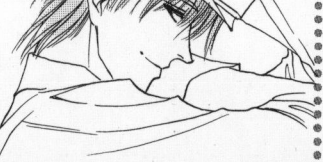

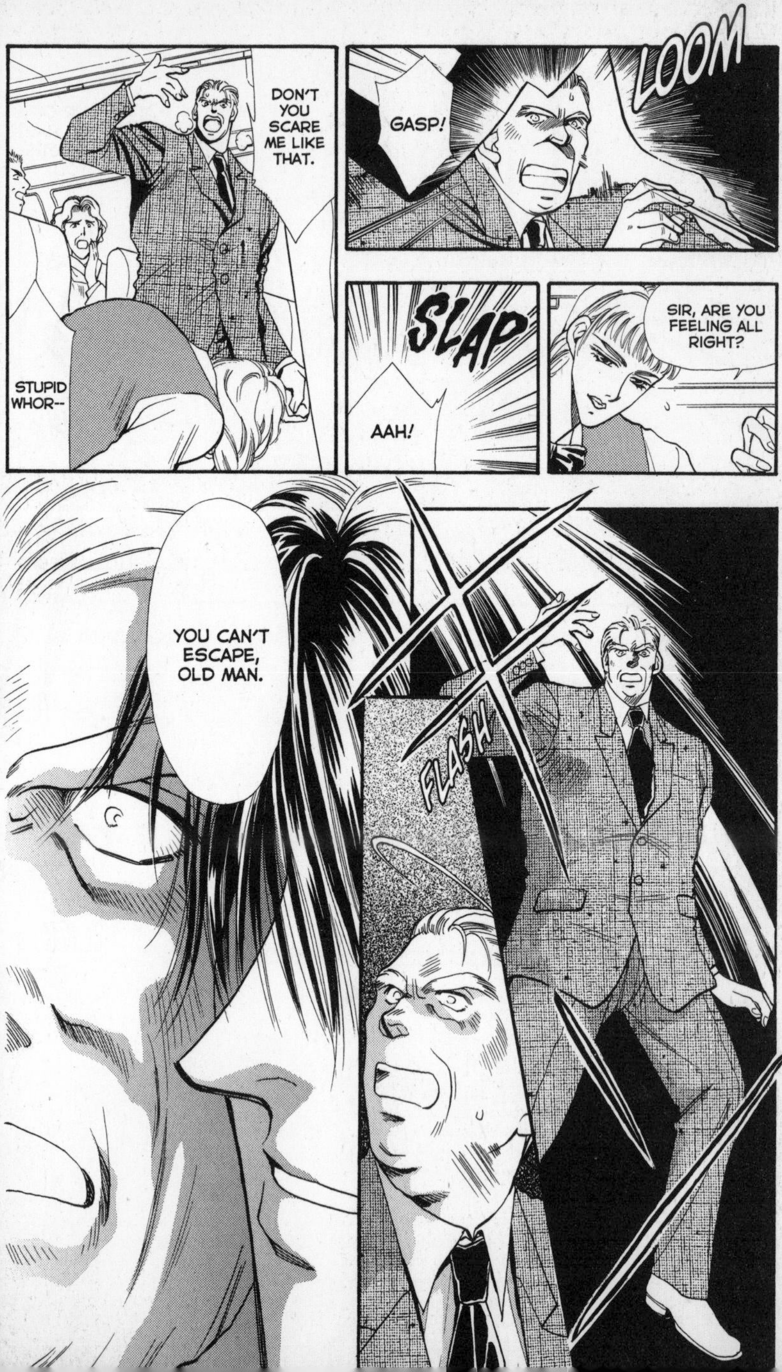
LOOM
GASP!
SIR, ARE YOU FEELING ALL RIGHT?
SLAP
AAH!
DON'T YOU SCARE ME LIKE THAT.
STUPID WHOR--
YOU CAN'T ESCAPE, OLD MAN.
FLASH

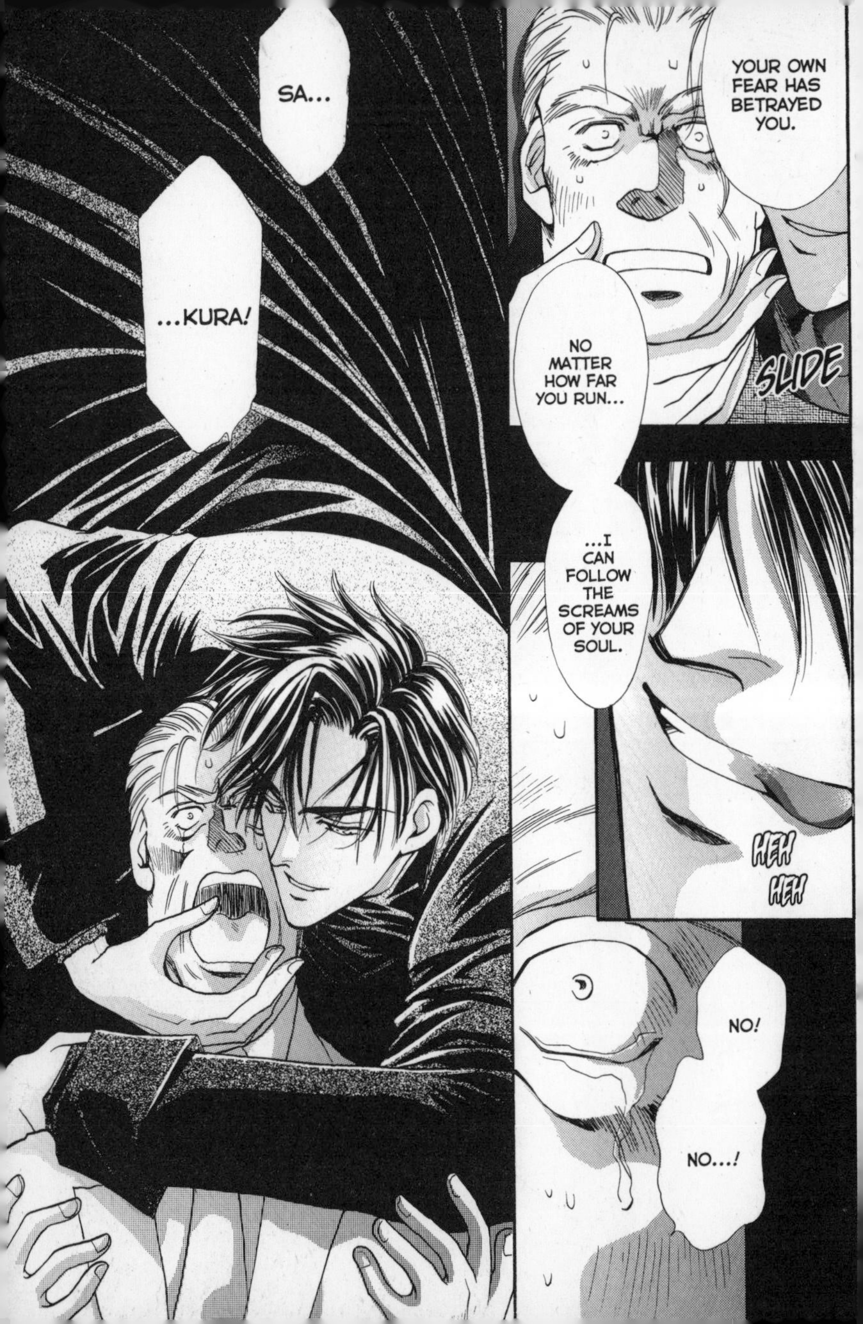
YOUR OWN FEAR HAS BETRAYED YOU.
NO MATTER HOW FAR YOU RUN...
SLIDE
...I CAN FOLLOW THE SCREAMS OF YOUR SOUL.
HEH HEH
NO!
NO...!
SA...
...KURA!

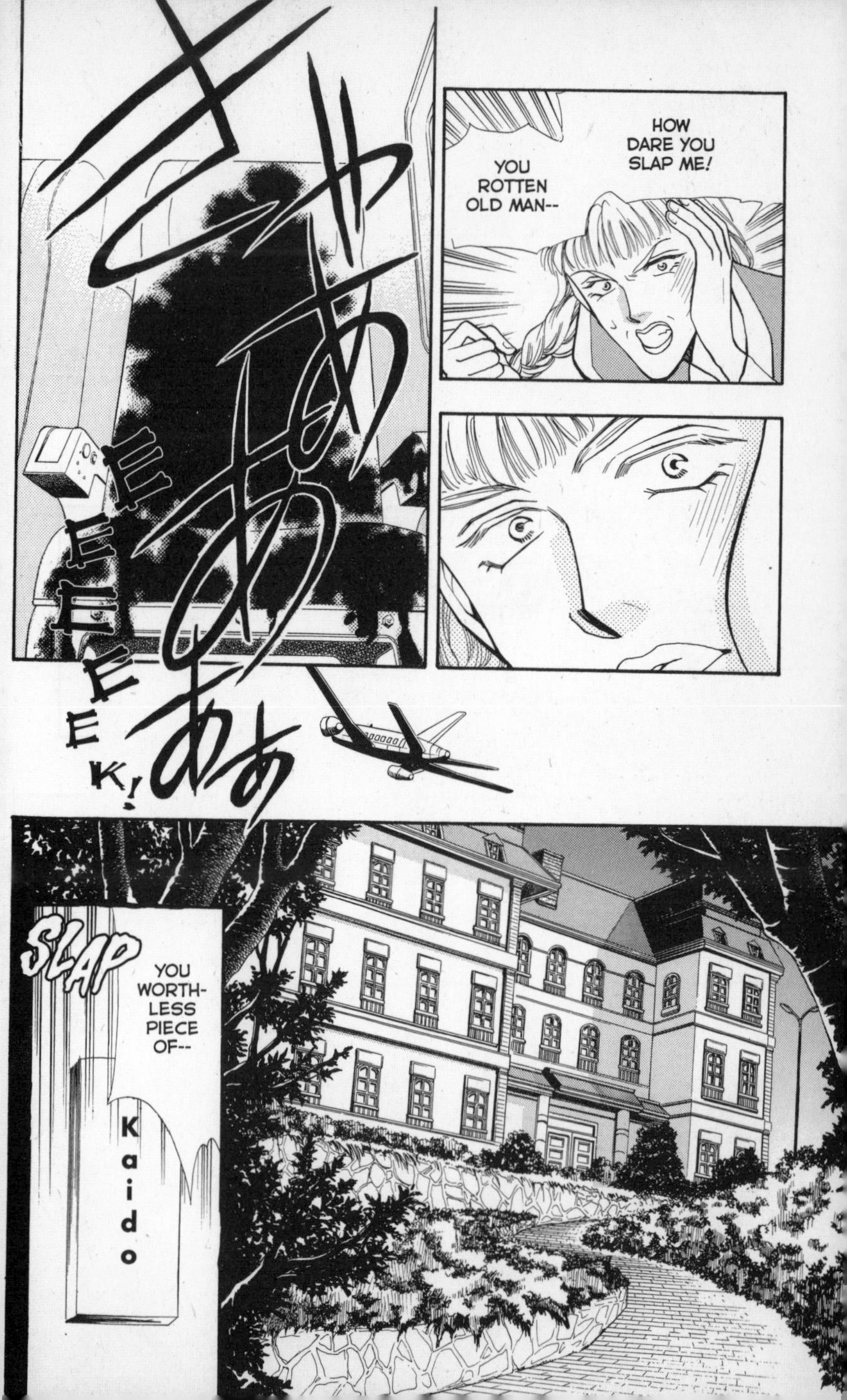
HOW DARE YOU SLAP ME!
YOU ROTTEN OLD MAN--
EEEEEEK!
YOU WORTHLESS PIECE OF--
SLAP
Kaido

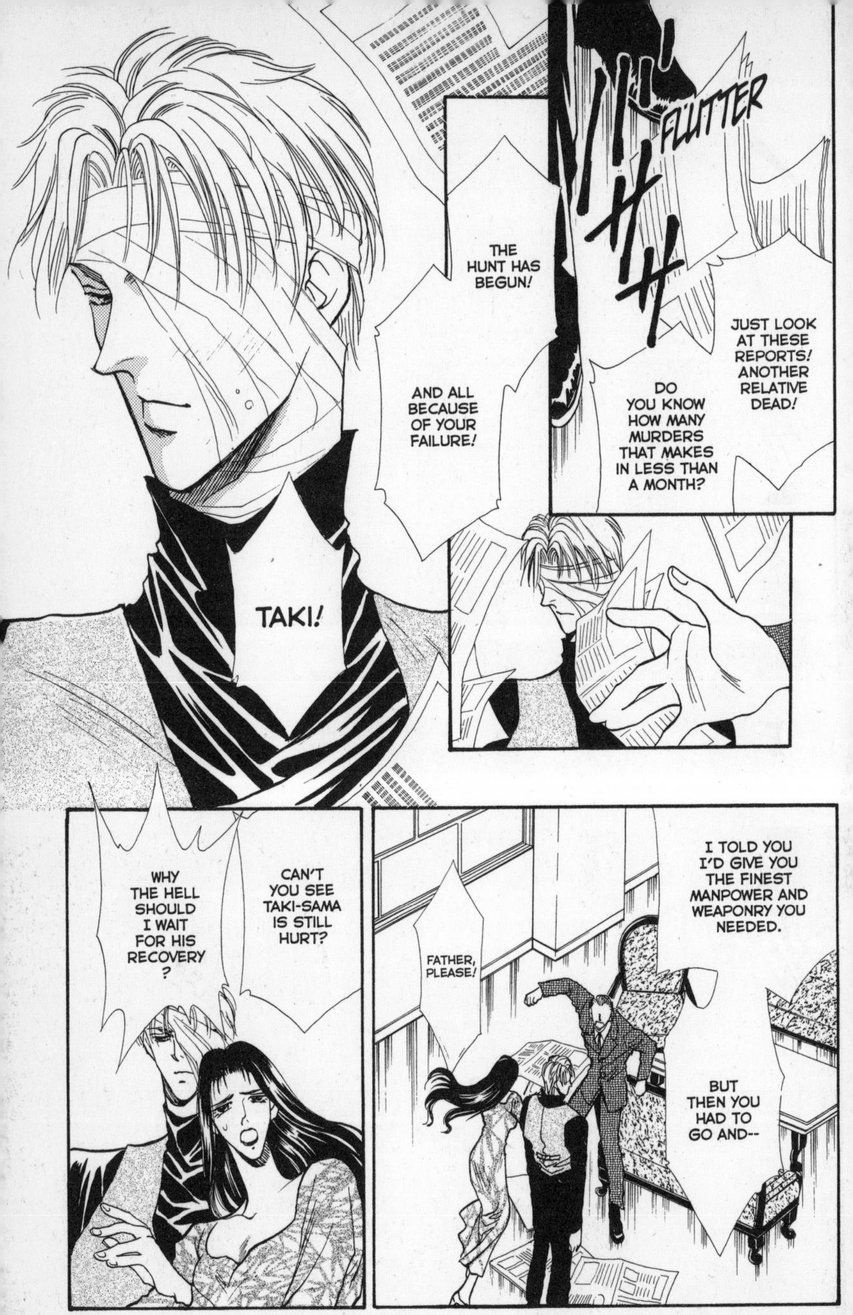
FLUTTER
JUST LOOK AT THESE REPORTS! ANOTHER RELATIVE DEAD!
DO YOU KNOW HOW MANY MURDERS THAT MAKES IN LESS THAN A MONTH?
THE HUNT HAS BEGUN!
AND ALL BECAUSE OF YOUR FAILURE!
TAKI!
I TOLD YOU I'D GIVE YOU THE FINEST MANPOWER AND WEAPONRY YOU NEEDED.
BUT THEN YOU HAD TO GO AND--
FATHER, PLEASE!
CAN'T YOU SEE TAKI-SAMA IS STILL HURT?
WHY THE HELL SHOULD I WAIT FOR HIS RECOVERY?

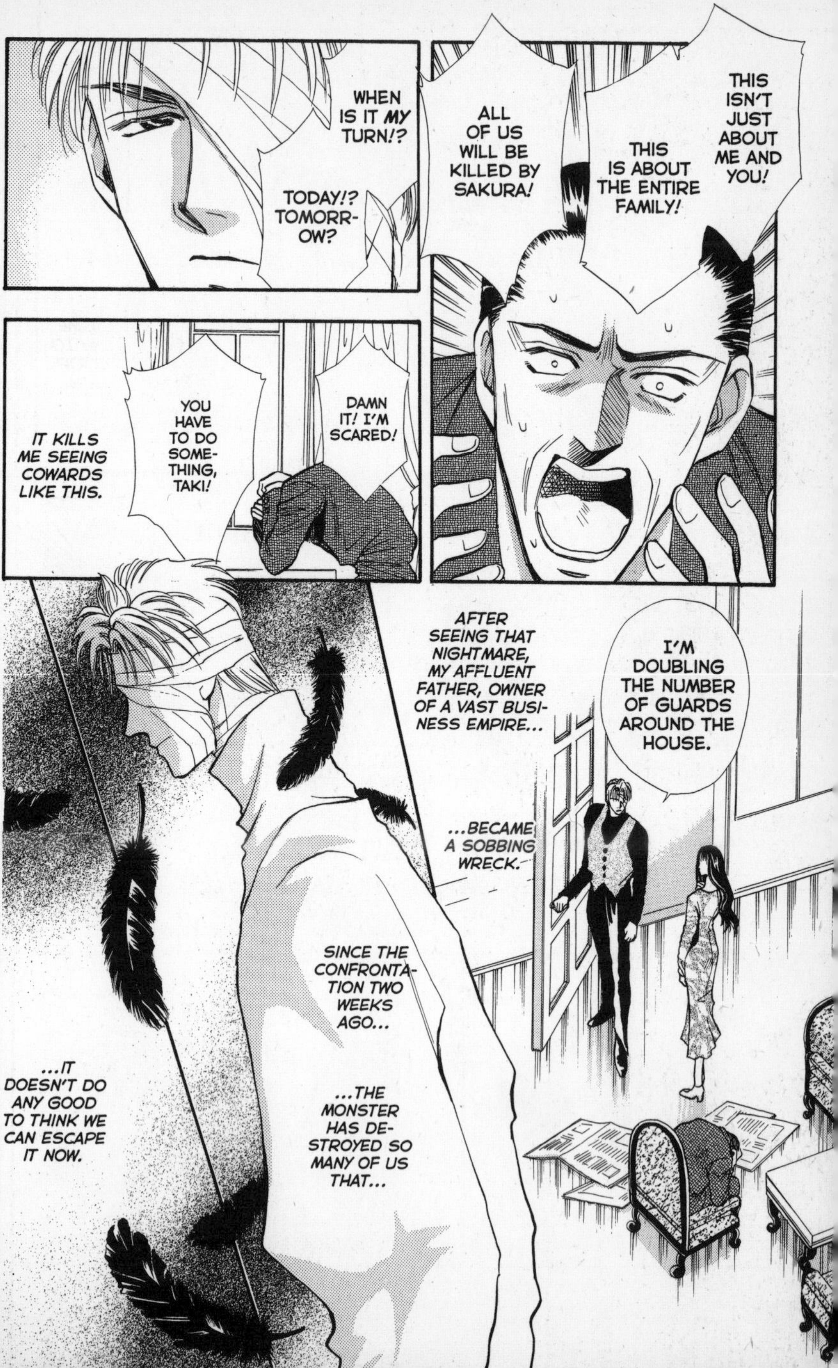
THIS ISN'T JUST ABOUT ME AND YOU!
THIS IS ABOUT THE ENTIRE FAMILY!
ALL OF US WILL BE KILLED BY SAKURA!
WHEN IS IT *MY* TURN!?
TODAY!? TOMORR-OW?
DAMN IT! I'M SCARED!
YOU HAVE TO DO SOME-THING, TAKI!
IT KILLS ME SEEING COWARDS LIKE THIS.
I'M DOUBLING THE NUMBER OF GUARDS AROUND THE HOUSE.
AFTER SEEING THAT NIGHTMARE, MY AFFLUENT FATHER, OWNER OF A VAST BUSI-NESS EMPIRE...
...BECAME A SOBBING WRECK.
SINCE THE CONFRONTA-TION TWO WEEKS AGO...
...THE MONSTER HAS DE-STROYED SO MANY OF US THAT...
...IT DOESN'T DO ANY GOOD TO THINK WE CAN ESCAPE IT NOW.

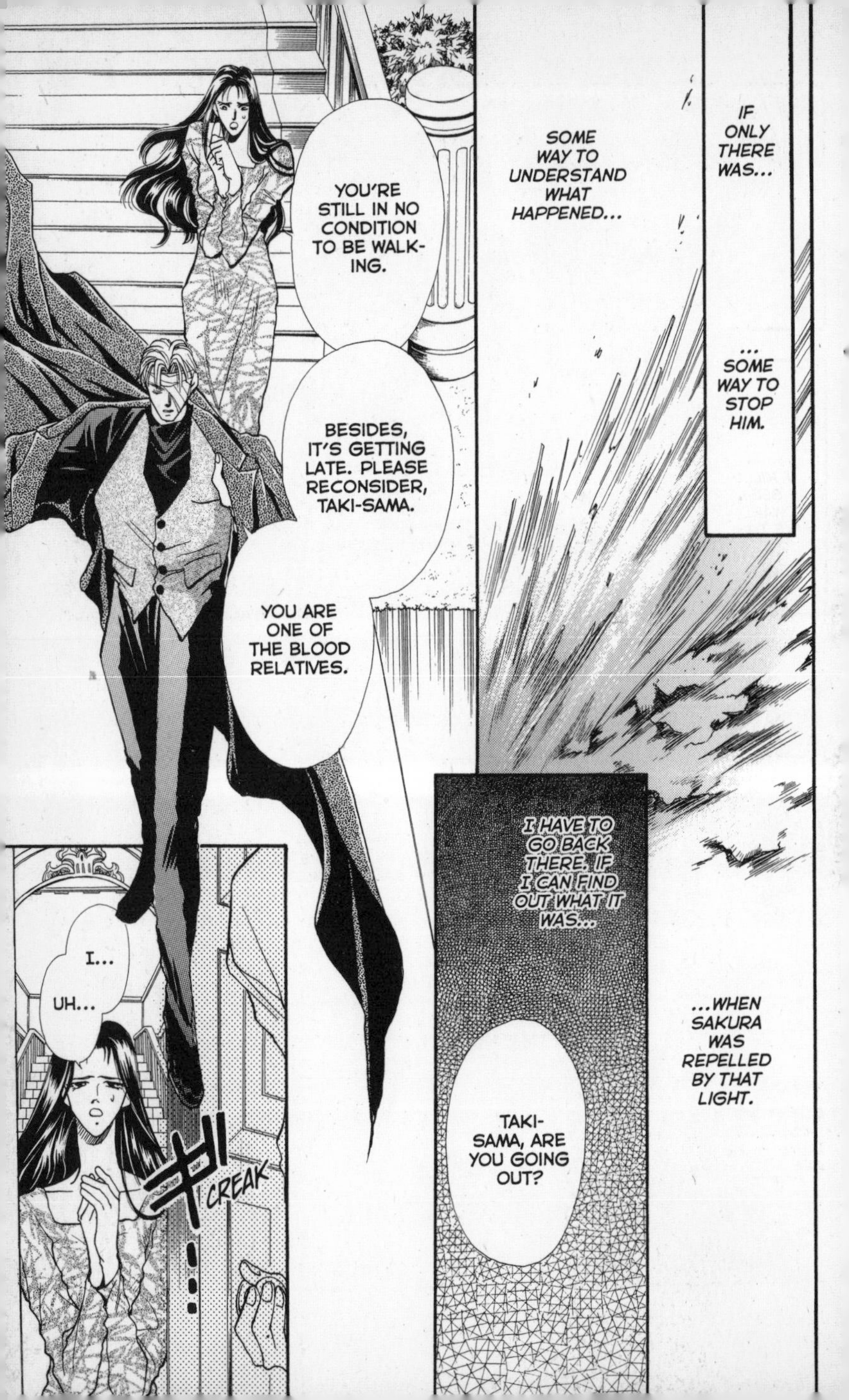
IF ONLY THERE WAS...
...SOME WAY TO STOP HIM.
SOME WAY TO UNDERSTAND WHAT HAPPENED...
...WHEN SAKURA WAS REPELLED BY THAT LIGHT.
I HAVE TO GO BACK THERE. IF I CAN FIND OUT WHAT IT WAS...
TAKI-SAMA, ARE YOU GOING OUT?
YOU'RE STILL IN NO CONDITION TO BE WALK-ING.
BESIDES, IT'S GETTING LATE. PLEASE RECONSIDER, TAKI-SAMA.
YOU ARE ONE OF THE BLOOD RELATIVES.
CREAK
I...
UH...

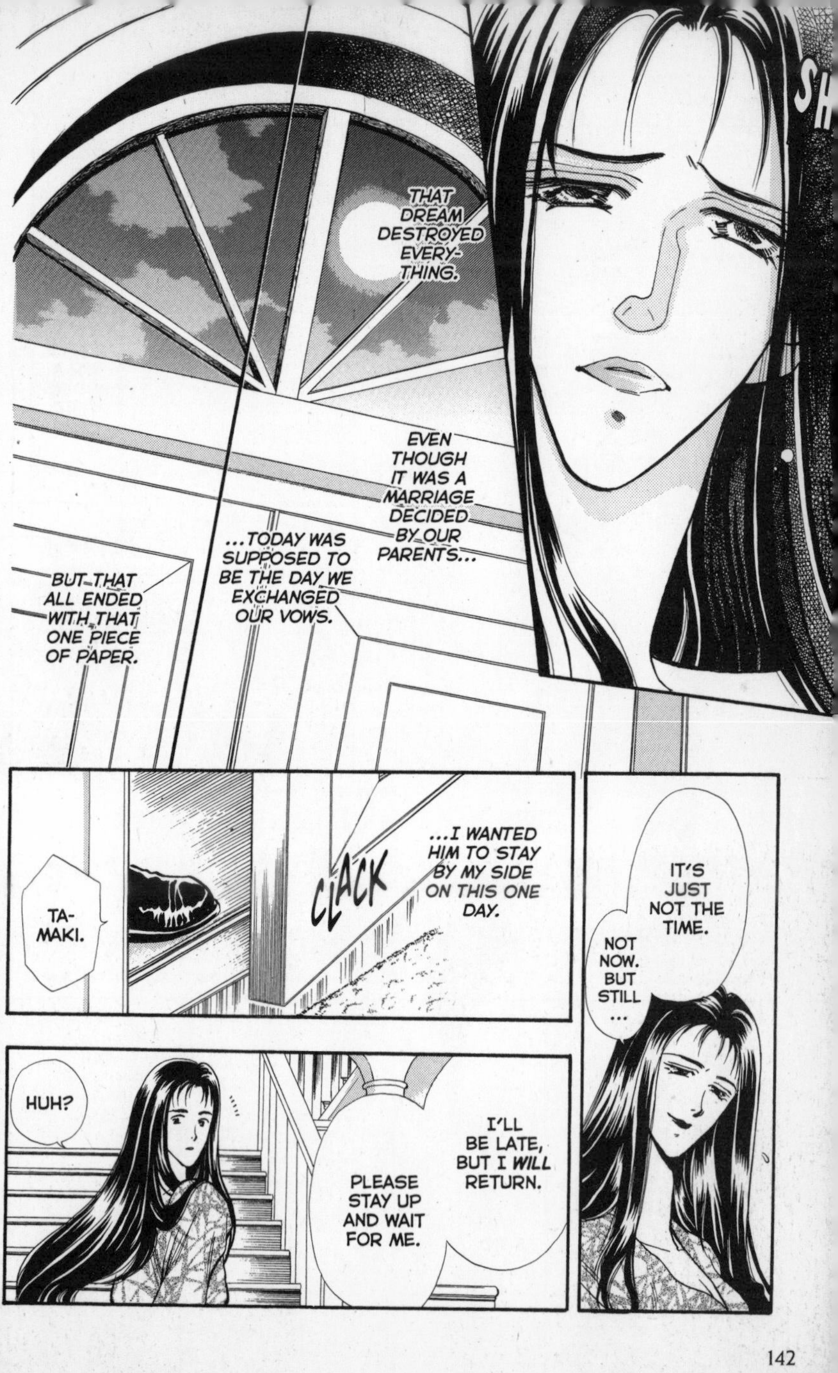
SH
THAT DREAM DESTROYED EVERY-THING.
EVEN THOUGH IT WAS A MARRIAGE DECIDED BY OUR PARENTS...
...TODAY WAS SUPPOSED TO BE THE DAY WE EXCHANGED OUR VOWS.
BUT THAT ALL ENDED WITH THAT ONE PIECE OF PAPER.
IT'S JUST NOT THE TIME.
NOT NOW. BUT STILL ...
...I WANTED HIM TO STAY BY MY SIDE ON THIS ONE DAY.
CLACK
TA-MAKI.
I'LL BE LATE, BUT I WILL RETURN.
PLEASE STAY UP AND WAIT FOR ME.
HUH?

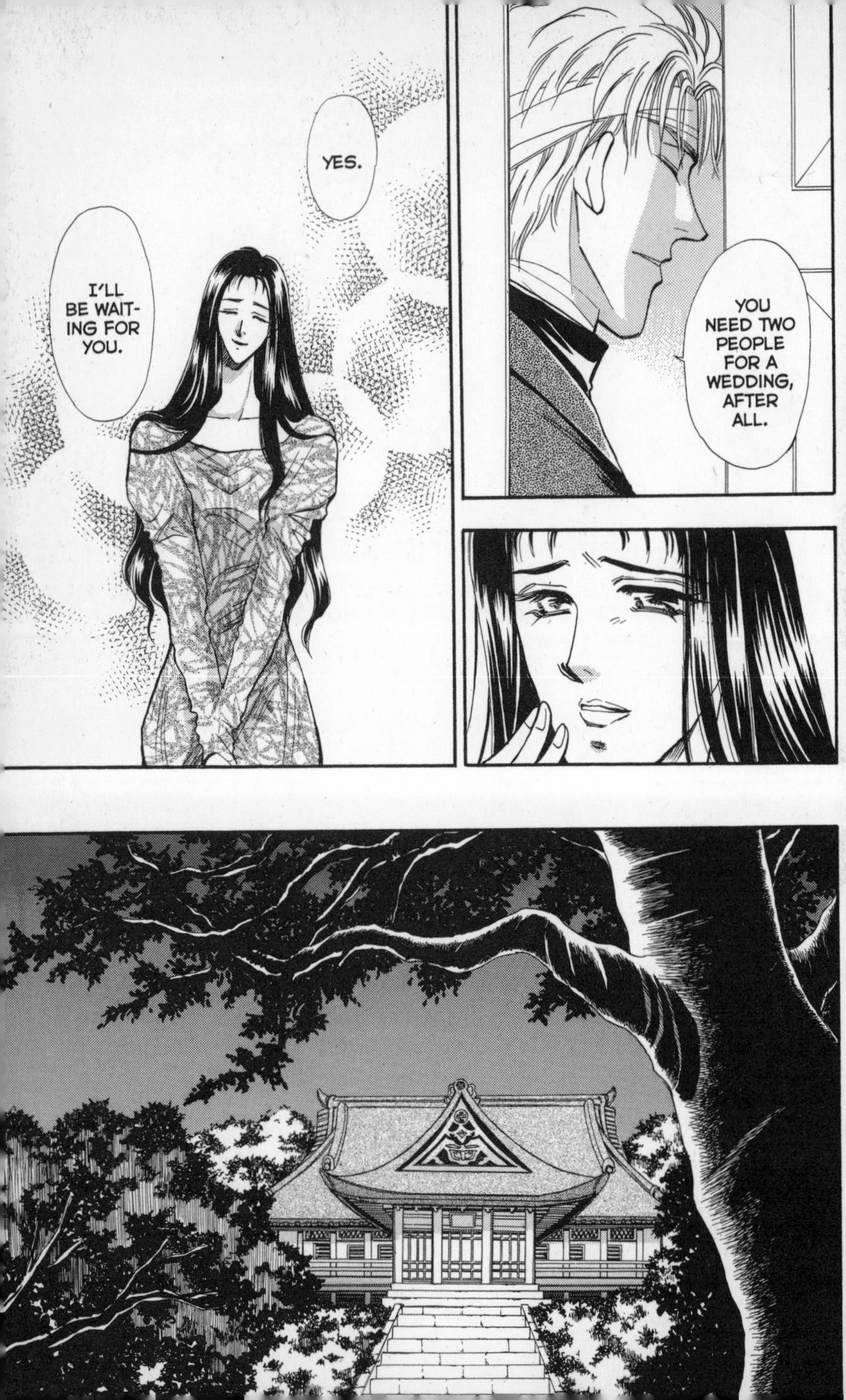
YOU NEED TWO PEOPLE FOR A WEDDING, AFTER ALL.
YES.
I'LL BE WAITING FOR YOU.

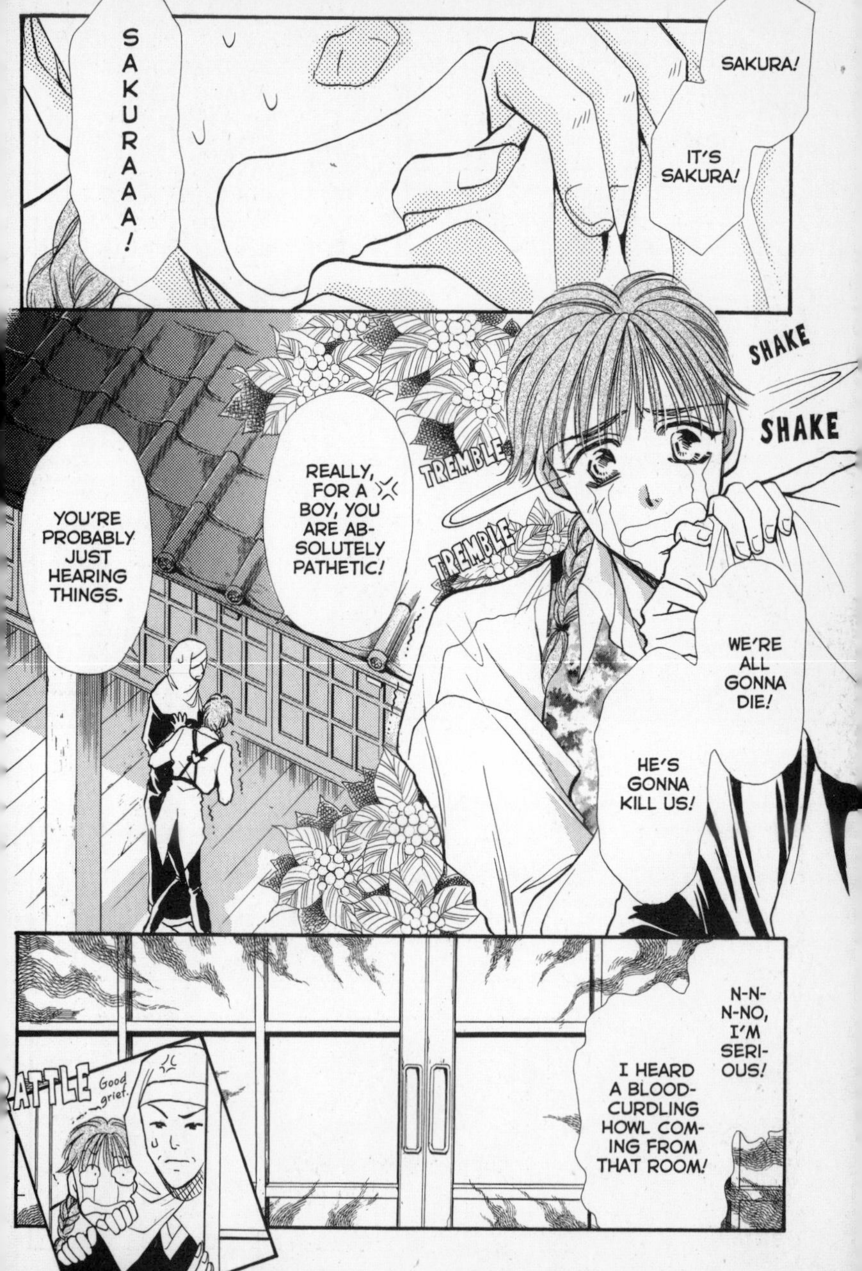
SAKURA!
IT'S SAKURA!
SAKURAAAA!
SHAKE
SHAKE
TREMBLE
TREMBLE
WE'RE ALL GONNA DIE!
HE'S GONNA KILL US!
REALLY, FOR A BOY, YOU ARE ABSOLUTELY PATHETIC!
YOU'RE PROBABLY JUST HEARING THINGS.
N-N-N-NO, I'M SERIOUS!
I HEARD A BLOOD-CURDLING HOWL COMING FROM THAT ROOM!
Good grief.
RATTLE

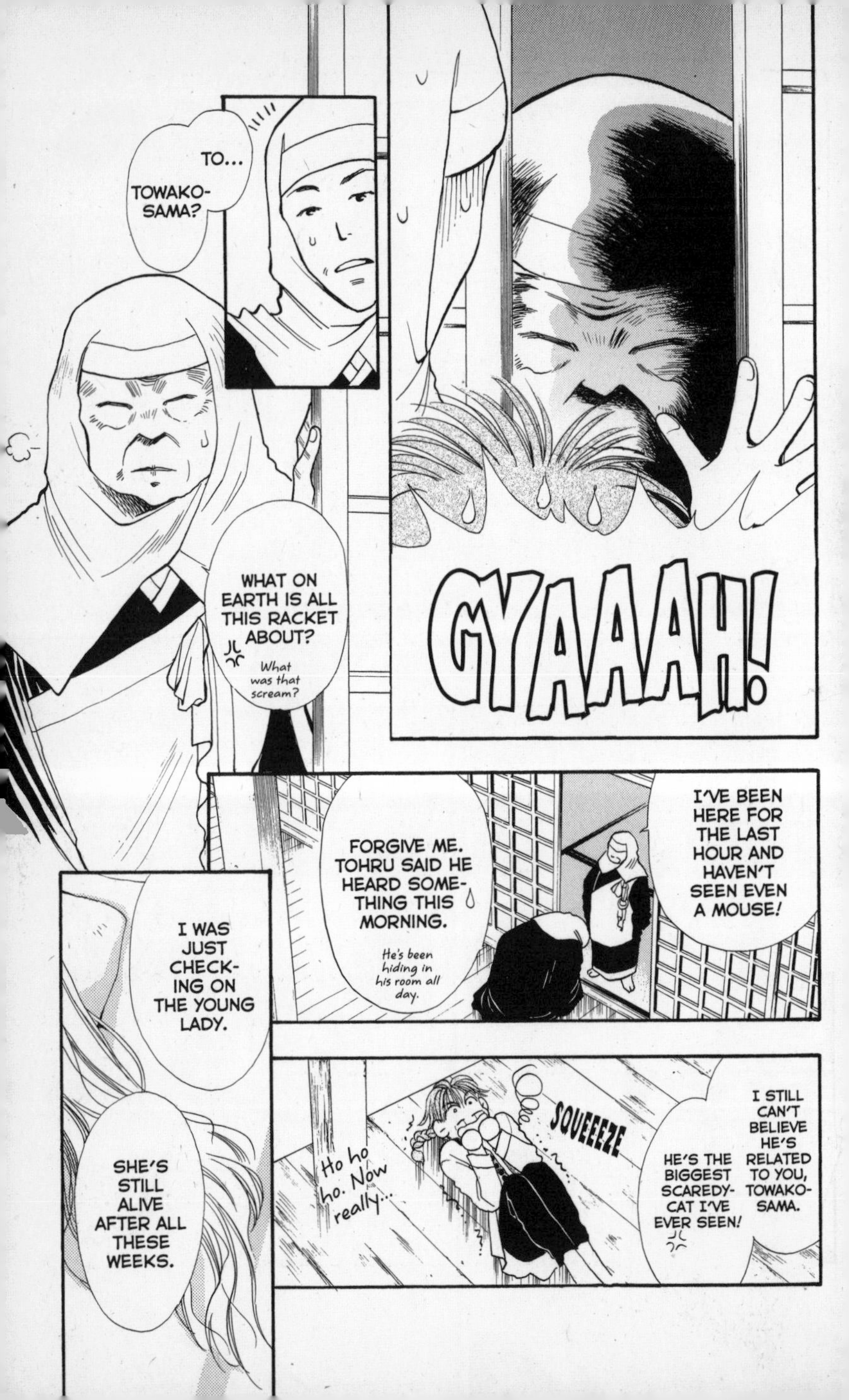
GYAAAH!
TO... TOWAKO-SAMA?
WHAT ON EARTH IS ALL THIS RACKET ABOUT?
What was that scream?
I'VE BEEN HERE FOR THE LAST HOUR AND HAVEN'T SEEN EVEN A MOUSE!
FORGIVE ME. TOHRU SAID HE HEARD SOME-THING THIS MORNING.
He's been hiding in his room all day.
I STILL CAN'T BELIEVE HE'S RELATED TO YOU, TOWAKO-SAMA.
HE'S THE BIGGEST SCAREDY-CAT I'VE EVER SEEN!
SQUEEEZE
Ho ho ho. Now really...
I WAS JUST CHECK-ING ON THE YOUNG LADY.
SHE'S STILL ALIVE AFTER ALL THESE WEEKS.

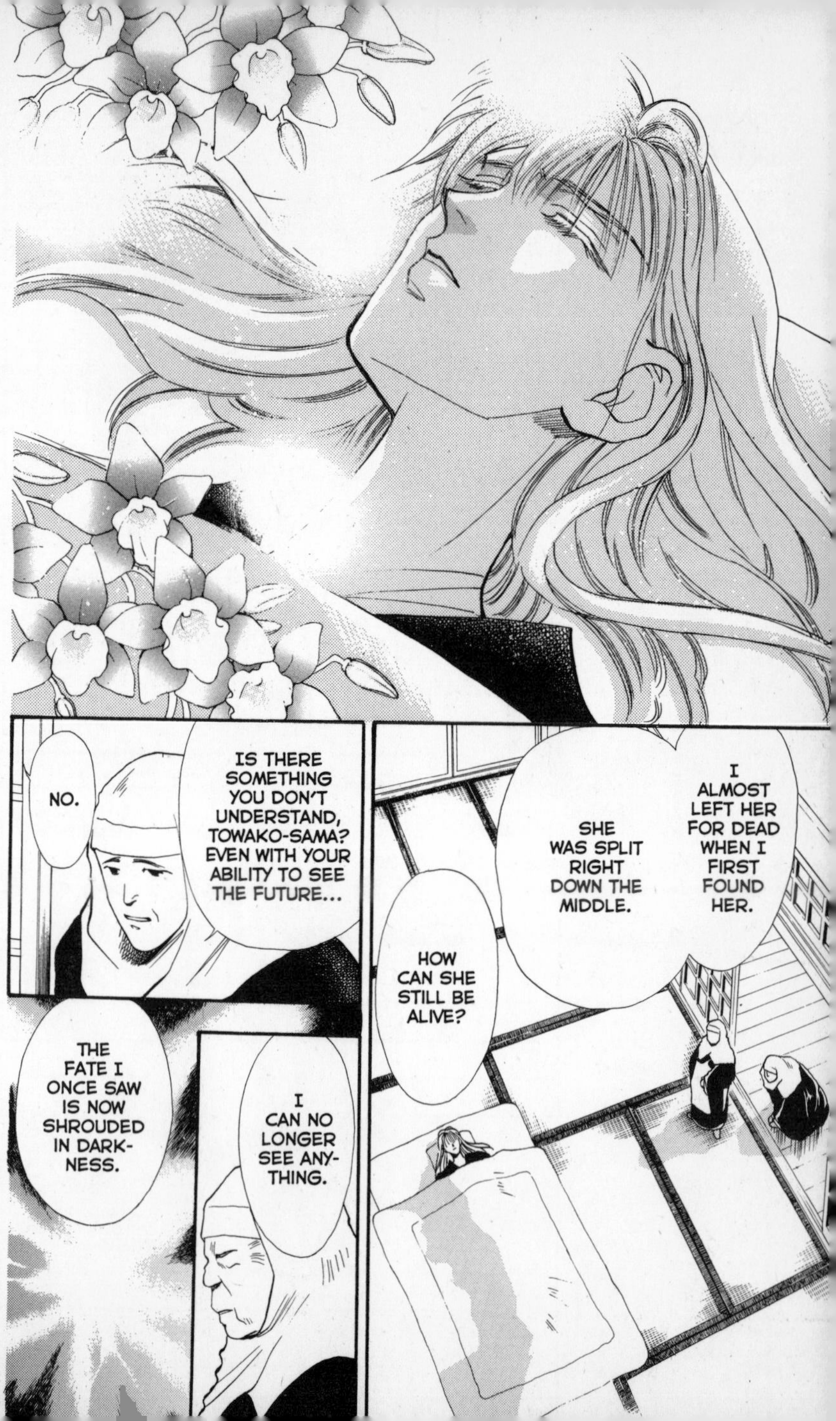
I ALMOST LEFT HER FOR DEAD WHEN I FIRST FOUND HER.
SHE WAS SPLIT RIGHT DOWN THE MIDDLE.
HOW CAN SHE STILL BE ALIVE?
IS THERE SOMETHING YOU DON'T UNDERSTAND, TOWAKO-SAMA? EVEN WITH YOUR ABILITY TO SEE THE FUTURE...
NO.
I CAN NO LONGER SEE ANY-THING.
THE FATE I ONCE SAW IS NOW SHROUDED IN DARK-NESS.

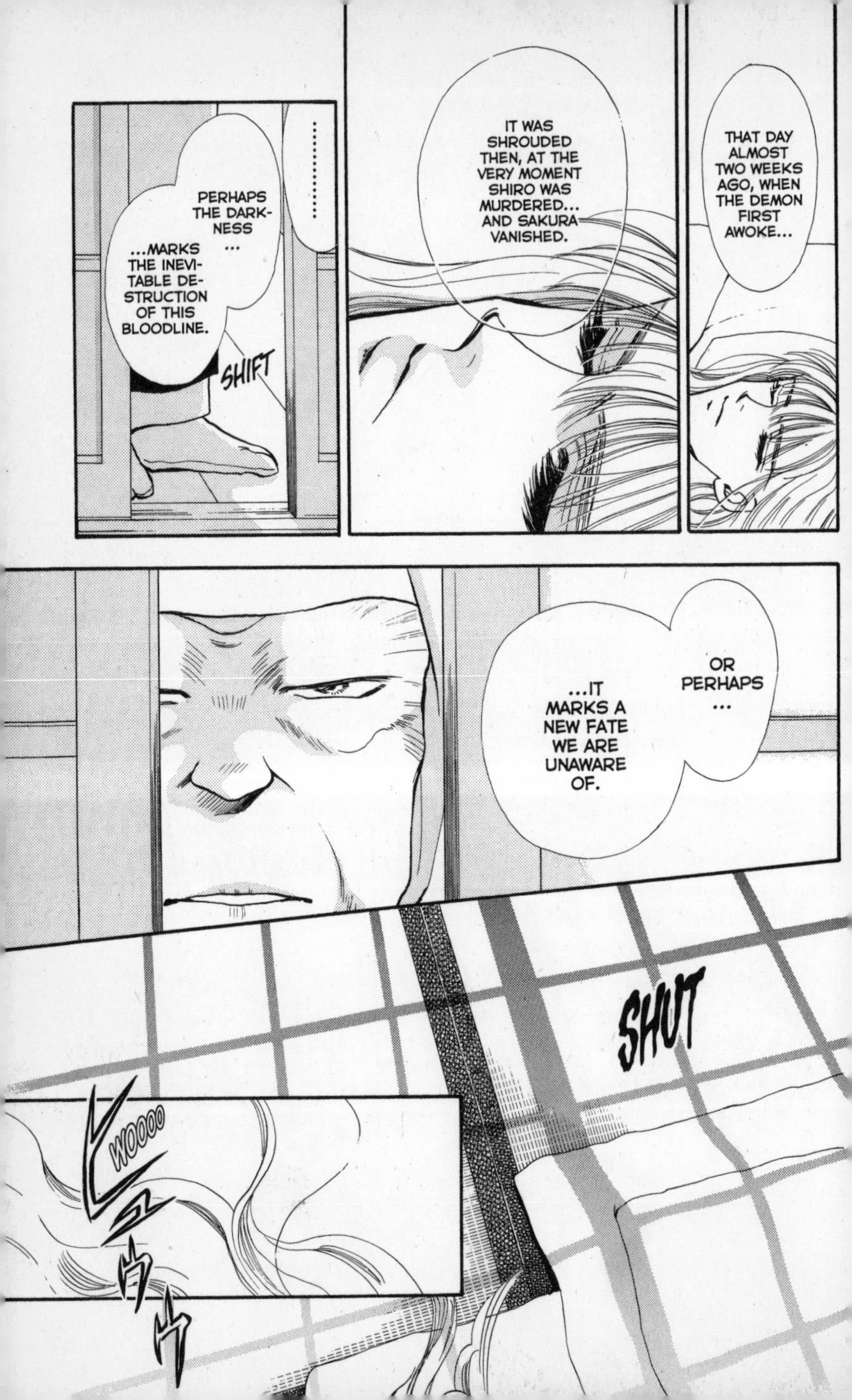
THAT DAY ALMOST TWO WEEKS AGO, WHEN THE DEMON FIRST AWOKE...
IT WAS SHROUDED THEN, AT THE VERY MOMENT SHIRO WAS MURDERED... AND SAKURA VANISHED.
......
PERHAPS THE DARKNESS ...
...MARKS THE INEVITABLE DESTRUCTION OF THIS BLOODLINE.
SHIFT
OR PERHAPS ...
...IT MARKS A NEW FATE WE ARE UNAWARE OF.
SHUT
WOOOO

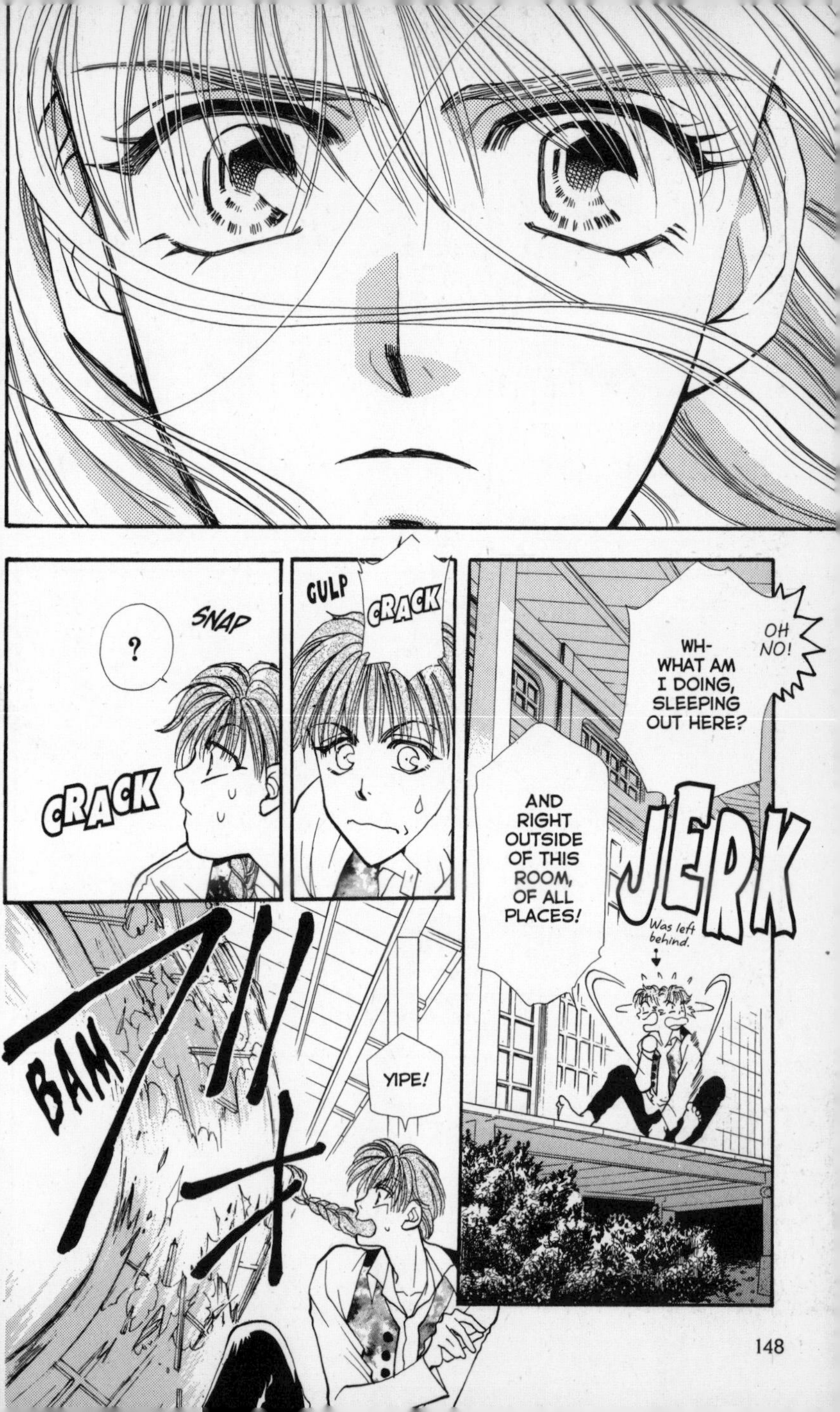

OH NO!
WH- WHAT AM I DOING, SLEEPING OUT HERE?
AND RIGHT OUTSIDE OF THIS ROOM, OF ALL PLACES!
JERK
Was left behind.
CRACK
GULP
?
SNAP
CRACK
YIPE!
BAM

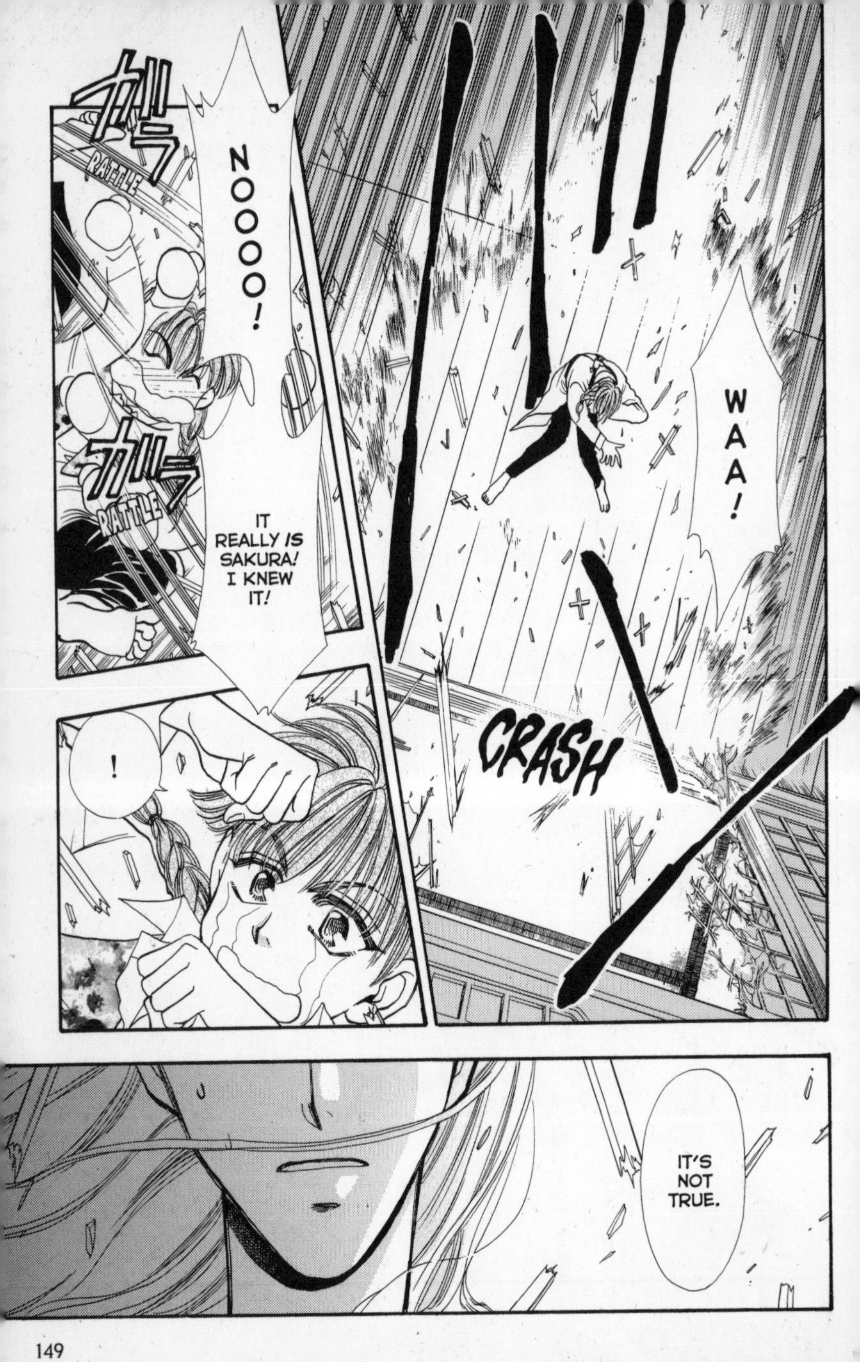
WAA!
CRASH
NOOOOO!
カラ RATTLE
IT REALLY IS SAKURA! I KNEW IT!
カラ RATTLE
!
IT'S NOT TRUE.

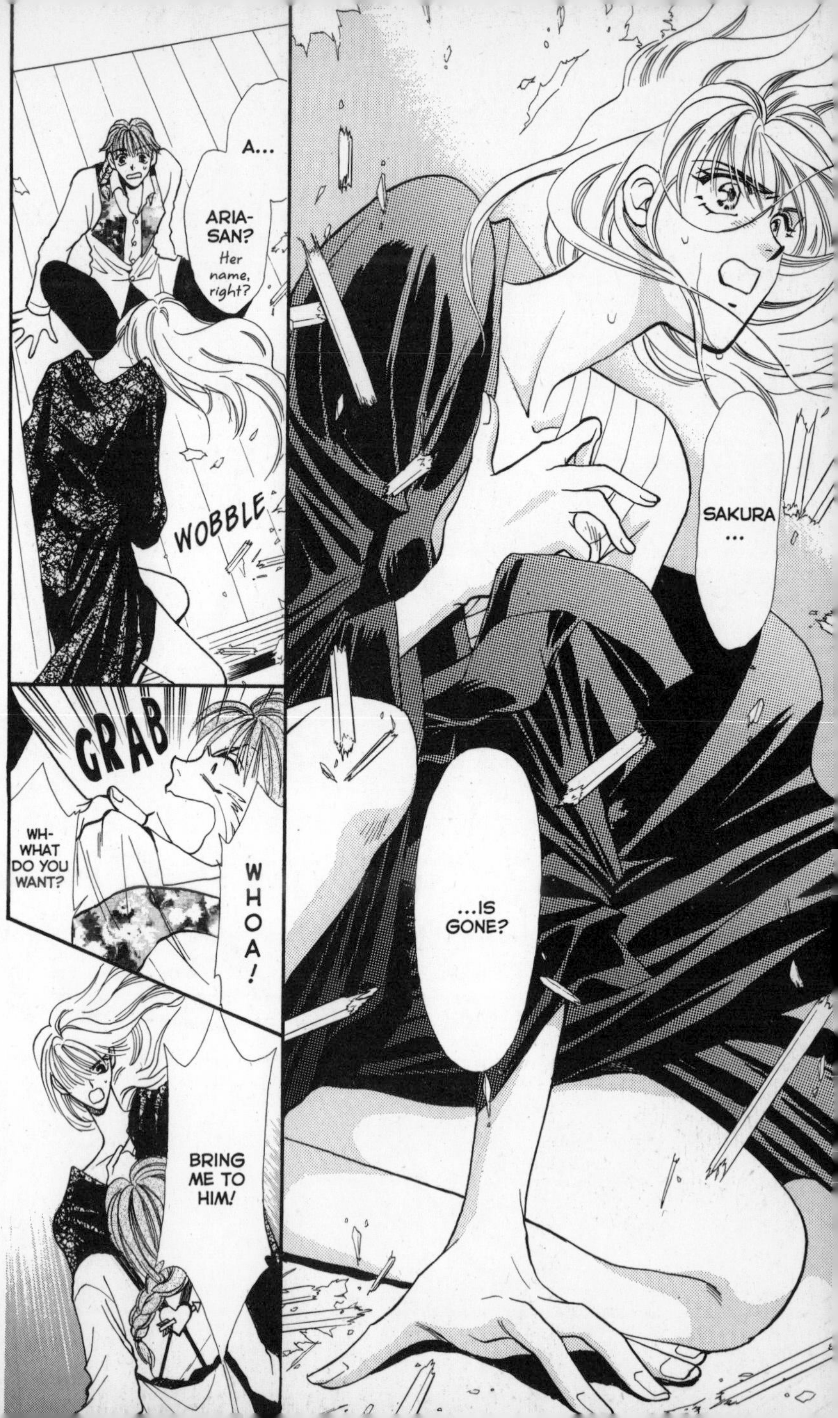
SAKURA ...
...IS GONE?
A...
ARIA-SAN? Her name, right?
WOBBLE
GRAB
WHOA!
WH-WHAT DO YOU WANT?
BRING ME TO HIM!

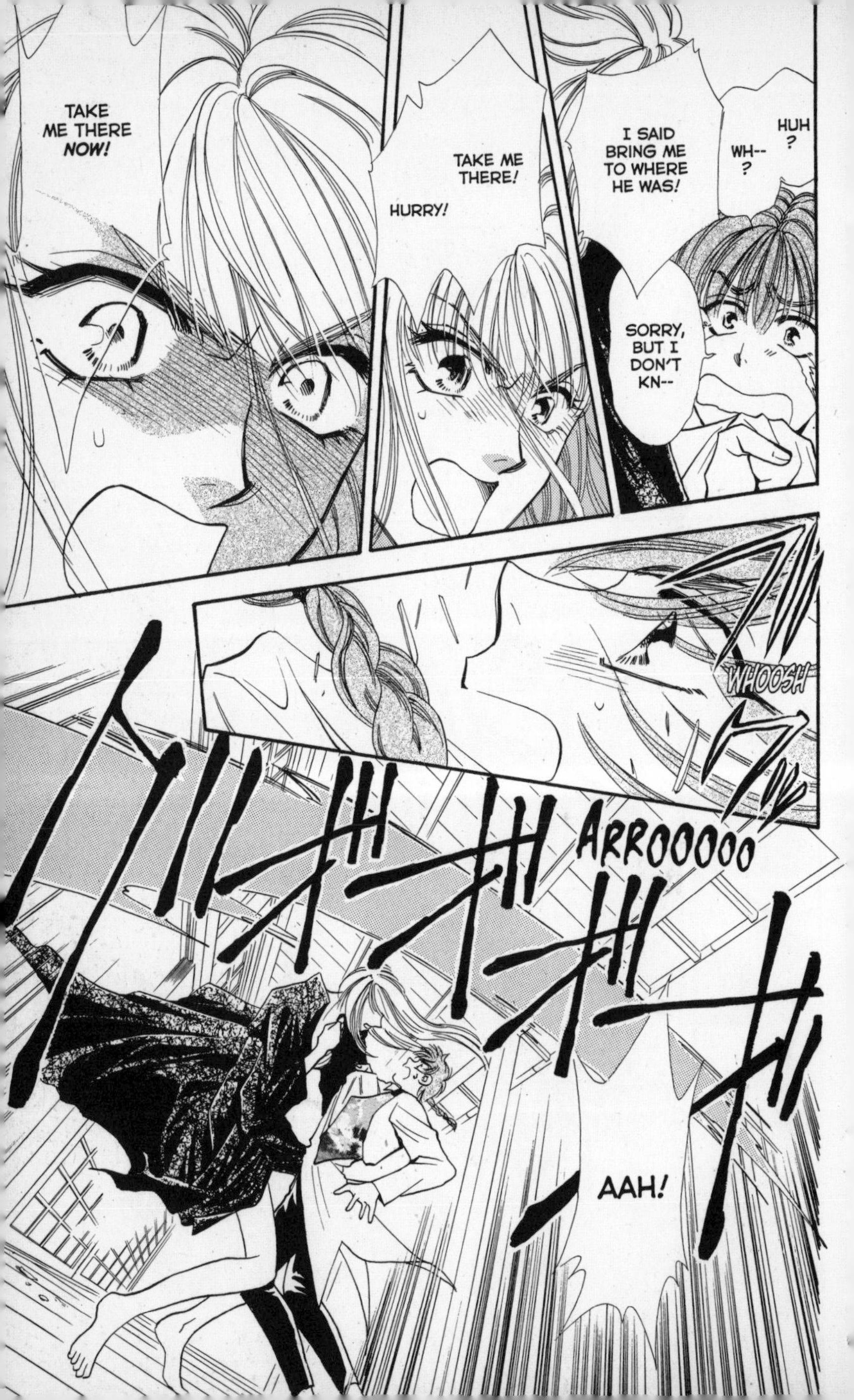

HUH ?
WH-- ?
I SAID BRING ME TO WHERE HE WAS!
SORRY, BUT I DON'T KN--
TAKE ME THERE!
HURRY!
TAKE ME THERE *NOW!*
WHOOSH
ARROOOOO
AAH!

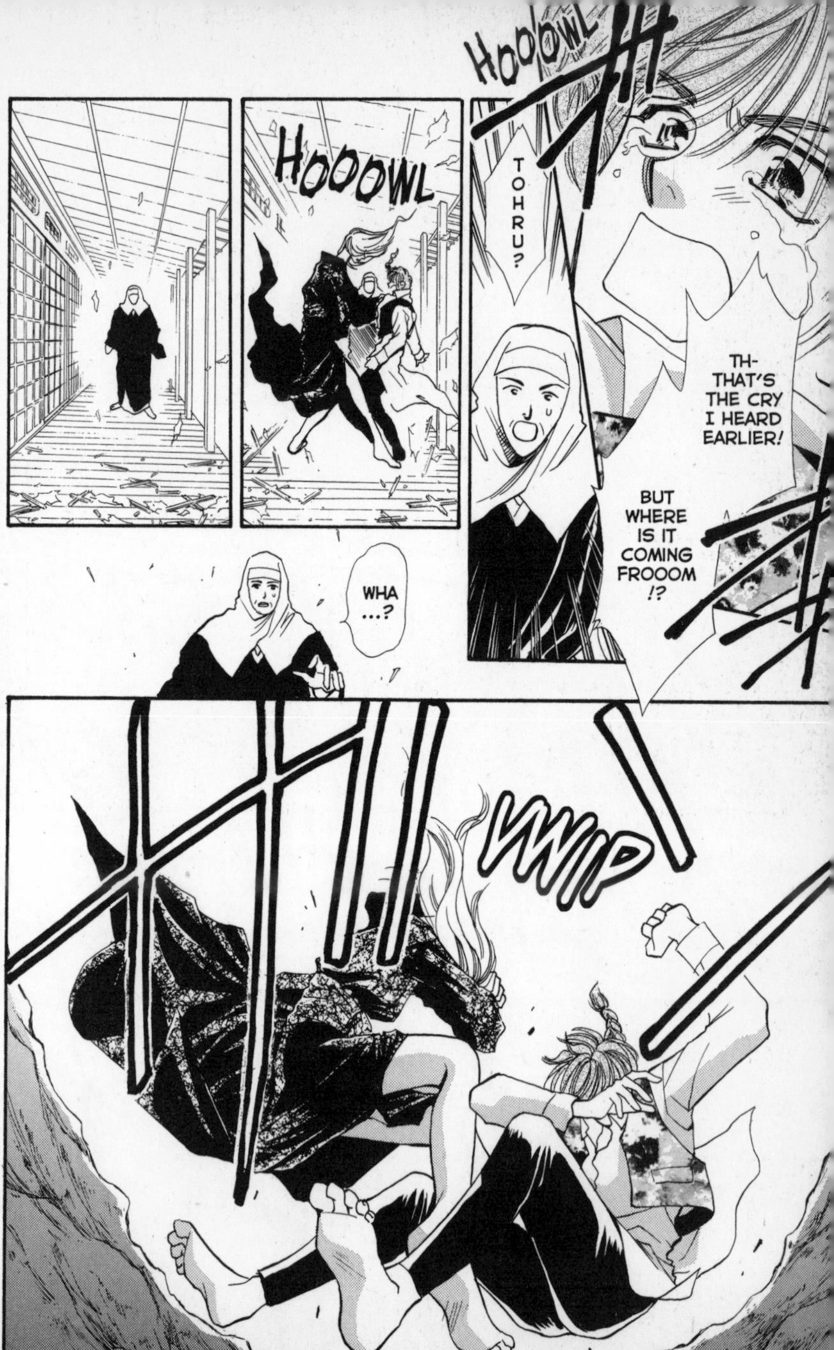
HOOOWL
TOHRU?
TH- THAT'S THE CRY I HEARD EARLIER!
BUT WHERE IS IT COMING FROOOM!?
HOOOWL
WHA ...?
VWIP

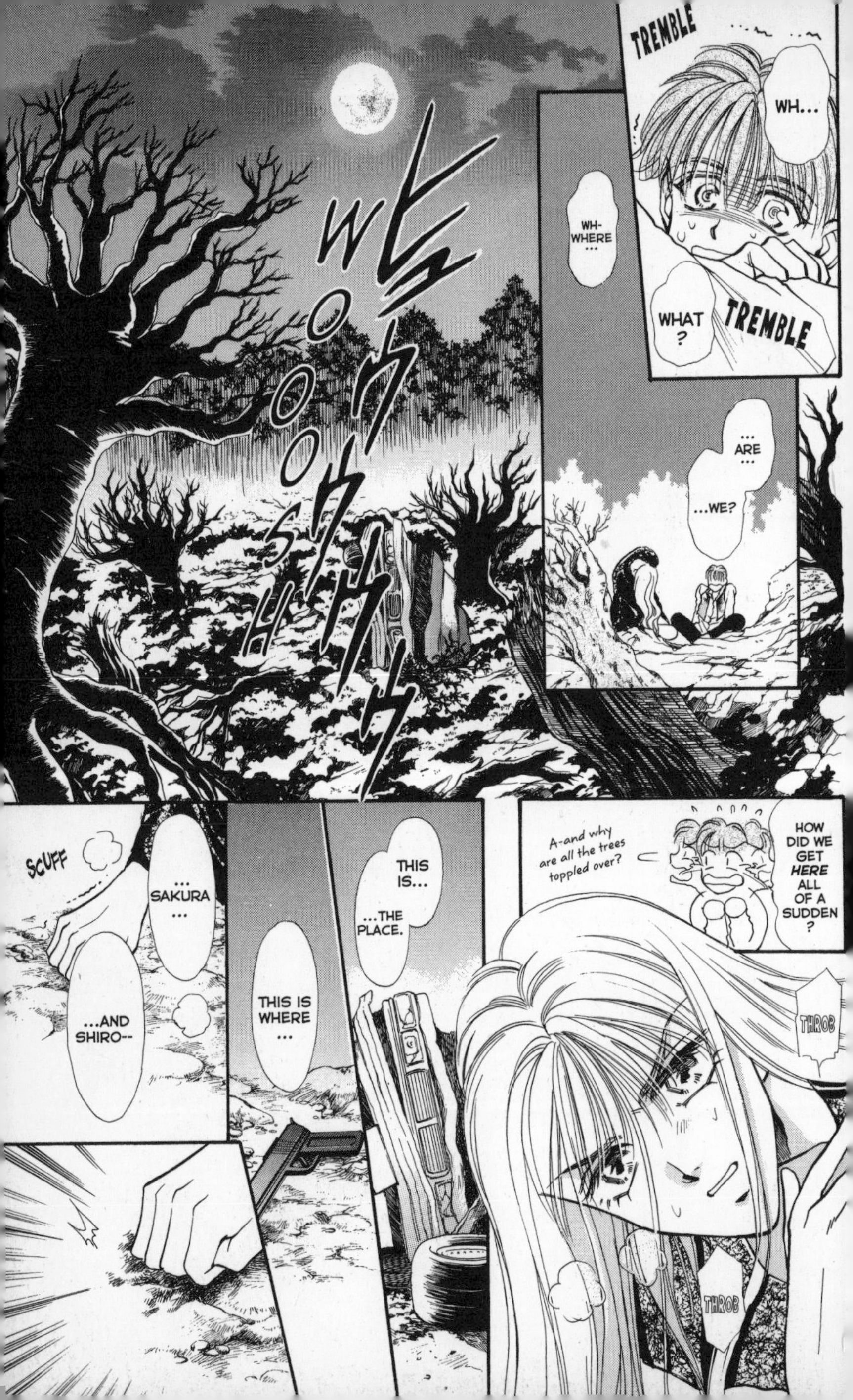

TREMBLE
...~ ...~
WH...
WHAT?
TREMBLE
WH-WHERE...
...ARE...
...WE?
HOW DID WE GET HERE ALL OF A SUDDEN?
A-and why are all the trees toppled over?
THROB
THROB
THIS IS...
...THE PLACE.
THIS IS WHERE...
SCUFF
...SAKURA...
...AND SHIRO--

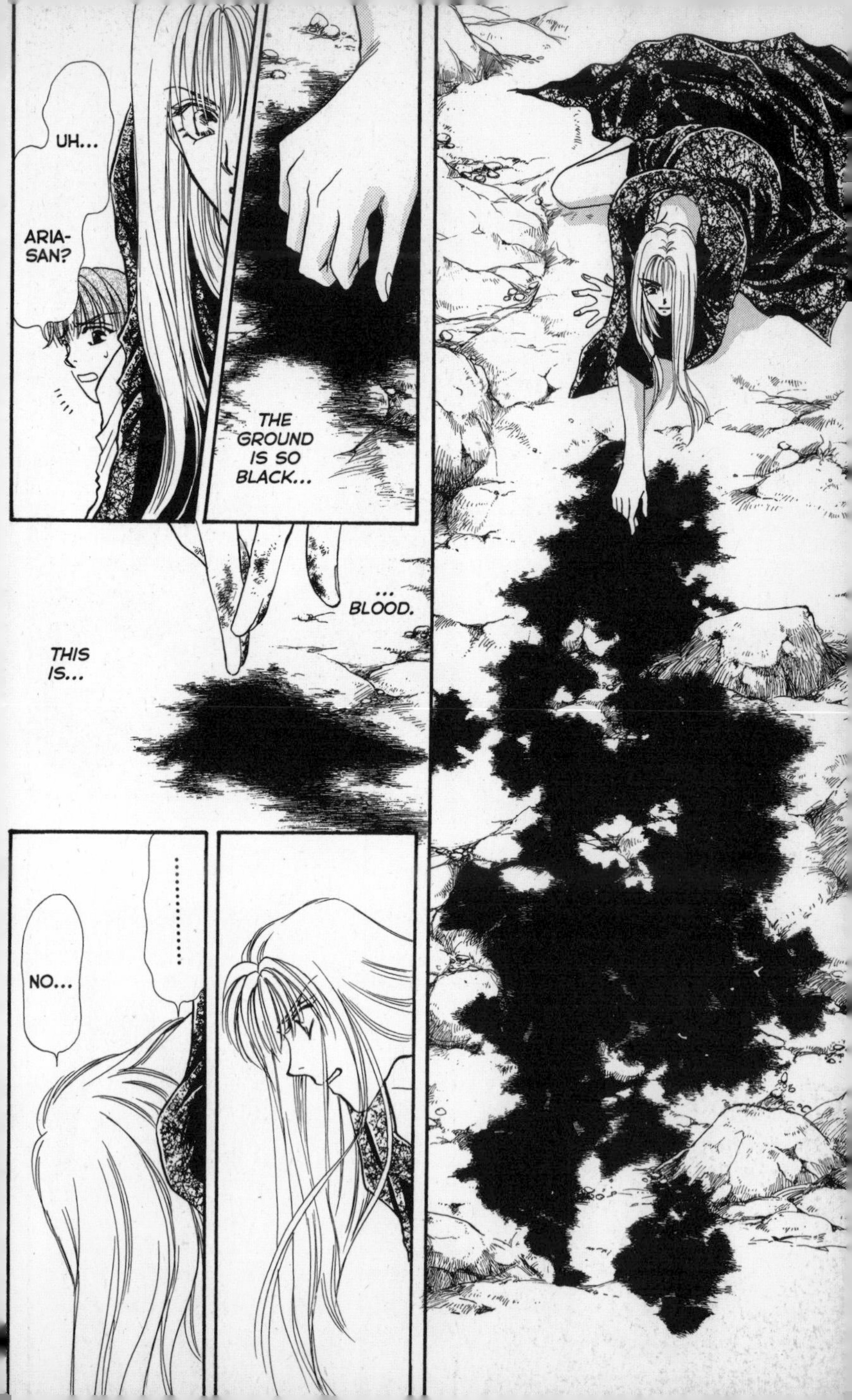
THE GROUND IS SO BLACK...
UH...
ARIA-SAN?
...BLOOD.
THIS IS...
....
NO...

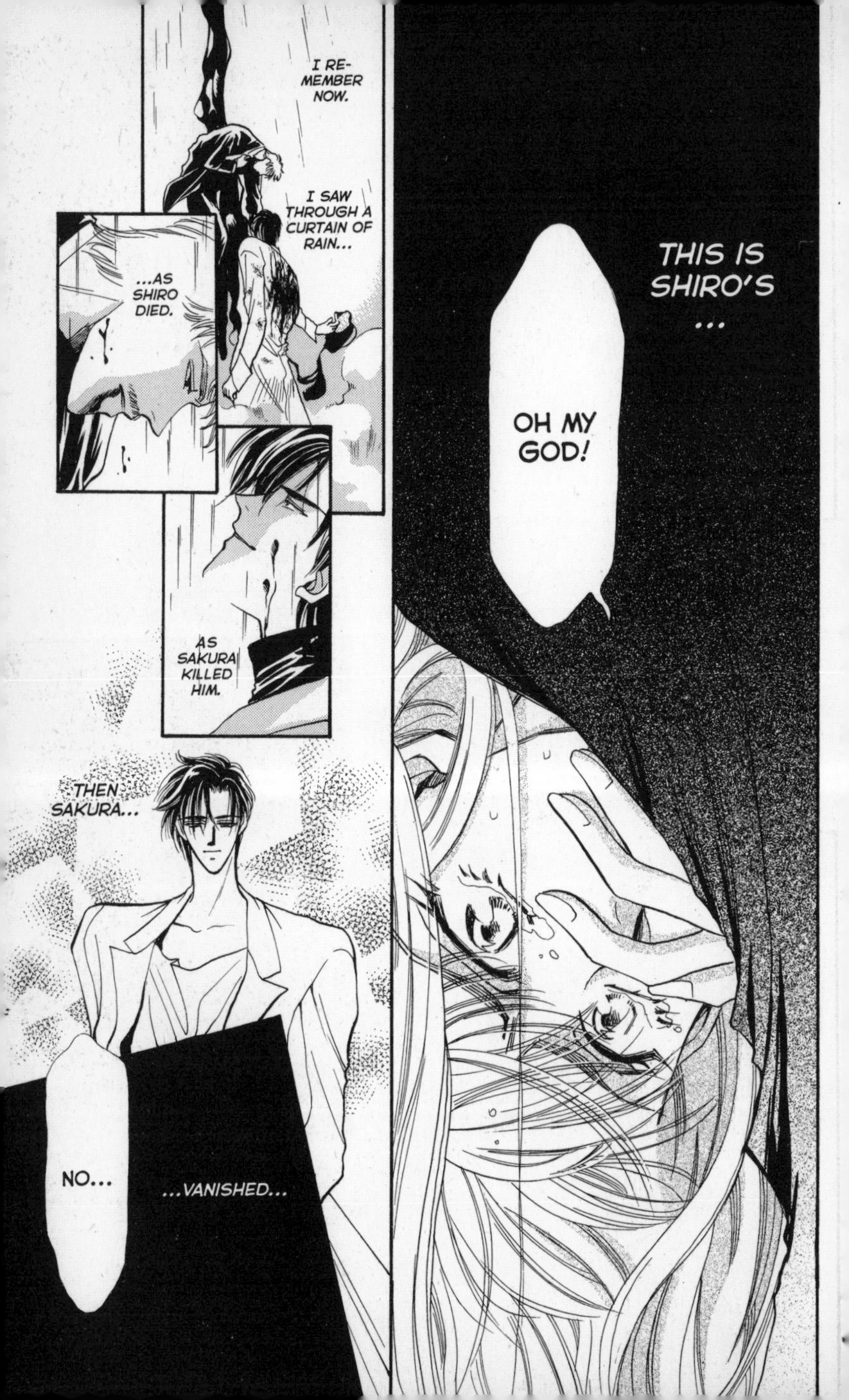
I RE-
MEMBER
NOW.
I SAW
THROUGH A
CURTAIN OF
RAIN...
...AS
SHIRO
DIED.
AS
SAKURA
KILLED
HIM.
THEN
SAKURA...
...VANISHED...
NO...
THIS IS
SHIRO'S
...
OH MY
GOD!

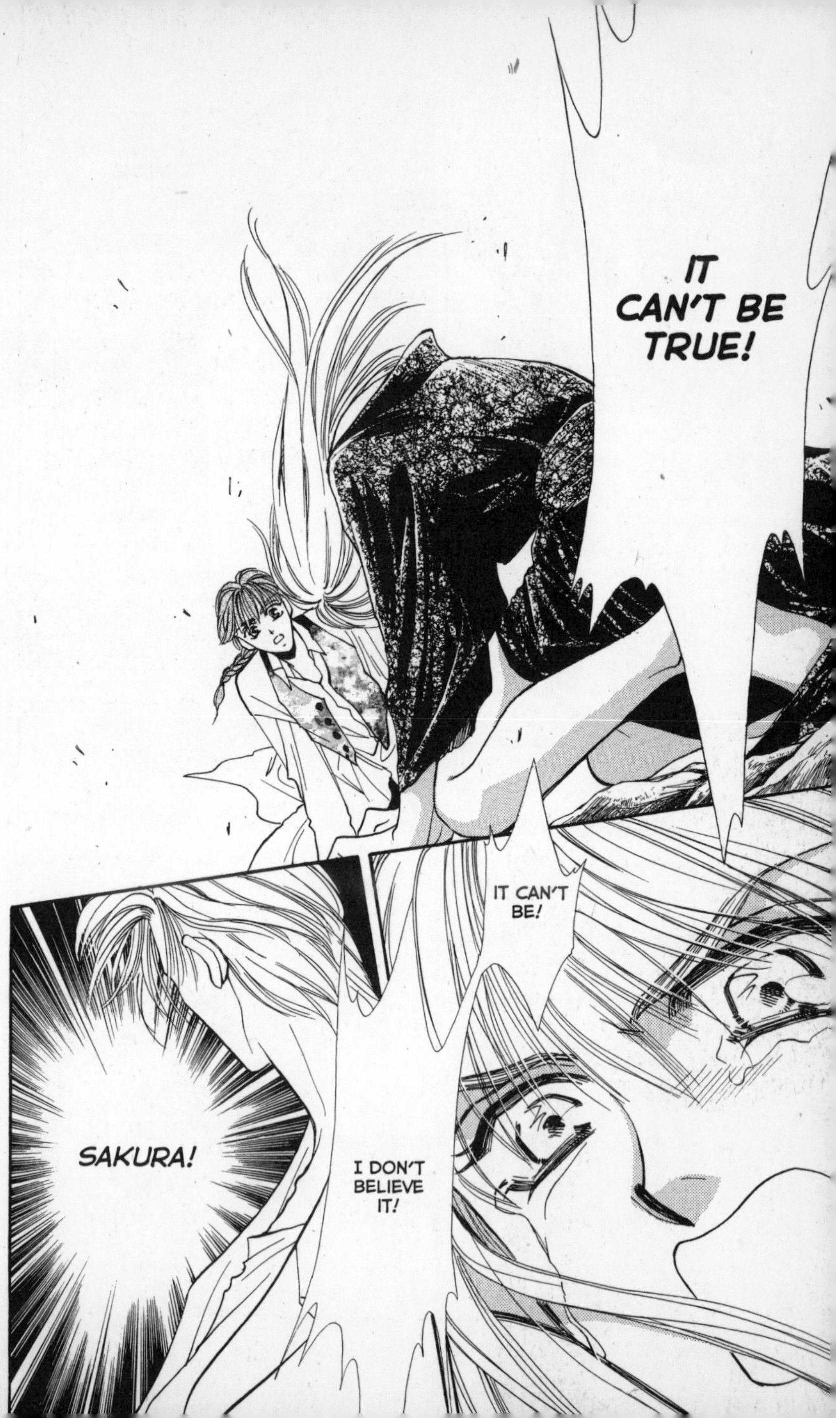
IT CAN'T BE TRUE!
IT CAN'T BE!
I DON'T BELIEVE IT!
SAKURA!

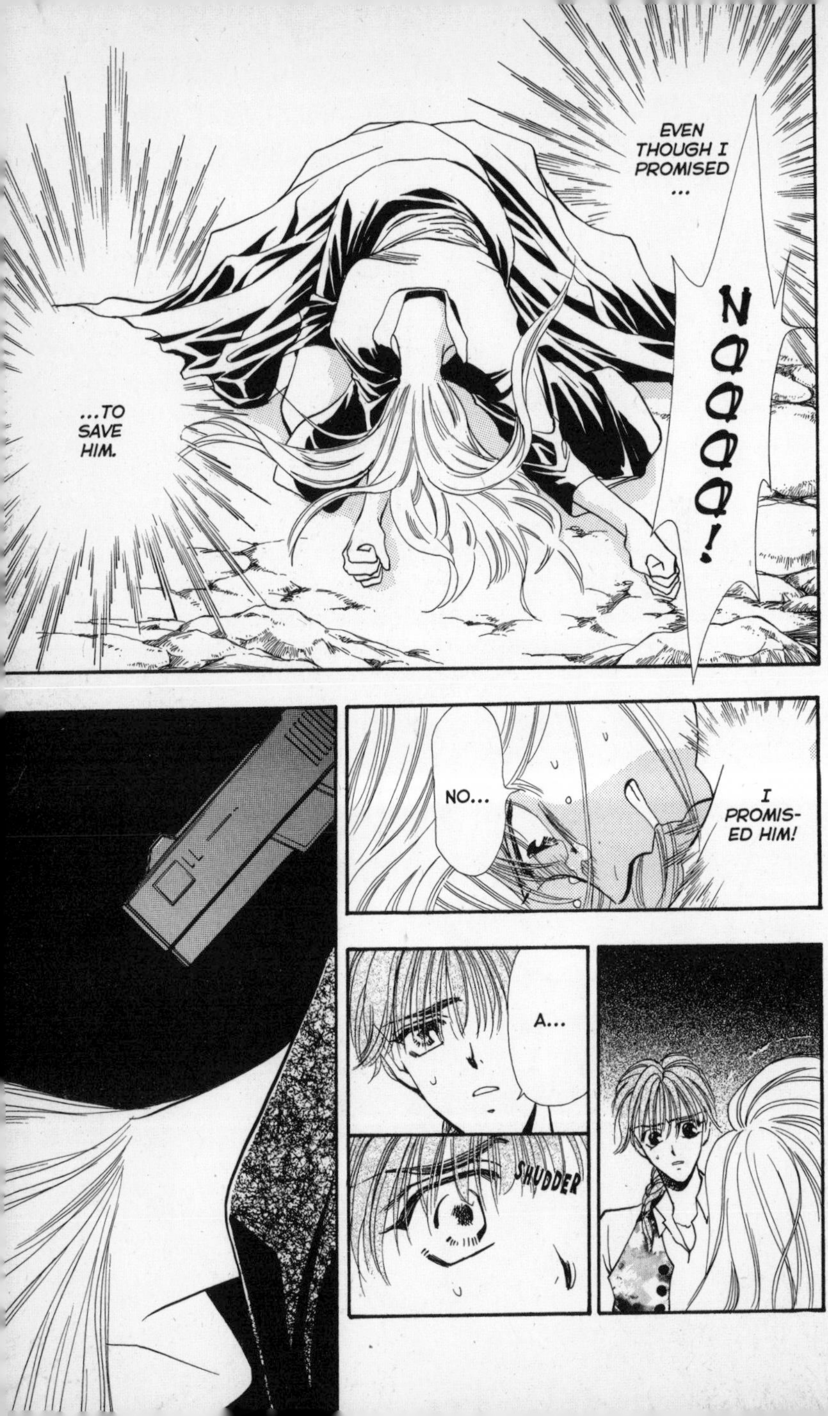
EVEN THOUGH I PROMISED ...
NOOOOO!
...TO SAVE HIM.
I PROMIS-ED HIM!
NO...
A...
SHUDDER

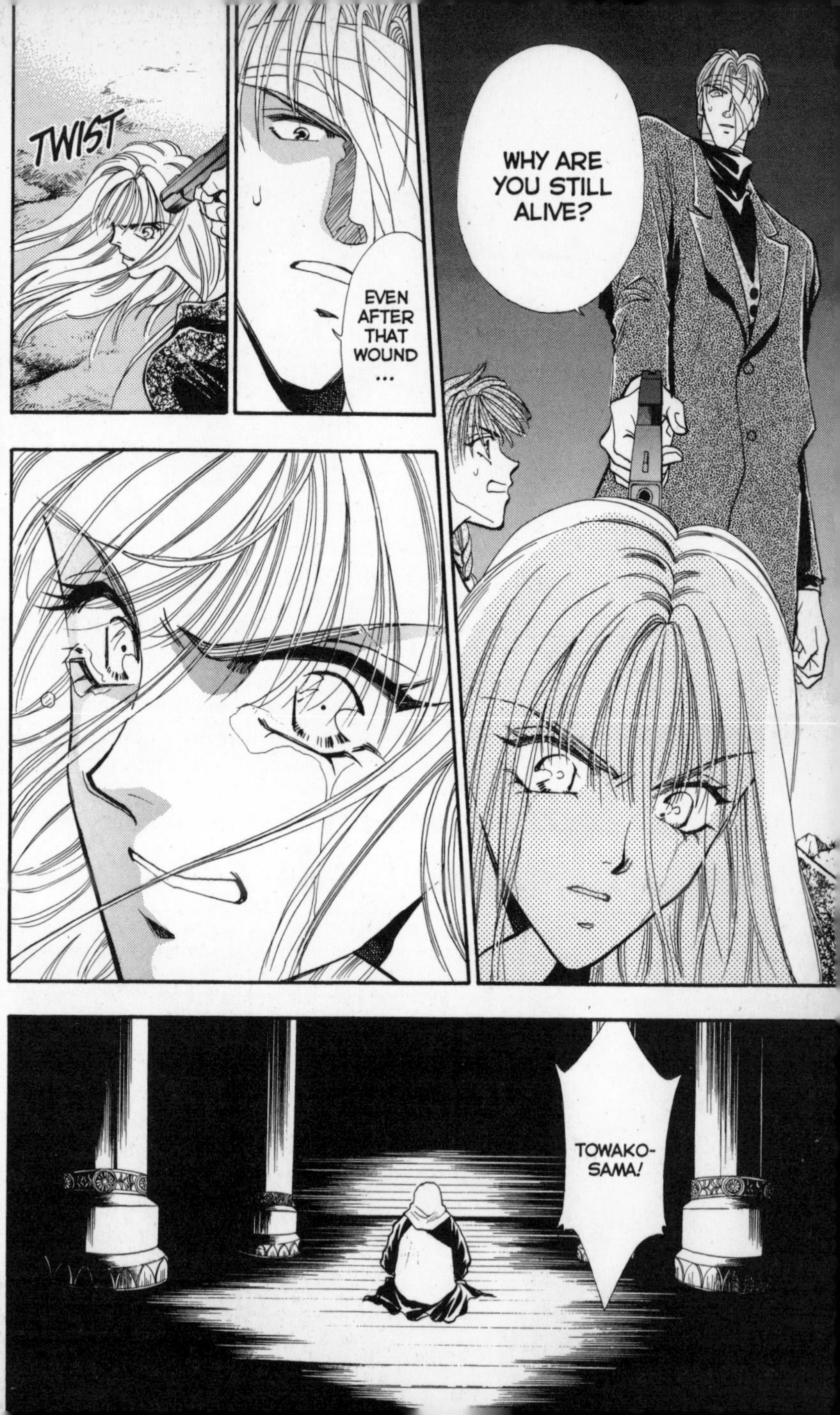
WHY ARE YOU STILL ALIVE?
EVEN AFTER THAT WOUND ...
TWIST
TOWAKO-SAMA!

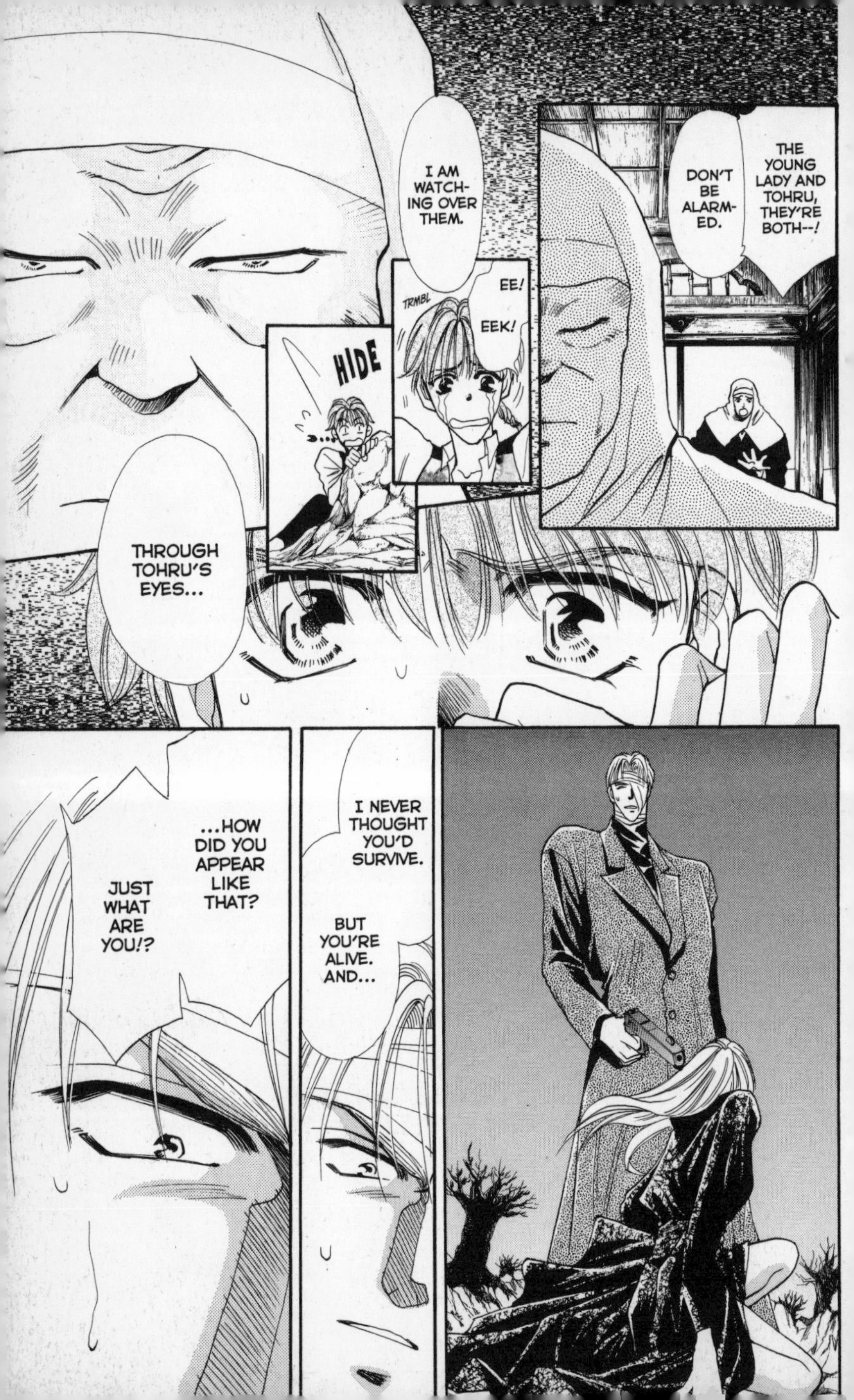
THE YOUNG LADY AND TOHRU, THEY'RE BOTH--!
DON'T BE ALARMED.
I AM WATCHING OVER THEM.
EE!
EEK!
TRMBL
HIDE
THROUGH TOHRU'S EYES...
I NEVER THOUGHT YOU'D SURVIVE.
BUT YOU'RE ALIVE. AND...
...HOW DID YOU APPEAR LIKE THAT?
JUST WHAT ARE YOU!?

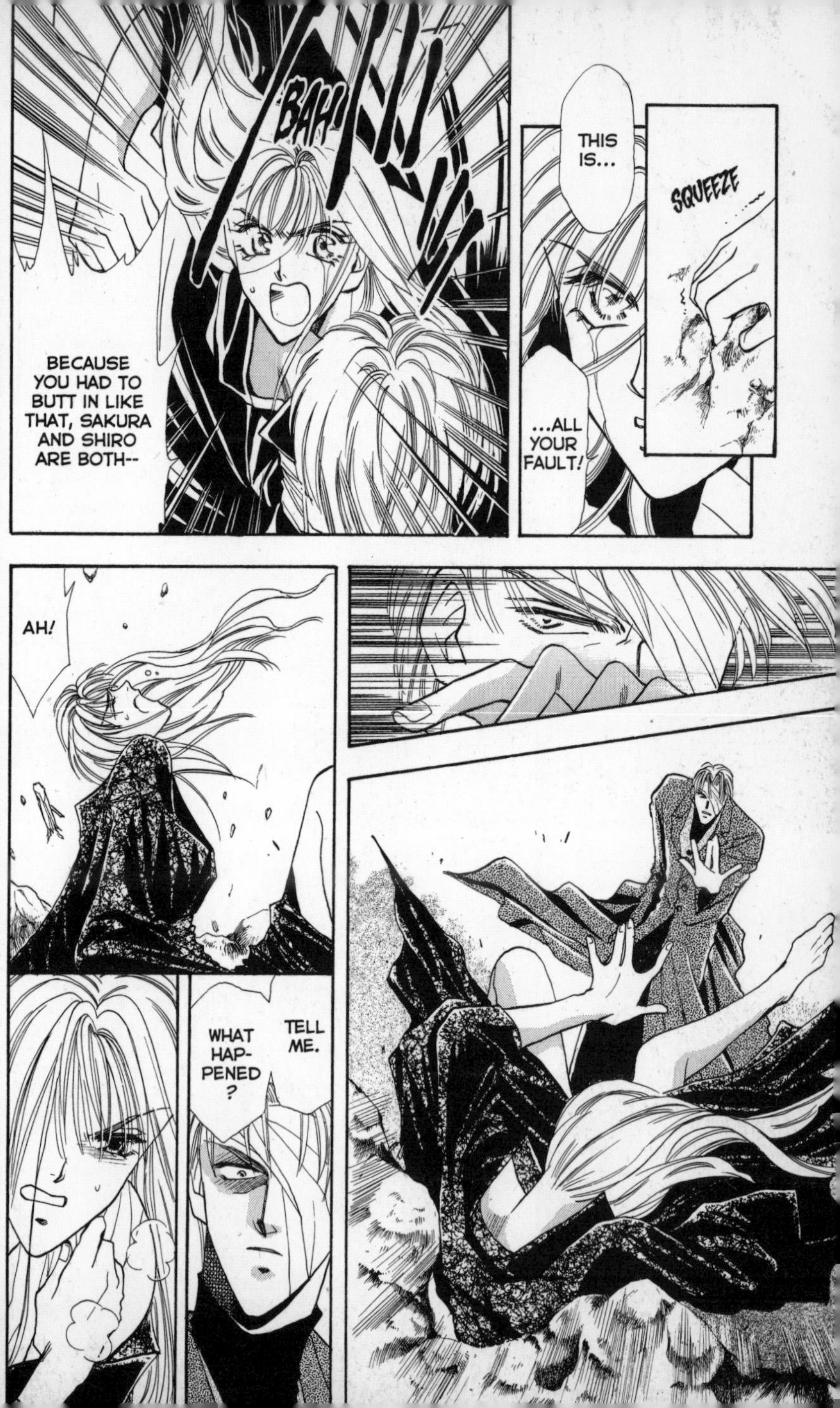
SQUEEZE
THIS IS...
...ALL YOUR FAULT!
BAH
BECAUSE YOU HAD TO BUTT IN LIKE THAT, SAKURA AND SHIRO ARE BOTH--
AH!
TELL ME.
WHAT HAP-PENED?

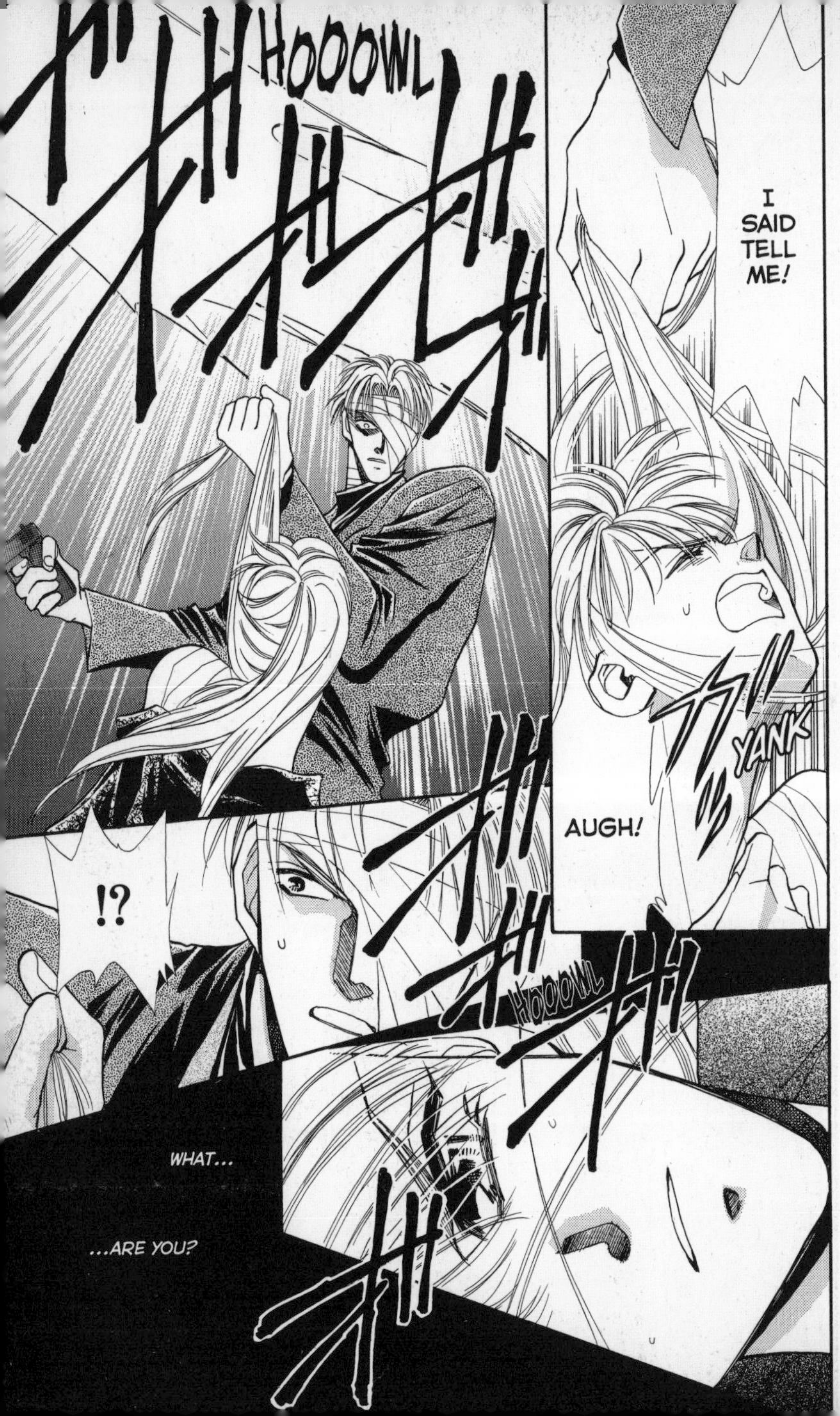
I SAID TELL ME!
YANK
AUGH!
HOOOWL
!?
HOOOWL
WHAT...
...ARE YOU?

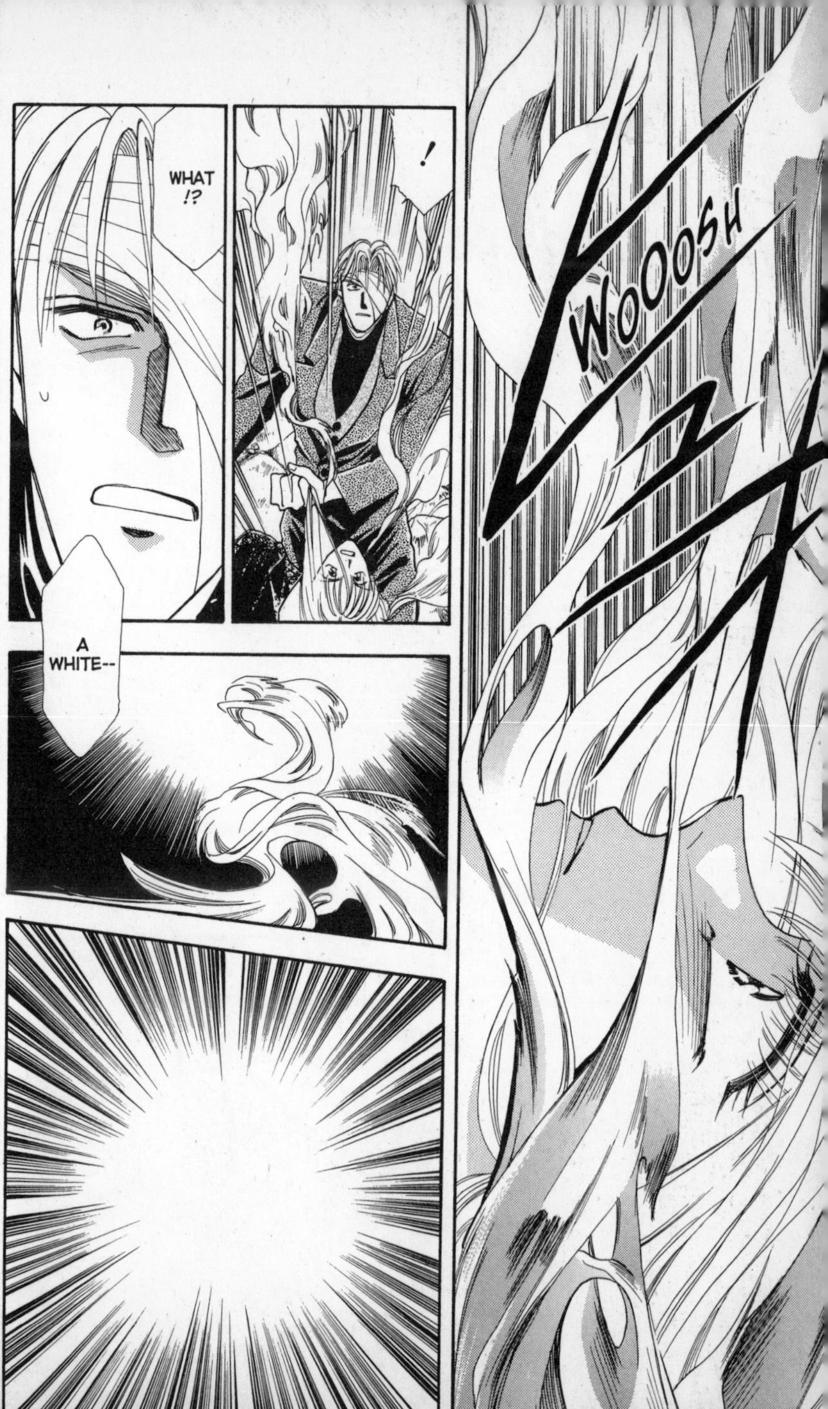
WOOOSH
!
WHAT !?
A WHITE--

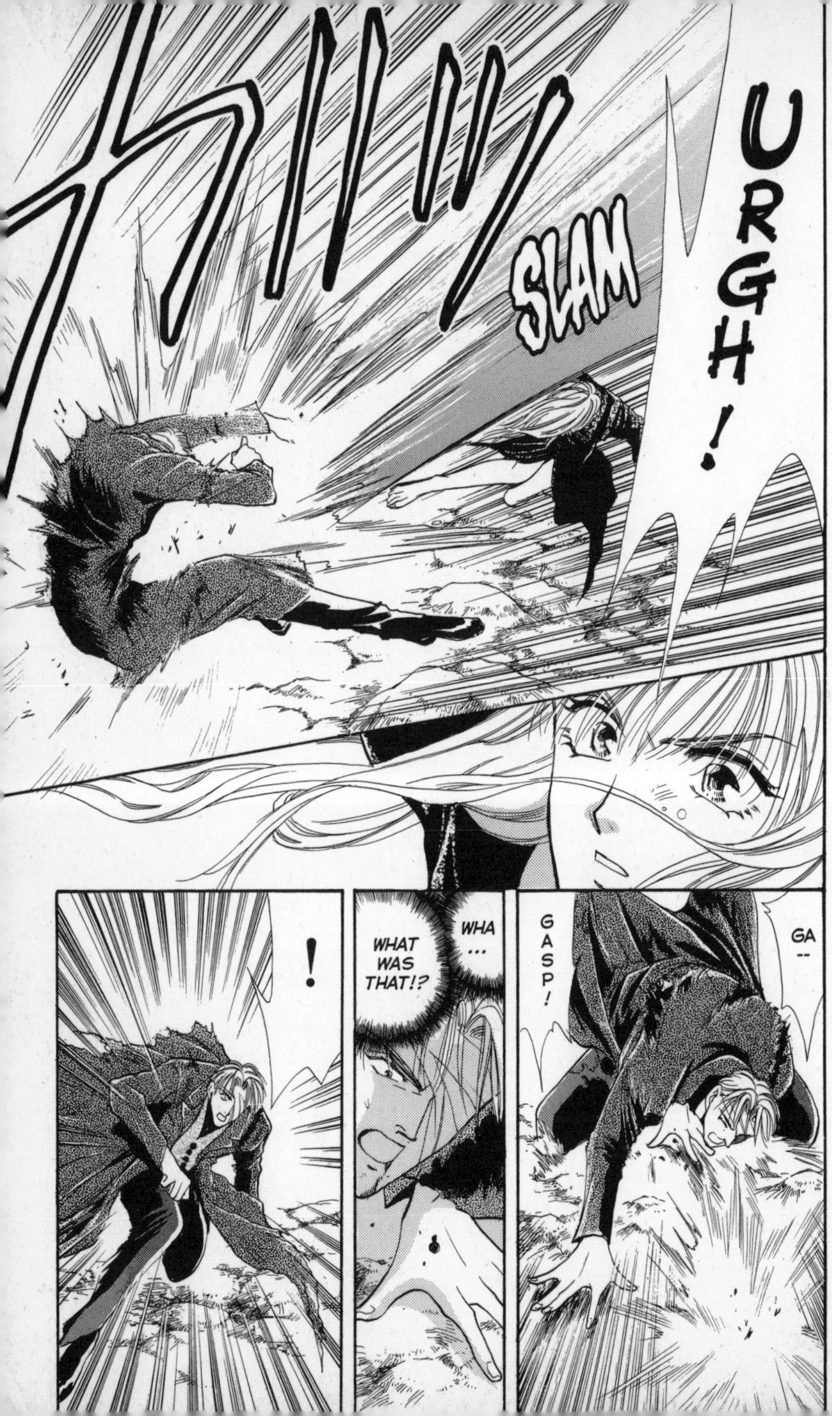
URGH!
SLAM
GA --
GASP!
WHA ...
WHAT WAS THAT!?
!

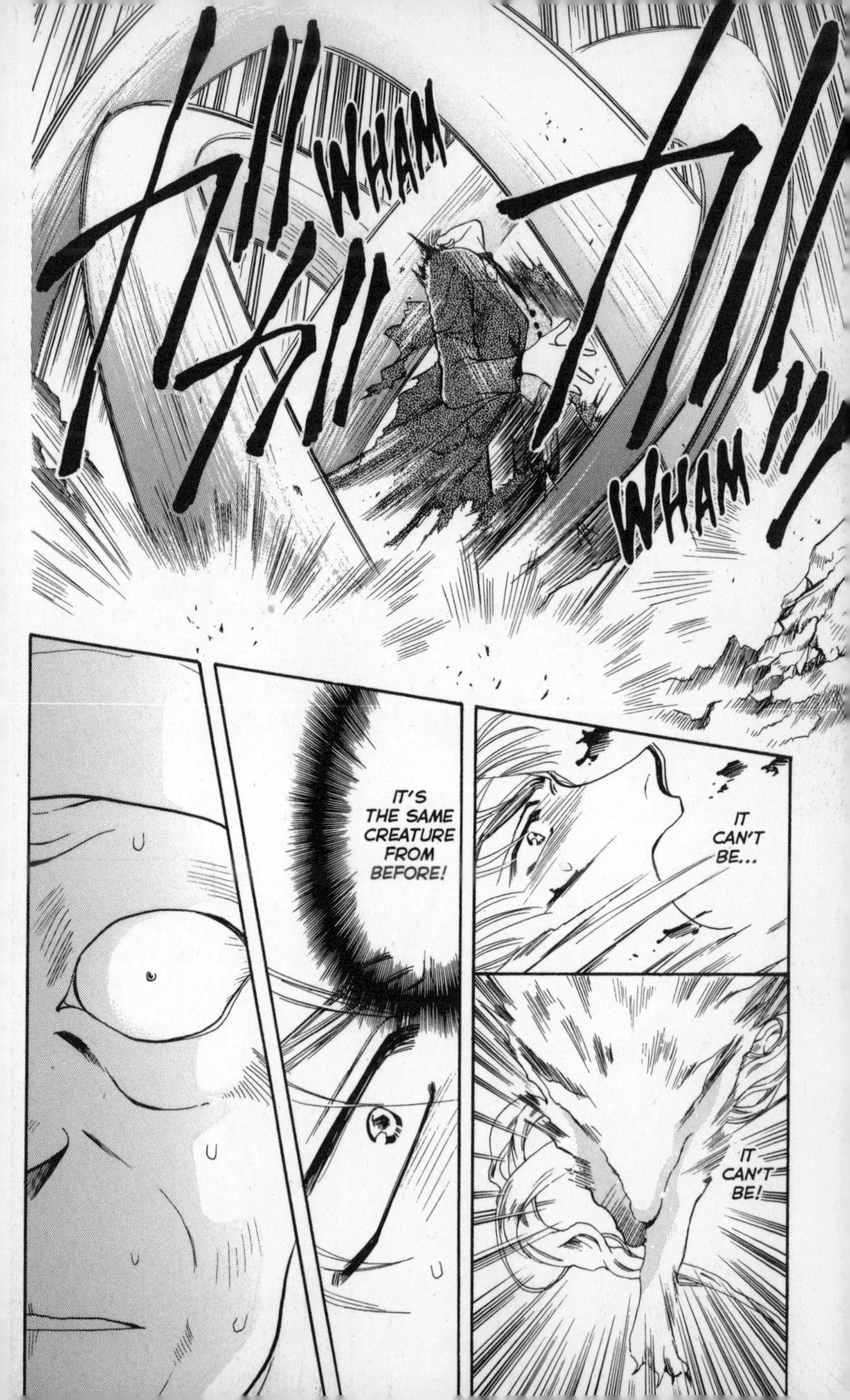
WHAM
WHAM
IT CAN'T BE...
IT CAN'T BE!
IT'S THE SAME CREATURE FROM BEFORE!

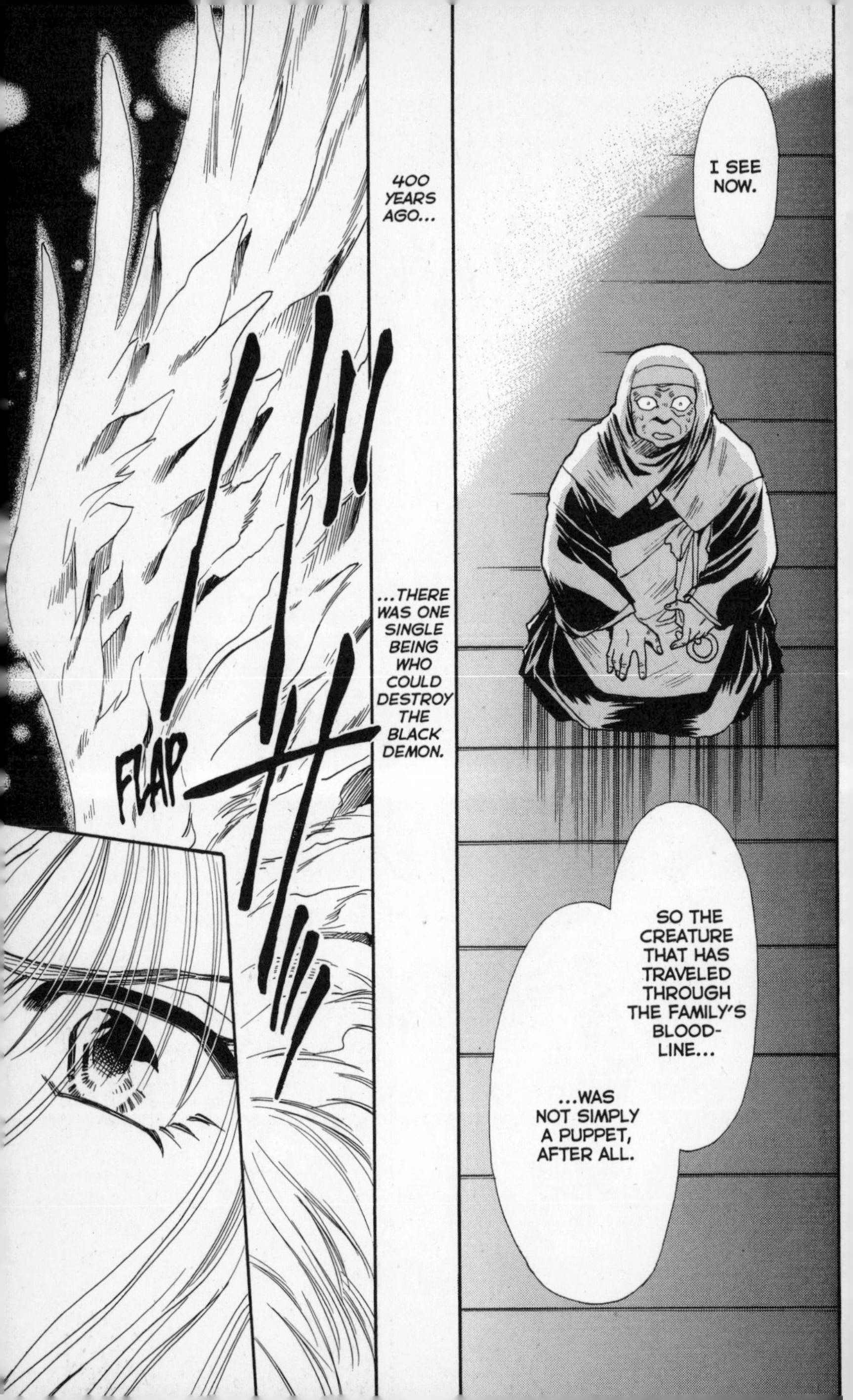
I SEE NOW.
SO THE CREATURE THAT HAS TRAVELED THROUGH THE FAMILY'S BLOOD-LINE...
...WAS NOT SIMPLY A PUPPET, AFTER ALL.
400 YEARS AGO...
...THERE WAS ONE SINGLE BEING WHO COULD DESTROY THE BLACK DEMON.
FLAP

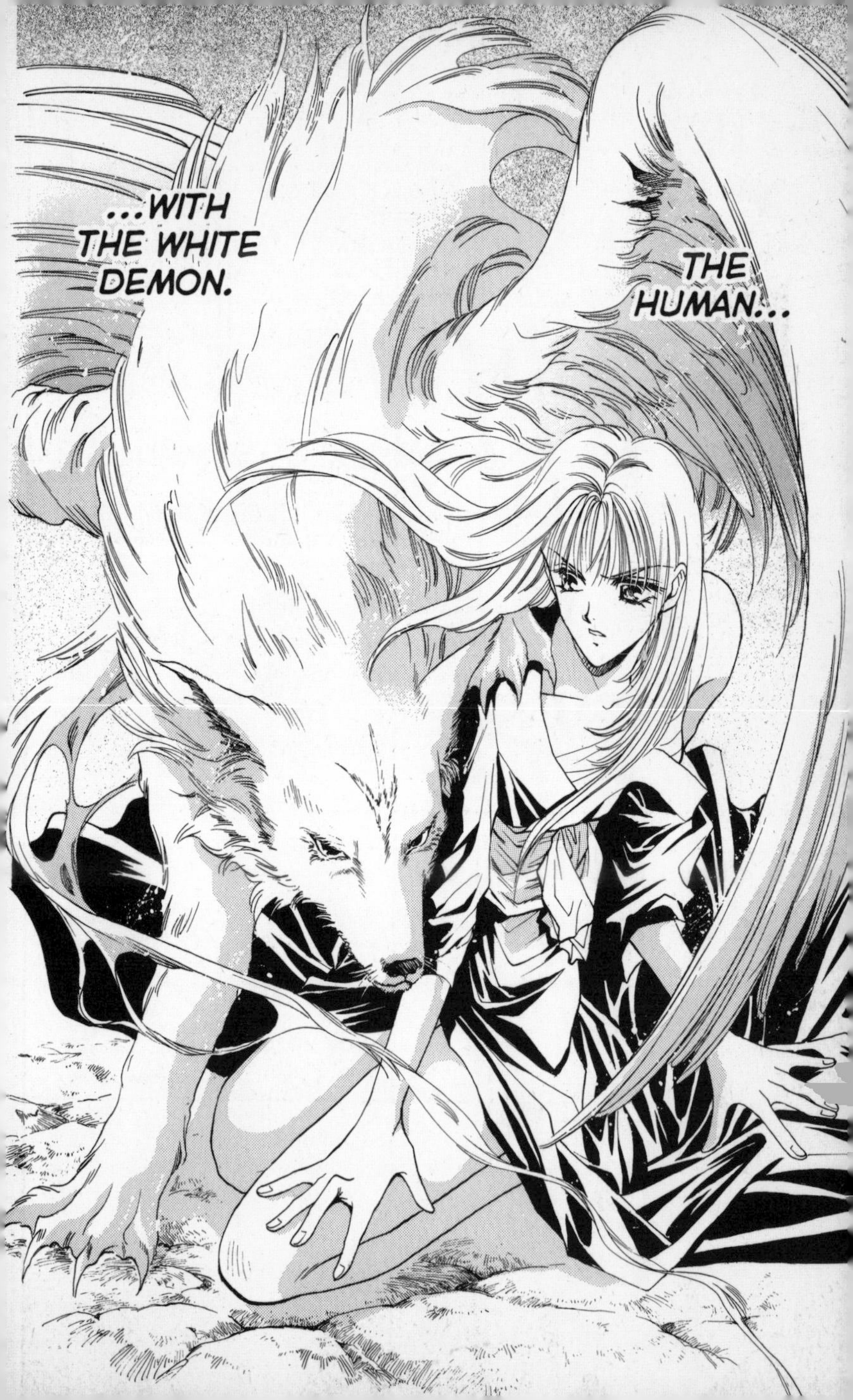
THE HUMAN...
...WITH THE WHITE DEMON.

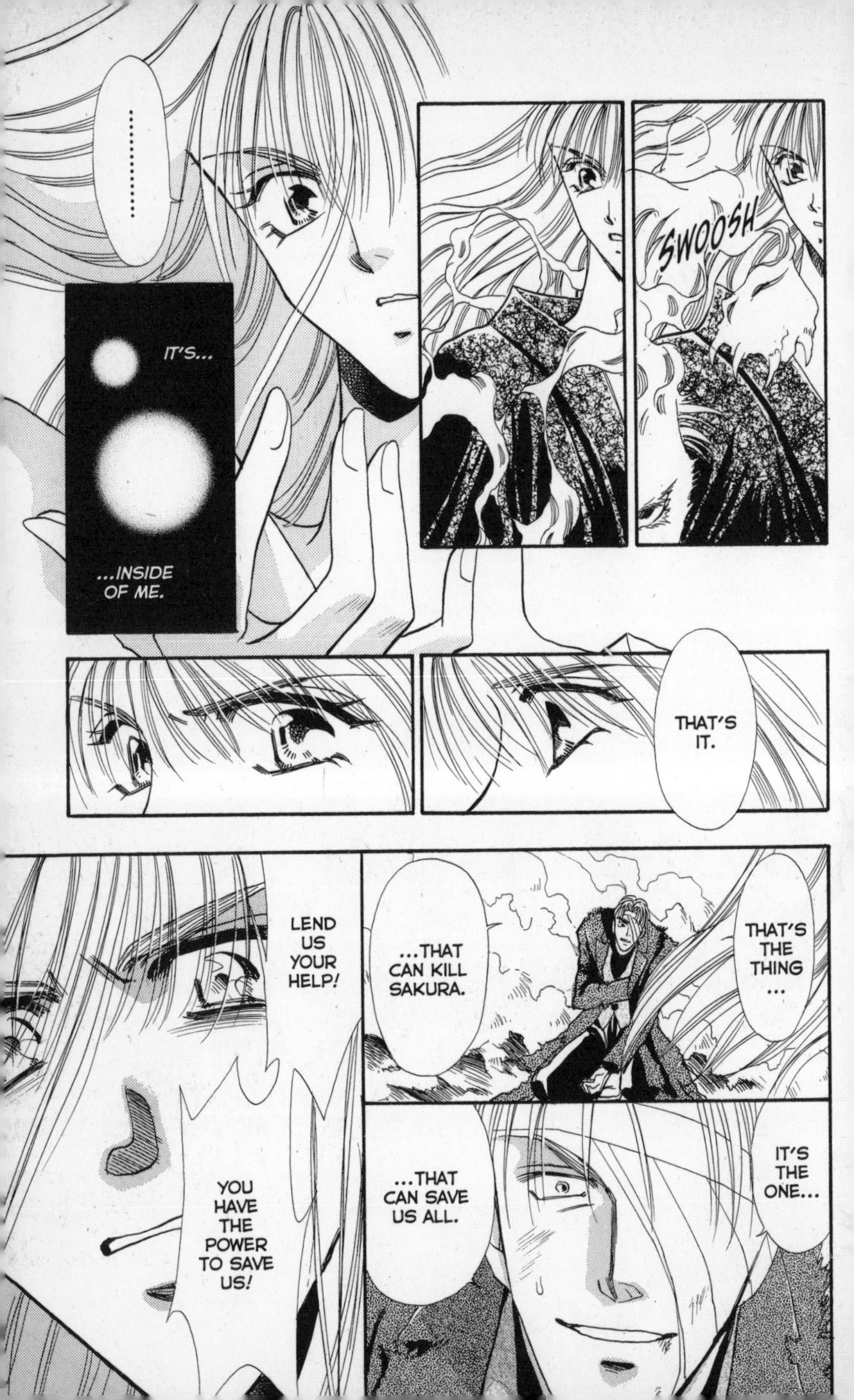
SWOOSH
......
IT'S...
...INSIDE OF ME.
THAT'S IT.
THAT'S THE THING...
...THAT CAN KILL SAKURA.
IT'S THE ONE...
...THAT CAN SAVE US ALL.
LEND US YOUR HELP!
YOU HAVE THE POWER TO SAVE US!

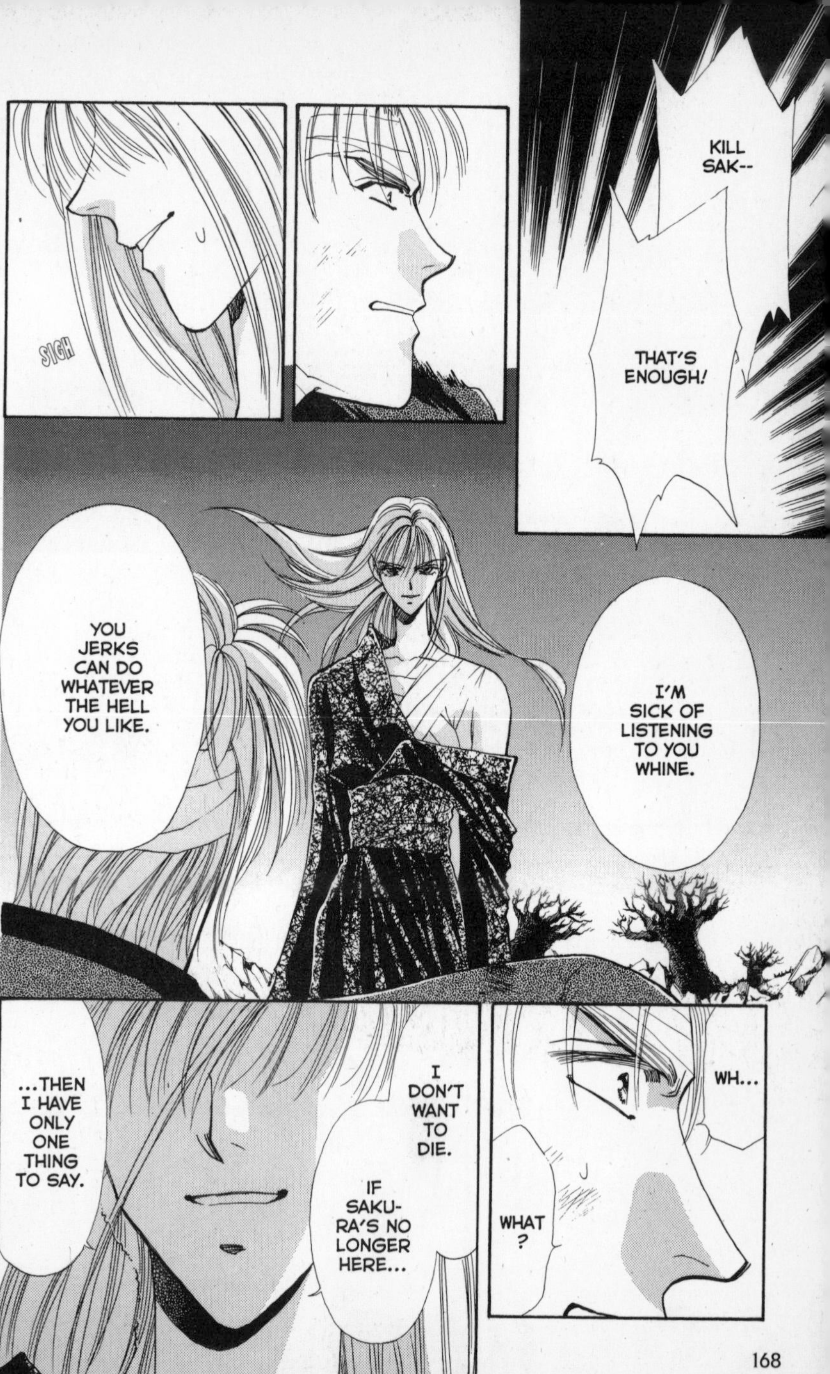
KILL SAK--
THAT'S ENOUGH!
SIGH
I'M SICK OF LISTENING TO YOU WHINE.
YOU JERKS CAN DO WHATEVER THE HELL YOU LIKE.
WH...
WHAT?
I DON'T WANT TO DIE.
IF SAKU-RA'S NO LONGER HERE...
...THEN I HAVE ONLY ONE THING TO SAY.

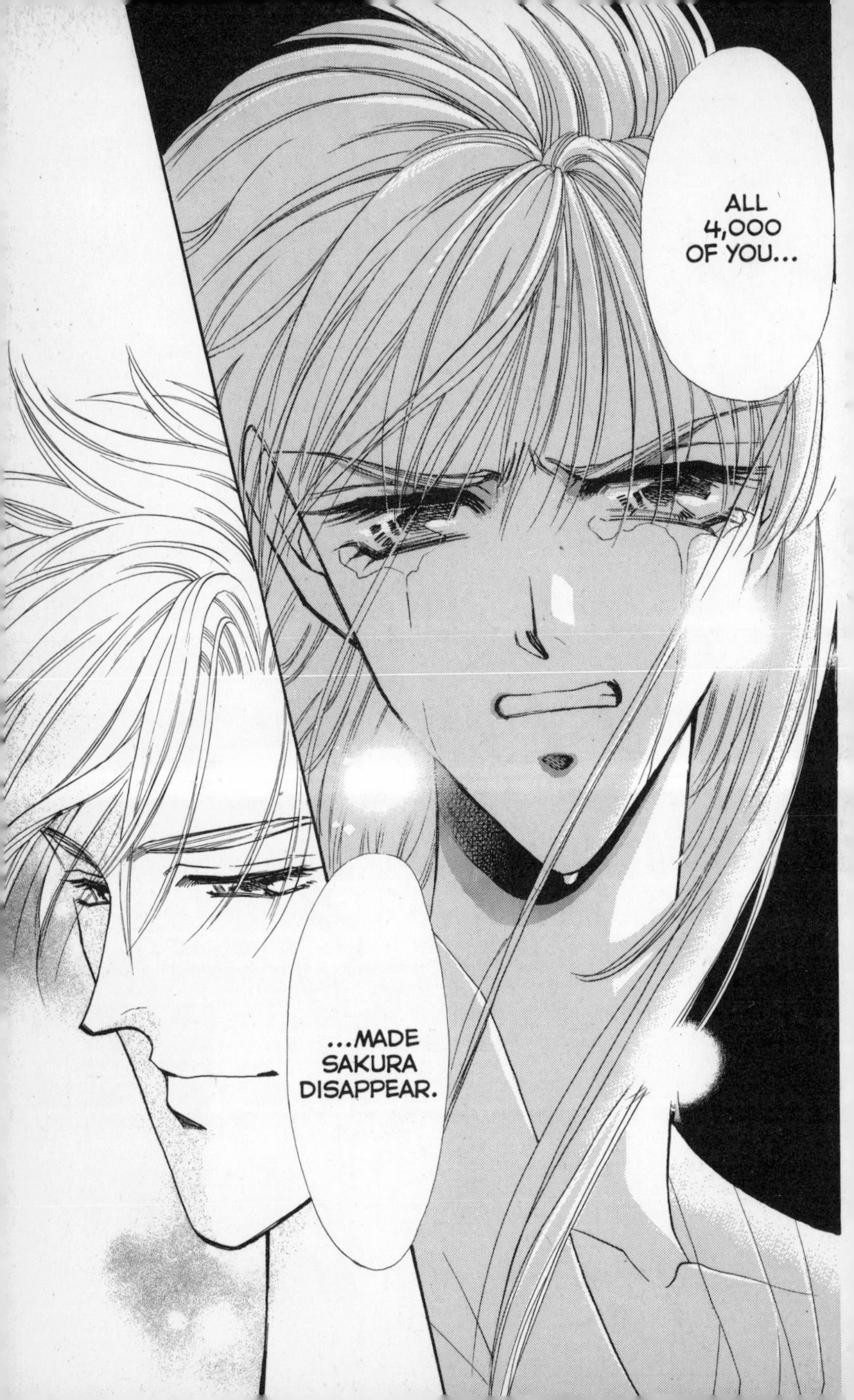
ALL 4,000 OF YOU...
...MADE SAKURA DISAPPEAR.

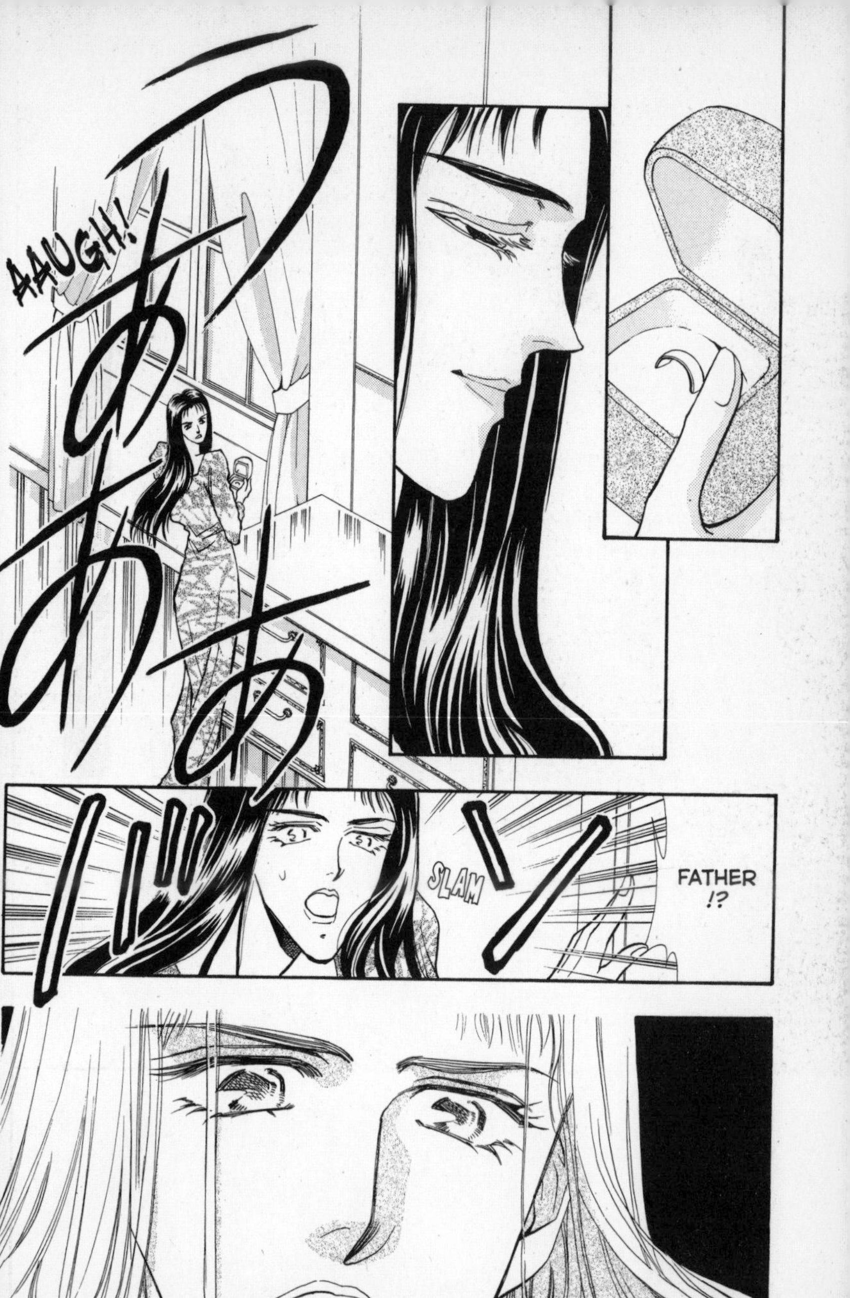
AAUGH!
SLAM
FATHER !?

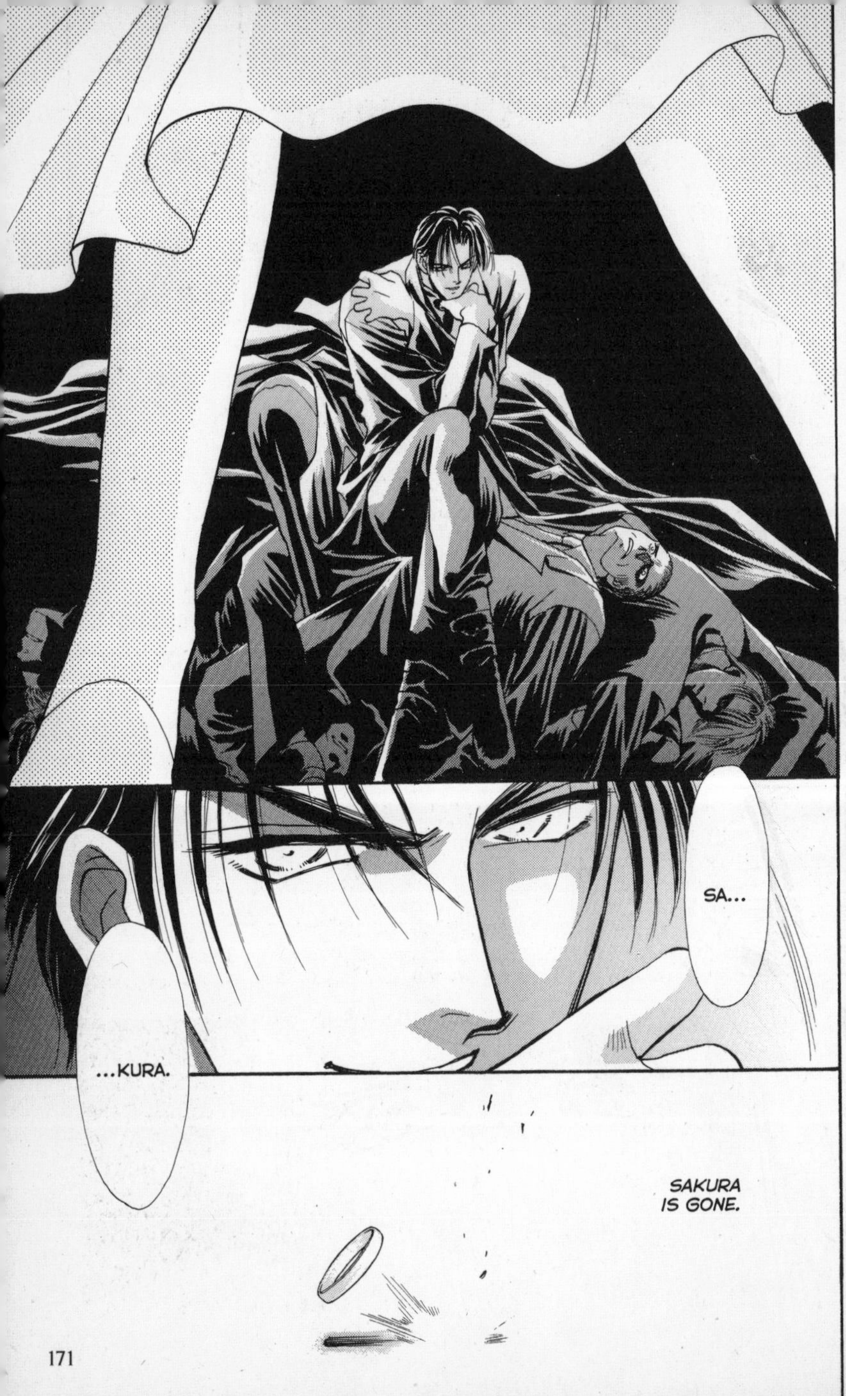
SA...
...KURA.
SAKURA IS GONE.

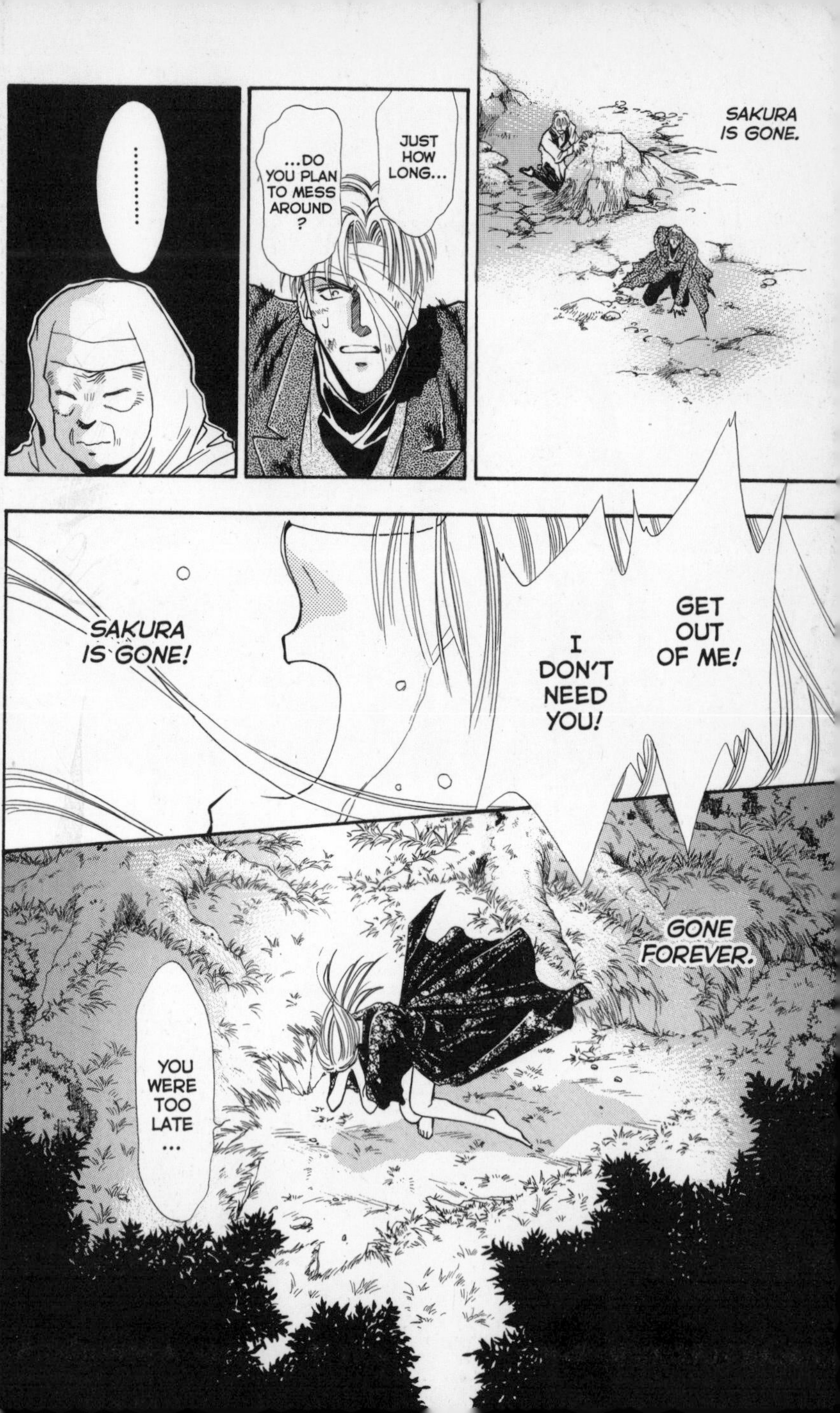
SAKURA IS GONE.
JUST HOW LONG...
...DO YOU PLAN TO MESS AROUND ?
......
GET OUT OF ME!
I DON'T NEED YOU!
SAKURA IS GONE!
GONE FOREVER.
YOU WERE TOO LATE ...

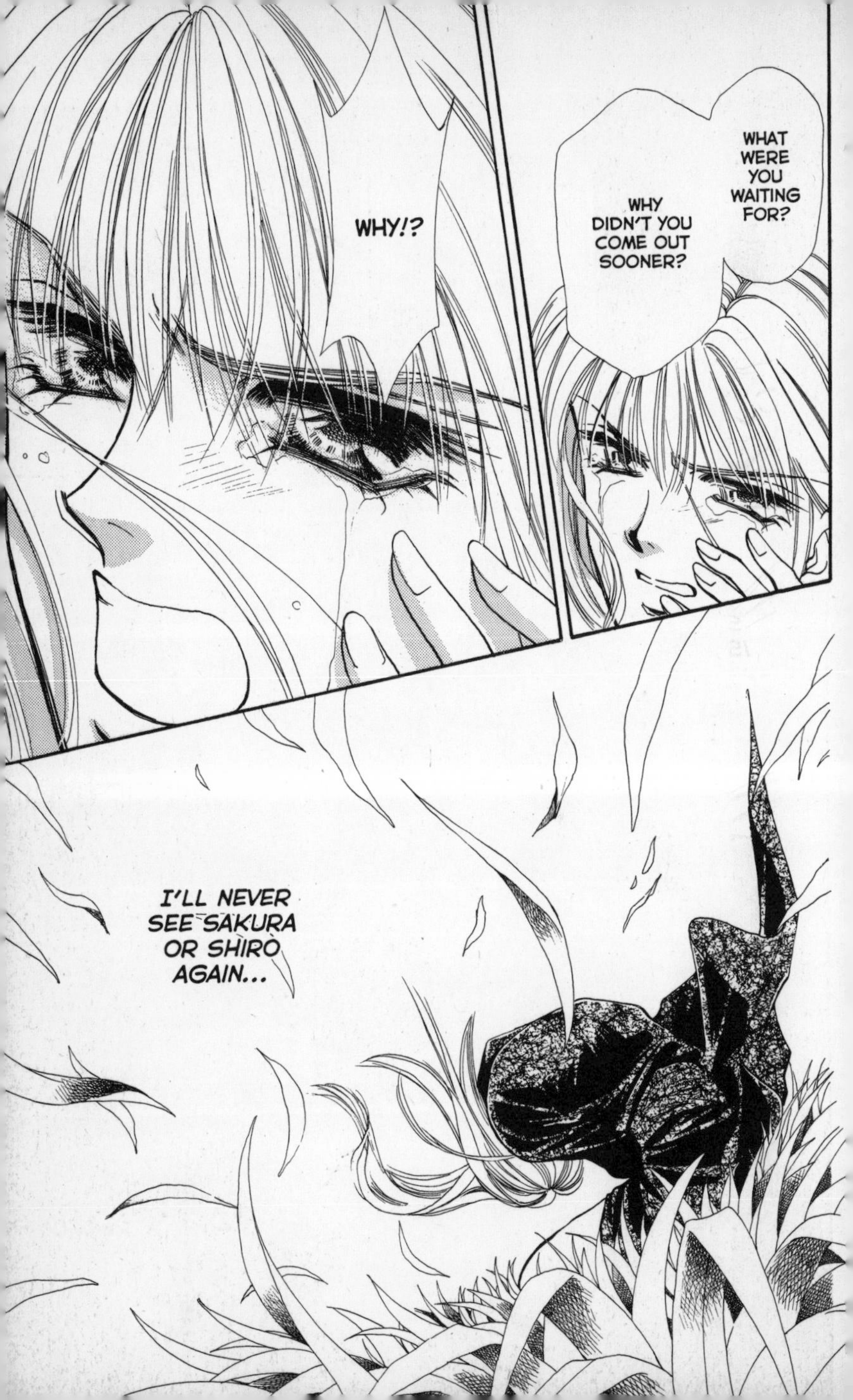
WHAT WERE YOU WAITING FOR?
WHY DIDN'T YOU COME OUT SOONER?
WHY!?
I'LL NEVER SEE SAKURA OR SHIRO AGAIN...

獣たちの夜

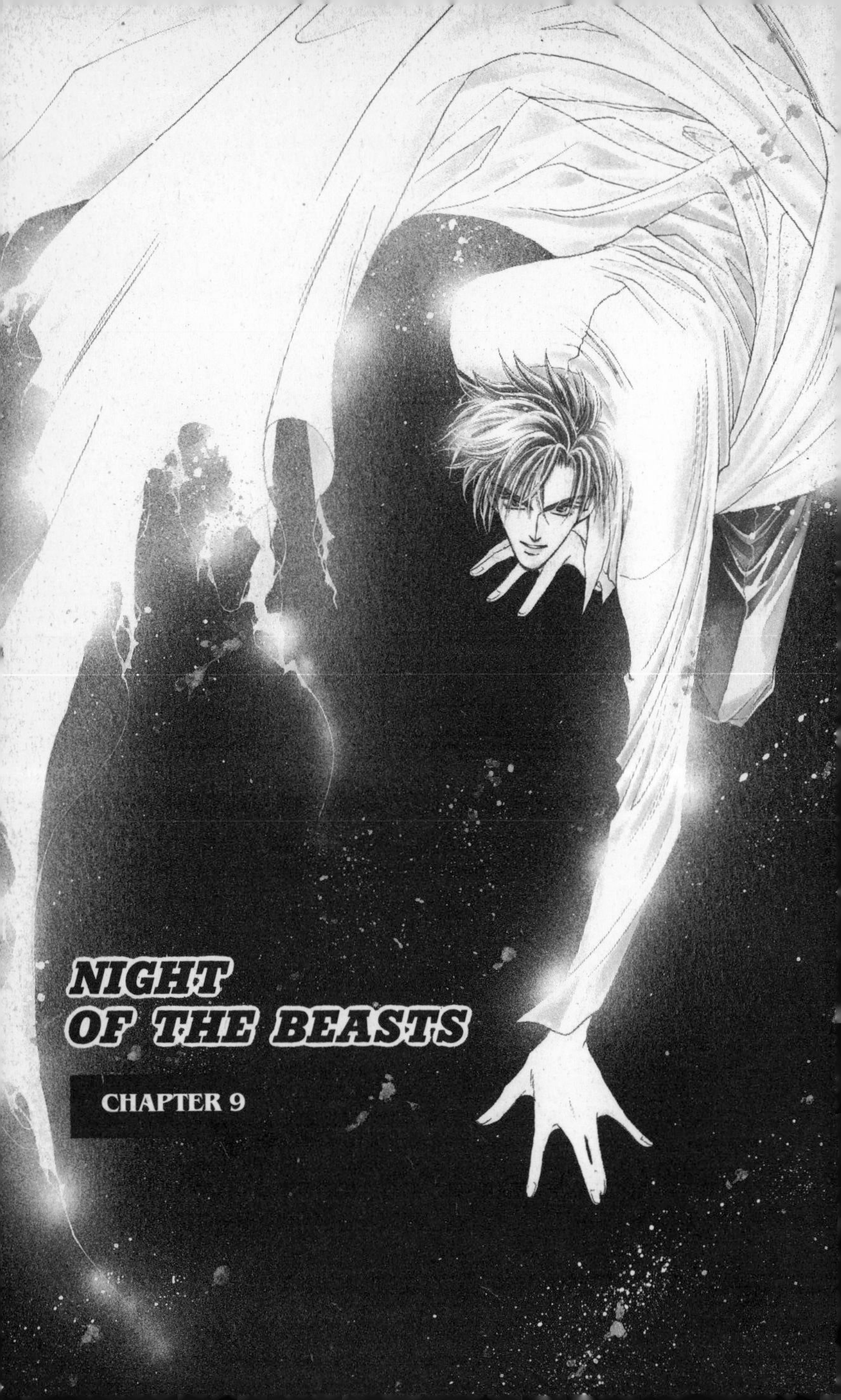
NIGHT OF THE BEASTS
CHAPTER 9

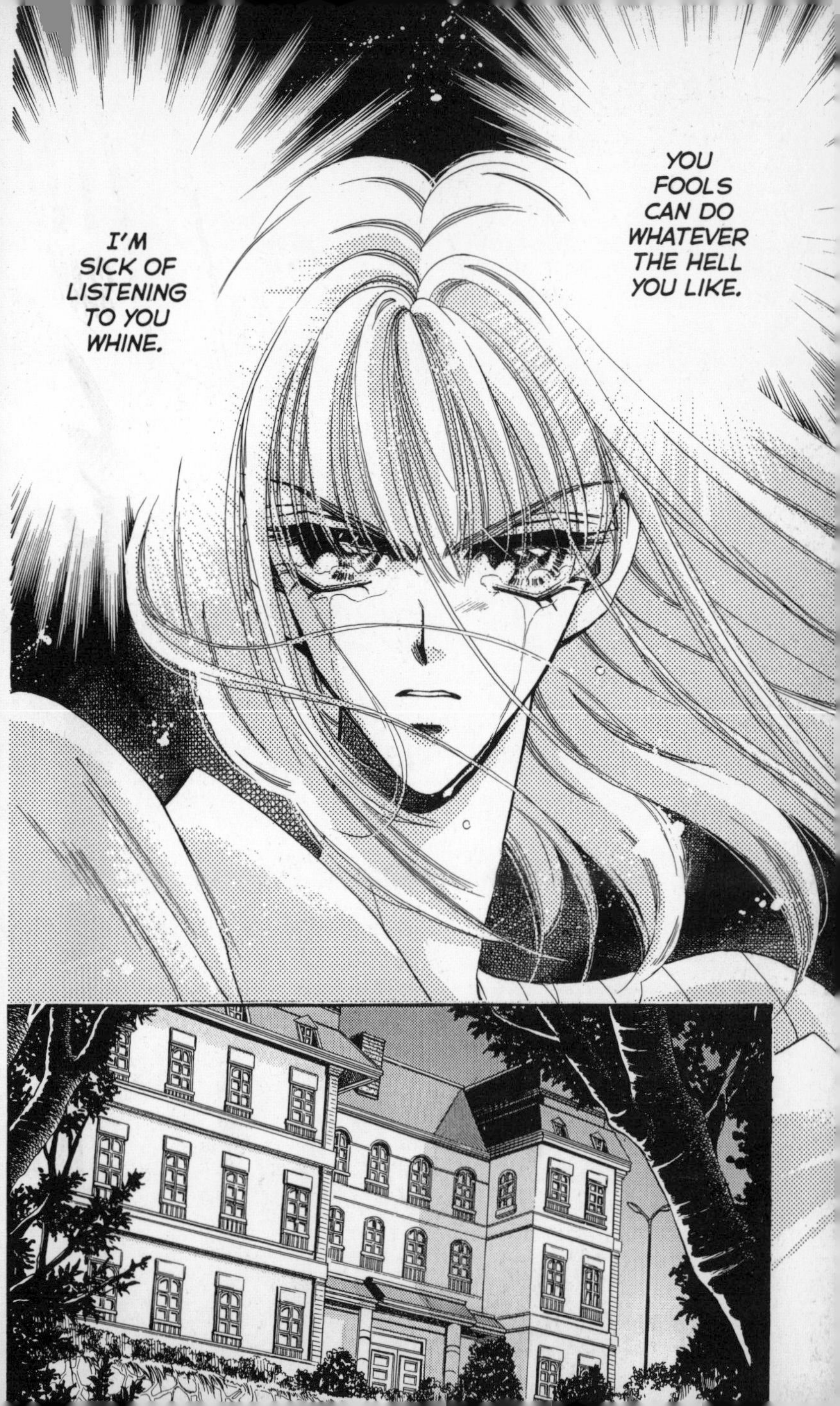
YOU FOOLS CAN DO WHATEVER THE HELL YOU LIKE.
I'M SICK OF LISTENING TO YOU WHINE.

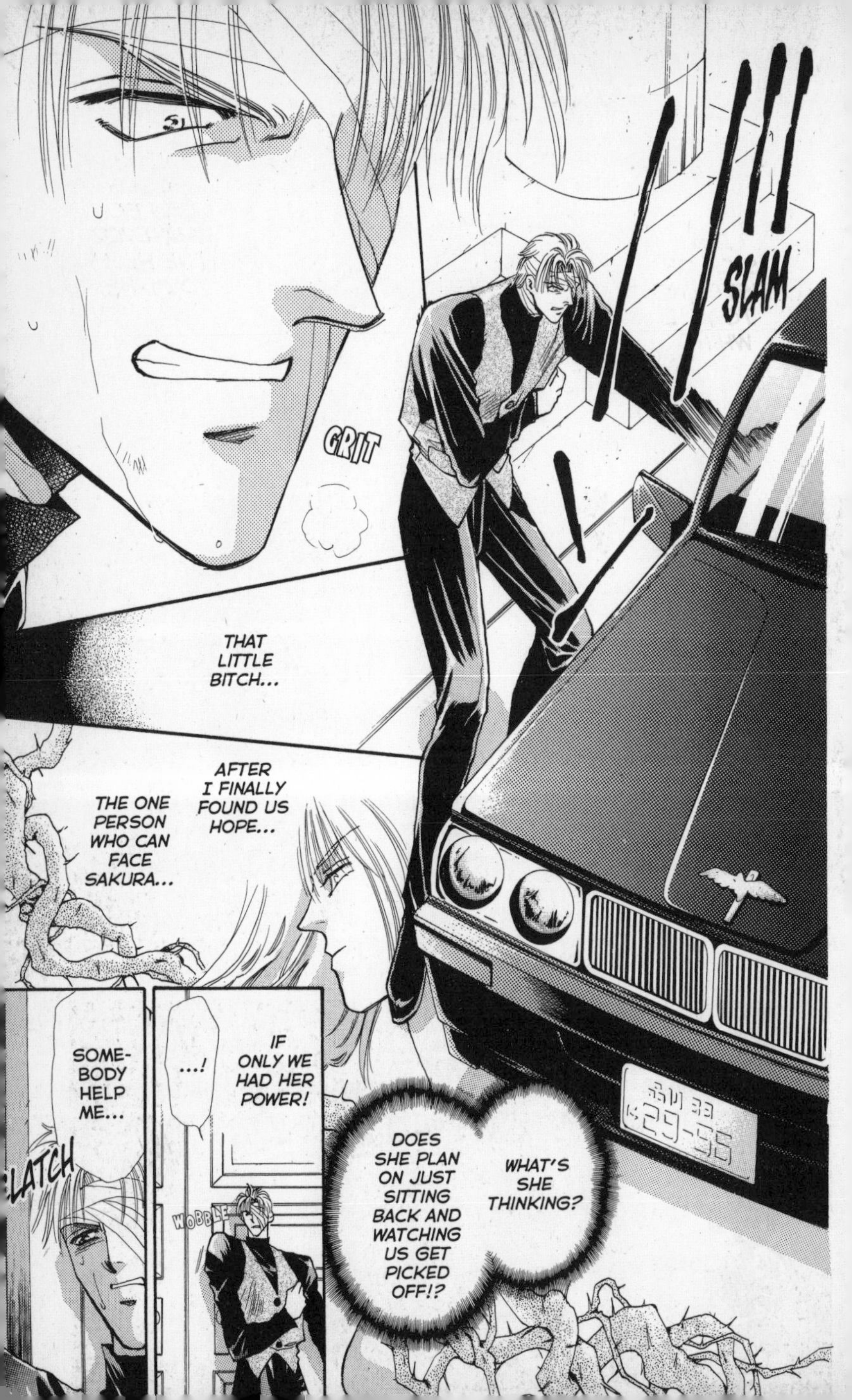
SLAM
GRIT
THAT LITTLE BITCH...
AFTER I FINALLY FOUND US HOPE...
THE ONE PERSON WHO CAN FACE SAKURA...
WHAT'S SHE THINKING?
DOES SHE PLAN ON JUST SITTING BACK AND WATCHING US GET PICKED OFF!?
IF ONLY WE HAD HER POWER!
...!
WOBBLE
SOME-BODY HELP ME...
LATCH

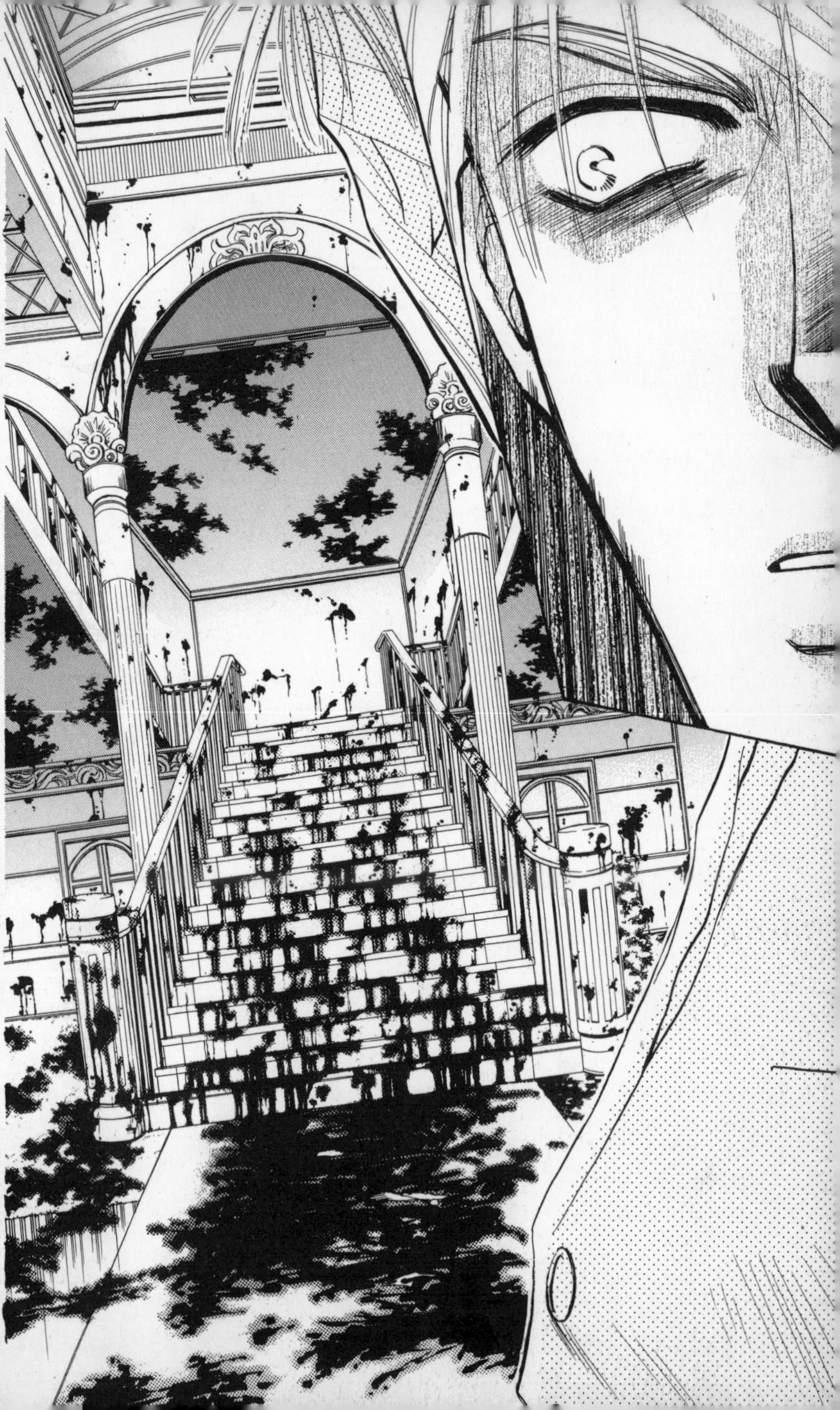

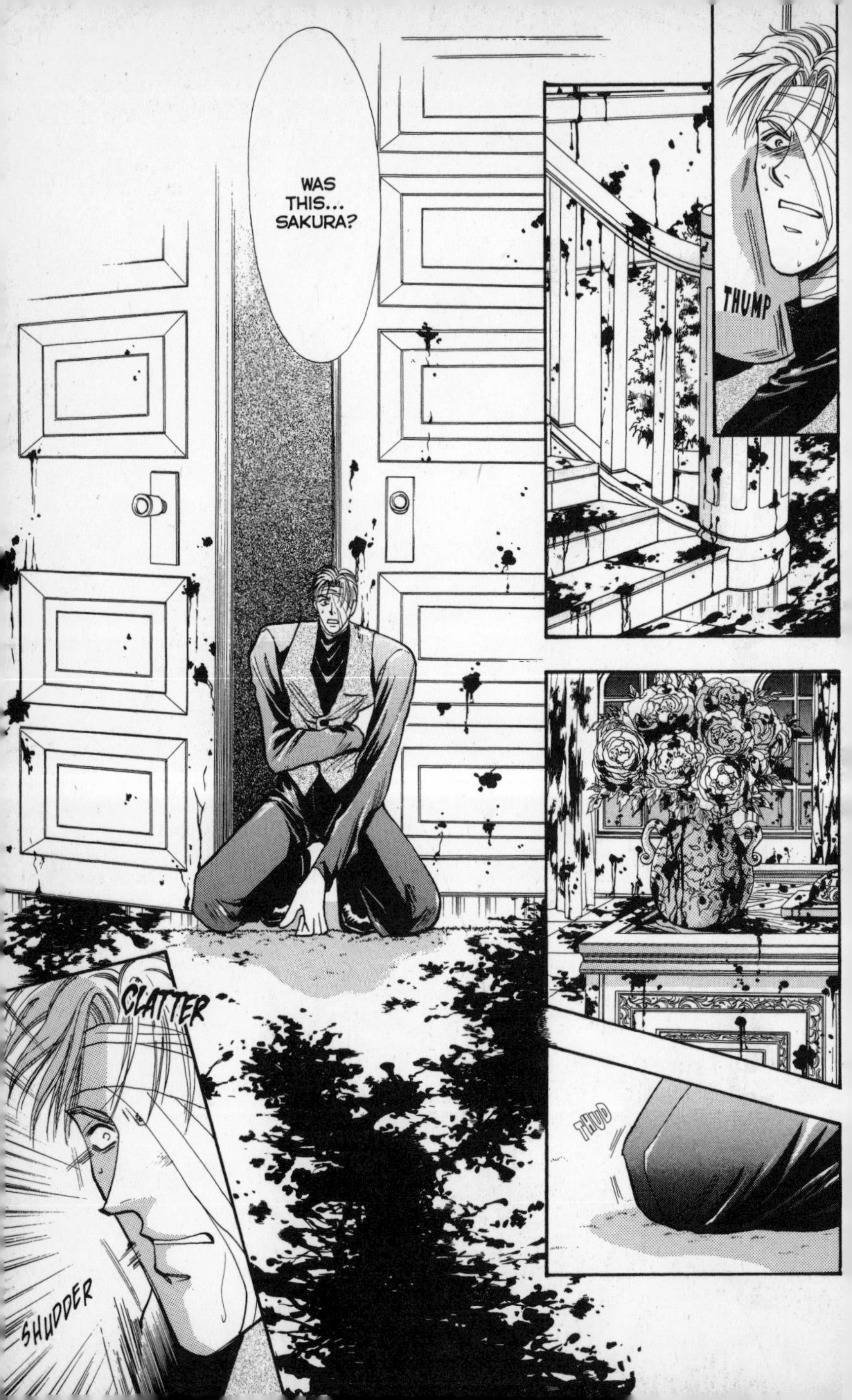
THUMP
THUD
WAS THIS... SAKURA?
CLATTER
SHUDDER

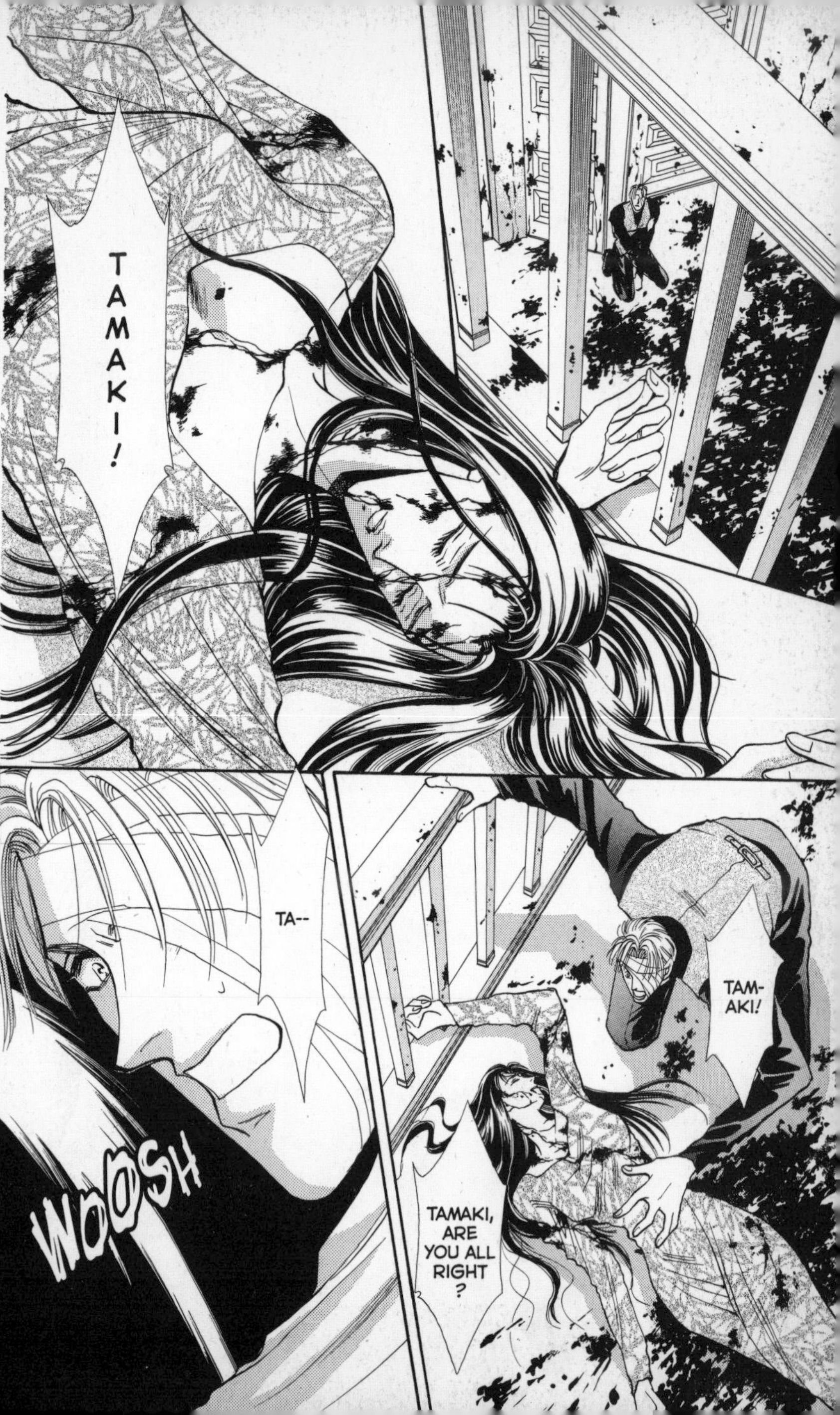
TAMAKI!
TAM-AKI!
TAMAKI, ARE YOU ALL RIGHT?
TA--
WOOSH

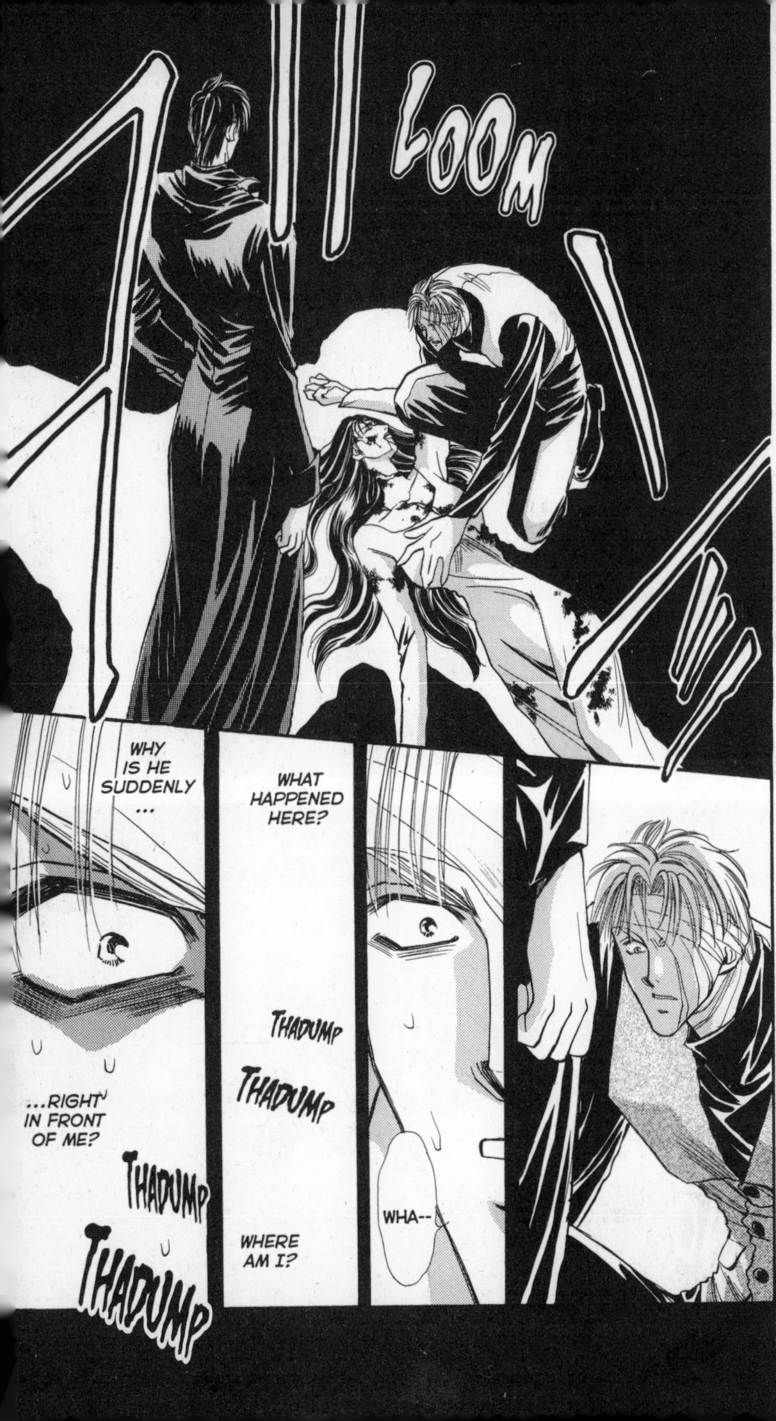
LOOM
WHA--
WHAT HAPPENED HERE?
THADUMP
THADUMP
WHERE AM I?
WHY IS HE SUDDENLY ...
...RIGHT IN FRONT OF ME?
THADUMP
THADUMP

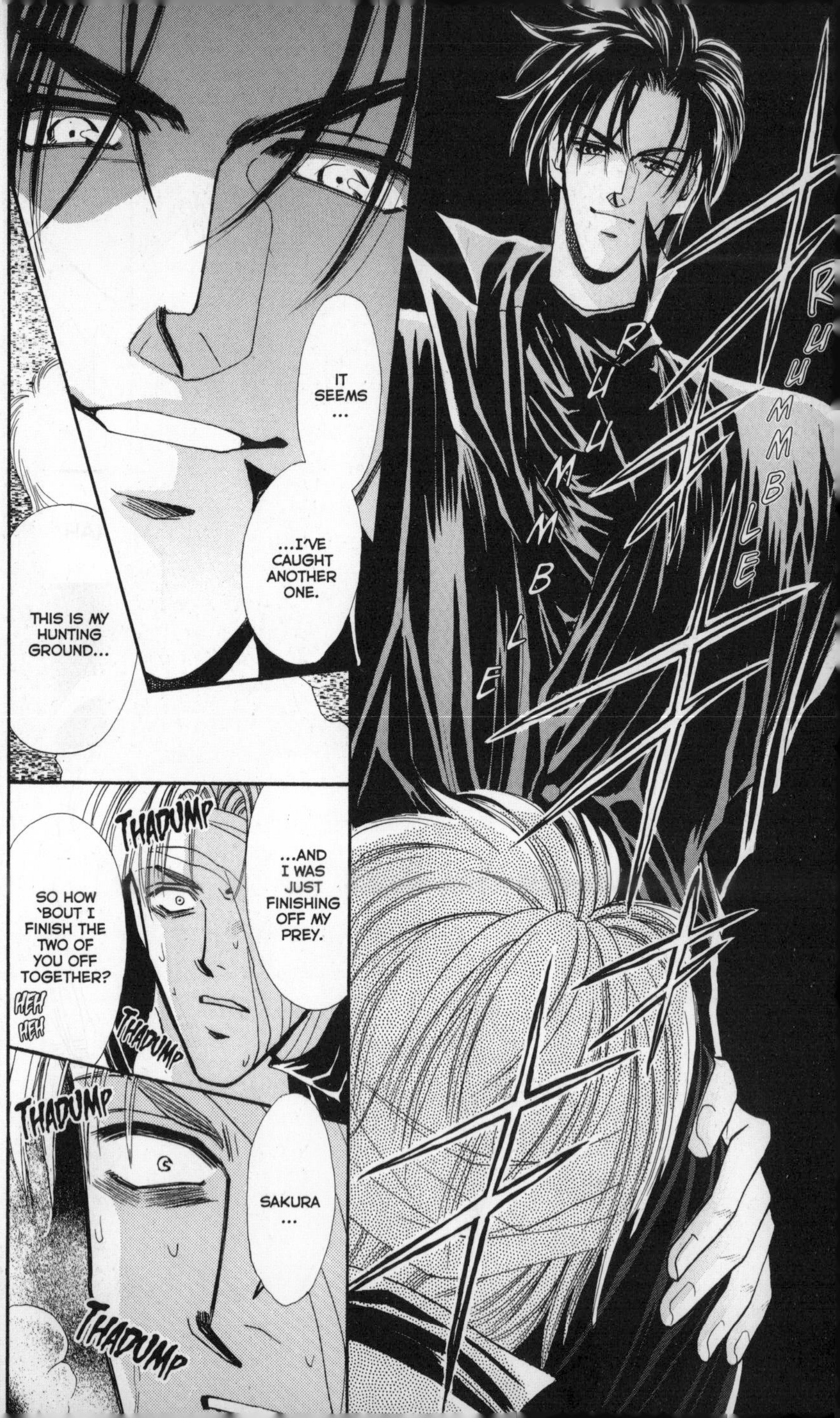
RUUMMBLE
RUUMMBLE
IT SEEMS ...
...I'VE CAUGHT ANOTHER ONE.
THIS IS MY HUNTING GROUND...
THADUMP
...AND I WAS JUST FINISHING OFF MY PREY.
SO HOW 'BOUT I FINISH THE TWO OF YOU OFF TOGETHER?
HEH HEH
THADUMP
THADUMP
SAKURA ...
THADUMP

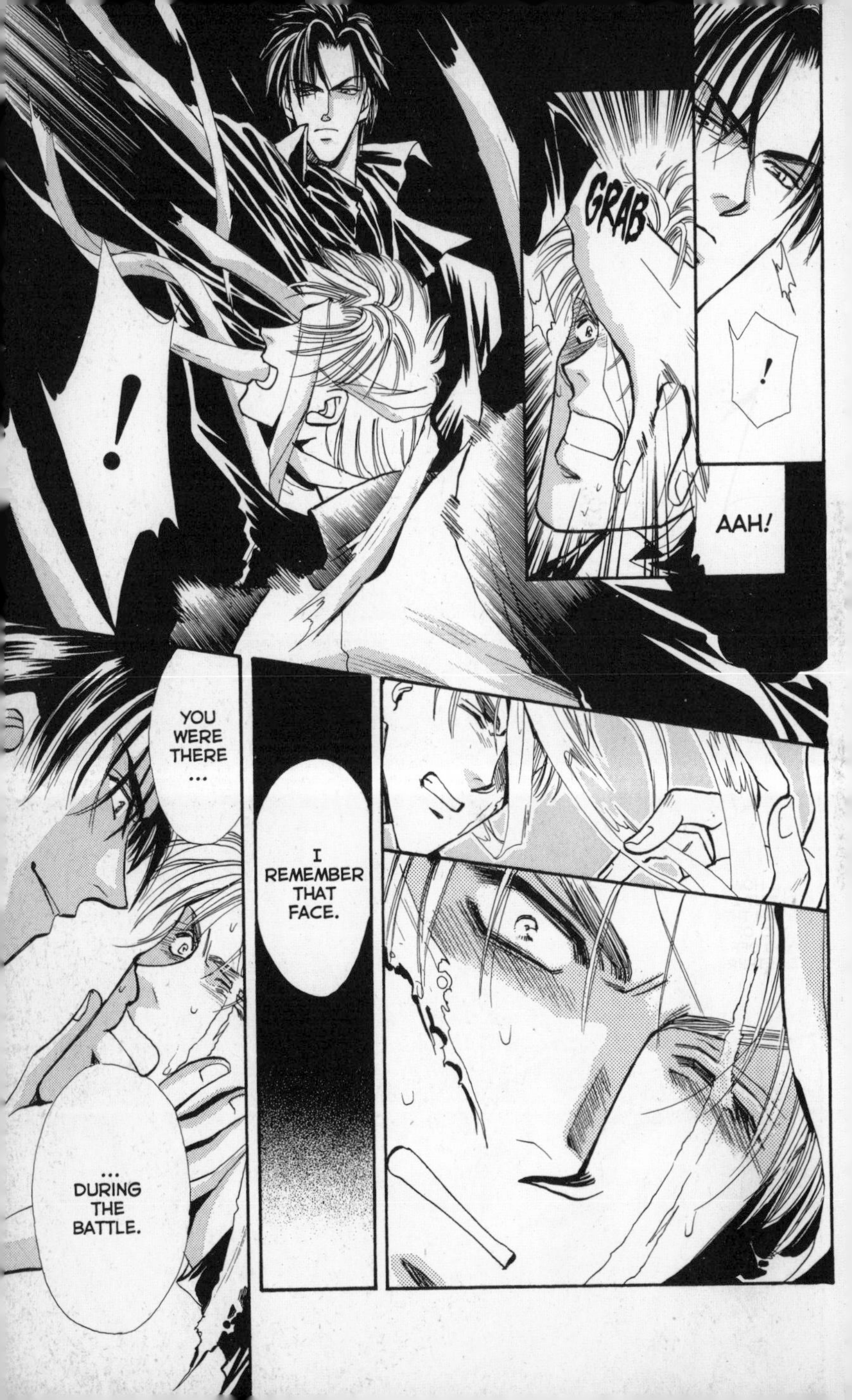
!
GRAB
AAH!
!
I REMEMBER THAT FACE.
YOU WERE THERE ...
... DURING THE BATTLE.

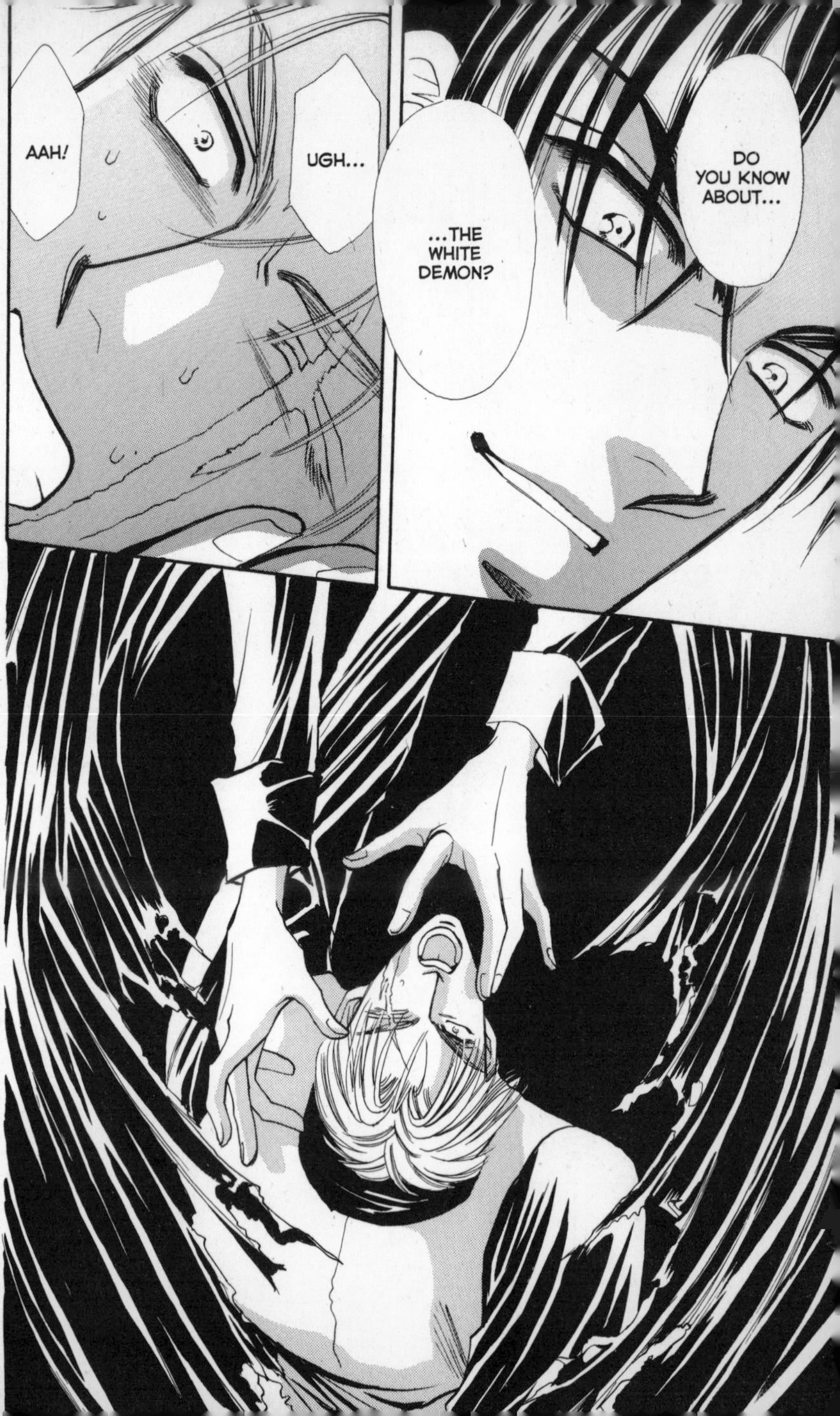
DO YOU KNOW ABOUT...
...THE WHITE DEMON?
UGH...
AAH!

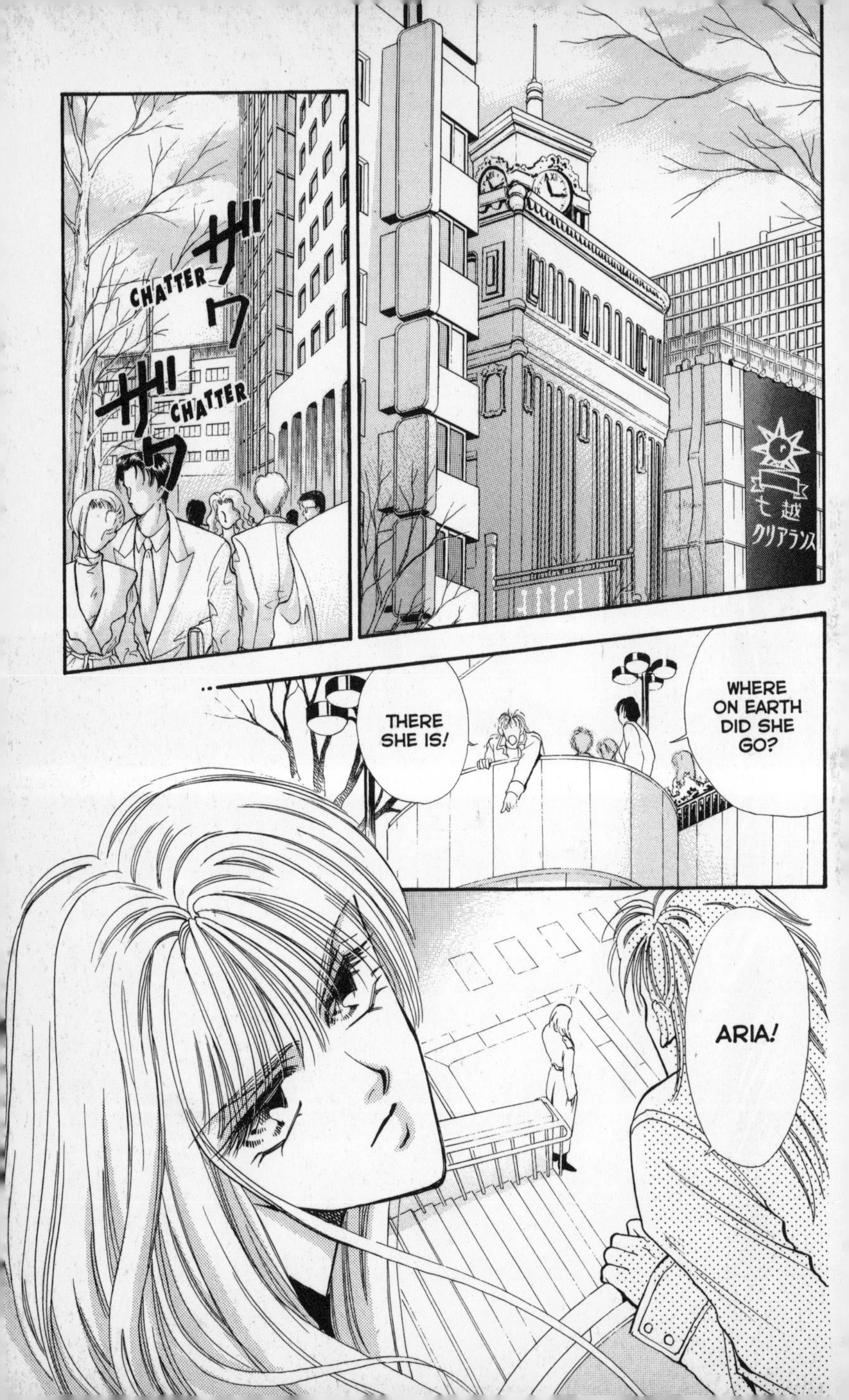
七越
クリアランス
ザワ
CHATTER
ザワ
CHATTER
WHERE ON EARTH DID SHE GO?
THERE SHE IS!
...
ARIA!

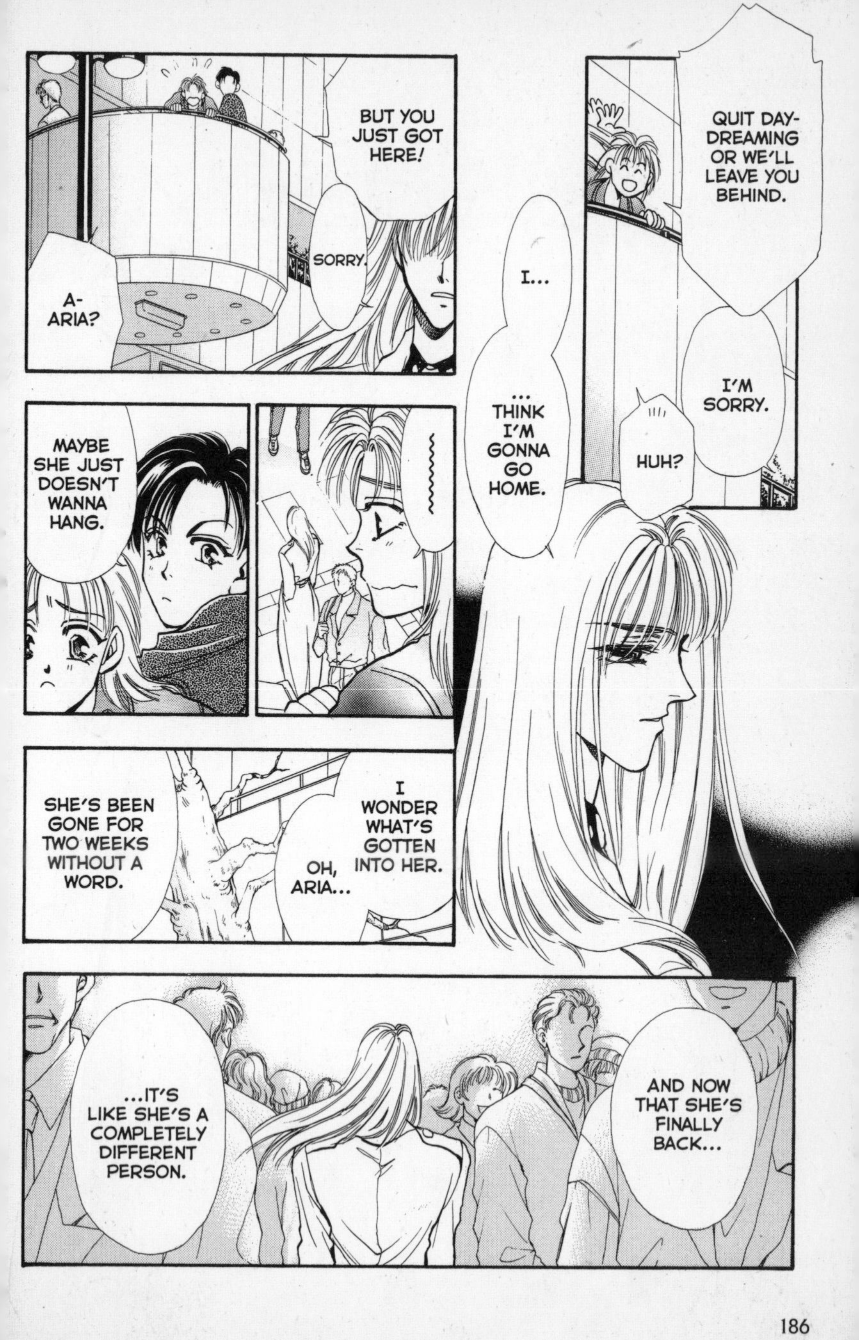
QUIT DAY-DREAMING OR WE'LL LEAVE YOU BEHIND.
I'M SORRY.
HUH?
I...
...THINK I'M GONNA GO HOME.
BUT YOU JUST GOT HERE!
SORRY.
A-ARIA?
MAYBE SHE JUST DOESN'T WANNA HANG.
I WONDER WHAT'S GOTTEN INTO HER.
OH, ARIA...
SHE'S BEEN GONE FOR TWO WEEKS WITHOUT A WORD.
AND NOW THAT SHE'S FINALLY BACK...
...IT'S LIKE SHE'S A COMPLETELY DIFFERENT PERSON.

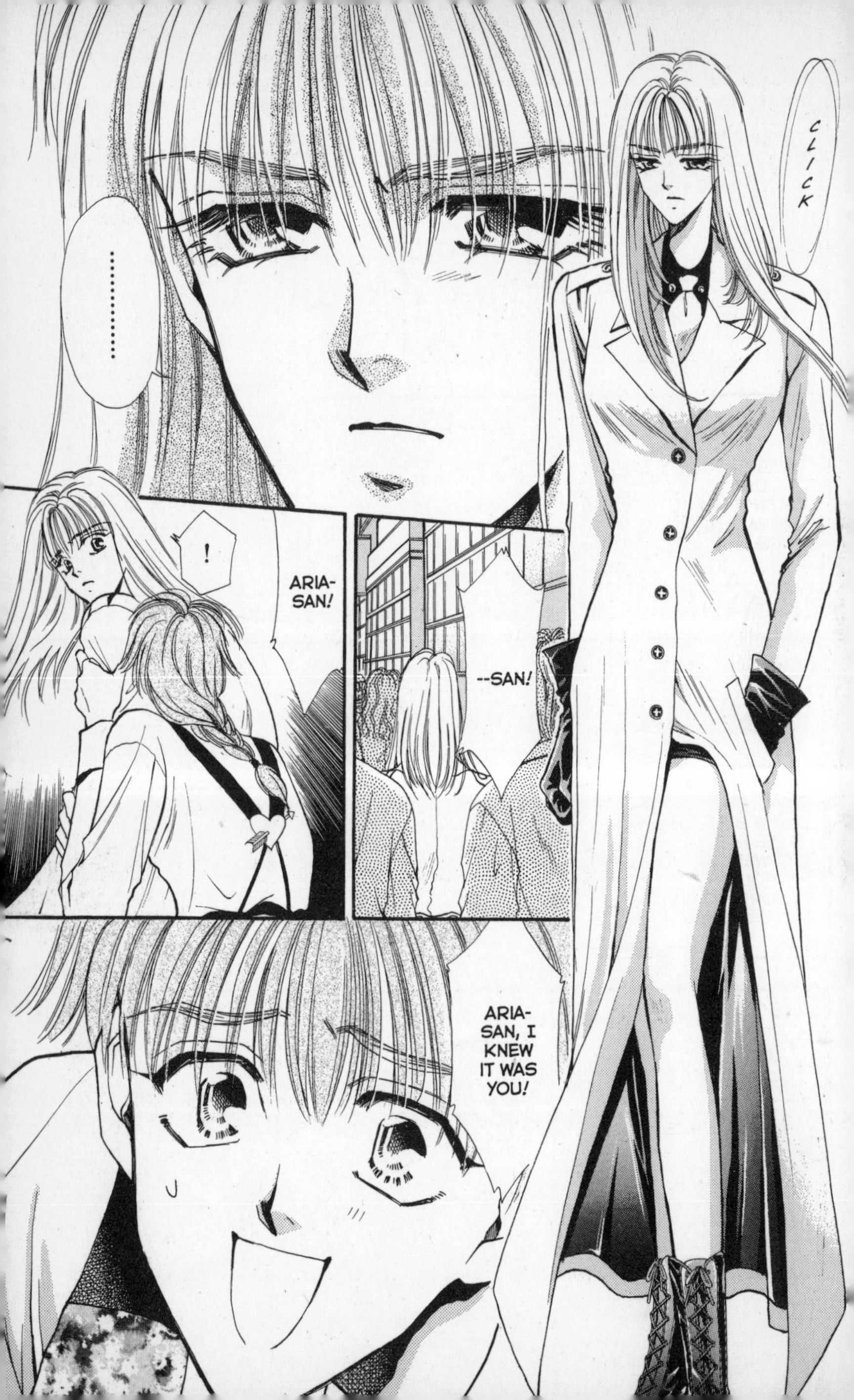
CLICK
......
--SAN!
ARIA-SAN!
!
ARIA-SAN, I KNEW IT WAS YOU!

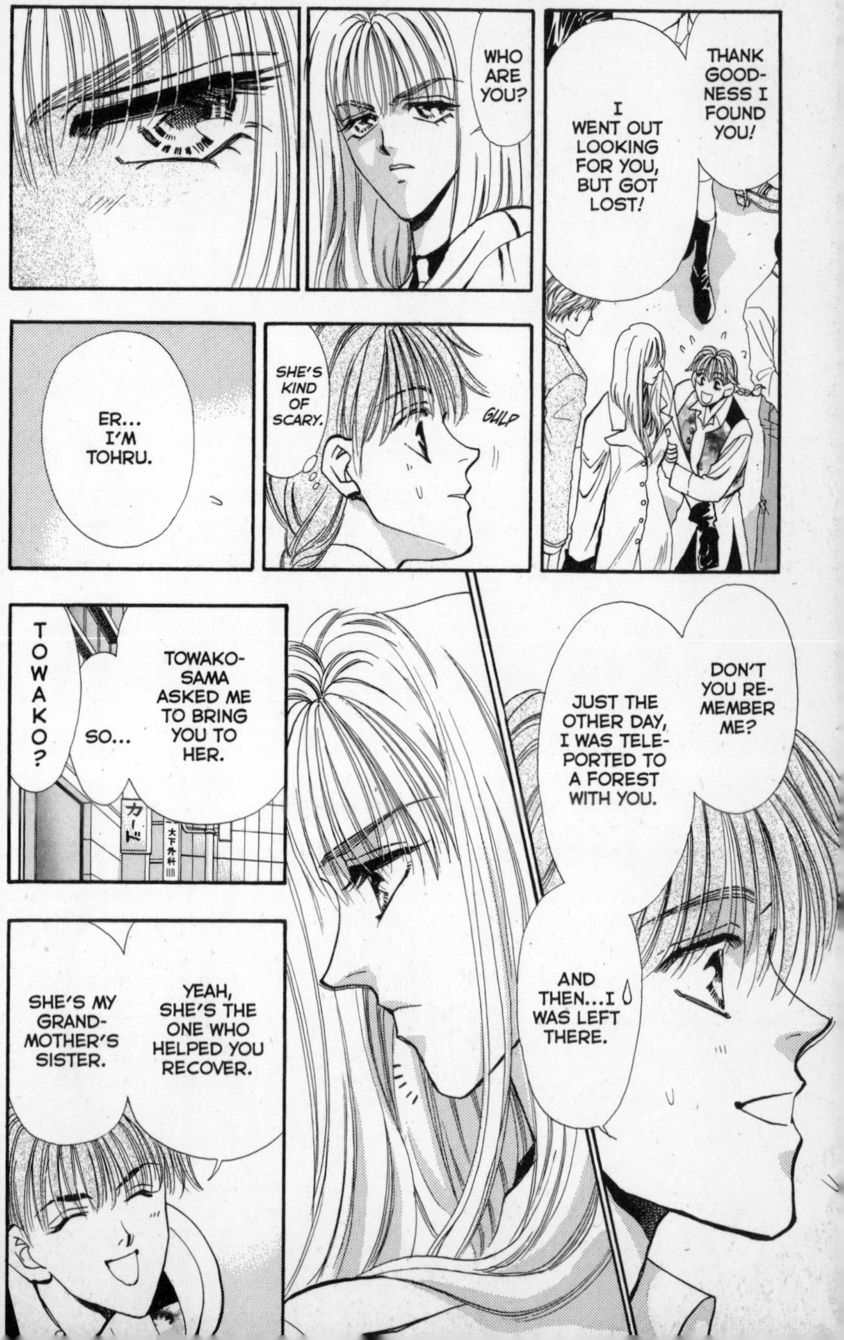
THANK GOOD-NESS I FOUND YOU!
I WENT OUT LOOKING FOR YOU, BUT GOT LOST!
WHO ARE YOU?
GULP
SHE'S KIND OF SCARY.
ER... I'M TOHRU.
DON'T YOU RE-MEMBER ME?
JUST THE OTHER DAY, I WAS TELE-PORTED TO A FOREST WITH YOU.
AND THEN...I WAS LEFT THERE.
TOWAKO-SAMA ASKED ME TO BRING YOU TO HER.
SO...
TOWAKO?
カード
YEAH, SHE'S THE ONE WHO HELPED YOU RECOVER.
SHE'S MY GRAND-MOTHER'S SISTER.

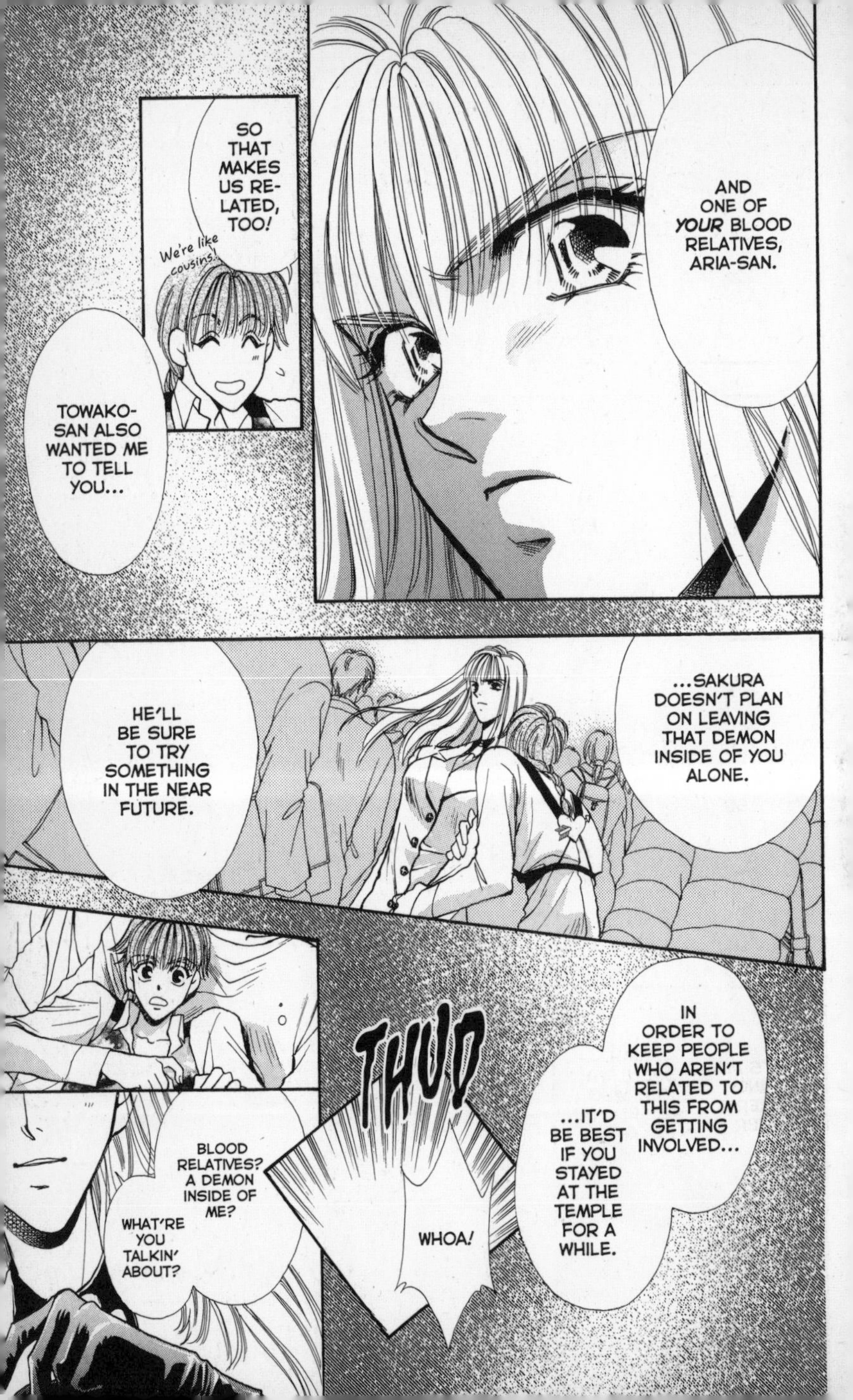
AND ONE OF *YOUR* BLOOD RELATIVES, ARIA-SAN.
SO THAT MAKES US RE-LATED, TOO!
We're like cousins!
TOWAKO-SAN ALSO WANTED ME TO TELL YOU...
...SAKURA DOESN'T PLAN ON LEAVING THAT DEMON INSIDE OF YOU ALONE.
HE'LL BE SURE TO TRY SOMETHING IN THE NEAR FUTURE.
IN ORDER TO KEEP PEOPLE WHO AREN'T RELATED TO THIS FROM GETTING INVOLVED...
...IT'D BE BEST IF YOU STAYED AT THE TEMPLE FOR A WHILE.
THUD
WHOA!
BLOOD RELATIVES? A DEMON INSIDE OF ME?
WHAT'RE YOU TALKIN' ABOUT?

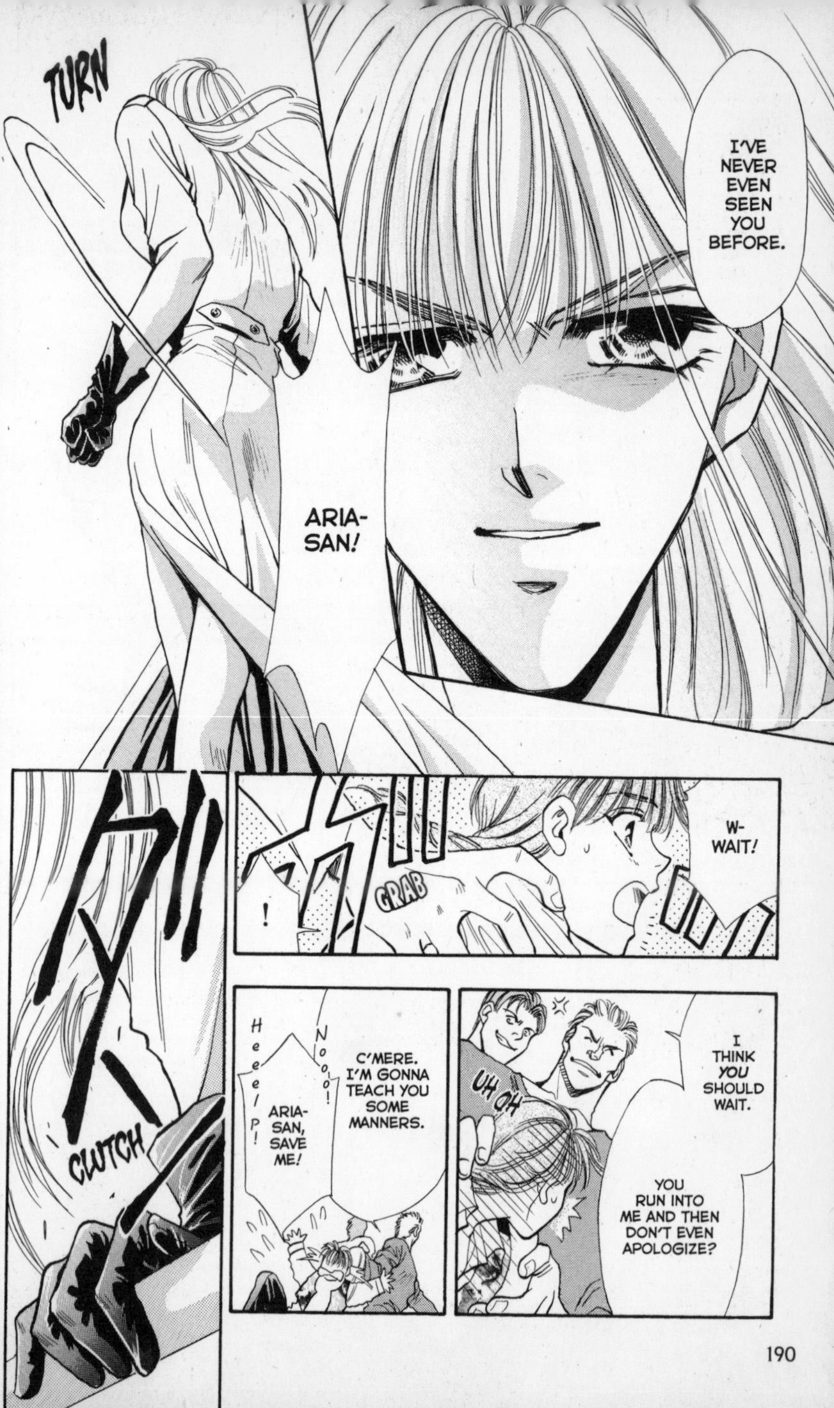
I'VE NEVER EVEN SEEN YOU BEFORE.
ARIA-SAN!
TURN
W-WAIT!
GRAB
!
I THINK *YOU* SHOULD WAIT.
UH OH
YOU RUN INTO ME AND THEN DON'T EVEN APOLOGIZE?
C'MERE. I'M GONNA TEACH YOU SOME MANNERS.
Nooo!
Heeelp!
ARIA-SAN, SAVE ME!
CLUTCH

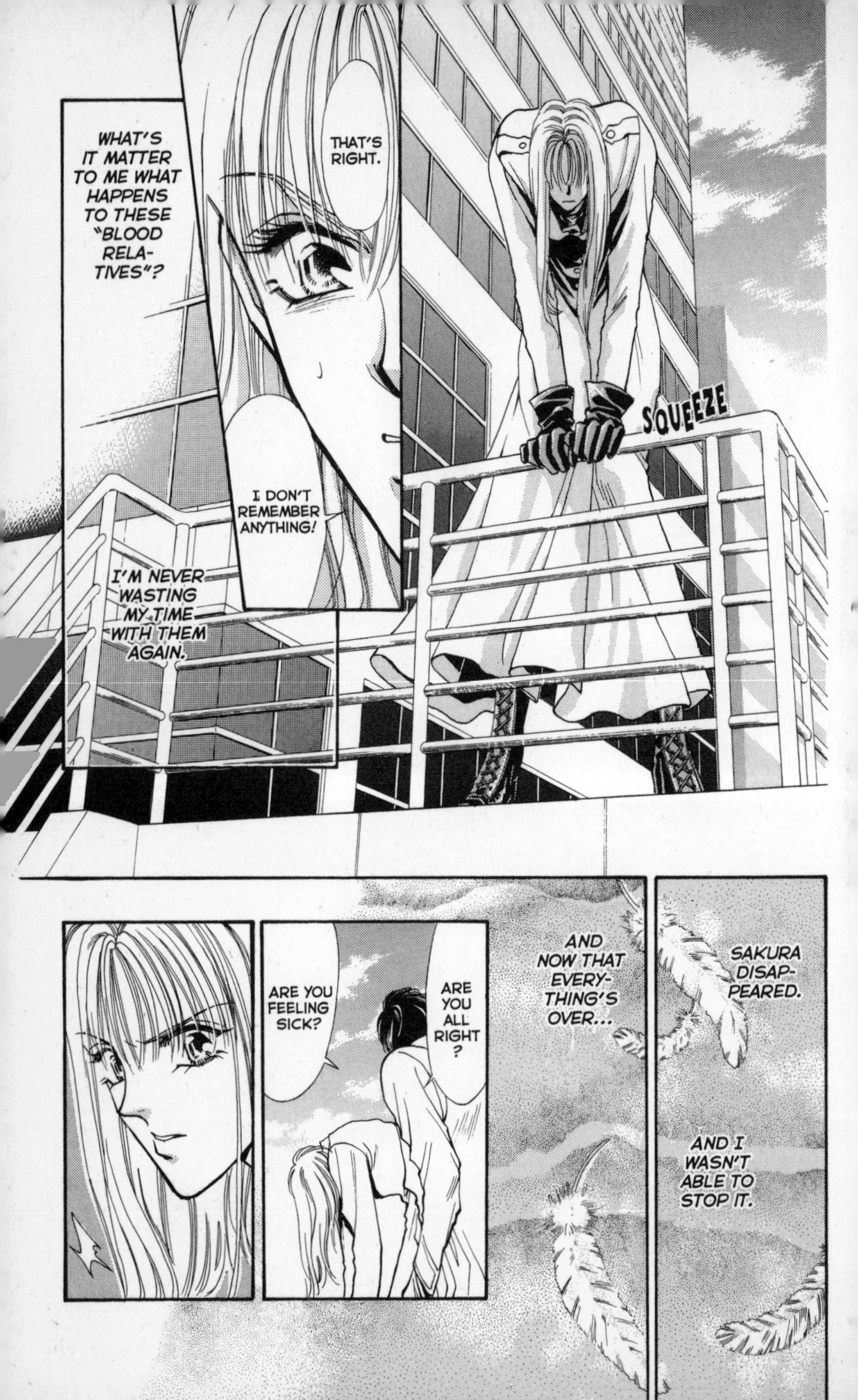
SQUEEZE
THAT'S RIGHT.
WHAT'S IT MATTER TO ME WHAT HAPPENS TO THESE "BLOOD RELATIVES"?
I DON'T REMEMBER ANYTHING!
I'M NEVER WASTING MY TIME WITH THEM AGAIN.
SAKURA DISAPPEARED.
AND I WASN'T ABLE TO STOP IT.
AND NOW THAT EVERYTHING'S OVER...
ARE YOU ALL RIGHT?
ARE YOU FEELING SICK?

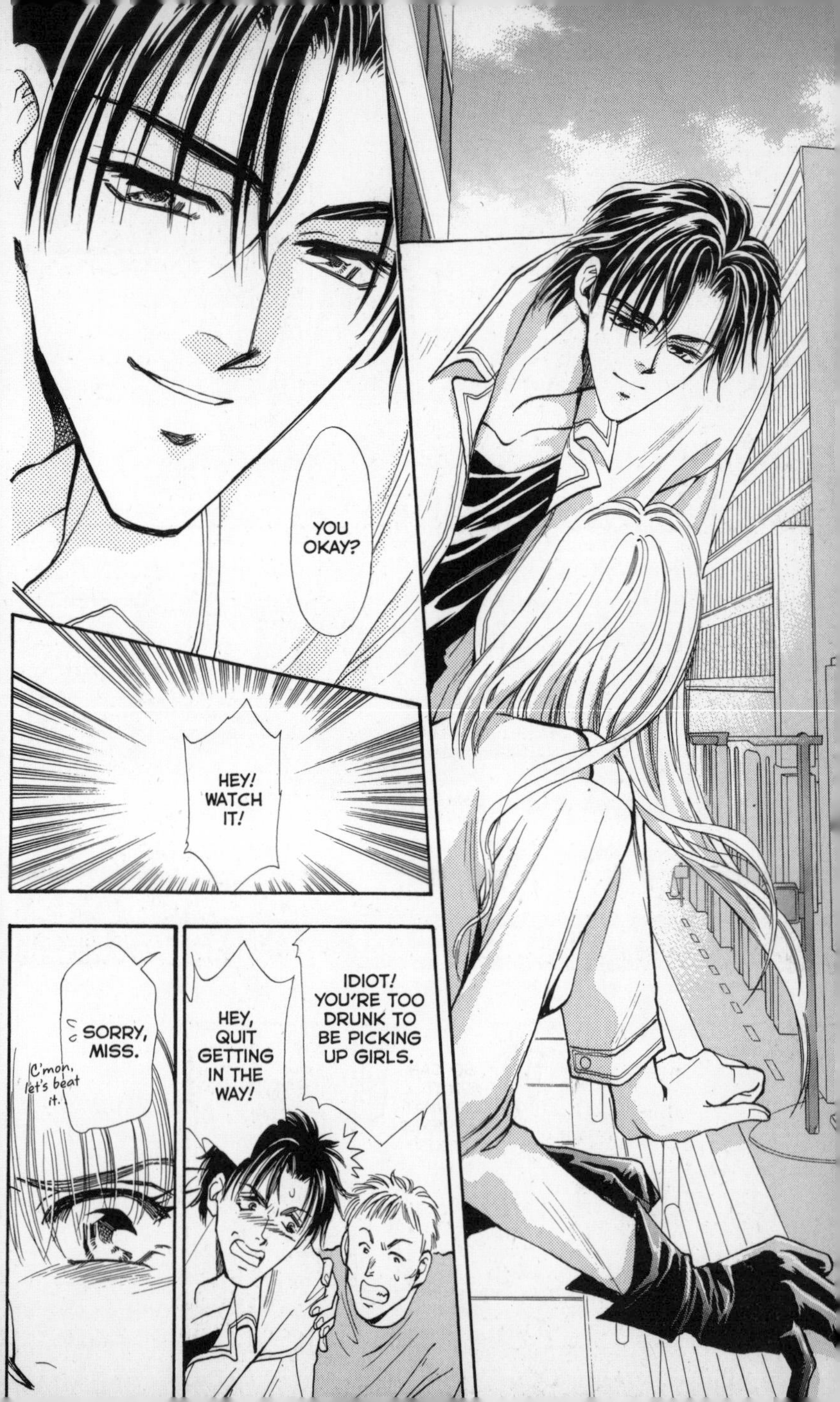
YOU OKAY?
HEY! WATCH IT!
IDIOT! YOU'RE TOO DRUNK TO BE PICKING UP GIRLS.
HEY, QUIT GETTING IN THE WAY!
SORRY, MISS.
C'mon, let's beat it.

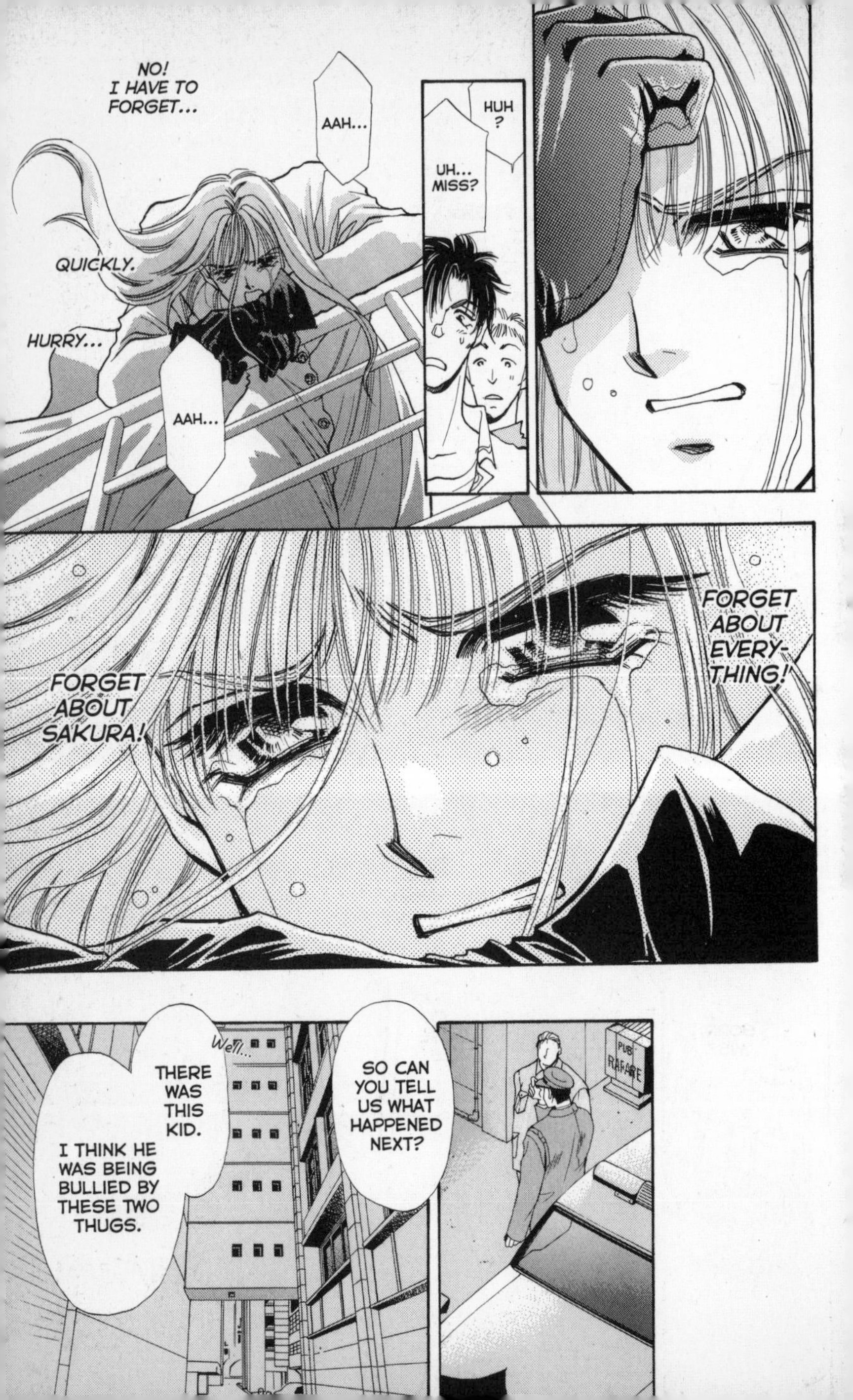
HUH ?
UH... MISS?
AAH...
NO! I HAVE TO FORGET...
QUICKLY.
HURRY...
AAH...
FORGET ABOUT EVERYTHING!
FORGET ABOUT SAKURA!
PUB RAFARE
SO CAN YOU TELL US WHAT HAPPENED NEXT?
Well...
THERE WAS THIS KID.
I THINK HE WAS BEING BULLIED BY THESE TWO THUGS.

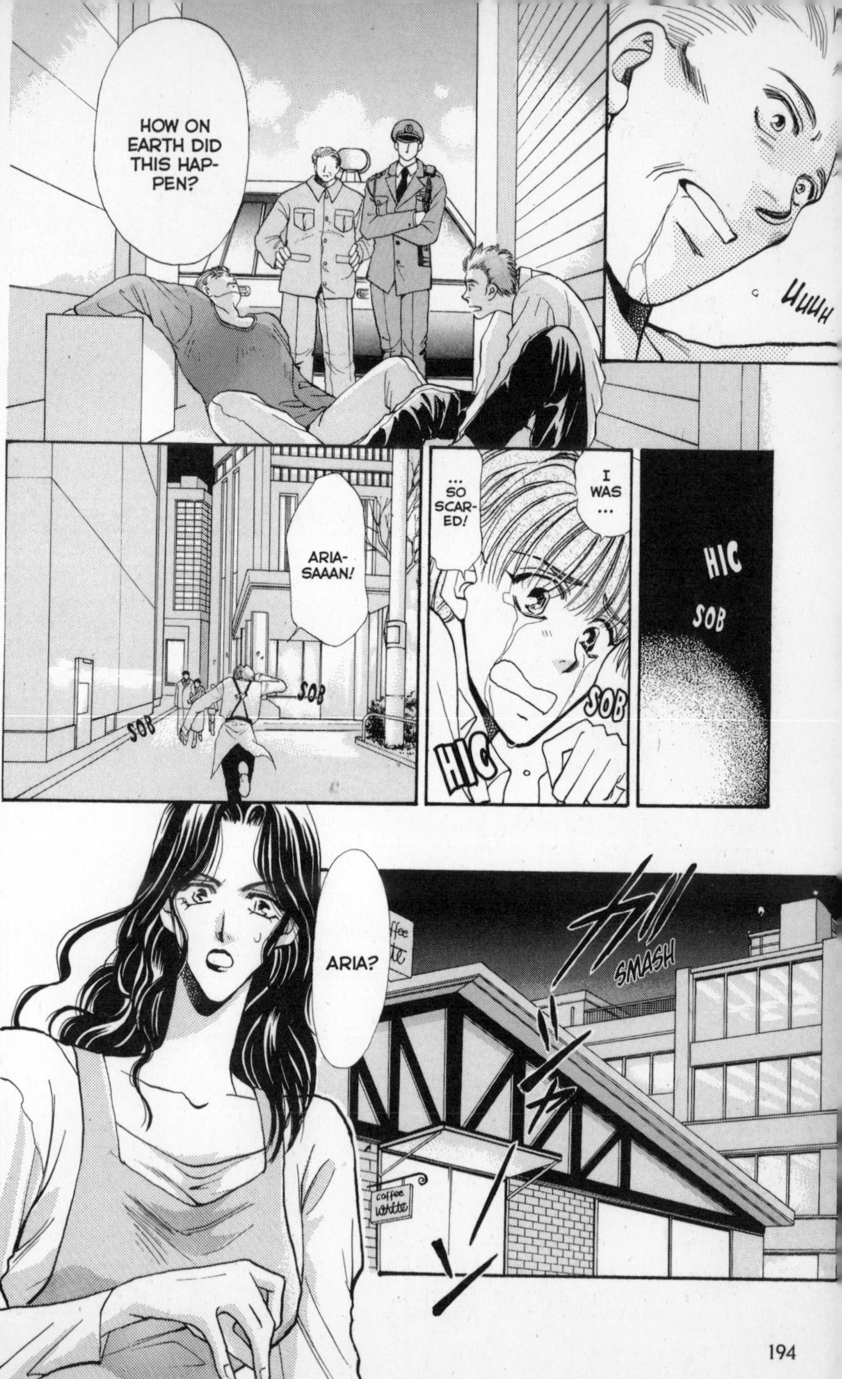
UUUH
HOW ON EARTH DID THIS HAPPEN?
HIC
SOB
I WAS...
...SO SCARED!
SOB
HIC
ARIA-SAAAN!
SOB
SOB
SMASH
ARIA?
coffee white

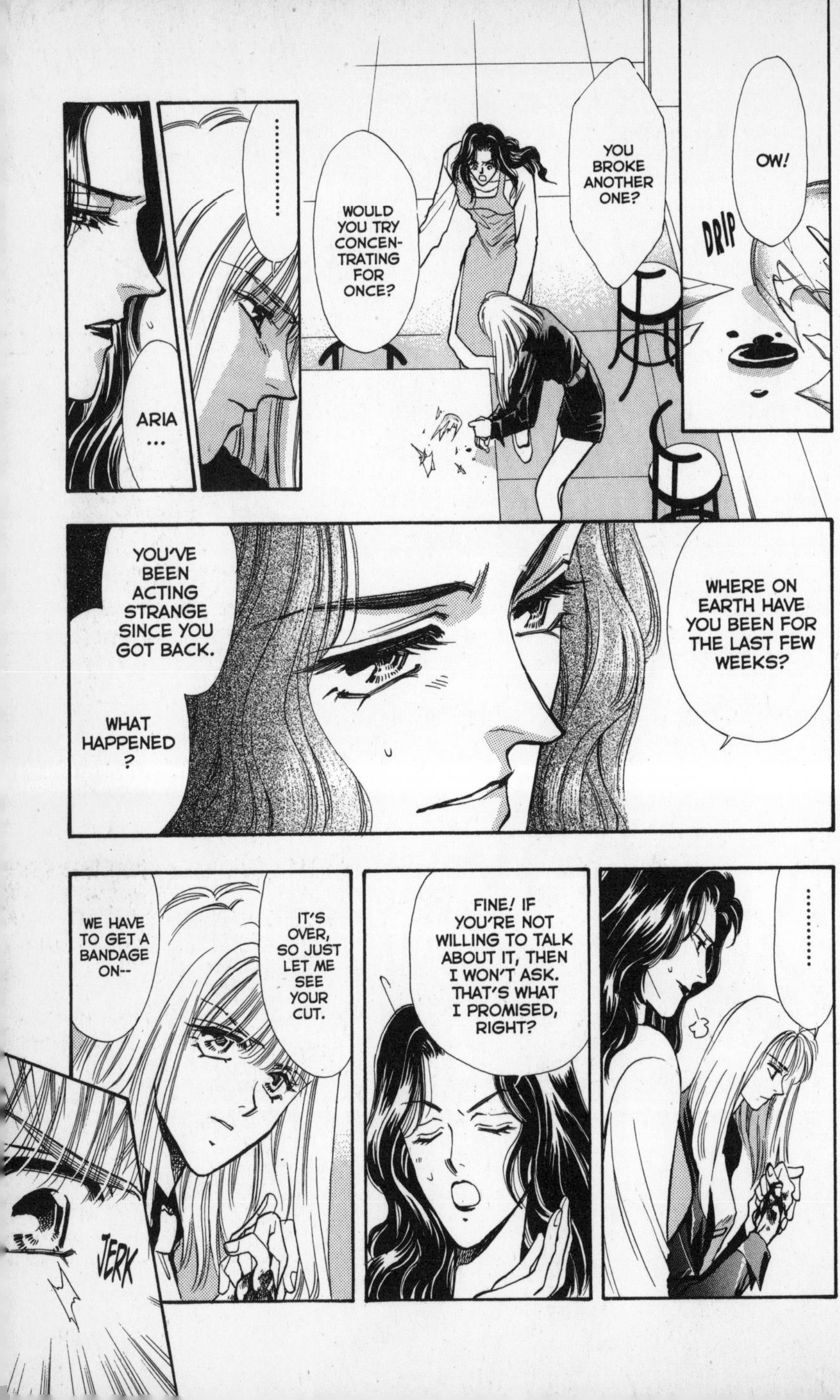
OW!
DRIP
YOU BROKE ANOTHER ONE?
WOULD YOU TRY CONCEN-TRATING FOR ONCE?
....
ARIA ...
WHERE ON EARTH HAVE YOU BEEN FOR THE LAST FEW WEEKS?
YOU'VE BEEN ACTING STRANGE SINCE YOU GOT BACK.
WHAT HAPPENED ?
....
FINE! IF YOU'RE NOT WILLING TO TALK ABOUT IT, THEN I WON'T ASK. THAT'S WHAT I PROMISED, RIGHT?
IT'S OVER, SO JUST LET ME SEE YOUR CUT.
WE HAVE TO GET A BANDAGE ON--
JERK

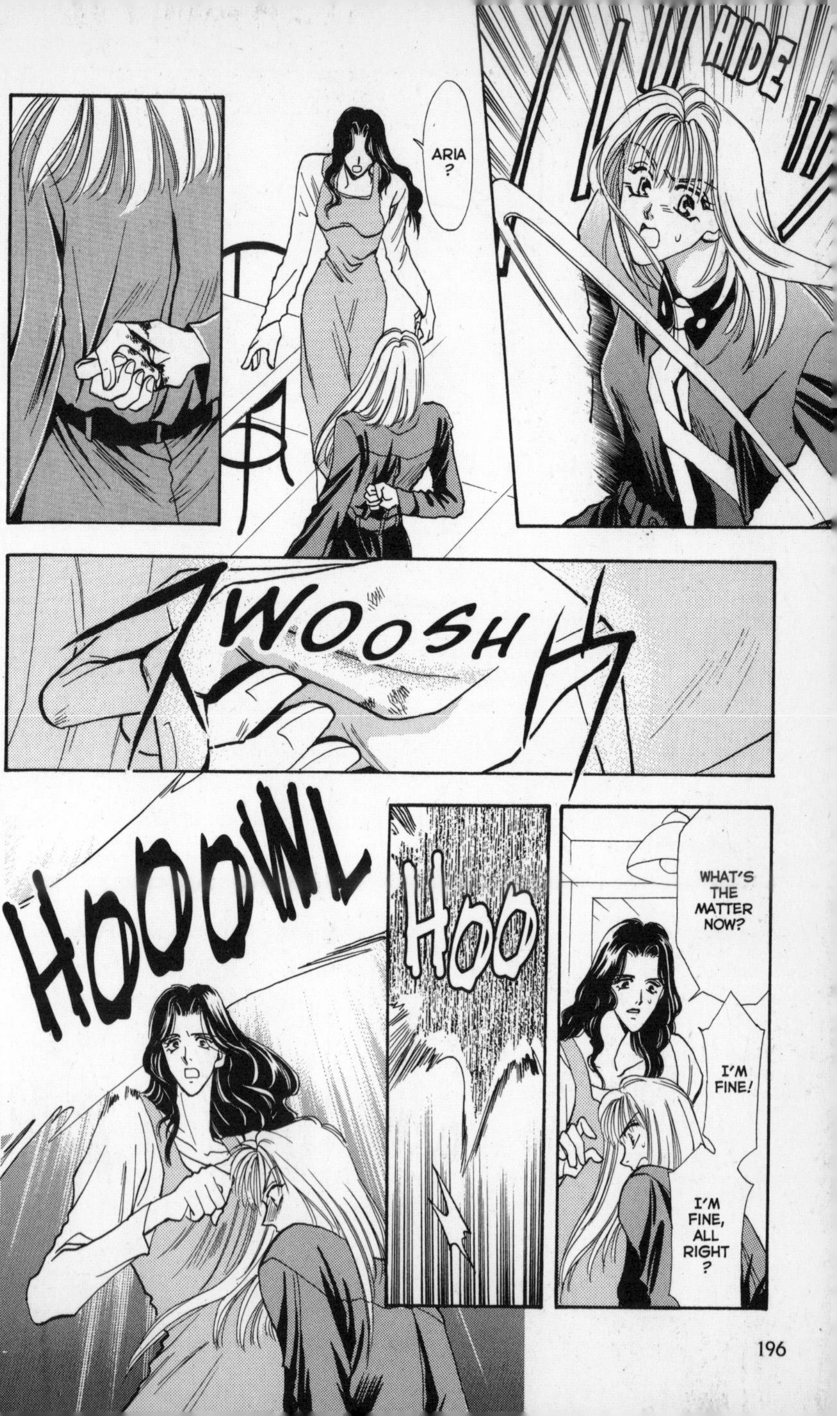
HIDE
ARIA ?
WOOSH
HOOOWL
HOO
WHAT'S THE MATTER NOW?
I'M FINE!
I'M FINE, ALL RIGHT ?

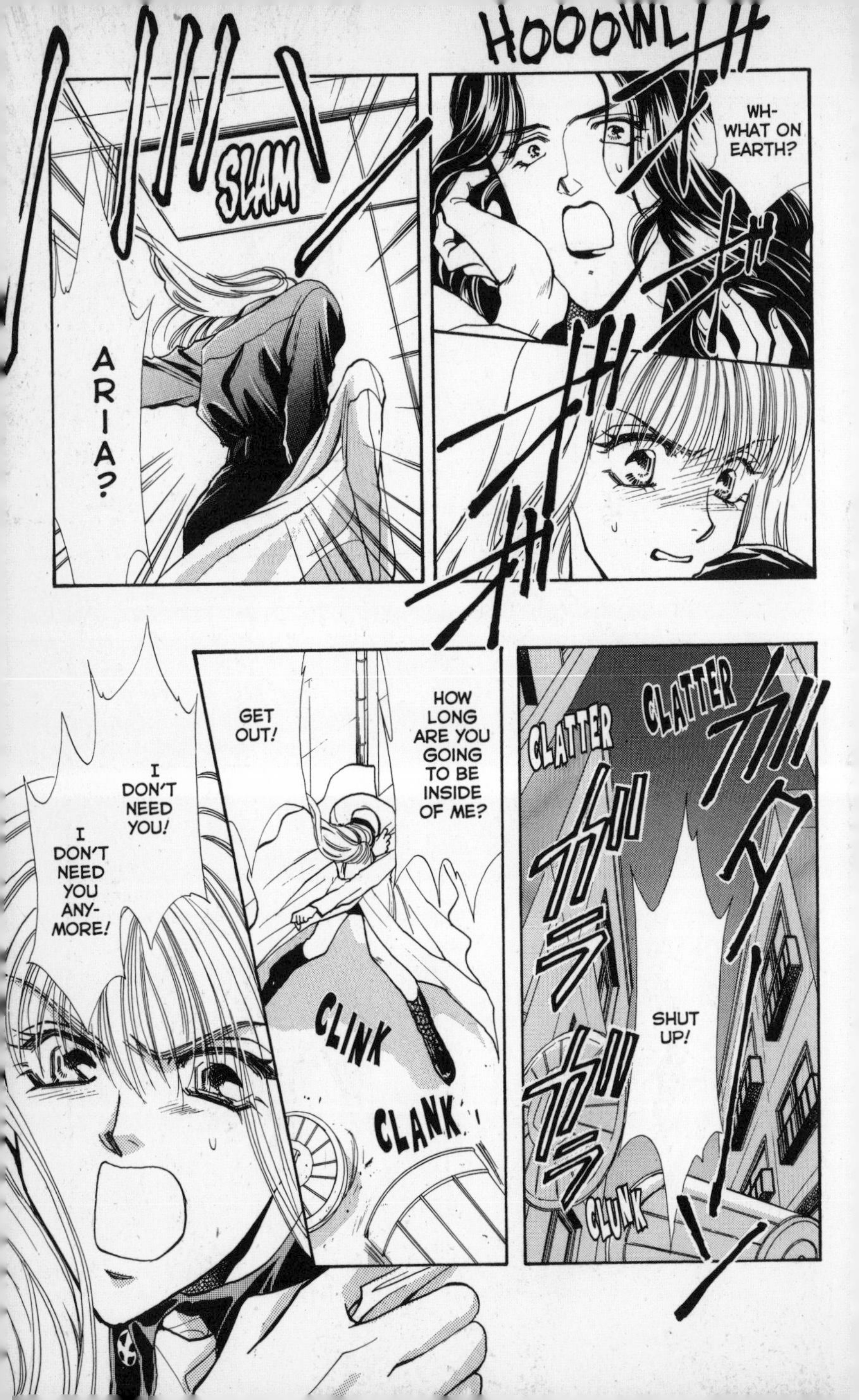
HOOOWL
WH- WHAT ON EARTH?
SLAM
ARIA?
CLATTER
CLATTER
SHUT UP!
CLUNK
HOW LONG ARE YOU GOING TO BE INSIDE OF ME?
GET OUT!
CLINK
CLANK
I DON'T NEED YOU!
I DON'T NEED YOU ANYMORE!

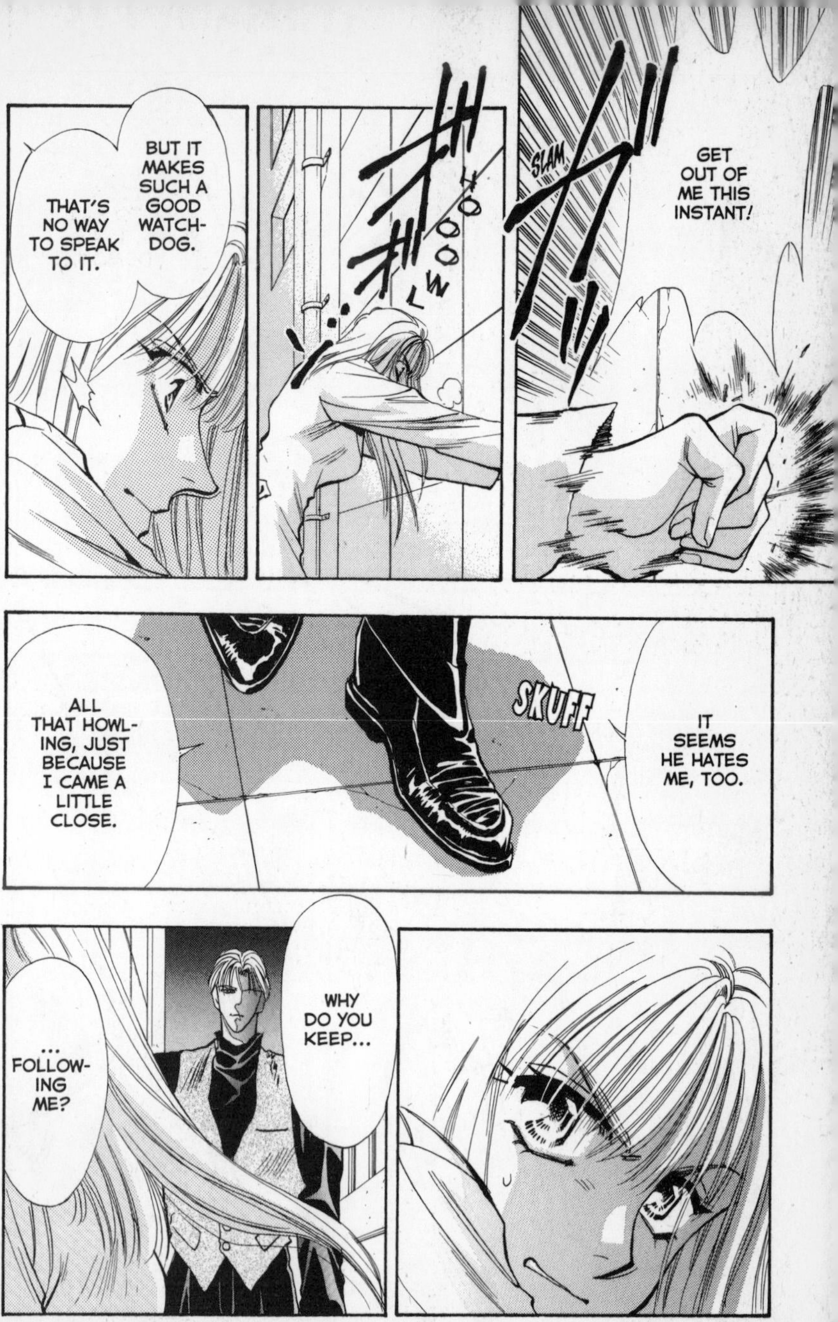
SLAM
GET OUT OF ME THIS INSTANT!
BUT IT MAKES SUCH A GOOD WATCH-DOG.
THAT'S NO WAY TO SPEAK TO IT.
IT SEEMS HE HATES ME, TOO.
SKUFF
ALL THAT HOWL-ING, JUST BECAUSE I CAME A LITTLE CLOSE.
WHY DO YOU KEEP...
... FOLLOW-ING ME?

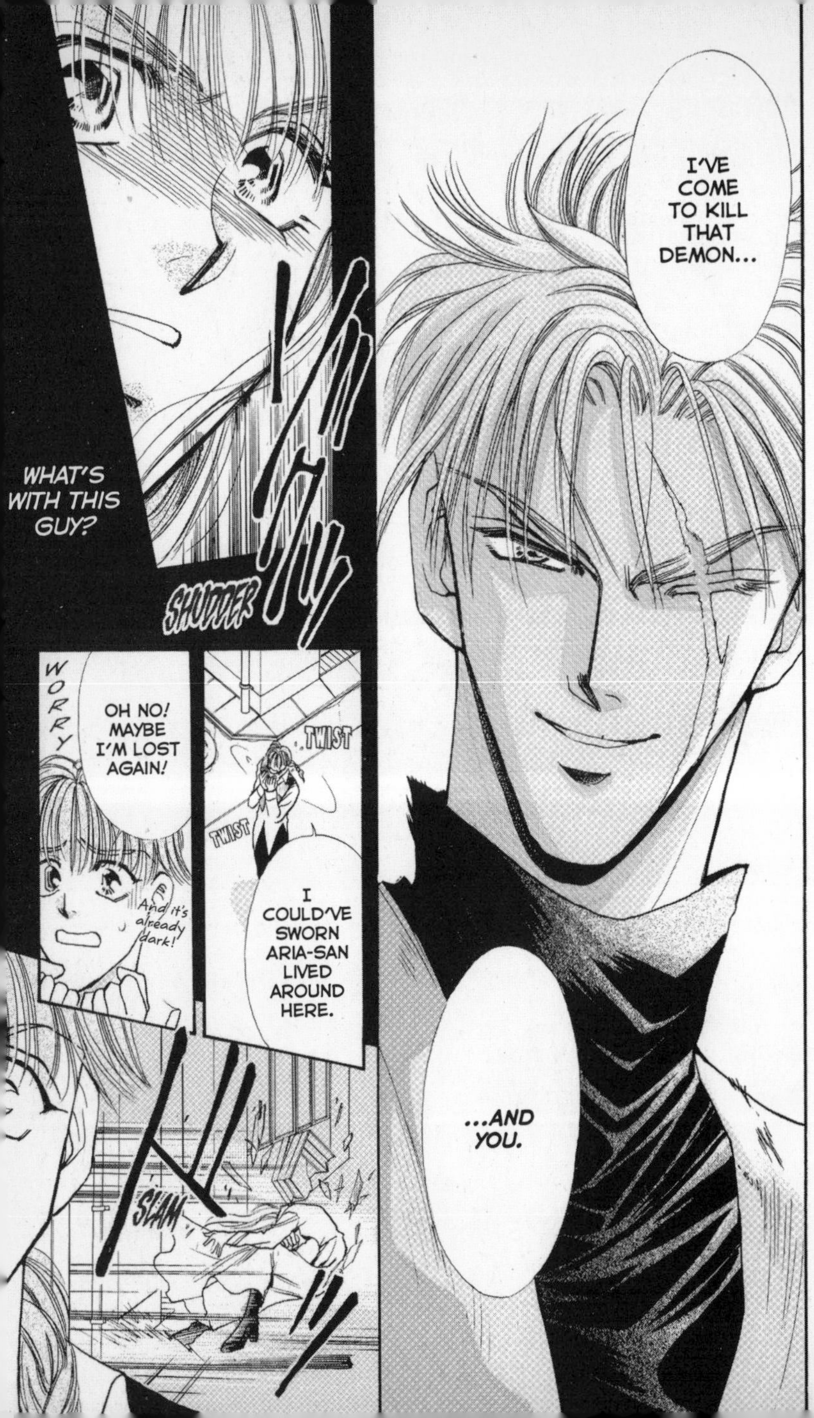
I'VE COME TO KILL THAT DEMON...
...AND YOU.
WHAT'S WITH THIS GUY?
SHUDDER
TWIST
TWIST
I COULD'VE SWORN ARIA-SAN LIVED AROUND HERE.
WORRY
OH NO! MAYBE I'M LOST AGAIN!
And it's already dark!
SLAM

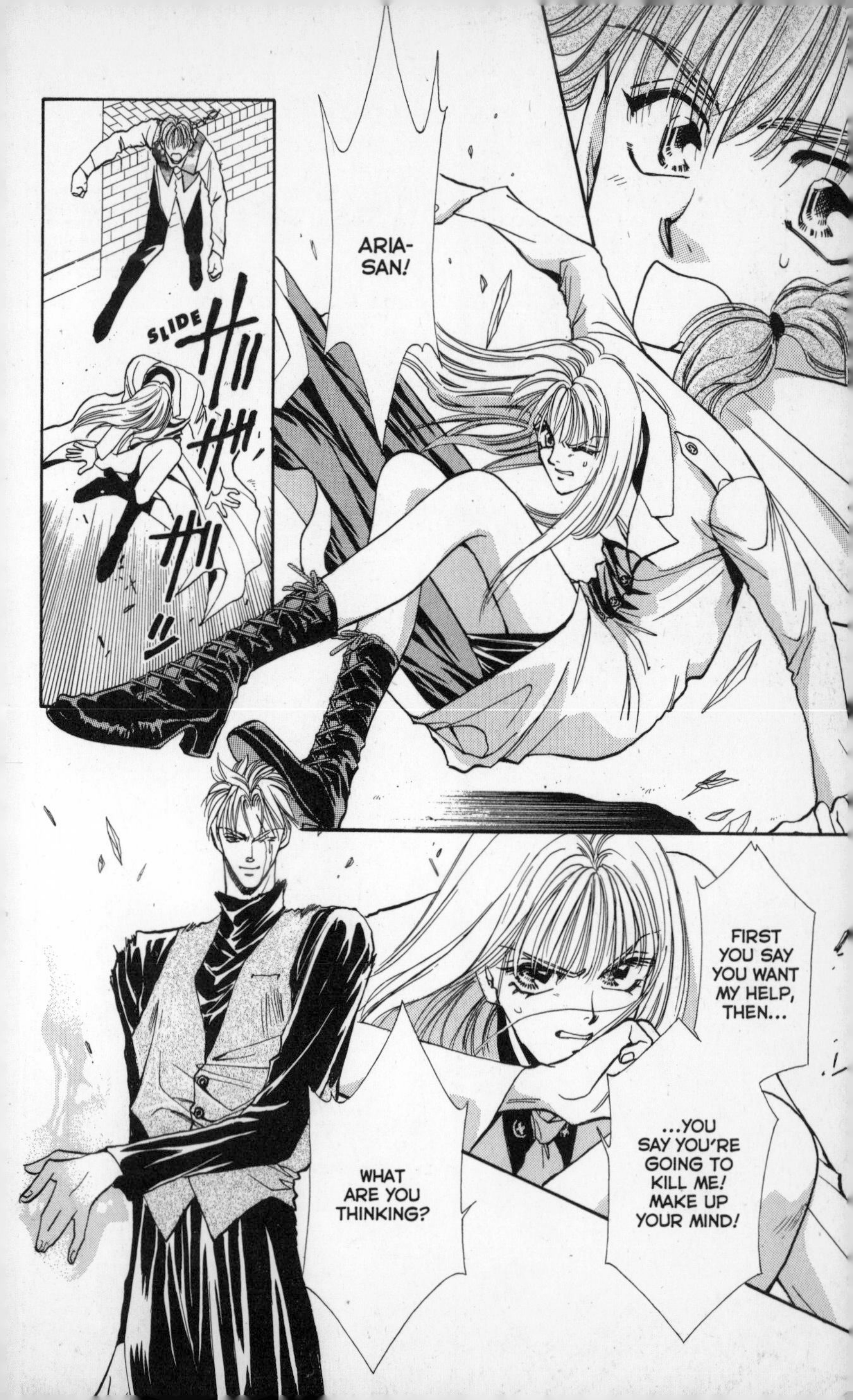
ARIA-SAN!
SLIDE
FIRST YOU SAY YOU WANT MY HELP, THEN...
...YOU SAY YOU'RE GOING TO KILL ME! MAKE UP YOUR MIND!
WHAT ARE YOU THINKING?

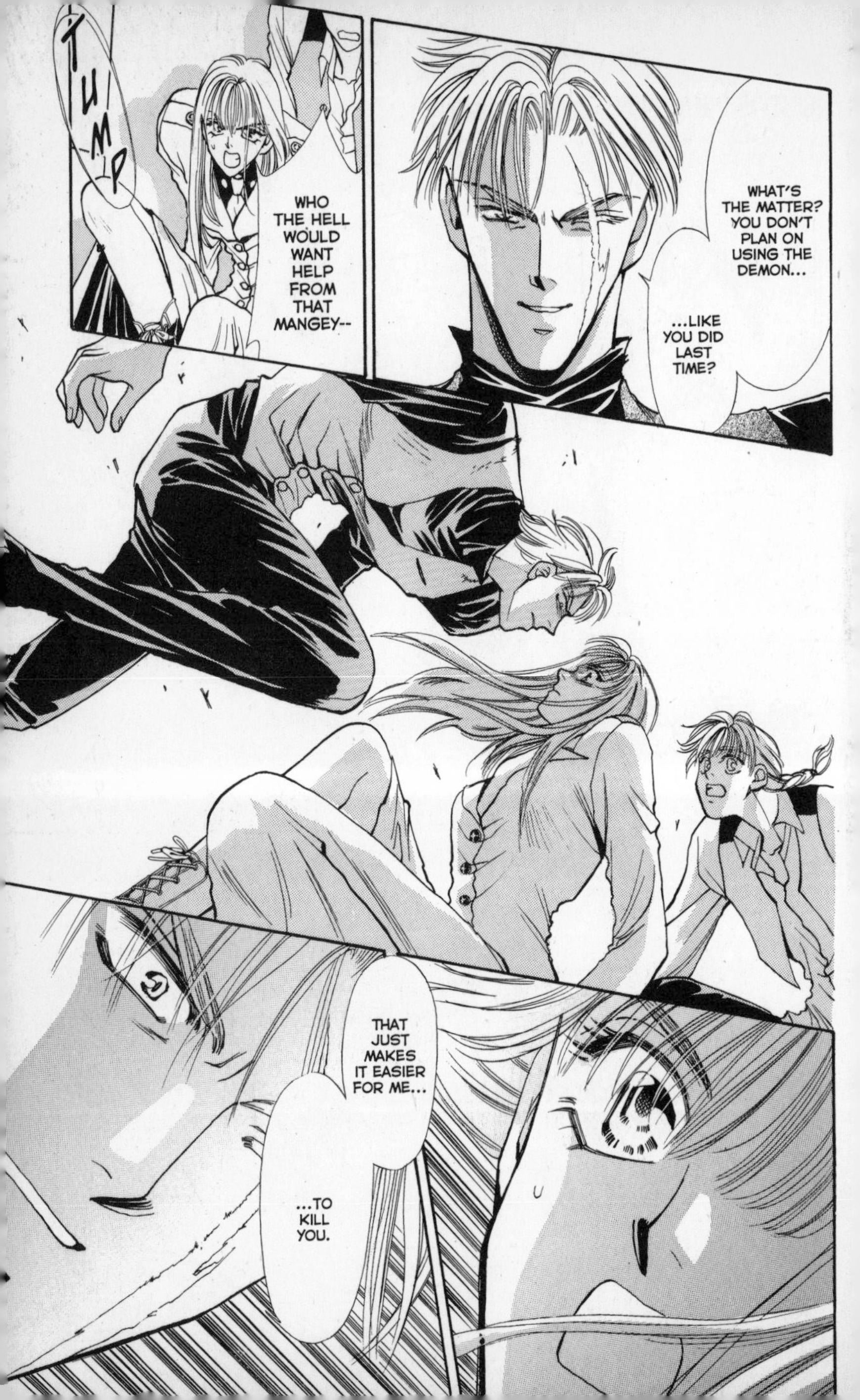
WHAT'S THE MATTER? YOU DON'T PLAN ON USING THE DEMON...
...LIKE YOU DID LAST TIME?
TUMP
WHO THE HELL WOULD WANT HELP FROM THAT MANGEY--
THAT JUST MAKES IT EASIER FOR ME...
...TO KILL YOU.

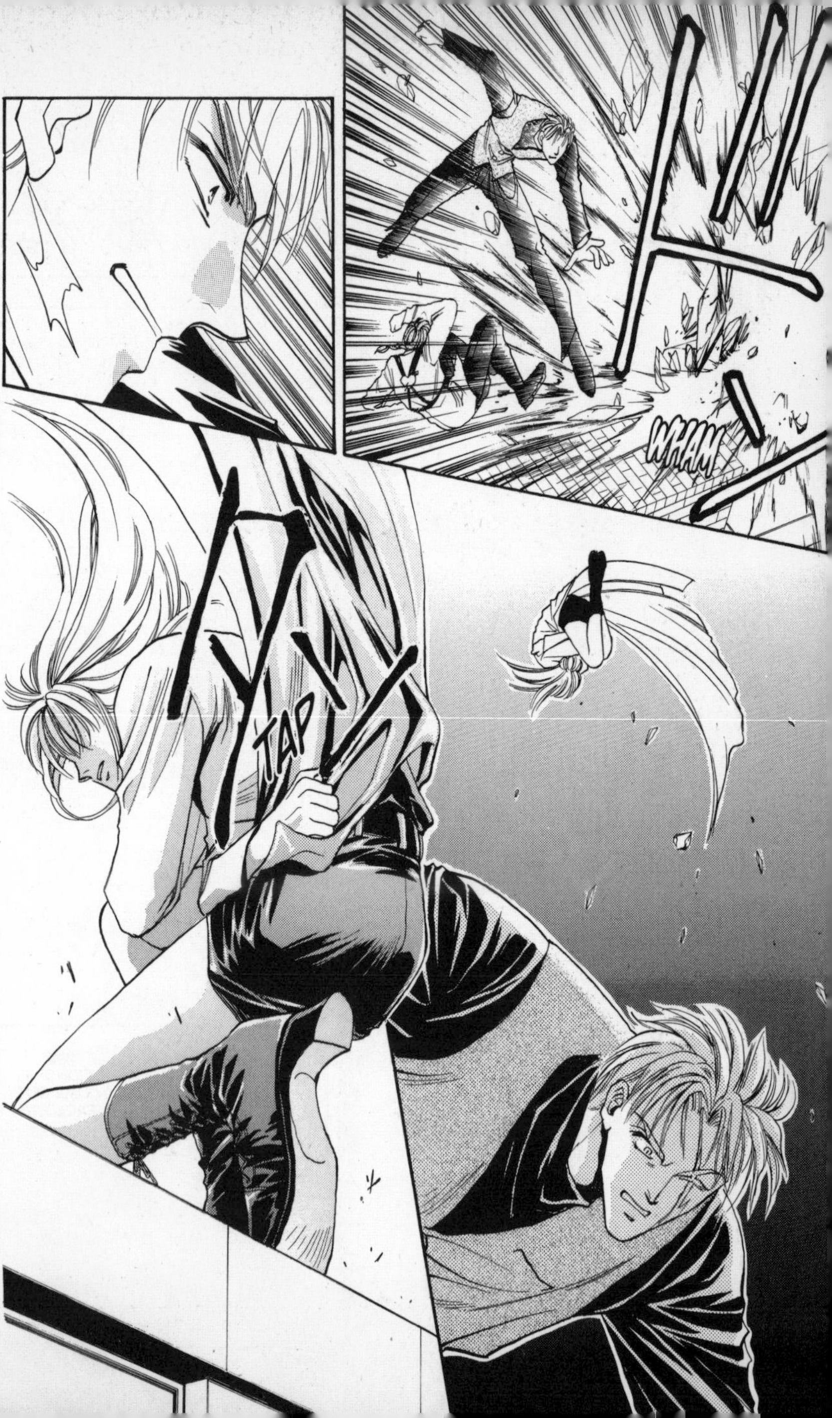
WHAM
TAP

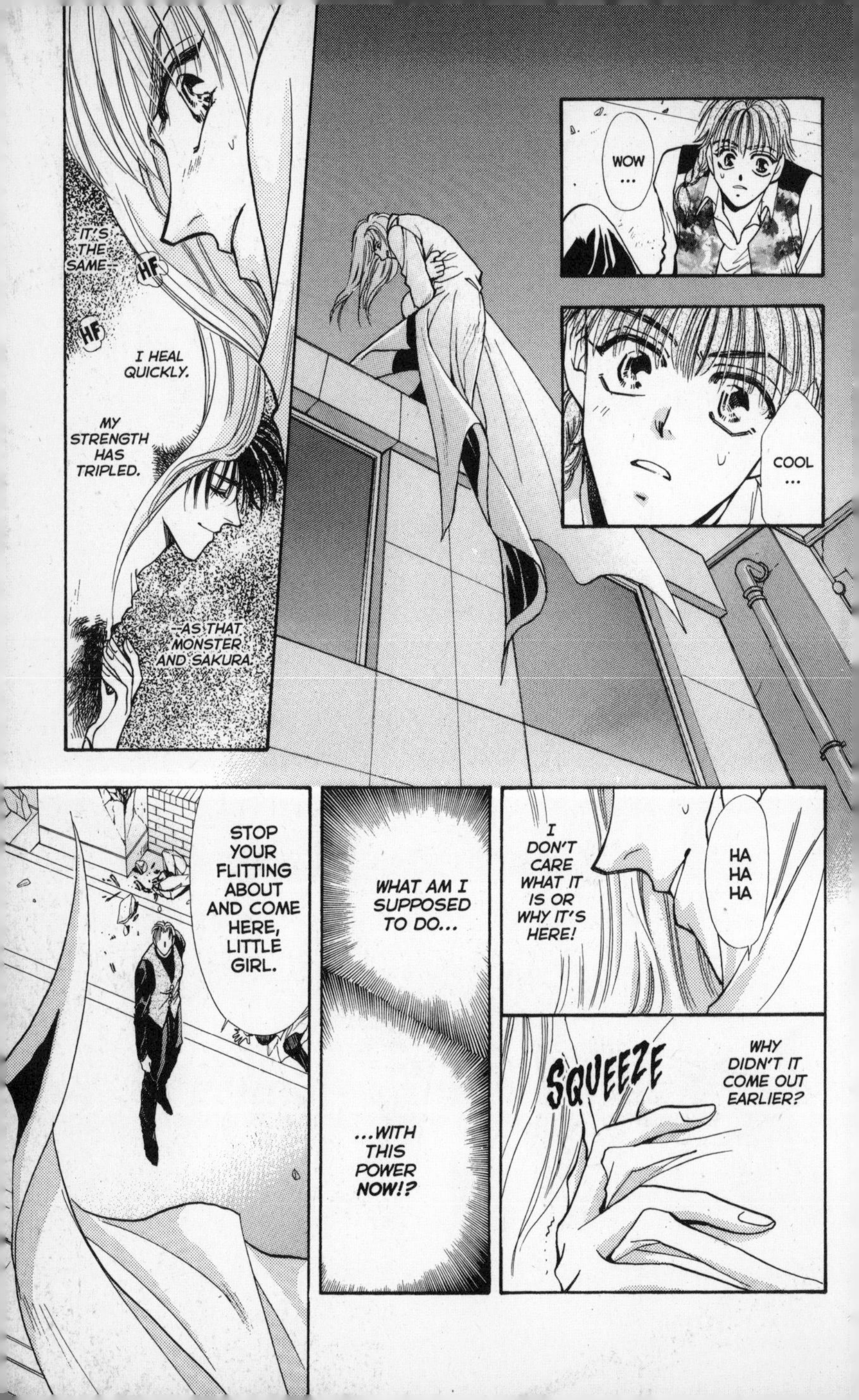

WOW ...
COOL ...
IT'S THE SAME--
HF
HF
I HEAL QUICKLY.
MY STRENGTH HAS TRIPLED.
--AS THAT MONSTER AND SAKURA.
HA HA HA
I DON'T CARE WHAT IT IS OR WHY IT'S HERE!
WHY DIDN'T IT COME OUT EARLIER?
SQUEEZE
WHAT AM I SUPPOSED TO DO...
...WITH THIS POWER NOW!?
STOP YOUR FLITTING ABOUT AND COME HERE, LITTLE GIRL.

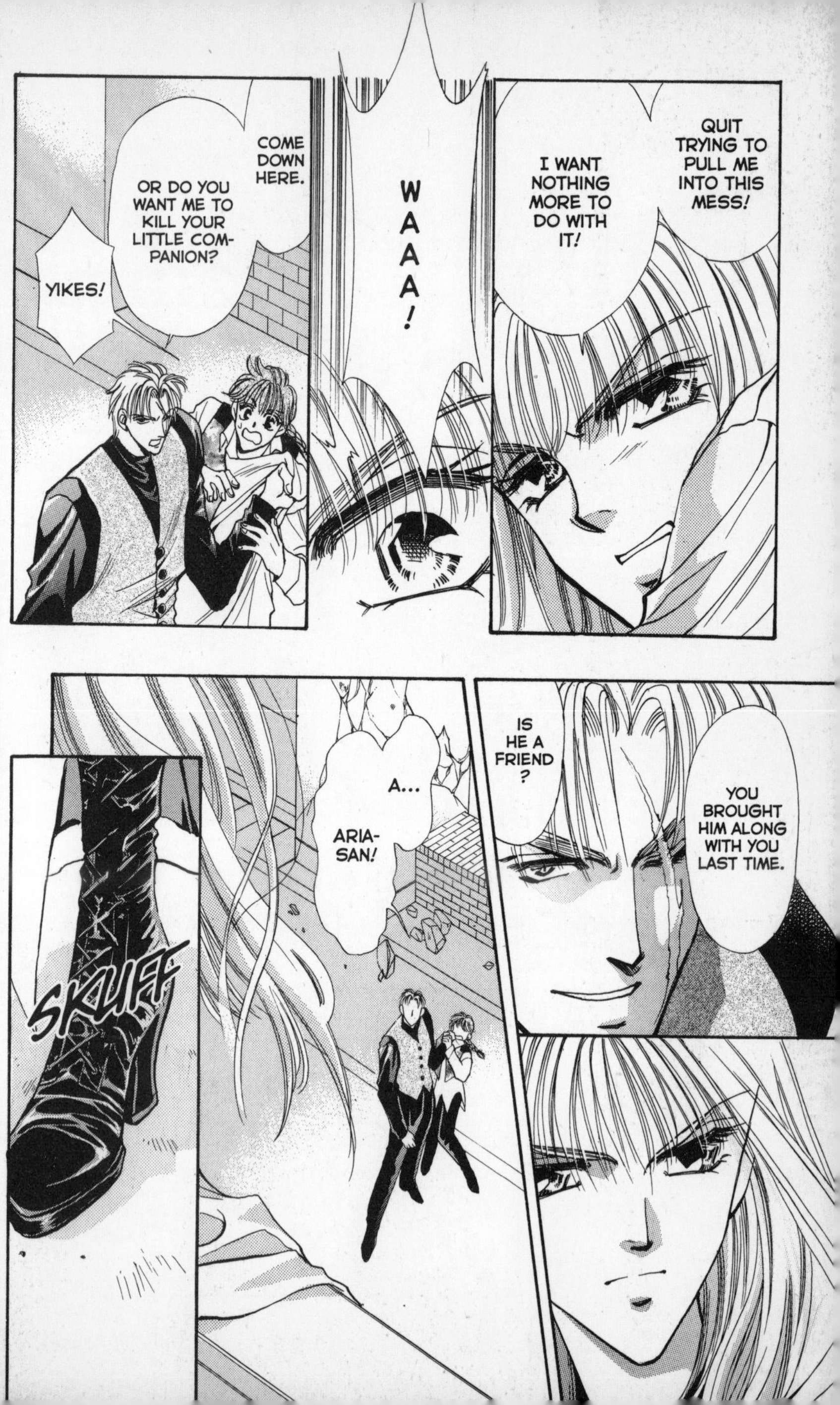
QUIT TRYING TO PULL ME INTO THIS MESS!
I WANT NOTHING MORE TO DO WITH IT!
WAAAA!
COME DOWN HERE.
OR DO YOU WANT ME TO KILL YOUR LITTLE COMPANION?
YIKES!
YOU BROUGHT HIM ALONG WITH YOU LAST TIME.
IS HE A FRIEND?
A...
ARIA-SAN!
SKUFF

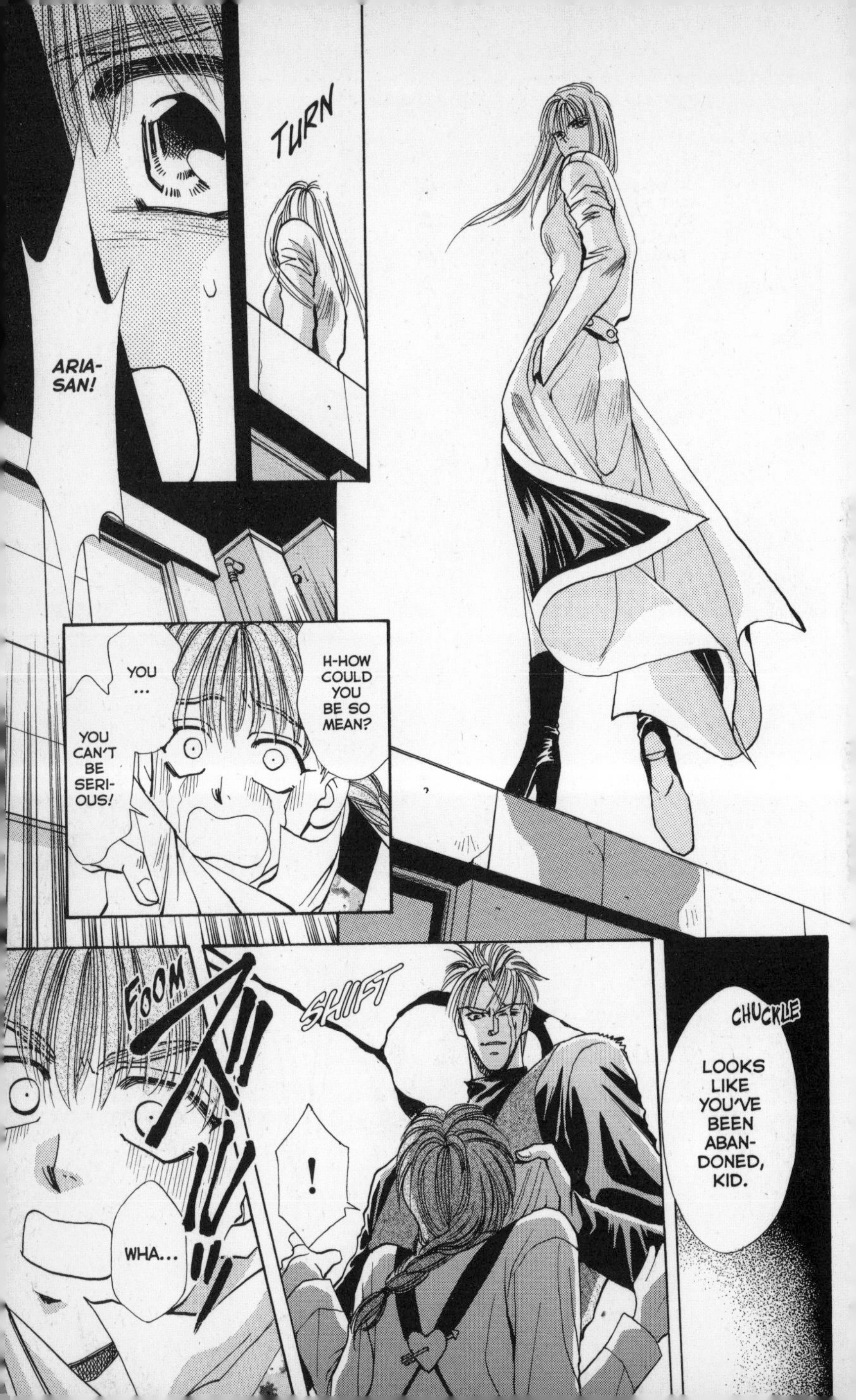
TURN
ARIA-SAN!
H-HOW COULD YOU BE SO MEAN?
YOU ...
YOU CAN'T BE SERI-OUS!
CHUCKLE
LOOKS LIKE YOU'VE BEEN ABAN-DONED, KID.
SHIFT
!
FOOM
WHA...

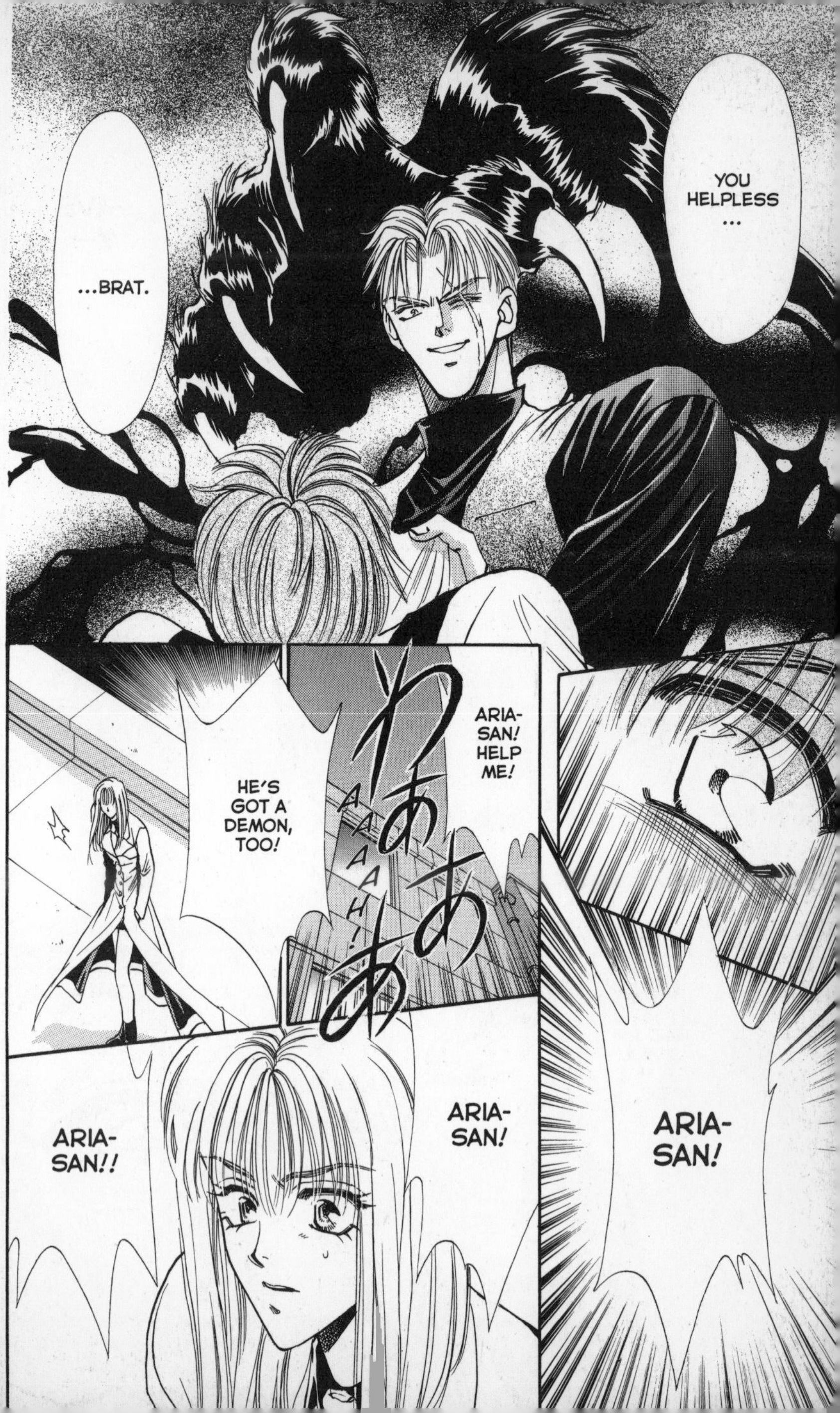
YOU HELPLESS ...
...BRAT.
ARIA-SAN!
ARIA-SAN! HELP ME!
わあああ
AAAAAH!
HE'S GOT A DEMON, TOO!
ARIA-SAN!
ARIA-SAN!!

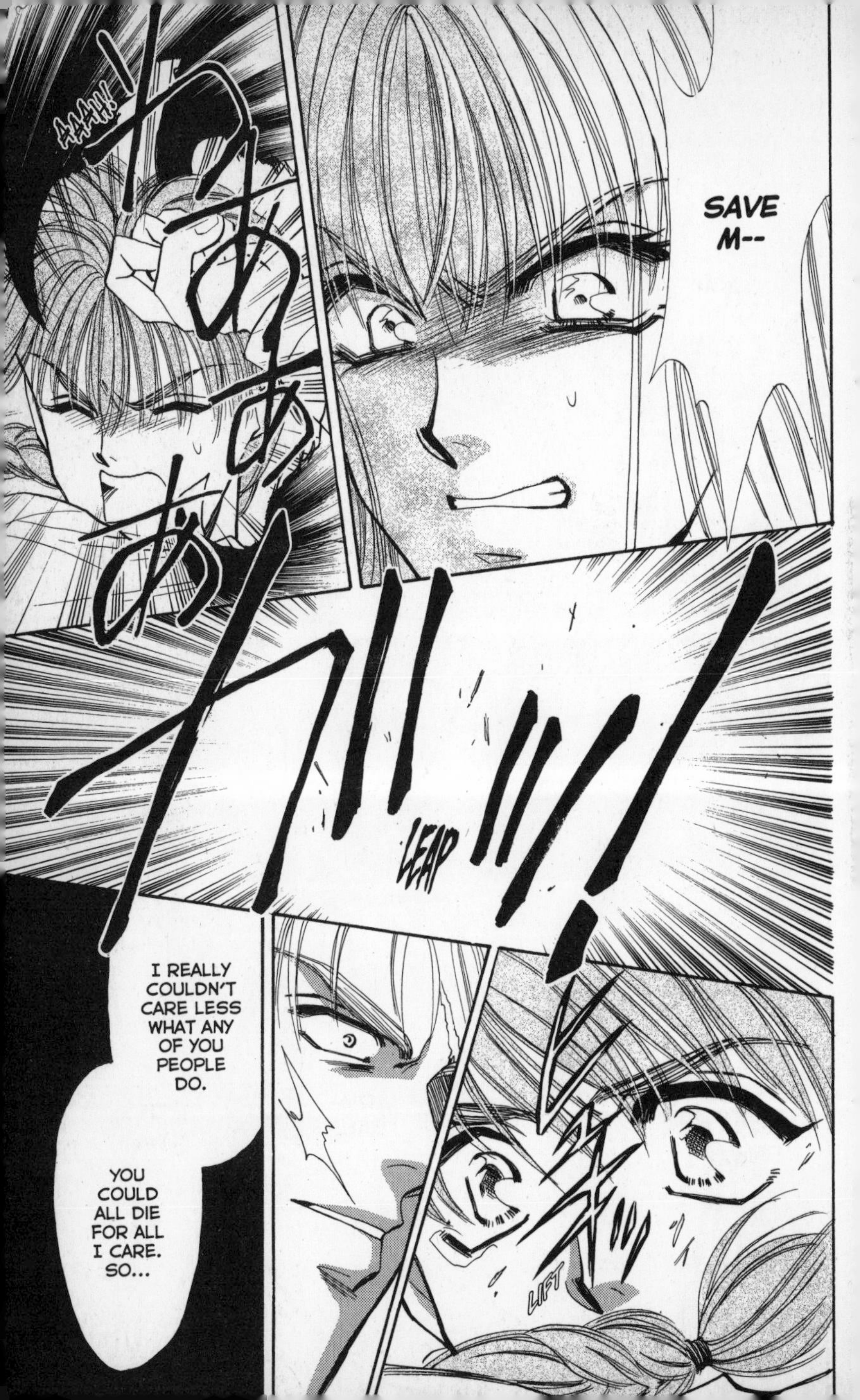
SAVE M--
AAAH!
LEAP
I REALLY COULDN'T CARE LESS WHAT ANY OF YOU PEOPLE DO.
YOU COULD ALL DIE FOR ALL I CARE. SO...
LIFT

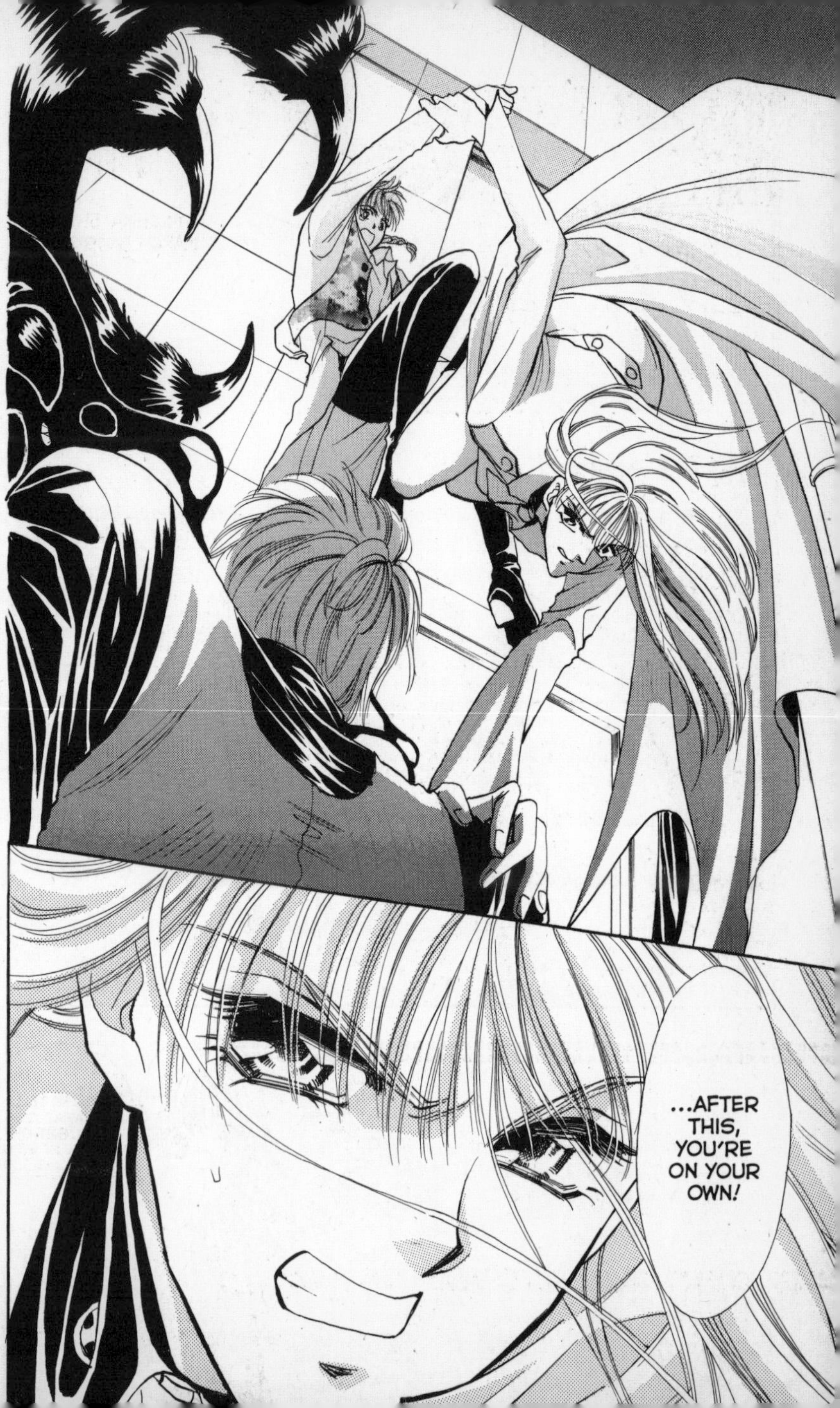
...AFTER THIS, YOU'RE ON YOUR OWN!

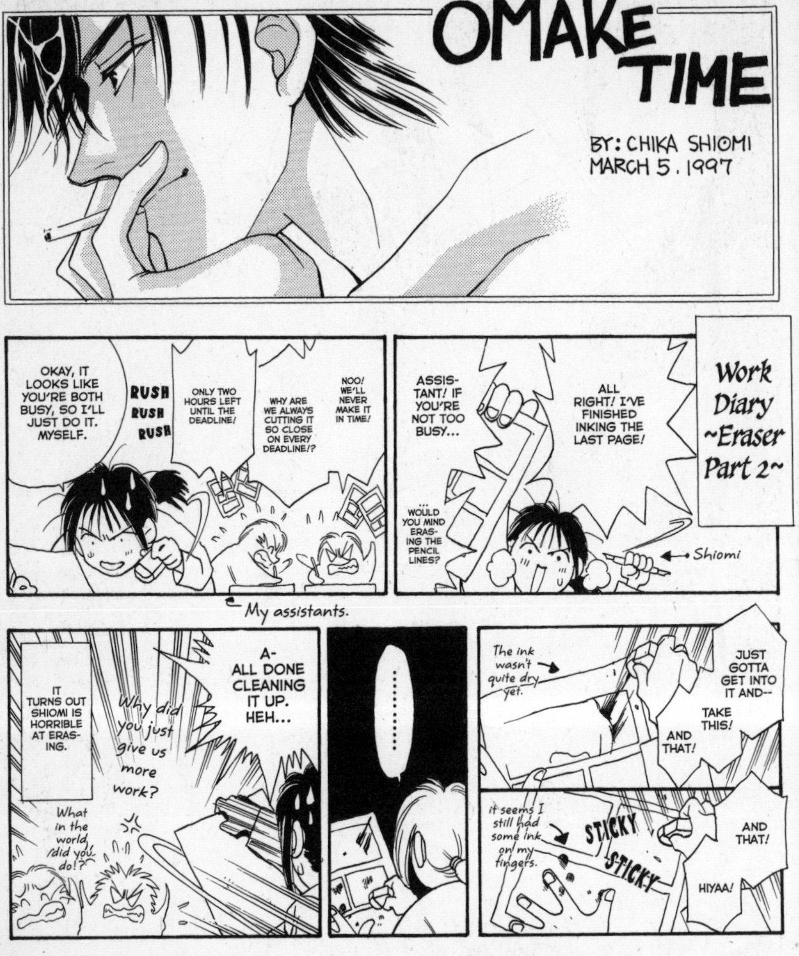
OMAKE TIME
BY: CHIKA SHIOMI
MARCH 5. 1997
Work Diary ~Eraser Part 2~
ALL RIGHT! I'VE FINISHED INKING THE LAST PAGE!
ASSISTANT! IF YOU'RE NOT TOO BUSY...
...WOULD YOU MIND ERASING THE PENCIL LINES?
Shiomi
NOO! WE'LL NEVER MAKE IT IN TIME!
WHY ARE WE ALWAYS CUTTING IT SO CLOSE ON EVERY DEADLINE!?
ONLY TWO HOURS LEFT UNTIL THE DEADLINE!
RUSH RUSH RUSH
OKAY, IT LOOKS LIKE YOU'RE BOTH BUSY, SO I'LL JUST DO IT. MYSELF.
My assistants.
JUST GOTTA GET INTO IT AND--
TAKE THIS!
AND THAT!
The ink wasn't quite dry yet.
AND THAT!
HIYAA!
STICKY
STICKY
it seems I still had some ink on my fingers.
....
A- ALL DONE CLEANING IT UP. HEH...
Why did you just give us more work?
IT TURNS OUT SHIOMI IS HORRIBLE AT ERASING.
What in the world did you do!?

Chika Shiomi
c/o Go! Media Entertainment
5737 Kanan Rd. #591
Agoura Hills, CA 91301

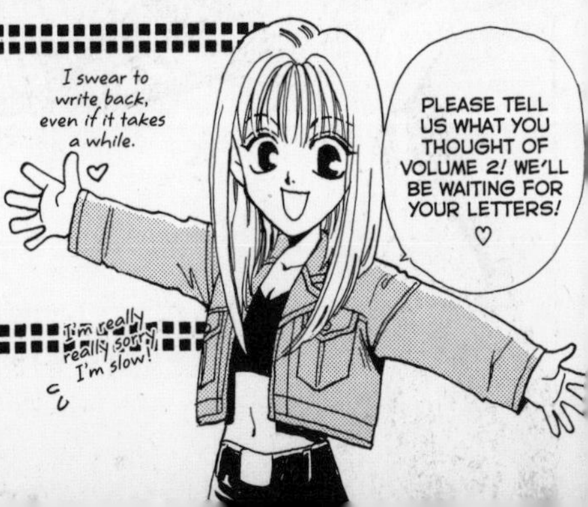
PLEASE TELL US WHAT YOU THOUGHT OF VOLUME 2! WE'LL BE WAITING FOR YOUR LETTERS! ♡
I swear to write back, even if it takes a while. ♡
I'm really really sorry I'm slow!

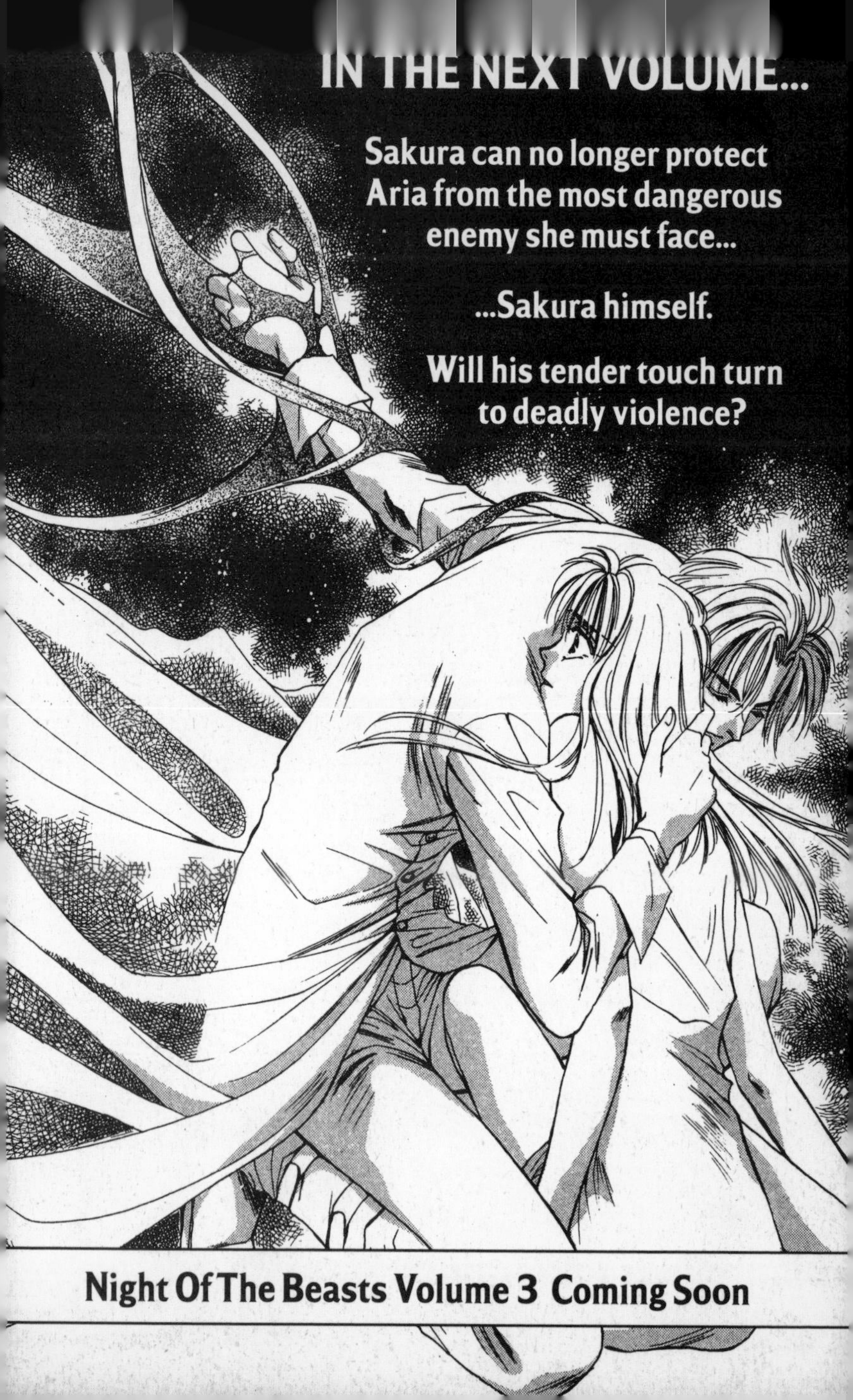
IN THE NEXT VOLUME...
Sakura can no longer protect Aria from the most dangerous enemy she must face...
...Sakura himself.
Will his tender touch turn to deadly violence?
Night Of The Beasts Volume 3 Coming Soon

INNOCENT.

PURE.

BEAUTIFUL.

DAMNED.

Cantarella

© 2001 You Higuri/Akitasho

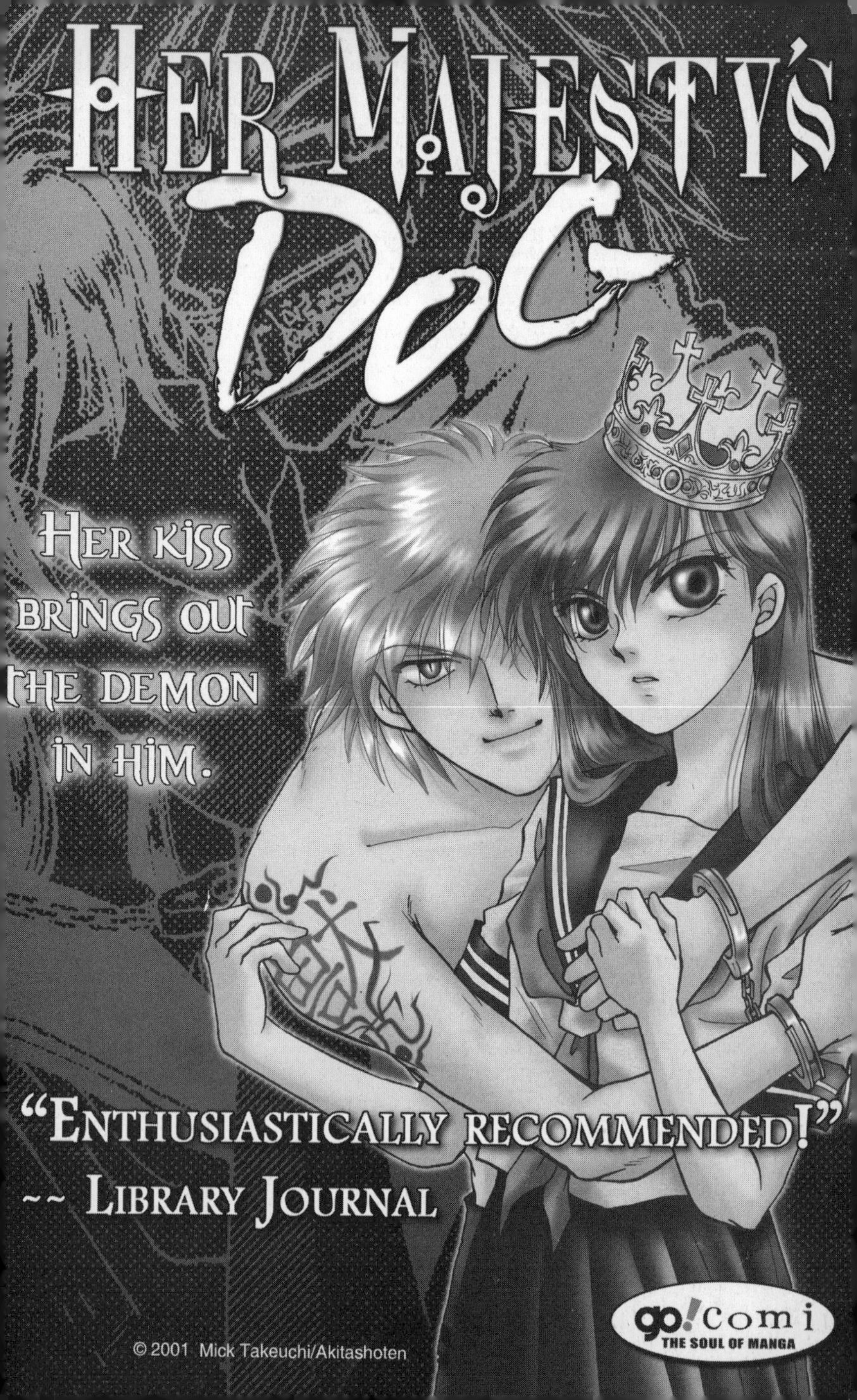
HER MAJESTY'S DOG
HER KISS BRINGS OUT THE DEMON IN HIM.
"ENTHUSIASTICALLY RECOMMENDED!"
-- LIBRARY JOURNAL
go!comi
THE SOUL OF MANGA

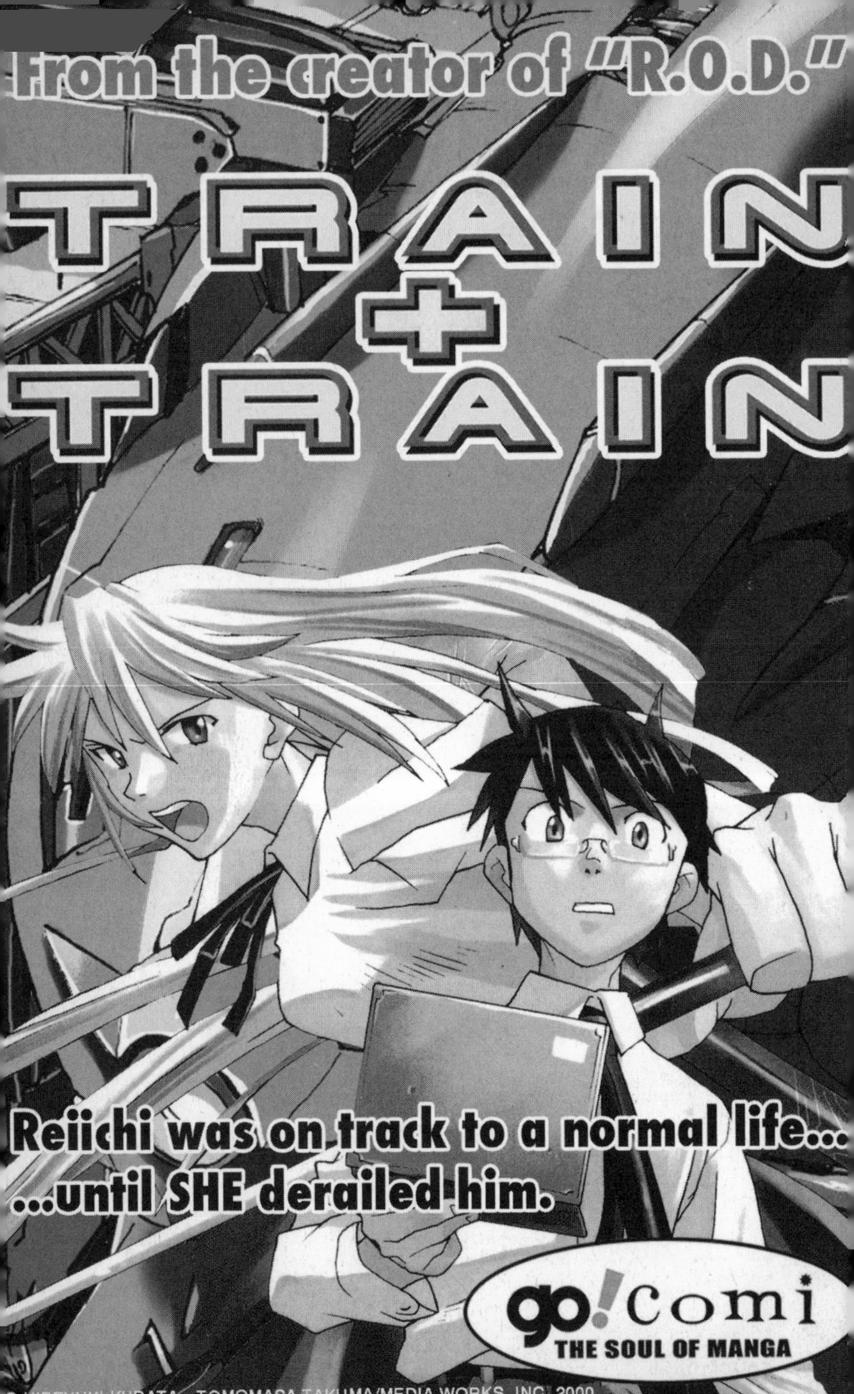
From the creator of "R.O.D."
TRAIN + TRAIN
Reiichi was on track to a normal life...
...until SHE derailed him.
go!comi
THE SOUL OF MANGA

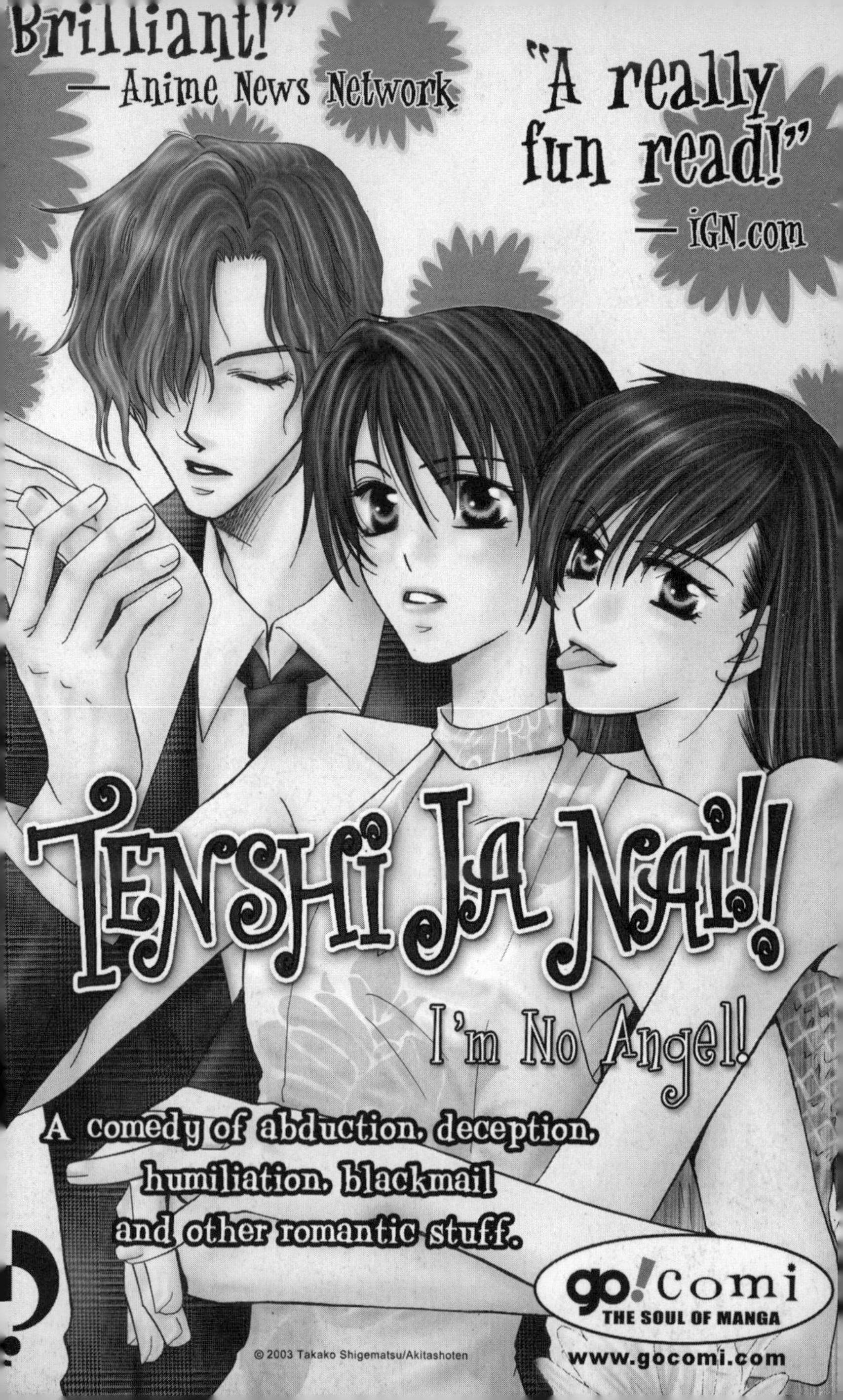

Brilliant!"
— Anime News Network
"A really fun read!"
— iGN.com
TENSHI JA NAI!
I'm No Angel!
A comedy of abduction, deception, humiliation, blackmail and other romantic stuff.
go!comi
THE SOUL OF MANGA
© 2003 Takako Shigematsu/Akitashoten
www.gocomi.com

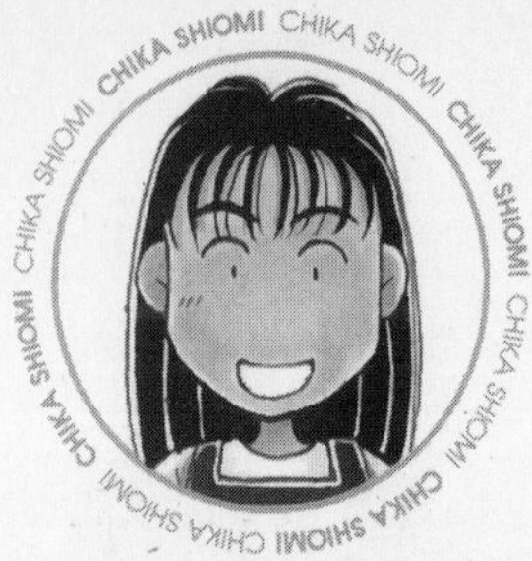
CHIKA SHIOMI CHIKA SHIOMI CHIKA SHIOMI CHIKA SHIOMI CHIKA SHIOMI CHIKA SHIOMI CHIKA SHIOMI

CHIKA SHIOMI

I wrote more than half of the second volume in a different house from the first. It was just a temporary stay, while we were waiting for renovations on our house to finish. But because of the move, I was forced to throw out my study desk, which I'd been using for decades. So during the temporary stay, I had to write out my manga on my mother's sewing machine table. It's sorta...or should I say REALLY small.

I was born February 21st. I come from Aichi Prefecture. I'm a Pisces, and my blood type is AB. My hobbies are skiing and going to hot water springs.

ABOUT THE MANGA-KA

Chika Shiomi has an amazing talent for depicting chilling and provocative horror stories that appeal to both shojo and shonen readers. Having created manga since 1993, starting with short stories in Akita Shoten's *Mystery Bonita* magazine, she has had a bountiful career of publishing both long-running series and short stories that have become popular both in Japan and abroad. Shiomi-sensei was born on February 21st and loves to travel and listen to Guns 'n Roses.